Expert Evidence Deficiencies in the Judgments of the Courts of the European Union and the European Court of Human Rights

EUROPEAN MONOGRAPHS

In the European Monographs series this book, *Expert Evidence Deficiencies in the Judgments of the Courts of the European Union and the European Court of Human Rights*, is the eighty-ninth title. The titles published in this series are listed at the end of this volume.

Expert Evidence Deficiencies in the Judgments of the Courts of the European Union and the European Court of Human Rights

George Cumming
Of the Inner Temple, Barrister

Wolters Kluwer
Law & Business

Published by:
Kluwer Law International
PO Box 316
2400 AH Alphen aan den Rijn
The Netherlands
Website: www.kluwerlaw.com

Sold and distributed in North, Central and South America by:
Aspen Publishers, Inc.
7201 McKinney Circle
Frederick, MD 21704
United States of America
Email: customer.service@aspenpublishers.com

Sold and distributed in all other countries by:
Turpin Distribution Services Ltd
Stratton Business Park
Pegasus Drive, Biggleswade
Bedfordshire SG18 8TQ
United Kingdom
Email: kluwerlaw@turpin-distribution.com

Printed on acid-free paper.

ISBN 978-90-411-4123-1

Printed and Bound by CPI Group (UK) Ltd, Croydon, CR0 4YY.

Table of Contents

Introduction*

This analysis will consider certain consequences of the application of the Rules of Procedure[1] (RP) of the Court of Justice[2] (CJ), to a limited extent those of the General

* Prof H Rasmussen had kindly accepted to write the preface for this book but regretfully his untimely death prevented him from so doing. I would however, like to express my thanks in memory of him, for his personal kindness and above all for the inspirational quality of his judicial analysis in this field of research.

1. KPE Lasok QC, T Millett & A Howard, *Judicial Control in the EU: Procedures and Principles*; Protocol (No 3) the Statute of the Court of Justice of the European Union. C83/201 OJ 30.3.2010; Rules of Procedure of the Court of Justice; www.curia.europa.eu Arts 45-53 and Art. 54 (a); R Barents 'The Court of Justice after the Treaty of Lisbon' (2010) *CMLRev* (47) 709 at 711 observes 'Under Art 245 EC The Statute with the exception of Title I (composition and independence of the courts) could be amended by the Council acting unanimously at the request of the Court of Justice and after consulting the European Parliament and the Commission or on a proposal of the Commission and after consulting the European Parliament and the Court of Justice.' KPE Lasok *The European Court of Justice: Practice and Procedure; ibid.*, Ch.1; Art. 19 (1) TEU (Treaty on European Union) provides the name 'Court of Justice of the European Union'. See R Barents 'The Court of Justice after the Treaty of Lisbon' (2010) *CMLRev* (47) 709 *ibid.*, at 709 'The treaty of Lisbon has introduced a new nomenclature for the judicial institution of the EU. According to Art. 19 (1) TEU this institution now bears the name 'Court of Justice of the European Union'. This modification is self-evident since the EC has ceased to exist. Moreover already before the entry into force of the Treaty of Lisbon the name 'Court of Justice of the European Communities' was not correct as the Treaty of Amsterdam had extended its jurisdiction to certain matters falling under the (old) Third Pillar of the EU (ex Art. 35 TEU). The institution consists of three judicial bodies (Art. 19 (1) TEU); the Court of Justice (Arts 251 to 253 TFEU), the General Court (Art. 254 TFEU) and specialized courts (Art. 257 TFEU). The institution consists of three judicial bodies (Art. 19 (1) TEU); the Court of Justice (Arts 251 to 253 TFEU); the General Court (Art. 254 TFEU) and specialized courts (Art. 257 TFEU). The Rules of Procedure may only with the approval of the Council: A Arnull, *The European Union and its Court of Justice*, 2nd edn (Oxford, OUP, 2006) at 29-30. Before the entry into force of the Treaty of Nice the Court had to wait for the unanimous approval of the Council before introducing changes to its Rules of Procedure. This sometimes entailed considerable delay. To enable it to act more rapidly the Court suggested to the re-Nice IGC that it should have the right to amend its Rules of Procedure without seeking the approval of the Council. That suggestion failed to attract the support of all the Member States but they did agree to permit the Council to grant its approval by a qualified majority (note 171 Art. 233 last paragraph). The maintenance of the requirement of Council approval (note 172 the abolition of that requirement would merely have put the Court on the same footing as the European Court of Human Rights and the International Court of Justice see Art. 26 (d) ECHR and Art. 30 of the Statute of the International Court of Justice. Particularly sensitive issues could have been dealt

Court (GC) as well as those of the European Court of Human Rights (ECtHR) with regard to the appointment of experts notably in the context of statutory interpretation: that is of the Treaty for the Functioning of the European Union (TFEU) and the European Convention of Human Right (ECHR). The central hypothesis of this analysis is that statutory interpretation[3] requires, in certain instances, notably as regards the

with in the Statute of the Court) reflected a certain wariness on the art of the Member States at the idea of giving the Court a free hand to organize its work (Meiji 'Guest Editorial: Architects or Judges Some Comments in Relation to the Current Debate' (2000) 37 *CMLRev* 1039, 1042.

2. The Court of Justice of the European Union now consists of the Court of Justice (formerly the European Court of Justice established by the ECSC Treaty of Paris 1952), the General Court (formerly the Court of First Instance). Art. 19 TEU defines the fundamental task of the Court of Justice of the European Union in its first paragraph which preserves the essence of the former EC Art. 220 in that it provides 'It shall ensure that in the interpretation and application of the Treaty the law is observed'.

   Consolidated Version of the Statute of the Court of Justice of the European Union:

   > Art. 23 'In the cases governed by Article 267 of the Treaty on the Functioning of the European Union, the decision of the court or tribunal of a Member State which suspends its proceedings and refers a case to the Court of Justice shall be notified to the Court by the court or tribunal concerned. The decision shall then be notified by the Registrar of the Court to the parties, to the Member States and to the Commission, and to the institution, body, office or agency of the Union which adopted the act the validity or interpretation of which is in dispute. Within two months of this notification, the parties, the Member States, the Commission and, where appropriate, the institution, body, office or agency which adopted the act the validity or interpretation of which is in May, within two months of notification, where one of the fields of application of that Agreement is concerned, submit statements of case or written observations to the Court. Where an agreement relating to a specific subject matter, concluded by the Council and one or more non-member States, provides that those States are to be entitled to submit statements of case or written observations where a court or tribunal of a Member State refers to the Court of Justice for a preliminary ruling a question falling within the scope of the agreement, the decision of the national court or tribunal containing that question shall also be notified to the non-member States concerned.'
   >
   > Art. 24 'The Court of Justice may require the parties to produce all documents and to supply all information which the Court considers desirable. Formal note shall be taken of any refusal. The Court may also require the Member States and institutions, bodies, offices and agencies not being parties to the case to supply all information which the Court considers necessary for the proceedings.'
   >
   > Art. 25 'The Court of Justice may at any time entrust any individual, body, authority, committee or other organisation it chooses with the task of giving an expert opinion.' www.curia.europa.eu, 20.10.2013.

3. MP Maduro 'Interpreting European Law: Judicial Adjudication in a Context of Constitutional Pluralism' (2007) *EJLS* (1) No 2, www.ejls.com, presents very succinctly a view of statutory interpretation which with due respect, is too narrow: 'Legal interpretation at the Court of Justice is governed by text, context and *telos* or purpose. These are the three methods indicated early on in the *Van Gend en Loos* judgment by the reference to "the spirit, the general scheme and the wording" of the legal provisions which the Court has to interpret. But the Court has done more than simply refer to these methods of interpretation. It has, in effect, deduced from the treaties a particularly hermeneutic framework distinct from that of traditional international law.': that is, the learned professor and Advocate General reduces without explanation statutory interpretation to the use of certain principles of interpretation: In truth statutory interpretation as approached in this book is very much the method adopted by such authors as R Sullivan, as in *Sullivan and Driedger on the Construction of Statutes*, 4th edn (Vancouver, Butterworths, 2002) which encompasses both principles of interpretation such as those evoked by Maduro as well as methods of interpretation which necessarily involves the application of the principles through

interpretation of technical words, the use of expert evidence in order to achieve a semantically[4] accurate meaning. This semantically accurate meaning of the technical words cannot be produced by a judge simply as a native speaker of a particular human language. In short, the failure by the CJ, the GC and the ECtHR in the interpretation of the TFEU and the ECHR which will be analysed in certain published judgments herein, can lead to the violation of notably Article 6 (1) ECHR[5] notably as interpreted and applied by the ECtHR in *Kraska v Switzerland*[6] and, implicitly, a concept of the Rule of

procedural methods and substantive rules of law such as the standard of proof, methods of proof etc. It is also very much connected with the discipline of Linguistics - see Robins below. Arguably, this narrow interpretation of the concept of judicial interpretation as presented by Maduro which divorces the use of the principles from the methods of application without any justification, in part leads to the complete absence of discussion and analysis of the application of the interpretative principles in the context of evidence, standards of proof and procedural imperatives such as case and fact management. Arguably, it is by reason of this exclusively principled basis which (in itself is not analysed as would for example R Dworkin, *Taking Rights Seriously* (Cam Masc, Harvard, 1977) in terms of policy as opposed to principles which in turn can be analysed in relation to theories of morality such as utilitarianism, or deontological ethics, etc.) that a corrective approach, such as that of H Rasmussen, *European Court of Justice* (Copenhagen, Gadjura, 1998) and others emerged which focussed ultimately on the form of statutory interpretation practised in the much wider context of evidence, proof, and concepts of civil procedure such as case and fact management. See also R Clayton QC & H Tomlinson QC, *The Law of Human Rights*, 2nd edn (Oxford, OUP, 2009), Chapter 6, General Principles under the Convention.

4. RH Robins, *General Linguistics*, 4th edn (London, Longmans, 1990) at 22: 'What one is really trying to do in semantics... is to explicate the ways in which words and sentences of various grammatical constructions are used and understood by native or fluent speakers of a language. Sentences consist of words in specific grammatical relations within constructions and words are used in speech and in writing as components of sentences. ... The meaning of a word therefore may be considered as the way it is used and understood as part of different sentences.'
5. Article 6 (1) ECHR 'In the determination of his civil rights and obligations or of nay criminal charge against him, everyone is entitled to a fair and public hearing within a reasonable time by an independent and impartial tribunal established by law....' A Zukerman, *Civil Procedure: Principles and Practice*, 2nd edn (London, Sweet & Maxwell, 2006), at 54 'Article 6 requires the State to respect certain due process principles when adjudicating upon such rights. Thus the court is duty bound to conduct a proper example of the submissions arguments and evidence adduced by the parties while maintaining the due process standards dictated by ECHR Art 6. Note 21 *Kraska v Switzerland* (1993) *EHRR* (18) para. 30)'; and at 55 'the general right to fair trial established by ECHR Art 6 consists of a bundle of specific rights. These may be divided into two groups: rights that are expressly mentioned in ECHR Art 6 and rights which have been held to be implicit in it by the ECtHR. There are four express rights: the right to a fair hearing; the right to a public hearing including the right to the public pronounce of judgment; the right to a hearing within a reasonable time; and the right to an independent tribunal. In addition the ECtHR has held the following rights are implied in the right of fair trial: the right to fair presentation of the evidence. the right to cross examine, the right of access to a court and the right to equality of arms and the right to a reasoned judgment.' It is submitted that the right involved in *Kraska v Switzerland* (1993) EHRR (18) para. 30, *ibid.*, constitutes an express rights in so far as it posits the right to a fair hearing as noted above by Zuckerman and therefore cannot be restricted.
6. *Kraska v Switzerland,* Application No. 13942/88, Judgement of 19 April 1993 (1993) *EHRR* (18) 188 at para. 30. 'It falls to the Court to decide whether the contested proceedings considered as a whole were fair within the meaning of the Convention. The effect of Article 6 para. 1 (Article 6-1) is, inter alia, to place the "tribunal" under a duty to conduct a proper examination of the submissions, arguments and evidence adduced by the parties, without prejudice to its assessment of whether they are relevant to its decision (see, among other authorities, mutatis mutandis, the *Barberà, Messegué and Jabardo v Spain* judgment of 6 December 1988, Series A no. 146, 31, para. 68). It has to be determined whether this condition was satisfied in the instant case.'

Law.[7] In truth, the inaccurate translation results in certain judgments, notably, those where expert evidence is required for the interpretation of technical meaning and in certain restricted instances, ordinary meaning, from a procedural error: namely, the failure on the part of a judge either in the CJ,[8] the GC or the ECtHR to exercise the requisite legal discretion so as to appoint an expert pursuant to the rules of procedure of the relevant court. With respect to the two Union courts, the CJ and the GC, the

7. LE Mulcahy (ed) *Human Rights and Civil Practice* (London, Sweet & Maxwell, 2001) at 95: 'The rules of law is inherent in the Convention as a whole. Interference with or restriction of a Convention right must be lawful for it to be justified. The legality principle is expressly contained in Articles 2,5,6, 8 and 11 and Article 1 of Protocol No. 1. ... An act may be lawful if it has 'some basis in domestic law' whether pursuant to statutory authority, the common law; European Community law or other sufficient source of guidance. The rule of law as interpreted by the European Court effectively requires a positive legal basis for the act in question. However the legal source must additionally be both clear and accessible for it to be compatible with the rule of law. (*Malone v UK* (1985) *EHRR* 14, para. 67). Interferences with Convention rights and freedoms are not permitted unless there is a clear legal basis for doing so. Similarly an individual should be able to predict with reasonable certainty when and under what conditions such interference may occur. A norm will not be regarded as a 'law' unless it is formulated with sufficient precision to enable the citizen to regulate his conduct. In *Sunday Times v United Kingdom* (1980) 2 *EHRR* 245, para. 49 the ECtHR held: 'If need be with appropriate advice – to foresee to a degree that is reasonable in the circumstance the consequences which a given action may entail.' It is submitted that one of the manifestations of the breach of the rule of law as expressed in Art 6 (1) ECHR is that statutory interpretations of the TFEU and the ECHR which are not based upon expert opinion evidence notably for the construction of the technical meaning of words prevent or render excessively difficult the possibility of a citizen of foreseeing the consequences of the application by the CJ, the GC and the ECtHR of the aforementioned treaties in that effectively, the evidentiary deficit may render the statutory interpretation therefore, unreasonable and unpredictable given that it is not based upon full use of facts and expert opinion which may be required for a fully accurate judgment following Bentham's procedural principle of rectitude of decision. See as regards the principle of rectitude of decision AAS Zukerman (ed), *Civil Justice in Crisis-Comparative Perspectives of Civil Procedure* (Oxford, OUP, 1999) 4-6. More generally I am grateful to Graham Child, Solicitor, *Bellamy & Child: European Union Law of Competition*, V Rose & D Bailey (eds) (Oxford, OUP, 2013) for remarks concerning the Rule of Law. The usual qualifications apply.
8. T Schilling 'Beyond Multilingualism: On Different Approaches to the Handling of Diverging Language Versions to a Community Law' (2010) *ELJ* (16) (1) 47 identifies a profoundly serious problem as regards variations in the translations of the various legal documents ranging from the TFEU through to directives and its breach of Art. 6 (2) TEU '[t]he Union shall respect fundamental rights as guaranteed by the [ECHR].' Schilling observes at p. 66 '... as the law now stands wile every language version of a law is declared to be authentic, in legal reality ie under the ECJ's uniform interpretation approach none of them truly is. Indeed, at present, while in theory no assistance of a translator is required to understand the meaning of a Community law, all language versions being equally authentic, for this very reason the assistance of even a posse of translators will not be able to resolve divergences between language versions but only to state them. Such a law, which must be looked for in 23 different places, the true importance of none of which is real clear, cannot be deemed easily or even truly accessible. The consequences of the present state of the law are thus at variance with both the quality requirements a law which interferes with liberties has to fulfil under the ECHR. Under both aspects the 'quality' of a Community law would be enhanced considerably if that law were authentic in one language only. There is no doubt in my mind that such a state of affairs would come much closer to the goal of permitting the citizen in his own language easy access to a Community law and to foresee its effects than the present one.' Arguably the analysis by Schilling has particular importance for the application of the principle of proportionality as well as the basic proof of the ordinary and technical meaning of the TFEU.

importance of considering the case law of the ECtHR arises by reason of Article 6 (2) TEU:

> Art 6 (2). The Union shall accede to the European Convention for the Protection of Human Rights and Fundamental Freedoms. Such accession shall not affect the Union's competences as defined in the Treaties.

As is clear from the above, the statutory interpretation of the ECHR carried out by the ECtHR will affect the judgments made by the two Union courts, CJ and GC involving ECHR rights by reason of the accession to the ECHR by the EU provided by Article 6 (2) TEU.[9]

In addition, as regards the CJ and the GC, it is submitted that such evidential deficiency can lead to a violation of Article 19 (1) TEU:

> It shall ensure that in the interpretation and application of the Treaties the law is observed. Member States shall provide remedies sufficient to ensure effective legal protection in the fields covered by Union law.

In short, it is submitted that 'the interpretation and application of the Treaties and law' can itself only be construed in the sense of accuracy of decision making: that is, rectitude of decision as conceived of by Bentham which is described by Zuckerman[10] in the following manner:

> In Bentham's terminology, the purpose of procedure is rectitude of decisions which requires the correct application of the law to the true facts. While rectitude of decision, or truth, is the aim of civil procedure it is acknowledged that our procedures are not perfect. There are always limitations to the ability of procedure to achieve rectitude of decisions. A system of procedure can strive to determine what happened in the past and to apply the law precisely but it cannot guarantee that errors will never occur. It is the mark of legal procedures that while the criterion of justice is external to the procedure (i.e. the true facts, the correct law) the procedure itself cannot always achieve a perfect correspondence between individual decisions and this criterion as Rawls observed (Note 2 pg 4 J. Rawls, A Theory of Justice – 85-86). ... Most if not all procedural requirements are concerned to secure rectitude of decision including the requirements of procedural justice. Measures such as the right to be heard or the right to an impartial tribunal are dictated by the desire for rectitude of decision. Of course, the appearance of justice is also important but it does not alter the fact that at the foundation of procedure lies the objective of getting at the truth. This objective lies behind the entire procedural organisation.

---

9. T Lock, 'Walking on a Tightrope: the Draft ECHR Accession Agreement and the Autonomy of the EU Legal Order' (2011) *CMLRev* (48) 1025; J-P Jacqué, 'The Accession of the European Union to the European Convention on Human Rights and Fundamental Freedoms' (2011) *CMLRev* (48) 995. See however the end footnote of this chapter, F van den Berghe 'The EU and Issues of Human Rights Protection' (2010) *ELJ* (16) 1, 112, at 149, as to possible deference by the ECtHR to certain types of cases involving CJ and GC rules of procedure and evidence despite full capacity to review pursuant to Art. 6 (1) ECHR.
10. AAS Zukerman (ed), *Civil Justice in Crisis- Comparative Perspectives of Civil Procedure* (Oxford, OUP, 1999), 6, *supra*.

In short, the real practical and jurisprudential difficulty which will result from the accession of the EU to the ECHR as provided by Article 6 (2) TFEU is as follows: namely that evidential deficits[11] arising from the failure by the CJ and the GC in preliminary references and direct actions to utilize expert evidence in statutory interpretation of TFEU will be aggravated by an analogous failure on the part of the ECtHR to employ expert evidence as regards the construction of the ECHR.

Arguably the objective of the rectitude of decision is present, as just noted, in so far as clearly Article 6 (2) TEU will function[12] in so far as the ECHR, and notably Article 61 thereof, will apply to the statutory interpretation of the TFEU by the CJ and the GC. Clearly, for the purposes of the instant analysis, the express right guaranteed by Article 6 (1) ECHR to fair trial, is the most significant of the bundle of rights contained judicially by that article.[13] Clearly the express right to due process or a fair trial guaranteed by Article 6 (1) ECHR applies to the judgments formed by the ECtHR itself and not simply to the CJ and the GC. Overall, for the purposes of the instant analysis, the element which relates the method of statutory interpretation used with respect to the ECHR and the TFEU by the ECtHR, the CJ and the GC is the following: namely, a deficit in the use of expert evidence[14] in the interpretation notably of technical terms which require expert opinion evidence but also words where the method of proof

11. E Barbier de la Serre & A-L Sibony, 'Expert Evidence before the EC Courts' (2008) *CMLRev* (45) 941.
12. The legal basis for accession is now provided for through Art. 6 (2) TEU, which actually includes an accession requirement in the wording of the provision: 'the Union shall accede to the ECHR'. As regards the Council of Europe, Art. 17 of Protocol n° 14 of the ECHR, which entered into force on 1 June 2010, amends Art. 59 of the Convention in order to provide for the possibility of accession for the Union. T Lock 'Accession of the EU to the ECHR: Who Would Be Responsible in Strasbourg' *Social Sciences Research Network PDF File 37,* 3.9.2010; 'EU Accession to the European Convention of Human Rights: A Legal Assessment of the Draft Accession Agreement', *Foundation Robert Schuman, European* Issues, No 218, 7.11.2011; 'EU Accession to the ECHR: Implications for Judicial Review in Strasbourg' (2010) *ELR* (35) 777; 'Walking on a Tight Rope' (2011) *CMLRev* (48) 1025; 'End of an Epic? The draft agreement of the EU's Accession to the ECHR', Yearbook of European Law (2012); D Ritleng 'The Access of the European Union to the European Convention of Human Rights and Fundamental Freedoms: A Threat to the Specific Characteristics of the European Union and union law', Uppsala Faculty of Law, Working Paper 2012:1.
13. A Zuckerman, *Civil Procedure: Principles and Practice* (London, Sweet & Maxwell 2006) p. 55 'The general right to fair trial established by ECHR Art 6 consists of a bundle of specific rights (*Ahmed v UK* (1995) *EHRR* CD 72). These may be divided into two groups: rights that are expressly mentioned in ECHR Art 6 rights which are expressly mentioned in ECHR Art 6 and rights which have been held to be implicit in it by the ECtHR. There are four express rights: the right to a fair hearing: the right to a public hearing including the right to the public pronouncement of judgment (subject to exceptions); the right to a hearing within reasonable time; and he right to an independent and impartial tribunal. In addition the ECtHR has held the following rights to be implied in the right of fair trial: the right of access to court, the right to fair presentation of the evidence, the right to cross-examination and the right to a reasoned judgement ... It has been held that the express rights are absolute in the sense that they may not be compromised or traded off against other Convention rights ... By contrast the implied right are not absolute and may be subject to limitations provided that the limitation is imposed in furtherance of a legitimate aim or public interest and provided that any limitation is reasonably proportionate to such aim or interest.'
14. E Barbier de la Serre and A-L Sibony 'Expert Evidence Before the EC Courts' (2008) *CMLRev* (45) 941.

known as judicial notice.[15] As regards judicial notice, the judge makes recourse to indisputable sources of information such as experts in the interpretation of the ordinary meaning of certain words in a statute. In short, this failure on the part of the ECtHR, the CJ and the GC to utilize expert evidence and, in particular, in the context of judicial notice as well as an assessor, may lead, through the evidential deficit caused by the absence of expert information, to inaccurate interpretation of both the TFEU and the ECHR. Therefore, by omitting to use its rules of procedure to obtain expert opinion evidence the CJ,[16] the GC and the ECtHR in interpreting the TFEU and the ECHR respectively, violate both Article 19 TEU and Article 6 (1) ECHR in the case of the former and Article 6 (1) ECHR as regards the latter court. Indeed, perhaps surprisingly, the ECtHR itself arguably breaches Article 6 (1) ECHR in actions brought by private individuals to enforce their rights pursuant to the ECHR:[17] that is, by failing to use the investigative measures which are provided by its rules of procedure[18] in its statutory

15. P Roberts & A Zuckerman, *Criminal Evidence*, 2nd edn (Oxford, OUP, 2010), 169-176 at 169 'Judicial notice may be conceptualized as an alternative and strikingly different procedural mechanism for managing the inferential process. Common law judges are empowered to take 'judicial notice' of certain facts. These noticed facts are then treated as settled for all purposes. Authorizing judges to decide factual issues by judicial fiat would pose issues of procedural fairness, transparency and epistemic reasonableness in any system of adjudication. It is an especially surprising way of resolving factual issues in an adversarial systems in which the proof through party evidence is the norm. The traditional rationalization is that noticed facts are too obvious and indisputable to require explicit proof which would be an unnecessary and time wasting formality.' KC Davis, 'Judicial Notice' (1955) *Colum L R* (55) 945.
16. Section 2. Measures of inquiry: Article 63: Decision on measures of inquiry 1. The Court shall decide in its general meeting whether a measure of inquiry is necessary. 2. Where the case has already been assigned to a formation of the Court, the decision shall be taken by that formation. Article 64: Determination of measures of inquiry 1. The Court, after hearing the Advocate General, shall prescribe the measures of inquiry that it considers appropriate by means of an order setting out the facts to be proved. 2. Without prejudice to Articles 24 and 25 of the Statute, the following measures of inquiry may be adopted: (a) the personal appearance of the parties; (b) a request for information and production of documents; (c) oral testimony; (d) the commissioning of an expert's report; (e) an inspection of the place or thing in question.
17. L-A Mulcahy (ed), *Human Rights and Civil Practice* (London, Sweet & Maxwell, 2001) notes at 33-34. 'Enforcement of the Convention. Contracting States and where the State at issue had accepted the right of individual petition, individual applicants could lodge complaints against Contracting States for alleged violations of Convention rights. The right of individual petition greatly strengthened the effectiveness of the Convention in securing protection for fundamental rights. On January 14, 1966, the UK lodged a declaration with the Secretary General of the Council of Europe in which it accepted the right of individuals to bring a petition before the European Commission in accordance with (what was) Art. 25. The acceptance was limited to petitions in relation to any act or decision occurring or any facts or events arising subsequent to the Convention recognising the European Court's jurisdiction subject to similar conditions, was filed on the same day.' E Bates, *The Evolution of the European Convention on Human Rights* (Oxford, OUP, 2010) in particular chapters 6, 7, 8 and 9 as regards the development of individual petition; also Lord Lester QC, Lord Pannick QC and J Herberg (eds) *Human Rights Law and Practice.* (London, Lexis Nexis, 2009) in particular, Chapter 1, History and Context.
18. European Court of Human Rights or their representatives prior to any proceedings taking place before the delegation. Rules of Court – 1 July 2013, Registry of the Court of Strasbourg Annex to the Rules1 (concerning investigations) Rule A1 – Investigative measures 1. The Chamber may, at the request of a party or of its own motion, adopt any investigative measure which it considers capable of clarifying the facts of the case. The Chamber may, *inter alia*, invite the parties to

interpretation[19] of the ECHR which provide for the appointment of an expert if necessary on its own motion, the ECtHR seeks to carry out a statutory interpretation notably of the technical meaning of the terms of that treaty without using expert evidence. This produces, arguably, an interpretation which is not infrequently defective in that it may be too wide in terms of, notably, the technical meaning of the words which compose the ECHR when applied in the legal and factual context of the litigation.[20] The process of statutory interpretation may also involve non-expert judges endeavouring to provide expert meaning when they are not, through their exclusively judicial training, qualified to so do. This in turn then leads to inaccuracy: namely, the wide interpretation based upon the ordinary meaning of words in a statute as opposed to the more narrow technical meaning. Further, the aforementioned evidentially deficient interpretations lack the overall cogency which arises from an interpretation based upon an expert evidence as opposed to that based solely upon non-detailed judicial reasoning where relevant expert evidence exists and is obtainable. In short, the absence of the expert opinion evidence may diminish the linguistic plausibility[21] of the statutory interpretations rendered by the CJ, the GC and the ECtHR of respectively the TFEU and the ECHR. The reason for this is that judges make recourse to various types of expertise by reason of certain experts being recognized by a particular society as beneficial, useful and credible. Accordingly, experts in these areas are deemed to be acceptable by the courts and accordingly add social plausibility, credibility and eventually contribute to the veracity of the judgment. In this regard Zuckerman[22] notes that an example of what might be termed or deemed socially acceptable experts in Europe would be those in the general medicine. A less well admitted field would be in certain countries experts in psychiatry. In short, this social recognition and acceptance

produce documentary evidence and decide to hear as a witness or expert or in any other capacity any person whose evidence or statements seem likely to assist it in carrying out its tasks', www.echr.coe.int.

19. See also Vienna Convention of the Law of Treaties: the European Convention of Human Rights is an international treaty and must therefore be interpreted in accordance with principles of public international law. (*Golder v UK* (1975) *EHRR* (1) at 524 paras 29-30) The primary source of law for the interpretation of treaties is the Vienna Convention of the law of Treaties 1969 and notably Art. 31 of this convention which provides: 'A treaty shall be interpreted in good faith in accordance with the ordinary meaning to be given to the term of their context and in the light of its object and purpose.'
20. R Sullivan, *Sullivan and Driedger on the Construction of Statutes*, 4th edn (Vancouver, Butterworths, 2002), *supra*, at 40-41: 'As defined above, ordinary meaning refers to the meaning that a reader understands from reading words in their immediate context. However in statutory interpretation the expression 'ordinary meaning' is also used to refer to the common or popular meaning of words as opposed to any technical or specialized meaning which they might bear...Technical or scientific terms are words or expressions that have no common or popular meaning; their only meaning derives from the specialized use by a distinct portion of the community. When technical or scientific terms are used in legislation there is no possibility of confusion; such terms automatically receive their technical or scientific meaning. Note2 see *Perma v R* (1984) 2 *SCR* 232 at 264 per Dickson J 'It is well established that technical and scientific terms which appear in statutes should be given their technical or scientific meaning.'
21. R Sullivan, *Sullivan and Driedger on the Construction of Statutes*, 4th edn (Vancouver, Butterworths, 2002, *ibid.*: at 125 'In principle the plausibility requirement is an important constraint on judicial interpretation. The range of meanings that can plausible be attributed to a text creates the limits within which interpretation can legitimately occur.'
22. A Zuckerman, *Criminal Evidence* (Oxford, OUP, 1989), *supra*, 62-71.

of certain types of expert evidence confers an element of plausibility[23] to statutory interpretations in which such expert evidence is used in addition to eventually, veracity. As such, it would appear that the element of plausibility arising from the use of expert evidence may contribute, at least in part, to creating a type of legitimacy, a credibility and, above all, an accuracy which appear, regretfully, in diminished or attenuated form with respect to certain judgments made by the CJ, GC and ECtHR.[24] Further, it is submitted that the use of such expert evidence prevents the statutory interpretation from being strained,[25] inaccurate and too wide notably in matters involving the competence of the governments of Member States signatories of the ECHR and the TFEU.

Further, certain types of rules are absent from the rules of procedure of both the CJ and the ECtHR: these rules provide the basis for a principled interpretation of the rules of civil procedure equivalent for example to the Overriding Objective in English civil procedure.[26] This deficit, in truth, can affect profoundly the manner in which the CJ and the GC ensure statutory interpretation pursuant to Article 19 TEU[27] in the

23. R Sullivan, *Sullivan and Driedger on the Construction of Statutes*, 4th edn (Vancouver, Butterworths, 2002), *supra*, Chapter 6 123-150.
24. My thanks to Dr E Bates for the numerous conversations I have had with him on this point. The usual disclaimers apply. See also E Bates, *The Evolution of the European Convention of Human Rights* (Oxford, OUP, 2010).
25. R Sullivan, *Sullivan and Driedger on the Construction of Statutes*, 4th edn (Vancouver, Butterworths, 2002), *supra*, 126-127.
26. Civil Procedure Rules Part 1 OVERRIDING OBJECTIVE 1.1 (1) These Rules are a new procedural code with the overriding objective of enabling the court to deal with cases justly. (2) Dealing with a case justly includes, so far as is practicable – (a) ensuring that the parties are on an equal footing; (b) saving expense; (c) dealing with the case in ways which are proportionate – (i) to the amount of money involved; (ii) to the importance of the case; (iii) to the complexity of the issues; and(iv) to the financial position of each party; (d) ensuring that it is dealt with expeditiously and fairly; and(e) allotting to it an appropriate share of the court's resources, while taking into account the need to allot resources to other cases. 1.2 The court must seek to give effect to the overriding objective when it – (a) exercises any power given to it by the Rules; or (b) interprets any rule subject to Rules 76.2, 79.2 and 80.2.
27. TFEU Treaty on the Functioning of the European Union and Treaty of European Union; the consolidated version of both treaties is reproduced at OJ 2010 C 83. Art. 19 (1) TEU. '1. The Court of Justice of the European Union shall include the Court of Justice, the General Court and specialised courts. It shall ensure that in the interpretation and application of the Treaties the law is observed. Member States shall provide remedies sufficient to ensure effective legal protection in the fields covered by Union law. 2. The Court of Justice shall consist of one judge from each Member State. It shall be assisted by Advocates-General. The General Court shall include at least one judge per Member State. The Judges and the Advocates-General of the Court of Justice and the Judges of the General Court shall be chosen from persons whose independence is beyond doubt and who satisfy the conditions set out in Articles 253 and 254 of the Treaty on the Functioning of the European Union. They shall be appointed by common accord of the governments of the Member States for six years. Retiring Judges and Advocates-General may be reappointed. 3. The Court of Justice of the European Union shall, in accordance with the Treaties: (a) rule on actions brought by a Member State, an institution or a natural or legal person;(b) give preliminary rulings, at the request of courts or tribunals of the Member States, on the interpretation of Union law or the validity of acts adopted by the institutions; (c) rule in other cases provided for in the Treaties.'

context of both direct actions, particularly of annulment Commission decisions involving EU competition law, as well as preliminary references[28] made pursuant to Article 267 TFEU.[29] This applies, it is submitted, also to the manner in which the ECtHR interprets the ECHR as regards the use of expert evidence. In short, as just noted, the evidentiary deficits may lead to inaccurate judgments[30] thereby provoking a violation of Article 19 TEU[31] which provides that as regards the CJ and the GC: 'It shall ensure that in the interpretation and application of the Treaties the law is observed' signifies the following: 'the correct application of the law to the fact'.[32] Further, this semantic and evidential inaccuracy impacts upon the distribution of the powers in that it may create harmonization which is devoid of any empirical justification, a redistribution of certain powers at the expense of the Member States: failure to connect the use of legal principles such as proportionality[33] and subsidiarity[34] to the

28. Article 267 TFEU 'The Court of Justice of the European Union shall have jurisdiction to give preliminary rulings concerning: (a) the interpretation of the Treaties; (b) the validity and interpretation of acts of the institutions, bodies, offices or agencies of the Union 3'.
29. References pursuant to Art. 267 refer to the Court of Justice.
30. This is particularly so with the use of the teleological method of interpretation when applied to words with a technical meaning where expert evidence is required in order in order to provide and prove a semantically accurate if not true technical meaning of the word. The failure by the court to use the rules for the appointment of an expert, or failure to utilize correctly the rules of case management which require amendment coupled with rules of pleading which are insufficiently precise all lead to a factual and evidential deficit which in turn may cause an inaccurate judgment with the consequential breach of Art. 41 of the CF and or Art. 6 (1). ECHR and thereby of Art. 19 TEU.
31. Article 19 (1). The Court of Justice of the European Union shall include the Court of Justice, the General Court and specialized courts. It shall ensure that in the interpretation and application of the Treaties the law is observed.
32. A Zuckerman (ed) S Chiarloni and P Gottwald (consultant editors) *Civil Justice in Crisis* (Oxford, OUP, 1999) at 1 'Dimensions of Justice: In all systems of procedure doing justice means arriving at decisions which give the arties before the court what is legally due to them. In order to do justice then the court has to determine the true facts and then correctly apply the law to the facts. In Bentham's terminology, the purpose of procedure is rectitude of decision which requires the correct application of the law to the true facts. Principles of Judicial Procedure in Collected Works of Jeremy Bentham (ed), Bowring (1938-43) Vol. ii).
33. A Portuese, 'Principle of Proportionality as Principle of Economic Efficiency' (2013) *ELJ* (19) (5) 612 at 613 'Even if the reader may have finally ended up to be convinced in the arguments developed throughout this paper the reader may be puzzled by the fact that a general principle of law be assimilated with the efficiency of some norms. Would it not be more intuitive to think of legal principles as having per se an anti-efficiency rationale or at least being efficiency neutral? This query is directly derived from the academic debate that has emerged between Posner (note 136: *The problems of Jurisprudence* (Harvard University Press 1990) and Dworkin (*Taking Rights Seriously* (Harvard University Press 1977). The former defends a reading of the law that I label as legal nihilism consisting of denying the existence of legal principles in favour of legal rules that are explainable most of the time from an efficiency perspective. The latter defends a reading of law that I label as legal formalism consisting of seeing the law as formed by legal principles derived from higher nature and that applies potentially with legal rules on grounds of moral values rather than on efficiency grounds. My contention is that beyond this simplistic dichotomy one can apprehend legal principles as such from an efficiency viewpoint and see whether or not they encapsulate an efficiency rationale. Legal principles do exist besides legal rules. But legal principles do not emerge from moral or higher nature (a top-down approach) but rather as a bundle of legal rules that are sufficiently settled to be self-argumentative (bottom up approach). Since legal principles are a bundle of legal rules it becomes very probably that an efficiency rationale supports them from a dynamic perspective.'

use of expert evidence aggravates the original failure to use expert opinion in the interpretation of the words contained within the articles of the TFEU the interpretation of which was effected without the use of such evidence. In reality, this evidential deficiency violates one of what might be termed, the linguistic restrictions upon interpretation: namely, that the consequences of the statutory interpretation must not be 'contrary to accepted norms of justice and reasonableness'.[35] Otherwise, according

34. R Van den Bergh, 'Economic Criteria for Applying the Subsidiarity Principle in the European Community: The Case of Competition Policy', *Int Review of Law and Economics* (1996) (16) 363, 381: 'An economic analysis of the subsidiarity principle allows for a better understanding of the fundamental issues in the allocation of competence between national antitrust authorities and a supranational agency. Decentralisation creates a scope for competition between legislators which at least theoretically allows firms and consumers to 'vote with their feet' by moving to their preferred jurisdiction. In reality an efficient outcome on the market of competition laws will not ensue because of insufficient choices information problems and restricted mobility. A more powerful argument in favour of decentralisation is the information advantage of national competition authorities. The danger of regulatory capture which is often advanced as an argument against decentralisation does not appear to be more serious than with a supranational authority. Industry general prefers the current decision making process under EC competition law o national procedures which provides support for the belief that regulatory capture may be even more worrisome than at the central level. A further powerful argument in favour of decentralization follows from a dynamic approach. Trial and error is most relevant in the field of competition policy. If antitrust rules vary across countries policy errors will be recognised more rapidly and better devices may be developed sooner.' The essential difficulty here is that the there is insufficient use of factual and in particular economic analysis of the application of the articles of the Treaty notably with respect to those articles which delimit the competence of the national governments in relation to the EU: this is particularly the case with Art. 5 TEU principles of conferral, subsidiarity and proportionality.
35. R Sullivan, *Sullivan and Driedger on the Construction of Statutes*, 4th edn (Vancouver, Butterworths, 2002), *supra*, at 235; on 'reasonableness' see Y Borgmann-Prebil 'The Rule of Reason in European Citizenship' (2008) *ELJ* (14) (3) 328 at 342 'It is submitted that by reason of analogy to the common conceptualisation of the mandatory requirements as derogation grounds that operate alongside and doctrinally in the same fashion as the express derogation grounds of the Treaty both the conditions and limitations referred to in Art 18 (1) EC and spelled out in the residence Directive ought to the understood analogously to the derogation grounds applicable to the economic free movement provisions. This means that they can be invoked by a Member State in order to restrict the prima facie right of residence enshrined in art 18 (1) EEC. The importance of the analogy lies at the conceptual level. All free movement rights of the rule of reason whether applied to the economic free movement provisions or to Art 18 (1) is that it provides for a balancing between the interest of migrating citizens and the interests of the host state.' Interestingly Borgman-Prebil at 346 refers to 'Sociologists like Delanty have defined citizenship as expressive of rights duties political participation and identity. Note 133 G Delanty' Models of Citizenship: Defining European Identity and Citizenship' (1997) Citizenship'. Interestingly, sociologists are considered in the Polygamy Reference as expert witnesses: see; *Re Polygamy Reference* 2011 BCSC 1588 (SO 97767) '[29] The expert witnesses represent a broad range of disciplines including anthropology, psychology, sociology, law, economics, family demography, history and theology'. Here the sociologist would present his expert evidence either through wide concept of judicial notice as presented by KC Davis or through the standard admission of expert evidence with cross examination of the witness; At p. 349 Borgmann-Prebil observes; 'Art 18 (1)EC is therefore best understood as a general wide ranging prima facie right that can be limited by virtue of countervailing 'objective considerations of public interest' whether specific manifestations of these are enshrined in specific provisions of (secondary) Community law or not. ... Once a measure is rendered a restriction there is a need to justify those rules constituting restrictions according to standards recognised by Community law. This is the most important aspect of the rule of reason analogy'.' Arguably however, Borgmann-Prebil has recognised in the sentence cited above that the limitation of Art. 18 (1) involves standards whether or not they are recognised by Community law. It is submitted that this recognition of a

to Sullivan,[36] they will be considered to be 'absurd' and 'not intended'[37] by the legislature. Further, there is the matter of Case Management Rules which as regards the CJ, GC and arguably also the ECtHRU are insufficiently proactive[38] and which also contribute to the deficiency of expert and non-expert evidence. This combination of the failure to use expert evidence in order to interpret in particular technical words which by definition have a more restricted scope than ordinary words coupled then with what can be an unjustifiably excessive reduction in the scope of the derogations which of course is not based upon any expert evidence is aggravated in the following manner: that the principle of proportionality is applied in a manner which lacks empirical objectivity: specifically, the application of the principle is not informed by the use of expert evidence. This can have a particularly deleterious effect as regards the interpretation of derogations from rights in those cases where derived rights are involved. As

wider evaluative basis corresponds more closely to the use of the term 'rule of reason' in the context of i.e. the Sherman Act (1890): see R Wish & D Bailey *Competition Law*, 7th edn (Oxford, OUP, 2012) '... the fact finder weights all the circumstances of a case in deciding whether a restrictive practice should be prohibited as imposing an unreasonable restraint on competition' 433 US 36, 49 (1977). This is as opposed to an evaluative basis which is limited to standards recognized by Community which may well conflict among other things with the allocation of powers established in Art. 165 TFEU. See also: Y Borgmann-Prebil, *The Rule of Reason in European Constitutionalism and Citizenship* (Routledge) to appear in 2013.

36. R Sullivan, *Sullivan and Driedger on the Construction of Statutes*, 4th edn (Vancouver, Butterworths, 2002), *supra*, Ch. 9 passim.
37. R Sullivan, *Sullivan and Driedger on the Construction of Statutes*, 4th edn (Vancouver, Butterworths, 2002) *ibid.*, 234: 'If adopting an interpretation would lead to absurdity the courts may reject that interpretation in favour of a plausible alternative that avoids the absurdity.' This leads to the question as to what constitutes 'absurdity'. Sullivan observes at 236: 'The modern understanding of the presumptions against absurdity includes the following propositions; (1) it is presumed that the legislature does not intend its legislation to have absurd consequences. (2) Absurd consequences are not limited to logical contradictions or internal incoherence but include violations of established legal norms such as rules of law; they also include violations of widely accepted standards of justice and reasonableness. (3) Whenever possible an interpretation that leads to absurd consequences is rejected in favour of one that avoids absurdity. (4) The more compelling the absurdity the greater the departure from ordinary meaning that is tolerated'. As regards the role of evidence in demonstrating what may constitute an absurd consequence arising from an incorrect statutory interpretation Sullivan observes: at 243 'To be successful a claim that certain consequences will follow from a particular interpretation must be grounded in real possibility. Evidence is admissible to establish the truth of this claim but normally the courts rely on judicial notice in judging a claimed absurdity to be convincing or 'merely speculative'. Courts may reject an absurdity based argument if the facts on which it depends are unlikely to occur or are unlike those at issues in the case.' Finally, Sullivan interestingly holds that there is or should be a symbiosis between the elimination of absurdities and the use of teleological interpretation and observes at 251 'The Court's jurisdiction to avoid absurd results parallels and complements is jurisdiction to promote legislative purpose. Whereas purposive analysis justifies the preference for interpretations that lead to good consequences which are presumed to be intended avoiding absurdity justifies the rejection of interpretations that lead to undesirable consequences which are presumed to be unintended. Like the purposive analysis consequential analysis should be part of every effort to apply legislation to particular facts.' For the instant purposes, absurdity in terms of unintended consequences is linked particularly to interpretations which are unreasonable in the sense of not being sustained by any notably expert opinion where such opinion could have been introduced by the court.
38. G Cumming, *Merger Decisions and the Rules of Procedure of the European Community Courts* (Alphen aan den Rijn, Kluwer Law Books 2012).

such statutory interpretation which does not employ expert evidence can distort the meaning of technical words particularly by enlarging their scope of application: that is because no expert evidence is utilized in the interpretation of the words, frequently, technical words, which form the basis of a 'right' in the TFEU or ECHR. In short, the 'right' is enlarged in terms of the scope of its application without any empirical basis and is in turn coupled with restrictive interpretations of derogations but, once again in a manner, which is not predicated upon professional expert opinion and facts. More specifically, failure to introduce expert evidence in order to define the terms of the principle of proportionality as it is applied in a specific context can lead to an interpretation of the aforementioned terms in their ordinary as opposed to technical sense which accordingly aggravates the violation of Article 19 TEU: that is, the legal competence of the Member States or vires,[39] is undermined and a form of harmonization is introduced, in violation of the principle of subsidiarity,[40] which has no empirical justification. The failure on the part of the CJ to envisage or to consider that certain of the words of the TFEU and of the secondary EU legislation such as Directives, contain not only ordinary meaning but also technical meaning is, in turn, aggravated by the failure on the part of that court to properly exercise its powers as provided by its rules of procedure. These rules[41] provide for the appointment of experts in order to properly evaluate the evidence provided by the parties pursuant to Article 6 (1) ECHR as interpreted in *Kraska v Switzerland*.[42] It is submitted that in the situation of a preliminary reference, the responsibility in such non-contentious proceedings is incumbent much more on the CJ as regards the assembling of the evidence than would be the case were the proceedings contentious.[43]

Moreover, and as just noted, the matter of the deficiency of expert evidence involves very much the duty of the judge according to Kraska,[44] therefore pursuant to

---

39. P Craig, 'The ECJ and Ultra Vires Actions: A Conceptual Analysis' (2011) *CMLRev* (48) (2) 357; T Horsley, 'Reflections on the Role of the Court of Justice as the 'Motor' of European Integration: Legal Limits to Judicial Law Making' (2013) CMLRev (50) (4) 931.
40. R van den Bergh 'Subsidiarity as an Economic Demarcation Principle and the Emergence of European Private Law' (1998) MJL 129 at 130.
41. The relevant rules of procedure are both cited and considered in subsequent chapters herein.
42. *Kraska v Switzerland,* Application No. 13942/88, Judgement of 19 April 1993 (1993) *EHRR* (18) 188, *supra,* at para. 30.
43. P Lasok, *The European Court of Justice- Practice and Procedure* (London Butterworths 1994) at 346:

> The role of evidence in non-contentious proceedings depends upon the nature of the proceedings and the relevance to them of findings of fact. In principle the fact that proceedings are non-contentious in nature means that fact finding is inquisitorial rather than accusatorial and in consequence that there is no evidential burden of proof (although there may well be a legal burden of proof arising as a matter of substantive law).

44. *Kraska v Switzerland,* Application No. 13942/88, Judgement of 19 April 1993 (1993) *EHRR* (18) 188 at para. 30. 'It falls to the Court to decide whether the contested proceedings considered as a whole were fair within the meaning of the Convention. The effect of Article 6 para. 1 (Article 6-1) is, inter alia, to place the "tribunal" under a duty to conduct a proper examination of the submissions, arguments and evidence adduced by the parties, without prejudice to its assessment of whether they are relevant to its decision (see, among other authorities, mutatis

ECHR Article 6 (1), to examine carefully the submissions, arguments and evidence presented by the parties notably however, from two points of view: firstly, from the point of view the point of view of the knowledge used by the judge to evaluate the evidence. This may require, in the context of Measures of Investigation[45] which exist in the rules of both the ECtHR, the CJ and the GC the appointment of a court expert, or assessor, to assist the judge in understanding the meaning of a technical word but also as serving as an indisputable source for judicial notice of the ordinary meaning of a word. It is clear that this duty necessitates that a judge consider making recourse to such expert opinion in order to ensure proper evaluation when his own knowledge from the point of view of statutory interpretation is insufficient. Indeed, depending upon the context of meaning and facts the duty may require that the judge specifically use expert evidence. This duty pursuant to Kraska[46] is arguably an express duty to ensure a fair trial through the correct application of the law to the true facts which of course may require recourse to the rules of procedure in order to appoint an expert to inform the judge possibly through the process of judicial notice or through cross examination by the parties in order to obtain and understand the correct and accurate information. The second aspect, however, of this duty of the judge is to carefully evaluate evidence in order to ensure that the rights of the defence are respected in the sense of the principle of contradiction. In short, this limb of the duty requires the judge to inform the parties of the criterion which are being used to evaluate the submissions: whether it is personal knowledge of fact or law on the part of the judge or whether it is an expert witness. This involves the use by the judge of his own or acquired, through an expert, knowledge of fact or law or both in the formation of this decision and effectively the right for a party to be able to comment upon the use of this knowledge by the judge in so far as it affects the party. According to Jolowicz:[47]

> The subject matter [the use by the judge of this own knowledge of fact or law in the formation of his decision] is at the heart of the judicial process and perhaps for that reason is one to which the rules of positive law seldom refer in explicit terms. It is more intractable than many: in the last resort it is concerned with the mental processes of the judge himself and those processes cannot ordinarily be known save to the extent that the judge is willing to disclose them in his exposition of the

---

mutandis, the Barberà, Messegué and Jabardo v Spain judgment of 6 December 1988, Series A no. 146, 31, para. 68). It has to be determined whether this condition was satisfied in the instant case.'

45. Measures of Organisation of Procedure and Measures of Inquiry Arts 62-64 Court of Just and the ECtHR CJ and the ECtHR Annex to the Rules1 Annexe (concerning investigations)

    Rule A1 – Investigative measures
    1. The Chamber may, at the request of a party or of its own motion, adopt any investigative measure which it considers capable of clarifying the facts of the case. The Chamber may, *inter alia*, invite the parties to produce documentary evidence and decide to hear as a witness or expert or in any other capacity any person whose evidence or statements seem likely to assist it in carrying out its tasks.
    2. The Chamber may also ask any person or institution of its choice to express an opinion or make a written report on any matter considered by it to be relevant to the case.

46. *Kraska v Switzerland*, Application No. 13942/88, Judgement of 19 April 1993 (1993) *EHRR* (18) 188 at para. 30.
47. A Jolowicz On Civil Procedure (Cambridge, CUP, 2000) 243.

> reasons for his decision or in the course of the proceedings leading up to his decision. Nor is it possible rigidly and accurately to enforce such rules as there may be which purport to restrict use by the judge of knowledge that he happens to have. ... For the time being only two means of control exist – a judge possessed of knowledge of which he cannot make legitimate use in a given case can be disqualified and a decision which is seen to be based in part on such knowledge can be set aside by a court of appeal or cassation.

It is clear that the primary concern at this point is protecting the rights of the defence concerning the rights of the parties to exercise a measure of control over the use made by the judge of his knowledge. This is arguably what Zuckerman[48] describes in the following manner:

> It is a basic requirement of procedural fairness that any person affected by a judicial decision should have an opportunity to be heard before the decision is made. The primary though not sole purpose of the right to be heard is to give the affected person and opportunity to present his side of the story and to respond to the evidence and arguments advanced against him. Since without knowledge of the case to be met a right to be heard would be of little value the right to be heard entails a right to prior and timely notice of the case that one has to meet and a reasonable opportunity to respond by presenting evidence or advanced argument. We may refer to this bundle of rights as the right to effective participation in the proceedings. ... The ECHR has recognised that the right to be heard is not absolute and that necessity may justify exceptions. However, an exception may only be made for legitimate purposes it must be strictly limited and it must be proportionate in the circumstances.[49] Furthermore exceptions must be accompanied by adequate safeguards to protect the interests of the party whose right to participation has been restricted.

The next matter to examine is the control of the types of knowledge which a judge may use. Jolowicz[50] observes:

> there is as might be expected virtual unanimity of view that the judge may use his personal knowledge of the ordinary course of human affairs his 'general knowledge' his 'common sense'. Otherwise it would be impossible for him to carry out his judicial function in relation to disputed questions of fact.

However, expert or technical matters are somewhat different. Here the matter turns once again upon the duty of the court to provide a proper evaluation of the submissions arguments and evidence of the parties in order to comply with the express and derived right pursuant to Article 6 (1) ECHR: that is in the instant circumstances to avail himself

48. A Zuckerman, 'Civil Procedure: Principles and Practise', 2nd edn (London, Thomson, 2006) at 112.
49. *Ashingdane v UK* (EHRR) 528 at (57) *Stubbings v UK* RJD 1996 – IV No 18 (1996) 23 EHRR 213 at 48. Zukerman also observes on p. 115 'Also, in non adversarial proceedings such as references it has been held by the ECtHR hqt the non-adversarial nature of the proceedings cannot displace altogether the right to fair trial under ECHR Art 6.1.' And at p. 118 'Even where court proceedings involving children are non-adversarial in the sense that the court is predominantly concerned to protect the interests of children, the court must respect the parents' right to an adversarial process.'
50. A Jolowicz, *On Civil Procedure* (Cambridge, CUP, 2000), *supra*, 256.

in the context of the Investigative Measures of the possibility to as to appoint a court expert. In this regard, Jolowicz observes:

> It is axiomatic that no judge is omniscient. We do not in reality demand of a judge a universal knowledge even of the rules of law in force in his own jurisdiction. Certainly we demand of the judges a certain intuitive on legal issues but above all we demand that they have the ability to understand and evaluate legal reasons put forward by other – the advocates and for the judges of appellate courts the reasoning of their colleagues in the courts below. As regards the facts since we cannot demand of the judges that they have knowledge of every branch of science of every art and of the mysteries of every profession we cannot demand either that they resolve question of fact requiring such knowledge unless they have help from suitable qualified experts.

In truth, the essence of the present analysis concerns the knowledge utilized by the judge in adjudicating a case, and in the instant situation, carrying out statutory interpretation. However, arguably, this knowledge of the judge is best analysed from two perspectives in the context of its impact upon Article 6 (1) ECHR: first, from the perspective of the rights of the defence in the sense of being able to challenge or contradict the knowledge of fact or law which the judge uses in order to adjudicate a particular case. This may be either through his own knowledge or through knowledge obtained from an expert. This expert knowledge, it is submitted, is necessary in order to ensure due process. Jolowicz[51] as will be seen shortly, refers to this aspect of the use of the knowledge of the judge as the principe du contradictoire; second, there is the perspective wherein the judge has a duty to analyse the facts or submissions presented by the parties pursuant to Kraska[52] noted earlier in a careful and appropriate manner. This deals with the duty of the court to ensure what might be termed the quality of the evaluation carried out by the judge when using his knowledge of laws or facts pursuant to a case such as Kraska[53] where in the court, as is recalled, observed as follows:

> 30. It falls to the Court to decide whether the contested proceedings considered as a whole were fair within the meaning of the Convention. The effect of Article 6 para. 1 (art. 6-1) is, inter alia, to place the 'tribunal' under a duty to conduct a proper examination of the submissions, arguments and evidence adduced by the parties, without prejudice to its assessment of whether they are relevant to its decision (see, among other authorities, mutatis mutandis, the Barberà, Messegué and Jabardo v. Spain judgment of 6 December 1988, Series A no. 146, p. 31, para. 68). It has to be determined whether this condition was satisfied in the instant case.

It is submitted that the meaning of 'proper examination' in the aforementioned judgment 'duty to conduct a proper examination of the submissions, arguments and evidence adduced by the parties' signifies that the court must analyse and examine the submissions, arguments and evidence with care. Arguably, this duty of care may extend to the appointment of an expert by the court on its own initiative or that of the

51. J A Jolowicz On Civil Procedure (Cambridge CUP 2000) Ch. 13 The use by the judge of his own knowledge (of fact or law or both) in the formation of his decision.
52. *Kraska v Switzerland* (1999) EHRR (18) 188.
53. *Kraska v Switzerland* (1999) EHRR (18) 188, *ibid.*

parties in order to obtain an accurate understanding in circumstances that the judge's own knowledge is insufficient: that is notably where the word to be interpreted are of a technical nature which because of their complexity require the knowledge of an expert and not the knowledge of a generalist; or the judge dispenses with formal proof and makes use of Judicial Notice[54] using as an indisputable source for the knowledge is an expert. In such circumstances the expert certainly in English civil procedure is known as an assessor.[55] Such an approach as regards the use of expert evidence, however, would require to be in conformity with two other procedural imperatives, namely, costs and time.[56] Accordingly, it has been necessary to consider both aspects of the duty which requires that the courts properly examine the submissions of the party or parties with respect to the technical meaning of words which the judge may or may not possess in addition to the right of the defence to respond to this judicial knowledge or interpretation in a contradictory manner.

I STATUTORY INTERPRETATION: METHODS OF INTERPRETATION AND PROOF OF MEANING

In large measure, the centerpiece of the instant analysis is effectively the comparative examination[57] of the use of expert evidence by various tribunals in the interpretation

54. The concept of Judicial Notice will be defined and examined in detail later in the analysis.
55. CPR Rules: The opinions presented by the assessor are not submitted for cross examination in so far as their use in the context of what may be termed the narrow use of Judicial Notice requires the subject area to be one which is indisputable. In contrast – would permit the use of cross examination. In so far as the scope of judicial notice may extend to include matters which are not indisputable. Certainly some such as Brewer appear to oppose the use of such court appointed experts based upon the view that judges should have specialist training which appear to be unrealistic: S Brewer 'Scientific Expert Testimony and Intellectual Due Process' (1998) Yale Law Journal (107) 1535 at 1681 'In Justice Breyer's view given this challenge judges should more actively solicit scientific information in order to perform their Daubert mandated role of "gatekeepers" vigilant against junk science for example by using court appointed experts (Fed R Evid 706) appointing special masters or specially trained law clerks or using pre-trial conferences to narrow the scientific issues. But for reasons suggested above this solution also fails to meet the needs of intellectual due process for any judge who is himself not epistemically competent in scientific methods and theories. For the judge is not capable of making an epistemically legitimate decisions about which a special master, a law clerk or a court appointed expert to consult. The only solution I see requires that one and the same legal decision maker wear two hats the hat of epistemic competence and the hat of practical legitimacy. That is whether it is a scientifically trained judge or juror or agency administrator the same person who has legal authority must also have epistemic competence in relevant scientific disciplines. In an age in which culture will increasingly take advantage of the massive intellectual power of science this is not too high a price for the legal system to pay to satisfy its own just intellectual aspirations.'
56. A Zuckerman 'Justice in Crisis: Comparative Dimensions of Civil Procedure', in A Zuckerman (ed) *Civil Justice in Crisis* (Oxford, OUP, 1999), *supra*, at 6 'There are further dimensions of justice which while having no direct bearing on rectitude of decision have powerful influence on both the justice of the system and on individual outcomes. These are time and cost.'
57. O Kahn Freund, 'On Uses and Misuses of Comparative Law' (1974) MLR (37) (1) 1 It is useful to be aware of the practical difficulties involved in the comparison of different legal systems and in particular of different systems of procedures which may be uniquely connected to the political system. Kahn-Freund observes in this regard at p. 19: 'However if we consider those institutions and procedures which express the power of the legal profession and the distribution of power

notably of international treaties and national laws. As noted earlier, the tribunals are those of the European Court of Human Rights (ECtHR), the Court of Justice of the European Union (CJ); the Supreme Court of the United States (USSC); the Supreme Court of Canada (SCC) and the Supreme Court of British Columbia, Canada (BCSC). The documents involved are the ECHR, the TFEU, the US Constitution and the Canadian Charter of Human Rights and Freedoms. Thus, it is necessary to consider in more detail the actual process of statutory interpretation in order to prepare for the analysis of judgments made by the aforementioned courts. One recalls that the essential legal and linguistic context in which this analysis has been placed is not just that of a reference to either the CJ or a direct action before the ECtHR, but rather something more specific: namely, statutory interpretation - or simply interpretation of statutes which in the case of the TFEU and the ECHR refers to the words contained within each of the component articles of those international treaties.[58] Dealing once again with the nature of technical meaning of words and proof thereof by experts in the context of the duty of a judge to properly consider the meaning of the statute presented by a party, Sullivan[59] observes:

> Whether a term has a technical meaning and what that meaning is are both questions of fact which must be established in a legally acceptable way. When a technical or specialised meaning is not something that everybody knows it cannot be judicially noticed but must be established through evidence normally expert opinion evidence. Such evidence is required to establish both that a term has a technical meaning and the content of that meaning.

At this point it is useful to consider briefly the concept of judicial notice and its use notably in the proof of the meaning of ordinary words. Roberts and Zuckerman[60] observe:

---

within the legal profession we see the barriers.' And at 20 'With renewed apologies to Maitland one may say that procedural law is tough law. All that concerns the technique of legal practise likely to resist change. In most respects the organisation of courts and of the legal profession, the law of procedure and the law of evidence help to allocate power and belong in Montesquieu's sense to the lois politiques. Comparative law has far greater utility in substantive law than in the law of procedure and the attempt to use foreign models of judicial organization and procedure may lead to frustration and may thus be a misuse of the comparative method.' It is to be noted that in the instant case a comparison of the rules can be made in so far as the rules of procedure of all of the courts considered, CJ, GC, ECtHR, USSC, SCC, and BCSC, specifically provide for the use of expert evidence and certainly in the case of the CJ, GC and ECtHR, appointment by the courts on their motion, of an expert. Accordingly, the comparison involves the different use of similar rules as regards the obtaining and the utilization of expert evidence by a court.

58. R Sullivan, *Sullivan and Driedger on the Construction of Statutes,* 4th edn (Vancouver, Butterworths, 2002), *supra;* P Côté, *Interprétation des Lois* (Cowainsville, Les Editions Yvon Blais Inc, 1982); R Bigwood, *The Statute: Making and Meaning* (Wellington, Lexis Nexis, 2004); M Beaupré Interpreting Bi-Lingual Legislation, 2nd edn (Toronto, Carswell, 1986); S Corcoran, *Interpretation* (Sydney, Federation Press, 2005) D Greenberg (ed) *Craies on Legislation,* 10th edn (London, Sweet and Maxwell, 2012); F Bennion, *Bennion on Statutory Interpretation,* 5th edn (London, Lexis Nexis 2008); O Jones *Bennion on Statutory Interpretation,* Supplement to the Fifth Edition (London, Lexis Nexis 2010).
59. R Sullivan, *Sullivan and Driedger on the Construction of Statutes,* 4th edn (Vancouver, Butterworths, 2002), *ibid.*
60. P Roberts and A Zuckerman, *Criminal Evidence* (Oxford, OUP, 2004), 173, *supra.*

> Requiring a party to prove a matter which is patently a forgone conclusion would saddle him with an excessive and unnecessary burden. The test of indisputability is therefore the key to identifying when a judge may properly dispense with the normal requirements of proof. However indisputability can be understood in two different senses. The first one corresponds to facts that 'everybody knows'. ... Indisputability in the second sense covers facts that can be ascertained definitively without necessarily being universally or even widely now. ... For the purpose of informing itself of such matters the court may have access not only to reliable documentary sources but also to experts. To summarize, facts may be indisputable either because they are generally accepted by the community at large or because they may be ascertained by consulting reliable and trusted sources (*McQuaker v Goddard* (1940 1 KB 687).

As noted, earlier, pursuant to Article 6 (1) ECHR and cases such as Kraska,[61] both the CJ, GC and the ECtHR are 'under a duty to conduct a proper examination of the submissions, arguments and evidence adduced by the parties 'in order to comply' in the round'[62] with the absolute duty to ensure a fair trial: it is submitted that in certain circumstances involving either the interpretation of technical words or the use of judicial notice of ordinary meaning where an indisputable source is used by the judge: then in order to comply with the duty of care and provide a 'proper evaluation of the evidence' the judge may be obliged to make recourse to an expert as opposed to relying upon its own knowledge. Indeed, arguably, an omission by the judge to make use of an expert in a context involving the statutory interpretation of such words and in some cases when judicial notice is employed, may lead to contravention of the obligation to ensure a 'proper evaluation of the submissions, arguments and evidence' tendered by the parties. This is particularly so given that an attempt to not use expert evidence, that is a restriction upon the right to 'proper evaluation', would thus not be justifiable by reason of the following considerations: namely, because a judge without a particular type of training such as in economics or political science would be unable to understand the technical words contained within the expert opinion and therefore the judgment would be taken effectively by the expert. Provision exists for appointment within the rules of both the CJ and the ECT for an assessor or a technician to be appointed in order to assist the judge to understand the expert opinion.[63]

---

61. *Kraska v Switzerland*, Application No. 13942/88, Judgement of 19 April 1993 (1993) *EHRR* (18) 188 at para. 30.
62. LA Mulcahy, *Human Rights and Civil Practice* (ed) (London Sweet and Maxwell 2001) at 369; and R Clayton QC and H Tomlinson QC, *The Law of Human Rights*, 2nd edn (Oxford, OUP, 2009) at 827 'Proceedings covered by Art 6 In order for the guarantees to apply there must be a right, obligation or charge in play and the proceedings must involve its determination. Proceedings are determinative in relation to civil rights and obligations when the outcome of the proceedings is decisive for them whether or not such determination is the primary purpose of the proceedings. *Ringeisen v Austria* No 1 (1971) 1 *EHRR* 455 (this case greatly expanded the scope of Art 6 in this context).' Accordingly, although the purpose of the reference procedure under Art. 267 TFEU may not be dispositive in fact overall, taking into account the national proceedings which involve the obligatory application of the CJ judgment and the ECtHR judgment on that precise point by national court – it remains to be see to what extent the judgments will bind the CJ – and therefore dispose effectively of the case. This is dealt with in more detail in a later chapter of this book.
63. E Barbier de La Serre and A-L Sibony 'Expert Evidence' (2008) *CMLRev* 941 at 984 'However it is striking that the EC Courts only rarely hear expert evidence despite the fact that they often deal

One notes the comments of former Judge Edward[64] as regards the nature of the decision to use an expert:

> What is the role of the expert in that context? I think the way to put it is this. The expert's report, the expert's investigations, are simply one tool in the judge's armoury of decision-making. They are one way in which a judge may go about deciding on an element in the case that needs to be established one way or another. Ultimately, the procedure, unlike the 'lay' procedure of the common law, is archetypally 'judicial' – the judge decides what are the crucial issues and what is the best way of resolving them.

While this statement is doubtless correct, one must add, however, that the judge exercises the discretion to use or not to use an expert in the context of certain principles of law. The judicial discretion is not untrammelled. Thus, the discretion will be affected notably by Article 6 (1) ECHR. Further, as was noted previously, the current expert evidence deficit may lead to a breach not only of the Article 6 ECHR but also to contravention of Article 19 TEU.[65]

It is recalled that the objective of statutory interpretation consists in providing an accurate interpretation of the words of the statute so as to permit in turn an accurate and judicious application of the law. In this regard, jurisprudentially, concepts of accurate and true applications of the law require attention. Thus, one might say that the scope of Article 19 TEU is subject to the following reflection by Jolowicz[66] as regards the notion of the correct application of law:

> The principle difficulty about the demand for correct decisions is for decisions which declare correctly the legal consequences that have come about through the operation of existing law on facts which have already occurred is that when we speak of law existing and operating in the society we use the language of metaphor. Or if that be too sceptical a view at least it is true that the results of the operation of law cannot be independently observed and verified. So far as the parties to litigation are concerned the judge has the last word subject only to appeal to other judges and we are schooled to accept as correct decisions which are not reversed especially if they are affirmed in appellate courts. The fact is however

with complex technical issues. It is even more striking that the type of expert evidence for which rules of procedure do exist under EC law i.e. evidence adduced by curt appointed impartial experts is the least frequently used while partial expert testimony adduced by the parties is more frequent but operates outside a clear procedural framework. This situation is not wholly satisfactory. It is submitted that improvements to the current law and practice o expert evidence before the EC courts should be guided by the principle expressed by the US Supreme Court in Kumho 'the expert must employ in the courtroom the same level of intellectual rigor that characterizes the practice of an expert in the relevant field'. Unfortunately current EC law does not guarantee systematic meaningful scrutiny of the reliability of scientific evidence in the EC Courts'.

64. Sir David Edward QC 'Evidence, Proof, Fact-Finding and the Expert Witness' *Expert Witness Institute* – 29 April 2004, 7th Sir Michael Davies Lecture at 8-9, //www.law.du.edu/documents/judge-david-edward-oral-history/2004-proof-fact-finding.pdf.
65. Article 19 TEU '1. The Court of Justice of the European Union shall include the Court of Justice, the General Court and specialised courts. It shall ensure that in the interpretation and application of the Treaties the law is observed. Member States shall provide remedies sufficient to ensure effective legal protection in the fields covered by Union law.'
66. A Jolowicz, *On Civil Procedure* (Cambridge, CUP, 2000) at 86.

> that no judicial decisions though final and binding on the parties can be more than an expression of opinion on a matter not susceptible of proof: there are no objective or external criteria capable of establishing the correctness or otherwise of a decision.

Notwithstanding what appears to be a positivist[67] description of law just presented by Jolowicz he nevertheless goes onto to consider what is necessary in his view for what might be termed the 'correct' as opposed to the 'incorrect' view of law:

> In these circumstances and however unfortunate some may consider the conclusion to be it has to be accepted that the nearest thing to a correct decision that it is possible to achieve is a decision reached by a judge who has all the information at his disposal that he personally considers necessary concerning both the facts - which means the facts that he considers to be relevant – and the law. Or to put the same point negatively the dangers of an incorrect decision are much greater where the parties have control of the information which the judge may use when he comes to his decision than where the judge has that control himself. All things being equal an inquisitorial type of procedure is therefore more likely to produce the correct decision than an accusatorial or adversarial procedure where the judge's role is only to decide between the rival contentions of the parties. Whatever we may ultimately mean by a correct decision it would be odd to describe as correct a decision that the judge himself believes to be wrong because he was deprived of information he considered he should have had or was debarred from apply the rule of law he thought appropriate to the case.

Jolowicz concludes by making the following remarks:

> ... The movement towards what is sometimes called the more active court which has undoubtedly taken place on the continent and also though to a lesser extent in common law countries [case management] is in part attributable to realisation that for a correct to be achieved the court must be able to obtain and to use the information which it considers necessary rather than that it should base its decision only on the information which the parties are willing that it should have.

Ultimately however, the ability of the judge to obtain evidence and, in particular, expert evidence in a somewhat inquisitorial procedural system such as that of the ECtHR the CJ and GC is arguably substantial: that is, by reason of procedurally being able to obtain information directly through the Measures of Inquiry which include the appointment of effectively a court expert the judge who is able not only to achieve correct application of the law but also to so do by augmenting the information presented by the parties. Thus, according to Jolowicz, 'a judge should endeavour to give the correct decision according to law on the facts before him without being restricted to the legal reasoning submitted by the parties or their counsel.'[68]

Interestingly, Jolowicz goes on to state his preference for rules such as those used in both the CJ, GC and the ECtHR which might be termed to be inspired or drawn from

67. In the tradition of J Bentham, *Theory of Legislation* (London, Kegan Paul, 1911); H L A Hart *The Concept of Law* (Oxford, OUP, 1961); in contra R Dworkin, *Taking Rights Seriously* (Cambridge, Massc., Harvard Press, 1977); R Dworkin, *A Matter of Principle* (Cambridge, Massc., Harvard Press, 1979); J Rawls, *A Theory of Justice* (Oxford, OUP, 1971).
68. A Jolowicz, *On Civil Procedure* (Cambridge, CUP, 2000), *supra*, at p. 86.

the 'inquisitorial' model of the civil law tradition as opposed to those from the accusatorial model of the common law tradition:

> Other things being equal an inquisitorial type of procedure is therefore more likely to produce the correct decision than an accusatorial or adversarial procedure where the judge's role is only to decide between the rival contentions of the parties. Whatever however we may ultimately mean by correct decision it would be odd to describe as correct a decision that the judge himself believes to be wrong because he was deprives of information he considered he should have had or was debarred from applying the rule of law he thought appropriate to the case.[69]

Arguably, therefore, Jolowicz's observations can be applied to the rules of the CJ, GC and the ECtHR generally and, in particular, with respect to the use of expert evidence and the appointment of court experts: that is, in so far as the function of a tribunal is to establish the truth by applying the law accurately to the correct facts the rules of procedure of these two courts are if correctly utilized by the judges capable of producing accurate judgments and ensuring compliance with both Article 6 TFEU and Article 6 (1) of the ECHR. For it is clear that both the rules of procedure utilized by the CJ, GC and ECtHR are fundamentally inspired by the inquisitorial tradition and in particular provide for the use of a court expert.

Bearing in mind once again, the constraints of the legal positivism which appear to characterize the position of Jolowicz one might also observe the following: namely, however difficult what might be termed an objectively accurate judgment may be to attain nevertheless ensuring that judgments contain an element of plausibility through the manner in which they have been interpreted is necessary: arguably, the presence or the use of expert evidence can confer upon a judgment an element of social legitimacy in so far as the domain of activity in which experts operate have become accepted, following the analysis of Zukerman, within a social group. In this regard, Zuckerman[70] observes:

> A judge deciding whether expert opinion should be accepted as an arbiter of a certain matter has to consider the state of public opinion on the point. If the community has come to defer to professional standards on the matter in question the courts will normally follow suit. Medical evidence is admissible on matters of health because we accept the authority of the medical profession in this regard. Psychiatry has not yet attained a like acceptance. Psychiatric evidence is admissible on the issue of insanity but not on the mental state of a normal person [in England]. It is arguable that the distinction is irrational; for to understand abnormality psychiatry has first to must the normal mental processes. However, as long as the community does not defer to psychiatry on matters such as intention and credibility the scope for expert evidence on such matters must remain limited and judicial difference of opinion of the kind we came across in Turner and Lowery are to be expected. Only when public opinion is clear one way or another can we demand consistency from the courts.

Therefore, the use of experts may serve to confer an element of social legitimacy upon a statutory interpretation particularly if the interpretation is somewhat strained or

69. *Ibid.*, at 86.
70. A Zuckerman, *Principles of Criminal Evidence* (Oxford, Clarendon, 1989), *supra*, 81-83.

marginally implausible. Arguably, this element of social legitimacy is critical in a legal system where it is difficult to speak of an absolute legal truth[71] notably in domains which touch upon national political powers as can be the case in interpretations of both the TFEU and the ECHR: that is, the interpretation achieves an acceptance in the sense of it being adopted by many speakers of a particular language group or several language groups primarily or in large measure because it is founded upon an expert view in a field of expertise accepted by a large segment of the population which speaks a particular language: such would perhaps be the case as illustrated earlier by Zuckerman of general medicine as opposed to psychiatry with the latter being increasingly absorbed within the former. This gradual absorption of the category of psychiatry would therefore have the effect of according thereby a certain legitimacy to statutory interpretation notably of technical words but possibly also ordinary meaning interpreted through judicial notice based upon the expert opinion of psychiatrists.

II THEORETICAL BASIS OF THE ANALYSIS IN THIS BOOK

Overall, it is submitted that the analysis herein follows generally from the theoretical position advanced by Rasmussen:[72] namely, the CJ while rightly pursuing a certain degree of judicial activism through statutory interpretation, nevertheless undermines the quality of its judgments by among other things, a lack of 'socio economic' facts and

71. One might contrast for example the positive view of law of perhaps H L A Hart, *The Concept of Law* (Oxford, Clarendon Press, 1961), *supra*, with the natural justice which underlies the operation of medieval Roman Catholic canon law (*Decretum Gratiani*, or *Codex Iuris Canonici* 1983) or the contrast between R Posner, *Economic Analysis of Law* (Kluwer Law Books, The Hague, 2007) and R Dworkin, *A Matter of Principle* (Cambridge MA, HUP, 1985), *supra*.

72. H Rasmussen, *On Law and Policy in the European Court of Justice* (The Hague, Martinus Nijhoff Publishers, 1986) at 512 'The prescriptions of my study are of a mixed nature as regards judicial activism in the Community. One the one hand I clearly recommend the containing of judicial translation of the political objectives of the Preamble into operational (constitutional) law. On the other hand, access to socio-economic fact and better docket controlling techniques are notions inseparably intertwined with the conduct of politically relevant judicial business. And that is where all signals point: 'Whether we like it or not whether we long for its furtherance or fight against it we have come to grips with politicisation of courts because it shapes the character of our time. Whether courts openly acknowledge that they are activist lawmaking institutions or not and whether existing constraints on judicial policy involvement are insurmountable or not judicial independence – if real – makes it extremely difficult to act upon if the judges themselves do not show commensurate restraint. At the end of a judicial activism running wild however: the frightening image of court curbing or even court destroying initiatives emerges. Therefore in the context of the Community the answer to a runaway courts is not a messenger boy court. The judges must not be allowed to like red robed kings but neither are they to be reduced to law finding puppets.... Between the clearly acceptable and the clearly unacceptable lies a presumably vast area of judicial involvement in public policymaking. Monitoring carefully the great variety of policy inputs the Court must in the first place define the scope of its legitimate action. There is a need for a strong Court acting clearly within the powers allotted to it by the provisions of the Treaties and by intervening constitutional developments.' See also TC Hartey, 'The European Court, Judicial Objectivity and the Constitution of the European Union' (1996) *LQR* (112) 95; in contra A Arnull, 'The European Court and Judicial Objectivity: A Reply to Professor Hartley' (1996) *LQR* (112) at 411; A Arnull *The European Union and its Court of Justice*, 2nd edn Oxford OUP 2006.

proof.[73] The analysis will however, not be restricted to the CJ but will include the ECtHR. It is submitted that the observations of Rasmussen as regards the lack of socio-economic facts can be best analysed in the context of what might be interpreted as a deficit of facts, both of expert and non-expert nature attributable in large measure to the rules of Civil Procedure which deal with the following: appointment of experts; case management and the drafting of pleadings. The primary focus of this study will however be the deficit of the expert facts and evidence, which would include among others the 'socio economic' facts referred to by Rasmussen. In this regard, the scope of

73. T Horsley 'Reflections on the Role of the Court of Justice as the 'Motor' of European Integration: Legal limits to judicial Law Making' (2013) *CMLRev* 931, *supra,* at 963 'The legal limits outline in this paper function alongside the Treaties' empowering provisions as sources of normative restraint on the Court's freedom to shape unilaterally the outer limits of EU law along both the vertical and horizontal axes.' It is submitted that with due respect Horsley, that the aforementioned 'legal limits' can only operate provided that in addition there are added the not only the TFEU but also procedural principles such as rectitude of decision, methods of statutory interpretation which include consideration of the semantic and evidential elements of the proof and analysis of the meaning of the words which constitute the TFEU in the official languages. Above all, legal limits will be established by explicit proof of meaning which will require consideration of the role of expert evidence in the context of ordinary and technical. It is the failure to consideration statutory interpretation and above all the necessary obligation to prove meaning and the exercise of the powers of the CJ GC and the ECtHR to obtain expert information which arguably leads to inaccurate interpretation of the 'legal limits' among other things and above all inaccurate application of the law to true facts in violation not only of the procedural principle of rectitude of decision but also of Art. 6 (1) ECHR. Similarly with P Craig 'The ECJ and Ultra Vires Action: A Conceptual Analysis' (2011) *CMLRev* (48) 395, *supra,* at 436-473 'The scope of intra vires action is an endemic problem for any polity that has limited power. The determination of those limits is often contestable, more specially in a polity such as the EU where the range of powers accorded to it are broad and certain powers are couched in language that renders it difficult to impose tight constraints on its exercise'. Craig's observation 'The determination of those limits is often contestable ...' is arguably a mirror image of the analysis of Horsley above and therefore requires in order to be functional explicit consideration to be given to methods of interpretation, proof of the meaning of the ordinary and technical meaning of the words in the TFEU notably through expert evidence in default of which violation of the principle of rectitude of decision and ECHR Art. 6 (1) will ineluctably follow and thereby prevent proper determination of the 'legal limits' or 'vires'. Finally, a similarly respectful criticism is directed to J Bengoetxea, N MacCormick and L M Soriano 'Integration and Integrity in the Legal Reasoning of the European Court of Justice', in G De Burca and J Weiler *The European Court of Justice* (Oxford, OUP, 2001) 41 at 51: the authors set forth Categories of Arguments. Although using the terms 'Linguistics or Semiotic categories, Ordinary Meaning EC Law Meaning and Language Version Arguments' the authors at no point connect the above theoretical constructs with the operation of statutory interpretation by the CJ and the GC in particular as regards the judicial proof of the meaning ordinary and technical of the component words of the TFEU. In so far therefore as evidential deficiency and its effect upon the proof of meaning, technical and ordinary, is not considered, the analysis proposed by the authors of judicial activism or more particularly operating within the 'legal limits' (Horsley) or 'vires' (Craig) must with due respect to the learned scholars, be considered as incomplete and incapable of justifying their conclusions. In short the authors have not considered the rules of procedure which are or may be used by the CJ and the GC and eventually the ECtHR which involve judicial proof of meaning notably in the context of the rules of procedure of those respective courts. Similarly as regards the analysis proposed by A Grimmel, 'Judicial Interpretation or Judicial Activism? The Legacy of Rationalism in the Studies of the European Court of Justice' (2012) *ELJ* (18) (4) at 518.

admissible evidence used by the Supreme Court of Canada in the judgment of Sauvé[74] as regards social sciences is particularly helpful and will be discussed in further detail in a later section of this book. Suffice it to say that for the Canadian court, evidence for proof involving concepts of the social sciences may include not just empirical data but also detailed logical analysis as presented in the form of political theories.

The actual corpus of data for the analysis will be restricted for reasons of convenience to certain early judgments of the CJ which involve European Competition and Union Citizenship, and in particular, student grants in the context of preliminary references pursuant to Article 267 TFEU: that is, basically the wording of what are currently, Article 18, 19, 20, 21, 101 and 102 TFEU coupled with Directives 17/62[75] and 2004/38[76] in addition to Article 165 TFEU which deals with jurisdiction and subsidiarity. Further, consideration will be given to direct actions and notably, actions which involve annulment of European Commission decisions involving European Competition law, the EU merger control Regulation 149/2004[77] and TFEU Articles 101 and 102. It is felt that these judgments in themselves constitute a cogent and heuristic valuable example of the method of interpretation utilized by the CJ. This method, as is well known, might be termed teleological.[78] However, it is most usefully analysed in a particular context: namely, when coupled with the evidentiary deficits which result from the teleological interpretation of the ordinary[79] and technical[80] meaning of the

74. *Sauvé v Canada (AG)* (2002) 3 *SCR* 519, *supra*.
75. Council Regulation No.s 17 (EEC): First Regulation implementing Articles 85 and 86 of the Treaty (at present Arts 101 and 102 TFEU) [Official Journal No. 013, 21.2.1962].
76. Formerly Art. 12 and Arts 17-21 of the Treaty Establishing the European Community. Directive 2004/38/EC of the European Parliament and the Council on the Right of Citizens of the Union and their Family Members to Move and reside Freely within the Territory of the Member States OJ 2004, 158/77.
77. Council Regulation (EC) No 139/2004 of 20 January 2004 on the control of concentrations between undertakings (the EC Merger Regulation) Official Journal L 24, 29.01.2004, 1-22.
78. R Sullivan, *Sullivan and Driedger on the Construction of Statutes*, 4th edn (Vancouver, Butterworths, 2002), Ch. 8 Purposive Analysis, *supra*; R Sullivan, *Statutory Interpretation*, 2nd edn (Toronto, Irwin Law Co., 2007), Ch. 5; J Bell & Sir G Engle, *Statutory Interpretation* (London, Butterworths, 1995), 105-112; H Kutscher 'Methods of Interpretation as Seen by a Judge at the Court of Justice' Judicial and Academic Conference, Luxemburg 197) part 1 ss 5-6; B Bennion, *Bennion on Statutory Interpretation: A Code*, 5th edn (London, Lexis Nexis, 2008) Part XXIX; Community Law and the European Court.
79. R Sullivan, *Sullivan and Driedger on the Construction of Statutes*, 4th edn (Vancouver, Butterworths, 2002), *ibid.*, Ch. 2 Ordinary Meaning.
80. R Sullivan, *Sullivan and Driedger on the Construction of Statutes*, 4th edn (Vancouver, Butterworths, 2002), *ibid.*, Ch. 3 Technical and Legal Meaning, 44: 'Faber's observations suggest that the key consideration in determining whether words should have their ordinary or their technical meaning should be the understanding of the audience at which the legislation is directed. As Lord Diplock said in Black Clawson (1975) AC 591 at 638: '... the court must give effect to what the words of the statute would be reasonably understood to mean by those whose conduct it regulates.' p. 46 'In deciding whether to adopt the ordinary or the technical meaning of words courts look to the usual range of factors: the purpose and scheme of the legislation, the consequences of preferring one meaning over another relevant common law principles and so on.'; at 46 'Whether a term has a technical meaning and what that meaning is are both questions of fact which must be established in a legally acceptable way. When a technical or specialized meaning is not something that everybody knows it cannot be judicially noticed but must be established through evidence, normally expert opinion evidence. (Note 29, 46 *Nova v R* (1988) 87 *NR* 101 (FCA) at 109; Township of Waters (1959) SCR 585 at 587-89; *Dentists Supply Co v*

words contained by the aforementioned articles of the TFEU and Directives 17/62 and 2004/38. In short, this method of teleological interpretation when examined in the context of the preliminary references based as, noted, upon an evidentiary deficiency and an absence of active case management[81] produces a particularly wide interpretation of Articles 18, 20 and 21, 101 TFEU and Directive 2004/38. Moreover, this method of interpretation also leads to specific consequences: that is, from the point of view of statutory interpretation, judgments which may be categorized as absurd[82] in the sense, as noted earlier herein, of unreasonable. In short, the statutory interpretations necessary for the judgments have been made without a consideration of relevant evidence, specifically expert evidence[83] as regards the interpretation of their constituent ordinary

---

Deputy MNR (1956) Ex. CR 450, 461-66.) Such evidence is required to establish both that a term has a technical meaning and the content of that meaning. The expert may introduce specialized dictionaries or encyclopedia, textbooks, publications of regulatory authorities or even legislation to support his or her testimony.'; Daniel A Farber 'The Inevitability of Practical Reason: Statutes, Formalism and the Rule of Law' (1992) 45 *Van L Rev* 533 at 552-53) '[Many] important statutes today are not addressed to the ordinary citizen. They are addressed to more specialized audiences – government agencies, legal specialists particular industries. Less sophisticated individuals often rely on official compliance guides or publications by experts to understand the statute rather than deciphering the statute themselves. The more sophisticated audience approaches the statute with a rich contextual understanding of previous law, the politics of the enactment, the affected activity, the dynamics of implementation in that area. It is artificial to ignore all this in interpretation.'

81. AA Zuckerman, *Zuckerman on Civil Procedure: Principles of Practice* (London, Sweet & Maxwell, 2006) Ch. 10 Court Management and Party Compliance, *supra*.
82. R Sullivan, *Sullivan and Driedger on the Construction of Statutes*, 4th edn (Vancouver, Butterworths, 2002) at 235: 'When a court is called upon to interpret legislation it is not engaged in an academic exercise. Interpretation involves the application of legislation to fact in a way that affects the well-being of individuals and communities for better or worse. Nor surprisingly, the courts are interested in knowing what the consequences will be and judging whether they are acceptable. Consequences judged to be good are presumed to be intended and generally regarded as part of the legislation purpose. Consequences judged to be contrary to accepted norms of justice and reasonable are labelled absurd and are presumed to have been unintended. If adopting an interpretation would lead to absurdity the courts may reject that interpretation in favour of a plausible alternative that avoids the absurdity. *In Morgenthaler v The Queen* (1976) 1 SCR 616 at 67, Dickson J wrote 'We must give the sections a reasonable construction and try to make sense and not nonsense of the words. We should pay Parliament the respect of not assuming readily that it has enacted legislative inconsistencies or absurdities'. Also at 239: 'To understand the current approach, the distinction between 'objective' and 'subjective' absurdity is unhelpful. Judges test consequences against a range of considerations: a) norms of rationality such as logical coherence and internal consistency; b) common law norms such as rule of law; c) shared community norms such as reasonableness and fairness.'
83. AA Zuckerman, Zuckerm*an on Civil Procedure: Principles of Practice* (London, Sweet & Maxwell, 2006), *supra*, Ch. 20 Experts and Assessors; D Dwyer, *Judicial Assessment of Expert Evidence* (Oxford, OUP,2008); D Dwyer 'The Causes and Manifestations of Bias in Civil Expert Evidence' (2007) CJQ (26) 425; D Dwyer 'The role of Experts under CPR Part 35' in D Dwyer (ed) *Changing the Role of Experts* (Oxford, OUP, 2009); M Zander 'The Woolf Reforms; what's the verdict' in D Dwyer (ed) *Changing the Role of Experts* (Oxford, OUP, 2009), *ibid.*; Ch. 23; R Turner 'Actively; the Word That Changed the Civil Courts' in D Dwyer (ed) *Changing the Role of Experts* (Oxford, OUP, 2009), *ibid.*, Ch. 23; A Jolowicz 'Civil Litigation: What Is It For' in D Dwyer (ed) *Changing the Role of Experts* (Oxford, OUP, 2009), *ibid.*, Ch. 3. See E Barbier de La Serre and A-L Sibony, 'Expert Evidence Before the EC Courts' (2008) *CMLRev* (45) 941, *supra*; G Cumming, *Merger Decisions and he Rules of Procedure of the European Community Courts* (The Hague, The Netherlands, 2012), *supra*. R Sullivan in *Sullivan and Driedger on the Construction of Statutes*,

4th edn (Vancouver, Butterworths, 2002), *supra*, identifies additional limitations to the teleological method of interpretation: in the context of a lack of empirical analysis of the consequences she observes at 232: 'The problem of limited means: Another reason for indeterminacy is the uncertain relationship between the objects of legislation and the rigour of the means chosen to pursue them. As Dickerson points out most statements of purpose describe the ultimate goals of the legislation using general often sweeping language and leaving out any mention of secondary purposes of inhibiting factors like costs (See R Dickerson, The Interpretation and Application of Statutes (Boston: Little Brown & Co). A legislature almost never wishes to pursue its goals at all costs or by any means regardless of other considerations. These considerations may not be mentioned in the legislation or referred to in legislative debate but if the drafter has done a good job of designing the legislative scheme they will be implicit in the details of the legislation both in what has been included and what has been omitted.'. C Barnard, observes in The *Substantive Law of the EU: The Four Freedoms*, 3rd edn (Oxford, OUP, 2010) at 515 'Free Movement of Persons; Derogations and limitations: Some of the justifications recognised in this fourth category come close to the very type of economic justifications which the Court has rejected in other cases ... The Court said such a justification had to be regarded as an 'economic aim [note 301 See also Case C-137/04 *Rockler v Försäkringskassan* (2000) *ECR* I-1141 para. 24. The Court will look to see if the expressed aim is genuinely economic or whether, viewed objectively, the rules actually serve another legitimate objective. This approach can be seen in Joined Cases C-49, 50, 54, 68 and 71 /98 Finalarte (2001) *ECR* I 7831.] For similar reasons the Court has rejected arguments based on a reduction in tax revenue as an overriding reason on the public interest (Case C-464/02 *Commission v Denmark* (2005) *ECR* I 2421) or the cost to the national exchequer (Case C-109/04 Kranemann (2005) *ECR* I 2421). Hatzopoulos explains the different treatment between public-order justifications which have been accepted by the Court and other cases where the aim is considered economic on the ground that the former serve a 'structural' purpose and so are regarded; or leniently than those which do not. [H. Hatsopulos, 'Recent development of the case law of the EJ in the field of Services (2000) 37 *CMLRev* 43, 79] At times the dividing line seems very fine '. It is submitted that the difference between public order and structural where the latter are rejected as being primarily financial in purpose and effect requires firstly, empirical demonstration and secondly empirical expert evidence for a demonstration as to why purely economic derogations can be disproportional and unreasonable or in what way they do not constitute an intra vires derogation to among other things citizenship rights. See further N Shuibne, 'Derogating from the Free Movement of Persons: When Can EU Citizens be Deported?' in (2005-6) *CYELS* 187 at 227 'In attempting to establish a justifiable derogation from Community law on the free movement of persons Member States have scant leeway. This was true even before EU citizenship thinking of the extensive legislative and judicial pruning of the public policy and security space. Citizenship is now used to defend further intrusions here but looking at other narratives – respect for family and forced dispensation with formalities in particular – it hardly seems to matter whether citizenship is used or not. In other words, the principle exposition of the substance of EC law on the free movement of persons has a momentum that seems to go beyond citizenship.' Arguably, Shuibne describes in this quotation the application by the CJ and the GC of specific sections of the TFEU as well as secondary legislation such as directives, where no expert evidence is used at all by the aforementioned courts to ensure the accurate statutory interpretation contained in the primary EU and secondary legislation. The judges of those courts rely exclusively on their own personal interpretations of technical words which they have no competence to interpret. For this reason not only is the scope of the rights of citizenship given an incorrectly large scope but the derogations such as the financial considerations are inaccurately minimized or ignored. Further, R Sullivan in *Sullivan and Driedger on the Construction of Statutes*, 4th edn (Vancouver, Butterworths, 2002), *supra*, at 230 makes the fundamental point which is that the interpretation of the objective is dependent upon the accurate interpretation of the component words that is the ordinary meaning which is particular subject to norms of plausibility which vary according to the community to which the judge belongs as a speaker of the language in with and the technical meaning which may vary in turn according to the expert. This all adds an element of indeterminacy to the interpretation: 'As noted above descriptions of legislative purpose tend to be vague and incomplete while inferences of legislative purposes are subjective and prone to error. Furthermore being able to identify the purposes sought does not necessarily

and technical words producing thereby from an expert point of view based upon empirical analysis, unreasonable or logically inconsistent consequences.

As regards the ECtHR, the judgments will involve two cases, *Hirst (2) v UK*[84] and *Scopolla v Italy*,[85] both of which concern disenfranchisement of prisoners and the effect upon Article 3 ECHR, the right to vote. The procedural approach of the CJ, GC and the ECtHR will in turned be analysed in relation to three judgments, one from the USSC, *Roper v Simmons*;[86] one from the SCC, *Sauvé v Canada*[87] and in particular the Minority Opinion therein expressed by Gonthier J.; and finally a judgment involving a reference by the SCBB in Re-Polygammy.[88] It is submitted that the judgments of the CJ, GC and the ECtHR examined herein contravene Article 6 (1) ECHR, the right to due process by reason of the evidential deficiency, that is, a lack of expert evidence. This is despite the existence of rules of procedure which permit both the CJ and the ECtHR to appoint experts if necessary on their own initiative. In short, the expert evidential deficiency is highlighted and contrasted with the very considerable use of such evidence in the three cases of *Sauvé v Canada*,[89] *Roper v Simmons*[90] and *Re: Polygamy*.[91]

More generally, it is contended that the absence of evidence expert and non-expert precludes a consequential empirical analysis of the application of the statutory interpretation of the TFEU and the ECHR carried out by the CJ, GC and ECtHR. In short, there is no restraint mechanism either in the internal linguistic form, i.e. arising from the ordinary or technical meaning of the words in the articles or in the external factual form, i.e. in the sense of expert evidence related to the statutory interpretation of the words in the articles of the TFEU or the ECHR. Therefore, particularly by reason of the absence of an obligation of an active case management duty[92] on the part of the

---

resolve the interpretative problem facing the courts. (Note 129 *R v Heywood* (1994) 3 *SCR* 761 at 812 per Gonthier J 'the objective is evident but "does not allow us to identify as easily the specific conduct prohibited" both the broad and narrow interpretations are consistent with the objectives'. As discussed above to get from the words of the text to the possible reasons for those words interpreters must rely on norms of plausibility. These consist of the assumptions and values that underlie and justify judgments respecting relevance coherence causation probability desirability and the like. Norms of plausibility resemble the conventions of language in that they are shared by members of a community. The more widely they are shared the more self-evident they appear to be to those who accept them. However the degree of assent or importance attaching to such norms can vary sharply among persons or groups of persons within society. Persons who do not share the same norms are unlikely to draw the same inferences. This is a significant source of indeterminacy.

84. *Hirst v UK (No. 2)* (2005) *ECHR* 681, *supra.*
85. *Scoppola v Italy (No. 3)* (2012) *ECHR* 868, *supra.*
86. *Roper v Simmons* (2005) 543 *US* 551, *supra.*
87. *Sauvé v Canada* (AG) (2002) 3 *SCR* 519, *supra.*
88. *Re Polygamy* 2011 BCSC 1588 Re: S 293 *CCC, supra.*
89. *Sauvé v Canada* (AG) (2002) 3 *SCR* 519, *supra.*
90. *Roper v Simmons* (2005) 543 *US* 551, *supra.*
91. *Re Polygamy* 2011 *BCSC* 1588 Re: S 293 *CCC, supra.*
92. G Cumming, *Merger Decisions and the Rules of Procedure of the European Community Courts* (Alpena aan den Rijn Kluwer Law Books, 2012) at 35 'It is necessary to ascertain the scope of the duty of case management as provided for by the Rules of Court of the GC namely, the Measures of Organisation contained within Article 64 (Note 164); As regards Article 64, R Plender, *Procedure in the European Court* (London, Sweet & Maxwell, 1997), observes at 148-149, 'Measures of organization of procedure are envisaged only in the Rules of Procedure of the Court of First Instance and those of the EFTA Court. The adoption of this innovation is a reflection of

aforementioned courts to seek out facts, the exceptions contained in certain articles of the TFEU[93] and the ECHR[94] are read down, in favour of the objective pursued by the

the nature and functions of the Courts. The Court of First Instance is required to undertake 'close examination of complex facts (note 538 Fourth recital in the preamble to Council Decisions 88/591. See also Case C-35/92P *Parliament v Frederiksen* (1993) *ECR* I-991 para. 19).' The EFTA Court for its part has clearly followed the model of the Court of First Instance … . Likewise the real difference between measures of organization of procedure of the Court of First Instance and the EFTA Court and the preparatory steps adopted by the Court of Justice is not clear…. The general purpose of these measures is to ensure that cases are prepared for hearing, procedures carried out and disputes resolved under the best possible conditions (Article 64 (1) CFI rules and Article 49 (1) EFTA Court Rules)' and those of Measures of Inquiry found in Art. 65 (Note 164 'Article 65. Without prejudice to Arts 24 and 25 of the Statute the following measures of inquiry may be adopted: (a) the personal appearance of the parties; (b) a request for information and production of documents; (c) oral testimony') which are specifically linked to the former. It is submitted that generally, the scope of the case management duty under both the specific rules and their judicial interpretation by the GC and the ECJ is when compared to power under the Civil Procedure Rules (CPR) and the rules of the Competition Appeal Tribunal (CAT) relatively narrow even in the context of a direct action for damages involving non-contractual liability. Specifically, the term 'active' is absent from the rules of Measures of Organisation and Measures of Inquiry. This is even more notably the case than in a direct action where the cause of action is non-contractual liability, pursuant to TFEU Art. 340 (2), and the court enjoys full jurisdiction to find a remedy in damages. Therefore, it is not constrained as in cases involving judicial review under Art. 263 TFEU which may impose restraints upon the operation of the scope of both the Measures of Organisation and Measures of Inquiry. In response to Plender it is submitted that the Measures of Organisation contained within Art. 64 of the General Court are slightly wider than the preparatory steps of the CJ in that the former include matters of law or points of law as opposed to exclusively facts and evidence as contained within the rules of the ECJ. In neither the case of the ECJ nor the GC do the courts have not active duty to implement these measures of organization or inquiry.

As regards the rules for active case management see the English CPR 1.41.4 '(1) The court must further the overriding objective by actively managing cases.(2) Active case management includes – (a) encouraging the parties to co-operate with each other in the conduct of the proceedings; (b) identifying the issues at an early stage; (c) deciding promptly which issues need full investigation and trial and accordingly disposing summarily of the others;(d) deciding the order in which issues are to be resolved; (e) encouraging the parties to use an alternative dispute resolution procedure if the court considers that appropriate and facilitating the use of such procedure; (f) helping the parties to settle the whole or part of the case; (g) fixing timetables or otherwise controlling the progress of the case; (h) considering whether the likely benefits of taking a particular step justify the cost of taking it; (i) dealing with as many aspects of the case as it can on the same occasion; (j) dealing with the case without the parties needing to attend at court; (k) making use of technology; and (l) giving directions to ensure that the trial of a case proceeds quickly and efficiently.' www.justice.gov.uk.

93. Article 21 (ex Art. 18 TEC) 1. Every citizen of the Union shall have the right to move and reside freely within the territory of the Member States, subject to the limitations and conditions laid down in the Treaties and by the measures adopted to give them effect.
94. DIRECTIVE 2004/38/EC OF THE EUROPEAN PARLIAMENT AND OF THE COUNCIL of 29 April 2004 on Equal Treatment: Article 24 1. Subject to such specific provisions as are expressly provided for in the Treaty and secondary law, all Union citizens residing on the basis of this Directive in the territory of the host Member State shall enjoy equal treatment with the nationals of that Member State within the scope of the Treaty. The benefit of this right shall be extended to family members who are not nationals of a Member State and who have the right of residence or permanent residence. 2. By way of derogation from para. 1, the host Member State shall not be obliged to confer entitlement to social assistance during the first three months of residence or, where appropriate, the longer period provided for in Art. 14 (4) (b), nor shall it be obliged, prior to acquisition of the right of permanent residence, to grant maintenance aid for studies, including vocational training, consisting in student grants or student loans to persons other than workers, self-employed persons, persons who retain such status and members of their families.

aforementioned articles to such an extent that the derogations effectively do not apply. Therefore, in truth, such a reading down of the provision for derogations constitutes a factually inaccurate interpretation in so far as it is devoid of any factual basis taking into account the wide concept of evidence proposed in *Sauvé v Canada*[95] which could be easily adopted by both the CJ, the GC and the ECtHR. In addition however, it also disproportionately introduces in violation of Article 164 TEFU a form of harmonization which once again has no basis in fact or economic argument.[96] Indeed, one observes that the concept of proportionality is applied without any foundation in expert evidence by the ECtHR.

Overall, the fundamental problem with the statutory interpretation practised by the CJ in the context of preliminary references and direct actions as well as the direct actions brought before the ECtHR can be identified by looking at the consequences of certain selected judgments. It is clear that the corpus containing the entirety of the judgments of both courts to date could not be examined physically in the confines of this book. Sullivan[97] observes:

> Interpretation involves the application of legislation to facts in a way that affects the well being of individuals and communities for better or worse. Not surprisingly, the courts are interested in knowing what the consequences will be and judging whether they are acceptable. Consequences judged to be good are presumed to be intended and generally are regarded as part of the legislative purpose. Consequences judged to be contrary to accepted norms of justice and reasonableness are labelled absurd and are presumed to have been unintended. If adopting an interpretation would lead to absurdity, the courts may reject that interpretation in favour of a plausible alternative that avoids the absurdity.

As noted earlier, from the point of view of statutory interpretation, the essential problem with the CJ, GC and the ECtHR judgments which will be examined herein is that the expert evidence deficiency[98] which characterizes the interpretation of the meaning of the ordinary and technical words in turn impinges upon the interpretation of the purpose of the legislation. This process leads to the following: in certain circumstances, consequences which are unreasonable and therefore following Sullivan, effectively absurd.[99] Above all it can be asserted that such consequences which

95. *Sauvé v Canada* (AG) (2002) 3 *SCR* 519, *supra*.
96. R van den Bergh 'Subsidiarity as an Economic Demarcation Principle and the Emergence of European Private Law' (1998) *MJL* 129 at 130.
97. R Sullivan, *Sullivan and Driedger on the Construction of Statutes* (Vancouver, Butterworths, 2002) at 255.
98. It is submitted that the absence of evidence as regards the proof of the ordinary and technical meaning of words is not to be confused with the use of the concept of judicial notice: if one adopts the restricted view of judicial notice as proposed for example by Zuckerman in P Robert & A Zuckerman, *Criminal Evidence*, 2nd edn (Oxford, OUP, 2010), *supra*, at pp169-175, namely, restricting it scope to indisputable propositions of fact which exclude proof as opposed to the much wider concept of KC Davis 'Judicial Notice' (195) Columbia LR () 945; which encompasses 'legislative facts' which are disputable and which may in certain circumstances require proof.
99. See discussion of the scope of the concept of legal absurdity in statutory interpretation in footnotes *supra* and in R Sullivan, *Sullivan and Driedger on the Construction of Statutes* (Vancouver, Butterworths, 2002), *supra*, 234-257.

manifest themselves as breaches of the principles of legal certainty, proportionality and subsidiarity were not intended by the legislature.[100]

By reason of these matters it is submitted that the CJ and GC would appear to have breached Article 19[101] TEU: specifically, 'It shall ensure that in the interpretation

100. It is submitted that the aforementioned analysis describes and explains the list of objections to ECJ judgments presented by P Craig 'The ECJ and Ultra Vires Actions' a Conceptual Analysis' (2011) *CMLRev* (48) 395, *supra,* at 397: 'Judicial interpretation of Treaty articles or EU legislation that is regarded as too broad, thereby widening the application of such provisions beyond what is felt to be warranted; judicial interpretation of particular Treaty articles that pays insufficient attention to internal limits expressed therein and thereby gives inadequate attention to important Member States values; Judicial decisions that are premised on interpretive principles such as effectiveness in order to extend the remit of a Treaty article or provision of EU legislation where the burden carried by such principles is felt to be over-broad and insufficiently justified; judicial use of general principles of law in order to expand the overall range of EU competence; judicial decisions within a particular area that treat EU action more leniently than Member State action; judicial interpretation of Treaty articles such as that on subsidiarity which is insufficiently searching and hence insufficiently protective of Member State autonomy.' It is clear also that these 'criterion' are not value free as indicated by terms such as 'too broad' as opposed to simply 'the scope of the judgments, wide or narrow'.

101. Article 19.1. TEU 'The Court of Justice of the European Union shall include the Court of Justice, the General Court and specialised courts. It shall ensure that in the interpretation and application of the Treaties the law is observed. Member States shall provide remedies sufficient to ensure effective legal protection in the fields covered by Union law.' R Barents 'The Court of Justice after the Treaty of Lisbon' (2010) *CMLRev* (47) 709 observes at 719 'Taking over the contents of Art 220 EC Art 19 (1) EU provides that the Court as an institution 'shall ensure that in the interpretation and application of the Treaties the law is observed'. Since Art 200 EC reflected that the EC is a 'Community of law' Art 19 (1) TEU confirms that the EU as the successor of the EC remains a 'community of law'. Accordingly, under the renewed treaties the most important 'constitutional' element of the judicial system of the EU is maintained. However it is striking that while the mandate of the EU Courts obliges them to ensure 'the observance of the law' according to the second sentence of Art. 19 (1) TEU the mandate of national courts is to ensure 'effective legal protection'. While the latter formula closely corresponds to Art 6 ECHR and Art 47 of the Charter of fundamental rights of the EU the former still reflects the philosophy of a 'recours objectif'. However Barents then goes on to say at p. 720 'As a consequence by virtue of the mandate set out in Art 19 (1) of the TEU the EU courts have to ensure that the rights freedoms and principles of the Charter are respect in the interpretation and application of the Treaties.' Accordingly, this duty pursuant to Art 6 (1) TEU to ensure respect of the Charter on Fundamental Rights would seem to exceed the exclusive role of a court the function of which are dictated exclusively by a 'recours objectif'. See also, European Union Committee House of Lords 'The Treaty of Lisbon, an impact assessment' 10h Report of Session 2007-08 No 5.86-5.87; M Dougan 'The Treaty of Lisbon 2007: Winning minds not hears' 45 *CMLRev* (2008) 617; Art 6 (2) TEU further obliges the EU to Accede to the ECHR. A protocol relating to that provision establish a number of conditions for the agreement to be concluded to that effect. One of the conditions is that this agreement must preserve 'the specific characteristics of the Union and Union law' and that it must ensure 'that accession of the Union shall not affect the competences of the Union or the powers of its institutions'.

Consolidated Version of the Treaty on the Functioning of the European EN. 30.3.2010. Official Journal of the European Union; P Lasok, T Millett & A Howard, *Judicial Control in the EU: Procedures and Principles,* observe at p. 375 as regards the application of Art. 19 the following: 'When interpreting a provision of EU law the function of the Court of Justice is to ensure that the law is observed (note 2778 EC Art 220). This means that the Court must construe the provision so that it is given its full effect and so that other provisions of EU law including the unwritten principles and fundamental rights on which the Communities are founded are observed. The characteristics of EU law which have the principal influence on how it is interpreted are: 1) EU legislation is drafted in several languages and the different language versions are all equally authentic (note 2779 See Art 100 first para) 2) EU law uses its own

and application of the Treaties the law is observed': this ultimately sounds as a breach of Article 6 (1) ECHR. However, it is also affirmed that the ECtHR in its own right as demonstrated by the two judgments which will be considered later contravenes Article 6 (1) through its failure to use expert evidence even more so that procedurally, like the CJ and GC, it has the capacity to so do.

More particularly, it is submitted that it is plausible that at least in the judgments considered herein that Article 6 (1) ECHR as interpreted in *Kraska v Switzerland*,[102] namely a failure to properly examine the merits of the case notably by means of the use of expert evidence obtained if necessary through appointment by the court of an expert.[103] Ultimately the ECtHR violates the rights of the defence in so far as by failing to use its discretion so as to appoint procedurally an expert may undermine the ability of the party to present his case to the court: accordingly, this breach of what is effectively a rights of the defence sounds in terms of Article 6 (1) ECHR, the right to due process.

III DETERMINATION OF RIGHTS, THE REFERENCE PROCEDURE PURSUANT TO TFEU 274

Given that vast majority of the judgments examined in the book have been rendered by the CJ pursuant to the reference procedure provided by Article 274 TFEU it is necessary to establish firstly that such a procedure is subject to control pursuant to Article 6 (1) ECHR. However there is one judgment which will be considered which also involves a direct action.

Pursuant to Article 340 (2)[104] for non-contractual liability[105] before the GC, namely, My Travel.[106]

---

terminology and legal concepts which do not necessarily have the same meaning in EU law as in the laws of the Member States. 3)Every provision of EU law must be placed in its context and interpreted in the light of the provisions of EU law as a whole regard being had to the objectives and state of evolution of EU law at the date on which the provision in question is to be applied.' Clearly the use of terminology which is specific to EU law in itself would justify in addition to other concepts which may be technical but not specific to EU law such as economic concepts and economic terminology, the use of experts.

102. *Kraska v Switzerland* (1999) *EHRR* (18) 188 para. 30.

103. Rules of Procedure Annex to the Rules1 (concerning investigations)

Rule A1 – Investigative measures 1. The Chamber may, at the request of a party or of its own motion, adopt any investigative measure which it considers capable of clarifying the facts of the case. The Chamber may, *inter alia*, invite the parties to produce documentary evidence and decide to hear as a witness or expert or in any other capacity any person whose evidence or statements seem likely to assist it in carrying out its tasks.

104. Article 340 (ex Art. 288 TEC) '(2) In the case of non-contractual liability, the Union shall, in accordance with the general principles common to the laws of the Member States, make good any damage caused by its institutions or by its servants in the performance of their duties.'

105. K Lasok QC, T Millett & A Howard, *Judicial Control in the EU: Procedures and Principles* (Richmond, Richmond Law & Tax Ltd, 2004), *supra*, at 78-95: Direct Actions Founded on Non-Contractual Liability.

106. *My Travel Group v Commission* Case T 212/035 (2008) *ECR* II 1967, *supra*.

[A] Determination of Rights by Article 274 TFEU and Applicability of Article 6 (1) ECHR Thereto

Andreangelli[107] argues that following the cases of Le Compte, Van Leuven and de Meyere[108] and Sramek[109] the expression 'in determination of civil rights and obligations' contained within Article 6 (1) ECHR can be interpreted so as to apply to the enforcement of Article 101 and 102 TFEU by the European Commission: that is in Le Compte the ECtHR took the view that the French term '"contestation" .... should not be construed too technically and .... should be given a substantive rather than formal meaning.'[110] It concluded that Article 6 (1) ECHR should be applicable to all proceedings be they judicial or administrative whose 'result .... is directly decisive'[111] for the existence or the exercise of a substantive right. Therefore in Sramek the ECtHR held that the outcome of proceedings before the Austrian Regional Property Transactions Authority was 'decisive for private rights and obligations'[112] of the applicant. In fact the task of the authority was to rule as to whether the contract for the sale of land satisfied the statutory conditions in order to produce its legal effects and consequently its 'unfavourable decision .... would and did mean that the transaction was null and void.'[113] Andreangelli then seeks to use what might be termed the criminal aspect the enforcement of Articles 101 and 102 TFEU, namely the fines which can be imposed upon undertakings for breach of Articles 101 and 102:

> ... the argument that the procedure for the enforcement of Art 81 and 82 EC can also be considered to be 'criminal' in nature according to the ECHR. In fact they concern the detection and sanction of violations of norms of general application adopted in the general interest namely the protection of free competition in the common market. As to the nature and severity of the sanction which the concerned undertakings risk incurring investigated firms may be fined up to 10 per cent of their worldwide turnover. It is therefore clear that such penalties are intended to be both deterrent and punitive.

As regards the merger proceedings Andreangelli observes:

> A parallel can be drawn with those proceedings provided by the law of some of the contracting states to the European Convention of Human Rights and aimed at the authorisation of land transactions such as those at issue in the Shramek case. In addition in its other Ringeisen judgement the European Court of Human Rights held that a procedure aimed at approving the contract for the purchase of land fell within the scope of Art 6 (1) ECHR being concerned with the determination of civil rights and obligations and 'decisive for the relations in civil law' between the applicant and his counterpart in the land transaction. Merger proceedings being aimed at verifying that the notified transaction is compatible with the rules of free

107. A Andreangeli, *EU Competition Enforcement and Human Rights* (Cheltenham, Edward Elgar, 2008), 24.
108. Le Compte, Van Leuven and De Meyere v *Belgium* (1982) 4 EHRR 1 para. 45.
109. *Shramek v Austria* (1985) 7 *EHRR* 351 at para. 34.
110. *Le Compte, Van Leuven and De Meyere v Belgium* (1982) 4 *EHRR* 1, para. 45, *supra.*
111. *Ibid.*, para. 47.
112. *Shramek v Austria* (1985) 7 *EHRR* 351 at para. 34.
113. *Ibid.*

> competition within the common market are 'decisive for the relations in civil law' between the merging parties. In fact it will depend on their outcome whether the parties will be allowed to carry out the concentration itself. They can thus be considered to be concerned with the determination of the parties' civil rights and obligations and must be subject to the requirements laid down by Art 6 (1) ECHR.

Accordingly, the conclusion of Andreangelli notably as regard direct actions which affect TFEU Articles 101, 102 and Merger Control Regulation 139/2004 is adopted herein as accurate: namely that errors of interpretation by the CJ in the context of direct actions such as annulment of European Commission decisions concerning the application of the aforementioned antitrust law could sound in a breach of Article 6 (1) ECHR: that is the judgments by the court directly determine the rights of the parties in the litigation. This would apply similarly to actions for non-contractual damage[114] pursuant to Article 340 (2) TFEU as in My Travel[115] which will be examined in a subsequent chapter herein.

By contrast the situation is perhaps less clear with respect to references made pursuant to Article 267 TFEU in the sense that the judgment of the CJ unlike in the aforementioned actions for annulment does not directly affect the rights of an individual as for example in the form of a penalty. That being said, ultimately it will be concluded that references pursuant to Article 267 TFEU determine rights and therefore can attract the application of Article 6 (1). ECHR. According to the CJ in Staatssecretaris van Financien[116] the effect of a preliminary reference is to be conceived of as follows:

> Under the division of functions provided for by Article 177 of the Treaty, it is for the national court to apply the rules of Community law, as interpreted by the Court, to an individual case. No such application is possible without a comprehensive appraisal of the facts of the case.

Thus, it would appear that although the interpretation made by the CJ is binding upon the referring national court, it is the application thereof to the facts of the case which can then affect the interests and the rights of the party in the sense of Article 6 (1) ECHR. This application of the interpretation of the EU law of course is carried out by the national court which has made the preliminary reference to the CJ pursuant to Article 267 TFEU. However, while the judgment of the CJ may be binding upon the national referring court the purpose of the reference is not to definitively determine the rights of the litigant in the national proceedings. In this regard, Lasok[117] observes specifically:

114. Article 340 (ex Art. 288 TEC):

> (2) In the case of non-contractual liability, the Union shall, in accordance with the general principles common to the laws of the Member States, make good any damage caused by its institutions or by its servants in the performance of their duties.

115. *My Travel Group v Commission* Case T 212/035 (2008) *ECR* II 1967.
116. *Staatssecretaris van Financien v Shipping and Forwarding Enterprise Safe* (1990) *ECR* I 285 at para. 2 of the Summary.
117. KP Lasok, *The European Court of Justice Practice and Procedure*, 2nd edn (London, Butterworth, 1994), *supra*, at 553.

> The object of the preliminary ruling procedure is not to determine the rights of the parties to the proceedings[118] but to lead to an authoritative ruling on a question of Community law. The procedure is dominated by the concept of the public interest which explains why the power to refer lies in the hands of the national courts or tribunals and also why the procedure itself is non-contentious, the parties appearing in order to submit their observations not as parties stricto sensu but more as amici curiae.

As regards the binding quality of the judgment which contains the 'authoritative ruling on community law' Lasok observes as follows:

> The ruling on the question is binding on the referring court which must apply it to the case in which the reference is made (note 1378; Case 320.88 Staatssecretaris van Financien v Shipping and Forwarding Enterprise Safe (1990) ECR I 285) although it is always open to the referring court to put supplementary questions either to detail with other issues which are seen to arise from the decision of the Court of Justice or even if necessary to clarify it. (note 1379: Case C 377/89 Cottand McDermot Minister for Social Welfare (1991) ECR I 1155) second reference following Case 286/85 McDermot and Cotter v Minister for Social Welfare (1987) ECR 1453). The ruling is also binding on appellate courts or courts of review dealing with the case although they may also put further questions to the Court of Justice to clarify the initial ruling. The extent to which such a ruling on interpretation is binding on other courts has been a matter of contention. The more commonly accepted view appears to be that such a ruling has persuasive force only in respect of other courts. They may follow and decided in consequence that it is not necessary to make a separate reference or they may seek to reopen it by posing a further question. The ruling is at least authoritative guidance on the question of interpretation raised.

Of interest are the following observations of Clayton and Tomlinson[119] as regards the ECtHR:

> Proceedings are determinative in relation to civil rights and obligations when the outcome of the proceedings is decisive for them whether or not such determination is the primary purpose of the proceedings (note Ringeisen v Austria (1971) EHRR (455) ... However the proceedings must be directly decisive for civil rights and obligations and a tenuous connection or remote consequences do not suffice. Determination or decisiveness in relation to civil rights and obligations refers to the decision on the merits of a case and its finality. Proceedings which are not determinative are not subject to Art 6 ECHR[120] guarantees.

---

118. Note 33 *Kledingverkoopbedriif de Geus en Uitengogerd v Robert Bosch GmbH*, Case 13/61 (1962) *ECR* 45 at 61 per A.G. Lagrange.
119. R Clayton QC & H Tomlinson QC, *The Law of Human Rights*, 2nd edn, vol. 1 (Oxford, OUP, 2009), 823, para. 11.330.
120. Article 6 (1) of the Convention provides: 'In the determination of his civil rights and obligations or of any criminal charge against him, everyone is entitled to a fair and public hearing within a reasonable time by an independent and impartial tribunal established by law ... .' R Clayton QC & H Tomlinson QC, *The Law of Human Rights*, 2nd edn (Oxford, OUP, 2009) at 827-828 'In order for the guarantees to apply there must be a right, obligation or charge in play and the proceedings must involve its determination. ... Proceedings are determinative in relation to civil rights and obligations when the outcome of the proceedings is decisive for them whether or not such determination is the primary purpose of the proceedings. (*Ringeisen v Austria (No 1)* (1971) EHRR 455) ... Determination or 'decisiveness' in relation to civil rights and

In truth, it may be possible to consider the use of Article 6 (1) ECHR pursuant to Article 267 TFEU both as regards the preliminary reference for an interpretation of a point of EU law and from the point of view of the non-conformity of EU or national legislation in a different manner: that is, as a process which on the contrary, fundamentally determines rights.

It is recalled that the ECtHR in Ringeisen[121] gave a wide interpretation to the type of proceedings which could be decisive for private rights and obligations:

> Para 94. For Article 6, paragraph (1) (art. 6-1), to be applicable to a case ('contestation') it is not necessary that both parties to the proceedings should be private persons, which is the view of the majority of the Commission and of the Government. The wording of Article 6, paragraph (1) (art. 6-1), is far wider; the French expression 'contestations sur (des) droits et obligations de caractère civil' covers all proceedings the result of which is decisive for private rights and obligations. The English text 'determination of ... civil rights and obligations', confirms this interpretation.

The character of the legislation which governs how the matter is to be determined (civil, commercial, administrative law, etc.) and that of the authority which is invested with jurisdiction in the matter (ordinary court, administrative body, etc.) are therefore of little consequence.

In the present case, when Ringeisen purchased property from the Roth couple, he had a right to have the contract for sale which they had made with him approved if he fulfilled, as he claimed to do, the conditions laid down in the Act. Although it was applying rules of administrative law, the Regional Commission's decision was to be decisive for the relations in civil law ('de caractère civil') between Ringeisen and the Roth couple. This is enough to make it necessary for the Court to decide whether or not the proceedings in this case complied with the requirements of Article 6, paragraph (1) (art. 6-1), of the Convention.[122]

---

obligations refers to the decision on the merits of a case and its finality. Proceedings which are not determinative are not subject to Article 6 guarantees'. As regards the nature of the reference proceedings KPE Lasok The European Court of Justice: Practice and Procedure, 2nd edn (London, Butterworths, 1994), *supra*, at 553: 'The object of the preliminary ruling procedure is not to determine the rights of the parties to the proceedings but to lead to an authoritative ruling on a question of Community law. Note Case 13/61 Ledingverkoopbedrijf (1962) *ECR* 45 at 61 (AG Lagrange)'. The difficulty arises from the terms of Art. 389 of the Code of Dutch Civil Procedure: except in cases where the judge orders provisions execution, the petition in cassation shall have a suspensory effect. 'I do not think however that the reference to the Court of Justice of a question for a preliminary ruling under Art 177 of the Treaty can be considered as a "measure of execution" in the procedural sense of this term, that is, as affecting the parties. The collaboration of the parties is not required and the action remains as it is. Furthermore there could be no question of provisions execution in such a case. The procedure is one which is largely governed by considerations of public policy; it operates without the active participation of the parties and does not affect their property or legal relations. Moreover even where there is doubt this Court would not be in a position to decide a question of national law. It can apply rules of national law only when they are clear and incontrovertible. In the present case, this Court has been properly seised and is bound to make a decision once it recognizes the question as one within its jurisdiction.'

121. *Ringeisen v Austria* (No 1) (1971) (1) *EHRR* 455.
122. *Ringeisen v Austria* (No 1) (1971) (1) *EHRR* 455, *ibid.*

One notes that the operative phrase in Tomlinson and Clayton[123] that 'Proceedings are determinative in relation to civil rights and obligations when the outcome of the proceedings is decisive ... whether or not such determination is the primary purpose.' This would appear to effectively override the interpretation of AG Lagrange as expressed by Lasok:

> The object of the preliminary ruling procedure is not to determine the rights of the parties to the proceedings[124] but to lead to an authoritative ruling on a question of Community law.

It is submitted that the scope of the purpose of Article 267 TFEU is wider than simply providing an authoritative ruling on a question of Community law but may also include the determination of the rights of the parties by proceedings the type and purpose of which may be widely interpreted following Ringeisen:[125] that is, the proceedings need not exist specifically in order to determine rights provided that they have a determinative effect. Accordingly, the CJ in Staatssecretaris van Financien[126] just cited does nothing more than describe the allocation of the functions between the CJ and the national court in the context of a request for interpretation. It is for the CJ to interpret the Union Law and the national court to apply it to the facts. The actual purpose of those two different processes is not discussed in the citation such that Staatsecretaris[127] does not exclude the possibility of determination of rights in the context of a preliminary reference. The real issue to be determined is whether or in what sense the 'authoritative ruling' to use the expression of Lasok, can, following Ringeisen,[128] exercise an outcome on the proceedings which is decisive for them whether or not such determination is the primary purpose of the proceedings.[129] Accordingly, it is appropriate to look at the preliminary reference pursuant to Article 267 TFEU in the context

123. R Clayton QC & H Tomlinson QC, The *Law of Human Rights*, 2nd edn, vol. 1 (Oxford, OUP, 2009), 823, para. 11.330.
124. Note 33: *Kledingverkoopbedriif de Geus en Uitengogerd v Robert Bosch*, GmbH Case 13/61 (1962) *ECR* 45 at 61 AG Lagrange.
125. *Ringeisen v Austria* (No 1) (1971) (1) *EHRR* 455, *supra*.
126. *Staatssecretaris van Financien v Shipping and Forwarding Enterprise Safe* (1990) *ECR* I 285 at para. 2 of the Summary.
127. *Ibid.*
128. *Ringeisen v Austria* (No 1) (1971) (1) *EHRR* 455, *supra*.
129. As regards the nature of civil rights and obligations within Art. 6 (1) ECHR Clayton and Tomlinson, *The Law of Human Rights*, 2nd edn (Oxford, OUP, 2009) at 834, para. 11.346 observe 'The basic principle is that public law matters are not excluded from being 'civil rights and Obligations' if they are directly decisive of private law rights', at 828, para. 11.330: 'Proceedings are determinative in relation to civil rights and obligations when the outcome of the proceedings is decisive for them whether or not such determination is the primary purpose of the proceedings. (*Ringeisen v Austrial* (1971) EHRR (1) 455). However the proceedings must be directly decisive for civil rights and obligations and a 'tenuous connection or remote consequences do not suffice' *Le Compte Van Leuven and De Meyere v Belgium* (1982*) EHRR* (5) 183 para. 47, at 835 para. 11.347: 'The most important consideration is whether the applicant has a financial interest at stake in relation to which the action of the state is directly decisive (*Le Compte Van Leuven and De Meyere v Belgium* (1981) EHRR (1) para. 45); the existence of such an interest is usually determinative (*Schouten and eldrum v Netherlands* (1994) EHRR (9) 432 at para. 50); finally at 829, para. 11.331 'Art 6 has been found to apply where a point of constitutionality' (*Deutchland v Germany* (1986) EHRR 448, 8 *Ruisz-Mateos v Spain* (1993) EHR (16) 505; *Kraska v Switzerland* (1993) *EHRR* 18; *Lizarraga v Spain* (2007) *EHRR* 45, 45) or a

of the larger procedural context: that is as a component which is part of the large composite composed of the national proceedings plus the interlocutory preliminary reference to the CJ which have been undertaken to preserve or enforce rights. It is submitted that it is useful to envisage the CJ preliminary reference procedure analogously to interlocutory orders such as injunctions in the English system of civil procedure.[130] Arguably, such an aggregate analysis may demonstrate more cogently the manner in which the preliminary proceedings may be considered to be determinative of the rights in the substantive proceedings. Zuckerman[131] cites Robins[132] as an example where the ECtHR held that court interlocutory and preliminary references proceedings may be considered to be determinative in so far as they form part of the continuation of the substantive dispute and that Article 6 (1) ECHR therefore applies. Conceived of in this manner the preliminary reference pursuant to Article 267 TFEU constitutes, as just noted, a segment of the overall procedure which the national court uses to determine definitively the rights which may arise in the substantive proceedings and which are affected by a point of EU law. Lester, Pannick Herberg et al.[133] observe as regards the application of the ECHR:

> In determining whether there has been a breach of the right to a fair hearing the ECtHR will consider the trial 'as a whole' as well as individual deficiencies in the trial process (Note 2 Barbera (1988) EHRR (11) 360 at para 68 and 89 (cumulative effect of a number of features of trial was unfair) including the decision of the appellate court whose procedure may be sufficient to remedy any unfairness caused at the trial unless satisfied that the applicant has been deprived overall of that right and it is often the combination of procedural deficiencies which it describes and which are described below on the acts of an individual case which lead to such an overall finding. The guarantee of a fair hearing relates to the implementation of judicial decisions as well as the trial itself (Note 1 Hornsby v Greece (1997) EHRR (24) 250 at para 40-41 (Greek authorities refraining for more than five years from taking necessary measures to comply with a judicial decision - held Art 6 (1) violated).

---

preliminary decision in the case (*Obermeier v Austria* (1990) *EHRR* (13) 290 (the preliminary question of the validity of the applicants dismissal from his employment was pivotal to his claim and thus Art. 6 applied)). Art. 6 thus applies in 'interim proceedings which have the effect of partially determining the rights of the parties by 'causing irreversible prejudice' to a party's interest. (*Markass Car Hire v Cyprus* where the Court applied Art. 6 to an application to set aside an ex injunction. In *Micallef v Malta* it was held that 'Article 6 applied to proceedings for an interim injunction. ... Art 6 is also applicable to separate court proceedings for the assessment of damages' (*Silva Pontes v Portugal* (1994) 18 *EHRR* 156 para. 33) and cost proceedings provided that the legal costs forming the subject matter of the proceedings are incurred during the resolution of a dispute which involves the determination of civil rights and obligations (*Beer v Austria*, Appl. 30428/96 judgment 6.2.2001) *Ziegler v Switzerland*.

130. The Court's power to grant an injunction is contained in section 37 (1) SCA 1981 (CCA section 38) as implemented by CPR rule 25.1.
131. A Zuckerman, *Civil Procedure: Principles and Practice* (London, Thomson, 2006), at 57.
132. *Robins v UK* (1997) 26 *EHRR* 527.
133. A Lester, D Pannick & J Herberg (eds), *Human Rights Law and Practice*, 3rd edn (London, Lexis Nexis, 2009), at 301.

In truth,[134] the interpretation rendered by the court pursuant to Article 267 TFEU operates in the following manner: the CJ provides an interpretation of the point of EU law such as in Delimitis[135] the meaning of terms in Article 101 TFEU 'all agreements between undertaking ... which may affect trade between Member States and which have as their object of effect the prevention ... of competition.' The interpretation given by the CJ pursuant to Article 267 TFEU is binding upon both the referring national court and the parties to the cause pending therein. Arguably, the interpretation is a form of declaration of the meaning of the EU law point which in turn through application by the national court to the facts of the pending case ultimately determines the rights of the respective parties involved in the substantive proceedings. It is the two together, namely, the interpretation given by the CJ coupled with its application by the national court to the fact which determine the rights involved in the pending case. Zuckerman[136] describes this phenomenon of the determination of rights in the context of interlocutory proceedings in the following manner:

> The view that the right to fair trial does not apply to interim proceedings or in other proceedings that are not determinative of rights cannot be taken at face value for clearly even in interim proceedings the court has to respect the right to be heard it must be impartial and independent and it must give a reasoned decision. The reason why the court must respect these and other similar rights in interim application is because civil proceedings cannot be readily compartmentalised so that breach of due process standards at one state in the proceedings would not affect the process as a whole. Interim decisions whether they take the form of an interim injunction or of the grant or refusal of an extension of time to fulfil a process requirement frequently impact upon the outcome of the litigation so that breach of due process standard at an interim stage would infect the process as a whole. Accordingly, the right to fair trial applies not only to the trial but to the entire process of determining rights of which the trial is but one component. ... It may be equally said that a biased interim decision may infect the process as a whole. It is therefore misleading to say that ECHR Art 6 does not apply to interim proceedings. The real position is that not every aspect of ECHR Art 6 must be fully implemented at every stage of the proceedings. The correct test of due process compliance is whether proceedings as a whole comply with ECHR Art 6.

134. KP Lasok, *The European Court of Justice: Practice and Procedure*, 2nd edn (London, Butterworth, 1994), 553.

135. *Stergios Delimitis v Henninger Brau* (1991) *ECR* I 935 Art. 101 (ex Art. 81 TEC) 1. The following shall be prohibited as incompatible with the internal market: all agreements between undertakings, decisions by associations of undertakings and concerted practices which may affect trade between Member States and which have as their object or effect the prevention, restriction or distortion of competition within the internal market, and in particular those which: (a) directly or indirectly fix purchase or selling prices or any other trading conditions; (b) limit or control production, markets, technical development, or investment; (c) share markets or sources of supply; (d) apply dissimilar conditions to equivalent transactions with other trading parties, thereby placing them at a competitive disadvantage; (e) make the conclusion of contracts subject to acceptance by the other parties of supplementary obligations which, by their nature or according to commercial usage, have no connection with the subject of such contracts.

136. A Zuckerman, *Civil Procedure* (London, Lexis Nexis, 2006), *supra*, at 57-58.

Anderson[137] describes the operation of the preliminary reference in the following manner which reinforces the need to view the proceedings as a whole which can be affected by in a determinative fashion by simply one part, namely the EU law point which is referred to the CJ:

> The function of the European Court in a preliminary reference is not that of an appeal court but rather that of a specialist tribunal which will give help when it is request and which sees its relations with national courts in terms of co-operation rather than hierarchy (Foglia v Novelleo Case C 244/80 (1981) ECR 3045. The preliminary reference is a step in the proceedings before the national courts which retains overall control of the case. Once given however, a preliminary ruling is binding not only upon the referring court but effectively on all courts and tribunals in the European Union (Note 3 Case 66/80SpA International Chemical Corporation (1981) ECR 1191 Case C 145/88 Torfaen BC (1989) EC 3851 at 3868).

As regards the so called binding effect of the preliminary reference, following one from the earlier observations of Lasok, Broberg and Fencher[138] observe as follows:

> While both the referring court and any subsequent appeal court are bound directly by the preliminary ruling the situation is different with regards to the parties to the main proceedings. These parties do not have the status of parties in the preliminary ruling procedure. They are thus no more bound by a preliminary ruling stemming from the main proceedings to which they are parties than by any other decision of the CJ. Whilst they may rely on the CJ's ruling in the proceedings before the national court in order to demonstrate the content of Community law it is only the national court's decision which they may require to be enforced. Moreover if they act in a manner incompatible with the preliminary ruling they will formally speaking not be in violation of the preliminary ruling as such but only of the relevant Community provision which was subject to the ruling.
>
> Further it is necessary to note that the preliminary reference procedure may use to determine not only rights which can be described as directly effective in EU law such as those which incorporated within Art 101 TFEU. Rather, the reference procedure may be used when for example directives do not have direct effect but nevertheless have a determinative effect upon the rights in the national proceedings as noted by A-G Reischl in Impressa Mazzalai:[139]
>
> It can therefore be said that, for the purpose of interpreting the said enabling Law it is material to know the scope of the directive concerning value added tax irrespective of the answer to be given to the question whether the effect of the reference contained in the enabling Law is that the Community provisions referred to have become national law. ...
>
> In my view, Article 177 of the EEC Treaty cannot be given such a narrow interpretation. It is clear that the jurisdiction to interpret embodied in that Article if the Treaty is disregarded applies in general to all Community legal measures. In fact it can readily be imagined that Community measures other than those which

137. D Anderson & M Demetriou, *References to the European Court*, 2nd edn (London, Sweet and Maxwell, 2002), 7, Ch. 2 Initiating a Reference: M Andenas, *Art 177 References to the European Court* (Butterworths, London, 1994).

138. M Broberg & N Fenger, *Preliminary References to the European Court of Justice* (Oxford, OUP, 2010), at 351.

139. *Impresa Constuzioni Comm Quirino Mazzalai v Ferrovia del Renon* (preliminary ruling requested by the Tribunale di Trento) Case 111/75 (1976) *ECR* I 657at 669-670.

> are directly applicable may be relevant in national legal proceedings. This is for example what happened in Case 32/74 Freidrich Haaga GmbH (1974) ECR 1201. In that case a Community directive was interpreted without any preliminary finding that it was directly applicable for the simple reason that it was relevant for determining the scope of a national law. There is a similar situation in the present case where the interpretation of the directive is important in relation to Article 5 of the enabling Law No 825 which contains clear references to Community law.

Following the assertion made by AG Reischel in Mazzalai,[140] namely, 'It can therefore be said that for the purpose of interpreting the said enabling Law it is material to know the scope of the directive ...' one might say the following: namely, that it is the application by the national judge of the interpretation of the EU law given by the CJ by which has the determinative effect upon rights which are being litigated nationally. Specifically, it is the national proceedings according to Reischel which are judicial and determinative of rights. Accordingly, transposing the earlier comment by Zuckerman, an inaccurate interpretation adopted by the CJ of the TFEU by reason of not having utilized expert evidence to establish the meaning of an expert term would profoundly affect the whole process when the interpretation is applied by the national court to the pending proceedings before it. As Zuckerman observes: 'It may be equally said that a biased interim decision may infect the process as a whole. It is therefore misleading to say that ECHR Article 6 does not apply to interim proceedings.' It is for this reason that Zuckerman seeks to include interlocutory proceedings in a wide interpretation of determination of rights pursuant to ECHR Article 6 (1).[141]

Additional examples of where the ECtHR has found a breach of Article 6 (1) of the ECHR in the context of preliminary proceedings which involved the determination of civil rights and obligation would be, as noted earlier herein, the case of Kraska[142] itself. The ECtHR observed in Kraska that the issue of decisive effect must be determined on a case by case basis. As such, even a constitutional court the objective of which is ostensibly not to decide issues involving rights may in fact and in law exercise a decisive effect upon rights and obligations. The ECtHR observed as follows:

140. *Impresa Constuzioni Comm Quirino Mazzalai v Ferrovia del Renon* (preliminary ruling requested by the Tribunale di Trento) Case 111/75 (1976) *ECR* I 657, *ibid.*, at 670.

141. In addition the CJ emphasizes the judicial nature of the national proceedings which are the basis of the preliminary reference by stating that only those proceedings which are of a judicial nature necessarily involving the determination of rights are therefore appropriate for the preliminary reference procedure. In *Job Centre* Case C 55/96 (1997) *ECR* I 7119 the CJ observed: 'Whilst Art 177 of the Treaty does not make reference to the Court subject to the proceedings during which the national court frames a questions for a preliminary ruling being inter partes it is none the less apparent from that provision that a national court may refer a question to the Court only if there is a case ending before it and if it is called upon to give judgment in proceedings intended to lead to a decision of a judicial nature. A court exercising administrative authority in 'non-contentious' proceedings concerning an application for confirmation of the memorandum of association of a company with a view to its registration cannot therefore make a reference to the Court. In such a situation it is acting independently of any dispute since a dispute and thus contentious proceedings may only arise if confirmation is refused.'

142. *Kraska v Switzerland* (1993) *EHRR* (18) 188 at 200 para. 26.

> As to whether Article 6 (1) also applied to the examination of Mr Kraska's public law appeal the Court reiterates that proceedings come within the scope of this provision even if they are conducted before a constitutional court where their outcome is decisive for civil rights and obligations (Ringeisen v Austria No 2 (1971) 1 EHRR 455 at para 94[143]) in order to determine whether this is so in a given case it is necessary to have regard to all the circumstances.[144]

In Ruiz-Mateos,[145] the constitutional court was described in terms which have also been used to characterize the preliminary reference procedure exercised by the CJ. As regards the activities of the constitutional court the Spanish government had claimed the following:

> The Government denied that Art 6 (1) was applicable pleading that the right in issues was not a 'civil right'. In support of this contention they cited the specific nature of the Constitutional Court's task and the features peculiar to questions of constitutionality. The Constitutional Court's role was to ensure that the legislature the executive and the judiciary respected the Constitution and not to rule on the rights and interests of individuals. This specificity of its functions appeared even more clearly in relation to proceedings of its type under review. Such proceedings were instituted by the ordinary courts and were intended to eliminate from the domestic legal system provisions contrary to the Constitution. In this instance there were no parties because institutional Act 2/1979 provided that only the representatives of the State authorities and the Attorney General need be heard. In addition the judgment was notified solely to the court which referred the question.

Despite the aforementioned description which also applies generally to the rules dealing with preliminary references to the CJ with one notable exception[146] the court looked carefully at the decision of the Constitutional Court on substantive proceedings to ascertain whether it had a decisive effect upon the substantive proceedings:[147]

> The Court observes that there was indeed a close link between the subject-matter of the two types of proceedings. The annulment, by the Constitutional Court of the

143. *Ringeisen v Austria* (No 1) (1971) *EHRR* (1) 455 at para. 94, 489: 'For Art 6 (1) to be applicable to a case (contestation) it is not necessary that both parties to the proceedings should be private persons which is the view of the majority of the Commission and of the Government. The wording of Art 6 (1) is far wider: the French expression 'contestations sur (des) droits et obligations de caractere' civil covers all proceedings the result of which is decisive for private rights and obligations. The English text 'determination of ... civil rights and obligations' confirms this interpretation. The character of the legislation which governs how the matter is to be determined (civil commercial administrative law etc) and that of the authority which is invested with jurisdiction in the matter (ordinary court, administrative body etc) are therefore of little consequence. In the present case when Ringeisen purchased property from the Roth couple he had a right to have the contract for sale which they had made with him approved if he fulfilled as he claimed to do the conditions laid down in the Act. Although it was applying rules of administrative law the Regional Commission's decision was to be decisive for the relations in civil law (de caractère civil) between Ringeisen and the Roth couple. This is enough to make it necessary for the Court to decide whether or not the proceedings in this case complied with the requirements of Art 6 (1) of the convention.'
144. *Kraska v Switzerland* (1993) *EHRR* (18) 188 at 200, *ibid.*, para. 26.
145. *Ruiz-Mateos v Spain* (1993) *EHRR* 505 at para. 55.
146. The parties are authorized to attend the proceedings and to make submissions Rules of Procedure CJ.
147. *Ruiz-Mateos v Spain* (1993) *EHRR* 505, *supra*, at para. 59.

> contested provisions would have led the civil courts to allow the claims of the Ruiz-Mateos family. In the present case the civil and the constitutional proceedings even appeared so interrelated that to deal with them separated would be artificial and would considerably weaken the protection afforded in respect of the applicants' rights. The Court notes that by raising questions of constitutionality he applicants were using the sole and indirect means available to them of complaining of an interference with their right of property: an amparo appeal does not like in connection with Art 33 of the Spanish Constitution.

The ECtHR then goes on in Ruiz[148] to establish that the Constitutional Court has many different functions only some of which may directly concern the rights of a specific group of individuals.[149] In such cases, the exercise of these powers is subject to Article 6 (1) and the concept of a fair trial with adversarial procedure. The ECtHR observes as follows:[150]

> The right to an adversarial trial means the opportunity for the parties to have knowledge of and comment on the observations filed or evidenced adduced by the other party. Admittedly proceedings before a constitutional court have their own characteristics which take account of the specific nature of the legal rules to be applied and the implications of the constitutional decision for the legal system in force. They are also intended to enable a single body to adjudicate on a large number of cases relating to very different subjects. Nevertheless it may happen that, as here, they deal with an act which directly concerns a restricted circle of persons. If in such a case the question whether that act is compatible with the constitution is referred to the constitutional court within the context of proceedings on a civil right to which persons belonging to that circle are a party those persons must as a rule be guaranteed free access to the observations of the other participants in these proceedings and a genuine opportunity to comment on those observations.

In light of the aforementioned cases of the ECtHR one may accordingly question the accuracy of the judgment in Bollman[151] Case 62/72 as regards compliance with Article 6 (1) ECHR:

> Proceedings instituted under Article 177 are non-contentious and are in the nature of a step in the action pending before a national court as the parties to the Main Action are merely invited to state their case within the legal limits laid down by the national court.

It is submitted that in those situations where a preliminary reference does have a definitive effect upon rights and obligations, then an interpretation which would accord with Ruiz-Mateos would require the following: that is one where the parties may have the right to cross examine in the context of a right to a fair trial and adversarial procedure.

148. *Ruiz-Mateos v Spain* (1993) EHRR 505 *ibid.*, at para. 63.
149. It is submitted that the second function pursuant to Art. 267 TFEU namely, the declaration of any incompatibility has an even more visible decisive outcome of the proceedings in the substantive pending proceedings before the national court. Text of Art. 247.
150. *Ruiz-Mateos v Spain* (1993) *EHRR* 505 *ibid.*, at para. 63.
151. *Bollman v Hauptzollamt Hamburg Watershof*, Case 67/72 (1973) *ECR* 269.

Arguably, the preceding analysis could apply to the functions of the CJ when making a preliminary reference involving in particular an Article 267 TFEU which has direct effect under EU law and possibly even a piece of EU legislation which does not have direct effect following AG Reischel in Impresa Mazzalai[152] but nevertheless affects the rights of the individual decisively in the substantive proceedings decisively. As regards evidence it is useful to consider the case of *H v France*[153] cases whist bearing in mind that the rules of evidence and the actual substantive content of a judgment generally do not attract the application of ECHR Article 6 (1) unless they have had an effect overall on the fairness of the trial.[154] In *H v France*[155] the ECtHR held that where a certain evidentiary threshold has not be achieved there is no need for the court to appoint an expert. Arguably, mutatis mutandis, where the evidentiary threshold has been attained the obligation to ensure a fair trial, pursuant to Article 6 (1) ECHR and Kraska,[156] *H v France*[157] would apply so as to require the appointment of an expert by a court:

> The Administrative Court held that no causal link had been established between the injection complained of and the alleged injury; it took the documentary evidence into account in particular the medical certificate of 9 May 1974. The Court notes that this certificate was drawn up 13 years after the event and nearly four years after the nature of the injection had been disclosed to the applicant. As Mr H had not made out any prima face case to the contrary the Administrative Court could reasonably hold that it was not necessary to test the accuracy of its conclusion by means of an expert's medical report.[158]

Accordingly, it is now appropriate to consider generally the scope and nature of the duty to ensure a fair trial which would attach to the CJ when exercising is powers pursuant to Article 267 TFEU. In so far as it is possible therefore to construe 'in the determination of his civil rights and obligations' of Article 6 (1) ECHR by aggregating the interim and the substantive proceedings whereby the interim proceedings before the CJ will directly affect the outcome of the substantive proceedings before the national court the following can be said to apply: specifically the application of the guarantees of ECHR Article 6 (1) to the interim proceedings as part of the substantive proceedings and in particular the following guarantee: 'the court is duty bound to conduct a proper examination of the submissions arguments and evidence adduced by

152. *Impresa Constuzioni Comm Quirino Mazzalai v Ferrovia del Renon (preliminary ruling requested by the Tribunale di Trento)* Case 111/75 (1976) *ECR* I 657, *supra*, at 670.
153. *H v France* (1989) 12 *EHRR* 74 at 91.
154. Lord Lester QC, Lord Pannick QC & J Herberg (eds), *Human Rights Law and Practice*, 3rd edn (London, Lexis Nexis, 2009), 310: 'The rules of evidence are in principle a matter for each contracting state. It is not generally for the ECtHR to substitute its own view as to the admissibility of evidence for that of the national courts although the court will nevertheless examine whether the proceedings as a whole were fair and in particular whether the manner in which evidence has been admitted (or not admitted) is such as to violate the principle of equality of arms.'
155. *H v France* (1989) 12 *EHRR* 74 at 91, *supra*.
156. *Kraska v Switzerland* (1993) *EHRR* (18) 188 at 200, *supra*.
157. *H v France* (1989) 12 *EHRR* 74 at 91, *supra*.
158. *H v France* (1989) 12 *EHRR 74* at para. 65.

the parties while maintaining the due process standards dictated by ECHR Art 6.' In *Kraska v Switzerland*[159] the ECtHR held:

> Paragraph 30. It falls to the Court to decide whether the contested proceedings considered as a whole were fair within the meaning of the Convention. The effect of Article 6 para. 1 (art. 6-1) is, inter alia, to place the 'tribunal' under a duty to conduct a proper examination of the submissions, arguments and evidence adduced by the parties, without prejudice to its assessment of whether they are relevant to its decision (see, among other authorities, mutatis mutandis, the Barberà, Messegué and Jabardo v. Spain judgment of 6 December 1988, Series A no. 146, p. 31, para. 68). It has to be determined whether this condition was satisfied in the instant case.

It is submitted that Kraska may be used to establish a duty on the part of both the CJ, GC and the ECtHR itself to seek expert evidence on its own behalf in order to correctly analyse expert evidence which has been tendered by the parties in order to ensure a fair trial pursuant to ECHR Article 6 (1). In addition arguably, in certain circumstances following *H v France*[160] once again both the CJ and the ECtHR may also be obliged notably when the threshold has been achieved to appoint an expert particular as regards matters of pure interpretation in the context of preliminary references. Therefore, the scope of the duty to ensure compliance with Article 6 (1) ECHR namely, to provide a fair trial would extend in certain circumstances to requiring the court to exercise its discretion and appoint an expert and possibly an assessor or a court expert pursuant to their respective rules of civil procedure.[161] The objective of such an appointment would be to ensure that the judges both the CJ, GC and the ECtHR may understand the expert evidence either presented to them by the parties or obtained through their own initiative by appointment of an expert on their own motion.

Accordingly, when viewed in terms of the preliminary reference procedure determining the rights which may involve simply that of the meaning of some terms arguably, the moment may well be that at which the national court applies the interpretation of the judgment to the facts of the national case. Such would correspond to the aforementioned analysis of Zuckerman whereby the violations of ECHR Article 6 (1) would be determined 'by reference to the proceedings as a whole'[162] It is

159. *Kraska v Switzerland* (1993) 18 *EHRR* at para. 30.
160. *H v France* (1989) 12 *EHRR* 74 at para. 65.
161. ECtHR: (European Court of Human Rights) Rules of Court – 1 July 2013: Annex to the Rules 1 (concerning investigations): Rule A1 – 'Investigative measures: 1. The Chamber may, at the request of a party or of its own motion, adopt any investigative measure which it considers capable of clarifying the facts of the case. The Chamber may, *inter alia*, invite the parties to produce documentary evidence and decide to hear as a witness or expert or in any other capacity any person whose evidence or statements seem likely to assist it in carrying out its tasks … .' www.coe.int/Dicyments/Rules_Cout_ENG.pdf, CJ. (Court of Justice of the European Union) Art. 64 Determination of measures of inquiry '1. The Court, after hearing the Advocate General, shall prescribe the measures of inquiry that it considers appropriate by means of an order setting out the facts to be proved. 2. Without prejudice to Articles 24 and 25 of the Statute, the following measures of inquiry may be adopted: (d) the commissioning of an expert's report'; www.curia.europa.eu.
162. A Zuckerman, *Civil Procedure: Principles and Practise* (London, Sweet & Maxwell, 2006), *supra*, at 57.

submitted that it is only in this manner that the necessary elements of ECHR Article 6 (1), namely, the direct influence of the interpretation upon the rights in the national proceedings can take place: that is at the level of the preliminary reference itself, just like the interlocutory proceedings before an English court, the rights have not yet been permanently and directly affected. If this analysis is accurate it would then be possible to utilize notably the right to a fair trial guaranteed by ECHR Article 6 (1), which is an absolute right, in order to control the interpretation made by the CJ in the context of the preliminary reference.

The essential difficulty however may well be that the ECtHR will be reluctant to apply this preceding analysis for the following reason: namely, that the same difficulty as regards the failure to use expert evidence in the interpretation of terms of the ECHR which may require expert evidence in interpretation as noted in the CJ and the GC, appears to exist within the ECtHR itself.[163]

IV CONCLUSION

In the course of this chapter, an attempt has been made to endeavour to present the general theoretical outline of this analysis. The essential position is that fundamentally a problem exists with respect to what has been termed by Bentham as rectitude of decision as regards the judgments of the CJ, the GC and the ECtHR. Effectively, the law, namely, the TFEU and the ECHR are not interpreted accurately by the aforementioned courts by reason of the failure to exercise their discretion and utilize expert evidence in order to ensure the most accurate statutory interpretation of the meaning both ordinary and technical contained within those two treaties. This failure which sounds in a breach of one of the principle objectives of civil procedure, namely, rectitude of decision, that is the correct application of the law to the true facts so as to produce a truthfully accurate judgment, also produces another consequence: namely, that the deficiency of expert evidence caused by the failure of the CJ, the GC and the ECtHR

163. F van den Berghe, 'The EU and Issues of Human Rights Protection' (2010) *ELJ* (16) 1, 112, at 149. 'Through the possibility of review by the Court of Human Rights of ECJ decisions, accession could completely eliminate the risk of divergences between both courts [ECJ and ECtHR]. However if the Court of Human Rights maintains the deferential attitude it adopted towards the ECJ in the Bosphorus case, divergences may persist but within the Court of Human Rights' case law. While this deference greatly reduces the risk of open conflicts between both legal orders it might prompt the Court of Human Rights to adopt a harsher stance vis-à-vis State measures than vis-à-vis EU acts leading to two lines of case-law. The Court of Human Rights' future stance is difficult to predict … . The EU being a High Contracting party to the Convention, direct complaints alleging the violation of human rights by either primary or secondary European law under any of all here Pillars could be brought before the Court of Human Rights. Here also the benefits of access might be rendered nugatory if the Court of Human Rights maintains its deference towards the ECJ. Unlike the ECJ's jurisdiction the Court of Human Rights competence covers situation falling outside the scope of Community law and by virtue of Protocol No 12, to the Convention any discrimination on grounds of nationality is prohibited. Lastly, as a specific human rights court external to the EU, the Court of Human Rights is in a position to examine whether the procedure before the ECJ conforms to the standards of Art 6 of the Convention.'

leads to a breach of the express right to a fair trial embodied within Article 6 (1) ECHR particular as interpreted in *Kraska v Switzerland*.[164]

It was argued in the course of the introduction that that Article 6 (1) ECHR can apply to notably the preliminary reference operated by the CJ by reason of the fact that when considered overall notably in relation to the national proceedings it can be said to determine rights.

This signifies the following in practical terms: namely, that in the context of the preliminary reference procedure before the CJ or direct actions before the GC or individual actions before the ECtHR, the evidence which is presented by the parties, and particularly national governments, in favour of a particular statutory interpretation of the TFEU or the ECHR is not properly in breach of ECHR Article 6 (1). There is no fair trial. This is specifically the case as regards evidence tendered by the parties in support of a specific interpretation of in particular the technical meaning of certain words contained within either the TFEU or the ECHR or indeed as well, the ordinary meaning. Rather as will be seen in the cases to be examined in the succeeding chapters, the CJ, the GC and the ECtHR basically substitute their own opinion concerning the meaning of technical words in particular in breach of their duty to examine the submissions including those which involve technical words properly in the sense of due care. This is even more so the case that the rules of procedure as will be noted in more detail in the succeeding chapters, specifically provide for all of the three courts to use experts, if necessary on their own initiative, to ensure that the interpretation of the treaties, and therefore the judgments are as accurate as possible. This inaccuracy of the judgments therefore fundamentally vitiates the operation of certain principles of interpretation such as proportionality and subsidiarity which require a strong empirical factual base in order to operate accurately. Further, the inaccurate statutory interpretations fundamentally undermine the operation of the doctrine of vires which is supremely important notably in the context of the TFEU but also, it is submitted, even with the ECHR. Further, and perhaps above all, the deficiency of expert evidence to sustain a particular statutory interpretation diminishes the credibility and legal certainty of the judgments produced by the aforementioned courts. Moreover, it is submitted that the deficiency of expert evidence is in large measure the factor to which Rasmussen directed his attention. At the end of the day however, these difficulties are facile to overcome in the sense that the requisite rules of procedure for the appointment of experts coupled with a wide scope for admissible expert evidence currently exist. The failure to use expert evidence which has been widely documented[165] requires simply a modification on the part of the CJ, the GC and the ECtHR. This is particularly grave as regards the CJ and the ECtHR from whom there is no appeal mechanism which may rectify the factually erroneous statutory interpretation and evaluation of evidence or indeed actual deficits of expert evidence.

Finally, consideration is given to judgments from three courts in the common law tradition rooted rather more in the adversarial as opposed to the inquisitorial tradition.

164. *Kraska v Switzerland* (1993) 18 *EHRR* at para. 30.
165. E Barbier de La Serre & A-L Sibony, 'Expert Evidence before the EC Courts' (2008) *CMLRev* (45) (4) 941, *supra*, passim.

These courts are the USSC, the SCC and the BCSC. Although in principle one might speak of a comparison of the judgments of these courts with those of the CJ, the GC and the ECtHR, in truth the purpose is to demonstrate how statutory interpretation based upon expert evidence coupled with judicial reasoning can take place. Arguably, the judgments of the USSC, the SCC and the BCSC possess a degree of credibility which is absent from the judgments of the CJ, the GC and the ECtHR, namely, the expert evidence. Criticisms of these judgments can focus directly on the cogency of the evidence involved which arguably achieve much more fully the principles of credibility and legal certainty and of course proper consideration of evidence than those of the CJ GC and the ECtHR considered herein.

CHAPTER 1

Brief Overview of Statutory Interpretation

It is heuristically useful to consider what may be generally thought of as forming certain general principles of statutory interpretation so as to be able to analyse and to identify better what might constitute deficiencies in the methods of interpretation of the TFEU and the ECHR by the CJ, GC and the ECtHR, respectively. Statutory Interpretation[1] may

1. 'Statutory': 'Pertaining to or consisting in statutes; enacted created or appointed by statute'; *Shorter Oxford Dictionary*, vol. II, 3rd edn (Oxford, Clarendon, 1973), 2115; 'Interpretation' 'The action of interpreting; explanation exposition; an explanation given; a way of explaining'. *Shorter Oxford Dictionary*, vol. I, 3rd edn (Oxford, Clarendon, 1973), 1099; 'Translation': 'The action or process of turning from one language into another: also the product of this; a version in a different language'. *Shorter Oxford Dictionary*, vol. II, 3rd edn (Oxford, Clarendon, 1973), 2347. It is to be noted that as regards 'translation' in the sense of the aforementioned 'action or process of turning one [human] language into another' the following analysis is proposed by T Shilling, 'Beyond Multilingualism: On Different Approaches to the Handling of Diverging Language Versions of a Community Law' (2010) *ELJ* (16) 47 at 49-50 argues that the use of multiple translations violates ECHR Art. 6 (2): 'According to Art 6 (2) of the EU Treaty.' The Union shall respect fundamental rights guaranteed by [ECHR]. According to Art. 6 (2) of the EU Treaty as to be amended by the Lisbon Treaty the EU shall even accede to the ECHR. The human rights law as developed by the Court of Human Rights under the ECHR requires under two aspects a certain quality of a national law that interferes with a human right: such interference can only be considered as justified by a law if that law is accessible to the citizen and if its effects are foreseeable. Accessibility of a law generally requires its publication in an official journal or in the case of jurisprudence in law reports or a law review. Foreseeability of its effects requires that the law is sufficiently clear for the citizen to foresee if need be with the assistance of a lawyer its effects i.e. what he must or must not do and what he may or may not expect or required from public authorities. As rule of law requirements these aspects must apply also beyond human rights. On the face of its EU laws clearly fulfil the requirement of accessibility: they generally are published in the Official Journal and most Court decisions including nearly all important ones are published in the European Court Reports. Existing problems stem from the EU's multilingualism concept under which it has as form 1 January 2007, 23 official languages. While Court judgments and individual administrative decisions even if published in the Official Journal in all official languages are authentic only in their respective language of procedure (Note 18 *P Kik v OHIM*, Case C-361/01 (2007) *ECR* I 10841, paras 37-38) the other versions being clearly marked as translations all 23 language versions of a legislative act are equally authentic (Note 19 for the founding treaties Art. 314 EC and Art. 53 for secondary legislation *CILFIT v Ministero della Sanita* (1982) *ECR* 3415 at para. 18: What are the

for the purposes of this analysis be conveniently divided into three different approaches in relation to the text of the statute: following Fitzmaurice[2] the divisions or approaches to the interpretation of the text involve, firstly, the intentions of the parties; secondly, the textual or ordinary meaning of the words; and thirdly, the teleological or aims and objects method. This classification is not exhaustive but it is felt that the categorizations therein contain the primary analytic methods involved in statutory interpretation. Fitzmaurice[3] observes:

> The ideas of these three schools are not necessarily exclusive of one another and theories of treaty interpretation can be constructed and (are indeed normally held) compounded of all three. However, each tends to confer the primacy on one particular aspect of treaty interpretation if not to the exclusion certainly to the subordination of the others. Each in any case, employs a different approach. For the 'intentions' school the prime indeed the only legitimate object is to ascertain and give effect to the intentions or presumed intentions of the parties: the approach is therefore to discover what these were or must be taken to have been. For the 'meaning of the text' school the prime object is to establish what the text means according to the ordinary or apparent signification of its terms: the approach is, therefore, through the study and analysis of the text. For the 'aims and objects' school it is the general purpose of the treaty itself that counts considered to some extent as having or as having come to have an existence of its own independent of the original intentions of the framers.

---

problems? Quite generally no two texts in different languages will ever have the exactly same meaning. Beyond this truism lies the fact that even significant divergences between different language versions of a text cannot fully be avoided. In the EU context there are two possible sources of this problem which is clearly more acute regarding secondary legislation than regarding the Treaties; in adequate translation and political meddling. In adequate translation is self-explanatory and to a certain degree inevitable: translators are fallible humans. Political meddling happens in the way that members of the different branches of the legislature sometimes develop an interest in the wording of specific language versions which is motivated more politically than linguistically.' Shilling concludes at p. 66 concerning the violation of ECHR Art. 6 (2) and the conformity of the current system of translations with the aforementioned article: 'The consequences of the present state of the law are thus at variance with both the quality requirements a law that interferes with liberties has to fulfil under the ECHR. Under both aspects the 'quality' of a Community law would be enhanced considerably if that law were authentic in one language only. There is no doubt in my mind that such a state of affairs would come much closer to the goal of permitting the citizen in his own language easy access to a Community law and to foresee its effects than the present one. The ECHR is all about protecting rights that are not theoretical or illusory but practical and effective (Noted 127 ECtHR *Artico v Italy*, Application 6694/74 Series A no 37, paras 15-16). The equal authenticity of 23 language versions is illusory, the authenticity of only one version accompanied by 22 official translations is effective. Now that the EU has 23 official languages for rule-of-law reasons a reform of its linguistics system is past due.'

2. GG Fitzmaurice, 'The Law and Procedure of the International Court of Justice: Treaty Interpretation and Certain Other Treaty Points' (1951) *BYBIL* (28) 1; FG Jacobs, 'Varieties of Approach to Treaty Interpretation: With Special Reference to the Draft Convention of the Law of Treaties before the Vienna Diplomatic Conference' (1969) *ICLQ* (18) 318; R Sullivan, *Sullivan and Driedger on the Construction of Statutes*, 4th edn (Vancouver, Butterworths, 2002); J Bell & G Engle, *Cross: Statutory Interpretation*, 3rd edn (London, Butterworths, 1994), *supra*.
3. GG Fitzmaurice, 'The Law and Procedure of the International Court of Justice: Treaty Interpretation and Certain Other Treaty Points' (1951) *BYBIL* (28) 1; *ibid.*, at 1-2; A Carty & RA Smith, *Fitzmaurice and the World Crisis 1939-1945* (The Hague, Martinus Nijhoff, 2000); JG Merrills, *Judge Sir Gerald Fitzmaurice and the Discipline of International Law* (The Hague, Kluwer Law Books, 1998).

It is appropriate at this point to consider each of these methods of interpretation in somewhat more detail:

(a) Intentional Approach: according to Jacobs[4] '[this method] attempts to elucidate the text of the treaty or statute which on this view is merely an expression of the will of the parties by reference to the whole course of negotiations leading to the conclusion of the treaty and seeks to investigate the actual intentions of the parties at the time of the adoption of the final text.'
(b) Meaning of the Text of Textual Approach: following Jacobs[5] 'the textual approach places the principal emphasis on the actual words of the treaty. ... Inevitably however an excessive literalism has to be qualified and every advocate of the textual approach readily admits certain qualifications: that extrinsic sources may be used if the text is ambiguous or if the meaning of the words leads to a conclusion which is obviously absurd or unreasonable.
(c) Teleological Approach: according once again to Jacobs.[6]

The teleological approach seeks to interpret the treaty in the light of its objects and purposes. The first question on this approach is not about the meaning of the particular clause which is the subject of interpretation but a broader inquiry into the objects and he purposes of the treaty taken as a whole and individual provisions of the treaty are construed so as to give effect to these objects and purposes.

Interestingly, Jacobs,[7] not unlike Fitzmaurice, does not see a marked distinction between the three approaches such that he goes on in the same paragraph to relate the teleological approach to the previous two methods:

> To a certain extent this approach is simply a combination of elements of the first two approaches. In so far as it relies on the objects and purposes of the treaty as they are expressed in the text and especially in the preamble or can be gathered from a reading of the treaty as a whole the teleological approach is essentially a variant of the textual approach. In so far as it goes beyond the text and seeks to ascertain the original aims of the parties in concluding the treaty by reference to the entire course of negotiations and the circumstances of its conclusion it is the subjective [intentional] approach in another guise. Certainly the classic controversies on the interpretation are based on the antithesis between the textual and the subjective approaches between the language used by the parties and their intentions. But the recent developments in the teleological approach now seem to justify its inclusion as a separate category. It is now generally recognised at least in the interpretation of constitutional documents and in particular of the United Nations Charter that the objects and purposes of a treaty may have to be construed in the light of subsequent developments in international organisation. According to the doctrine of the 'emergent purpose' the objects and purposes which determined the true interpretation of a treaty may be those which can be found to exist at the

4. FG Jacobs, 'Varieties of Approach to Treaty Interpretation: With Special Reference to the Draft Convention of the Law of Treaties before the Vienna Diplomatic Conference' (1969) *ICLQ* (18) 318, *supra*, at 319.
5. *Ibid.*, at 319.
6. *Ibid.*
7. *Ibid.*, at 319.

> time of interpretation not at the time of its conclusion. Clearly, this version of the teleological approach is not textual since the emergent purposes cannot be fathered from the text; nor is it subjective [intentional] since it is independent of the original intentions of the parties and perhaps also of their subsequent attitudes. Rather it regards the creation of the parties as having acquired a separate existence at any rate within the necessary limits imposed by the original text.

§1.01 GENERAL PRINCIPLES OF STATUTORY INTERPRETATION

It is however, useful to consider the aforementioned principles of statutory interpretation rather more from the point of view of the interpretation of law with its procedural and substantive elements such as the burden and standard of proof coupled with certain concepts emanating from the discipline of General Linguistics:[8] that is, notably, semantics. This broader view, arguably, is more useful methodologically than is the consideration of statutory interpretation simply in the context of the methods of interpretation as utilized by the CJ or the ECtHR. The broader view of statutory interpretation permits, as just noted, the inclusion of substantive legal concepts such as the standard of proof particularly as regards expert evidence. In addition, this widened scope of the concept of statutory interpretation would include the availability of procedural rules which, as noted previously, permit the courts to appoint by office experts who may inform judges of the meaning of words as well as rules of fact management. The latter may also lead to introduction of facts through the documents used in pleading as well as the use of overall fact management in order to ensure that all of the facts are available in order to ensure an accurate interpretation of both the ordinary and technical meaning of words contained within a statute or treaty. However, arguably, for the purposes of the instant analysis, the category for the use of expert as opposed to non- expert is the basic theoretical construction for statutory interpretation: namely, technical as opposed to ordinary meaning of words. The latter in particular, may require an expert through the process of judicial notice where the expert constitutes along with books and encyclopaedias, a source of knowledge which is authoritative and non-disputable.[9] As noted earlier, the heuristic value achieved through adopting a wide interpretation of the concept of statutory interpretation is that it necessarily leads to a consideration of the introduction and use of evidence and notably expert evidence as well as the use of concepts such as the standard of proof.

8. RH Robins, *General Linguistics*, 4th edn (London, Longman, 1990), at 22: 'What we are really trying to do in Semantics ... is to explicate the ways in which words and sentences of various grammatical constructions are used and understood by native or fluent speakers of a language. Sentences consist of words but of words in specific grammatical relations within constructions and words are used in speech and writing as components of sentences.' Accordingly, in the context of Linguistics semantics involves examining the meaning of words and sentences notably in the context of various grammatical constructions.
9. P Roberts & A Zuckerman, *Principles of Criminal Evidence* (Oxford, OUP, 2010), 169-175.

[A] Ordinary Meaning of Words

It is useful to commence by considering one of the two basic semantic units: namely, ordinary as opposed to technical meaning. The ordinary meaning[10] may be defined as the natural meaning, which appears when a word is simply read. The ordinary meaning rule can be said to consist of the following propositions which in turn can serve to relate it to the other two methods of interpretation, intentional and teleological and indeed form the necessary initial basis upon which they can be utilized:[11]

(1) It is presumed that the ordinary meaning of a legislative text is the meaning intended by the legislature. In the absence of a reason to reject it, the ordinary meaning prevails.
(2) Even if the ordinary meaning is plain, courts must consider the purpose and scheme of the legislation and the relevant legal norms. They must consider the entire context.
(3) In light of these considerations the court may adopt an interpretation which modifies or departs from the ordinary meaning provided that the interpretation which is adopted is plausible and that the reasons for adopting it are sufficient to justify the departure from the ordinary meaning.

According to Sullivan:[12]

> Ordinary meaning is the natural meaning which appears when the provision or word is simply read through. ... The immediate context relied on in reading has both an internal and an external aspect. The internal aspect is literary consisting as much of the surrounding text as is needed to make sense of the words being read. ... The external aspect of the immediate context is supplied by the reader and consists of the knowledge stored in his or her brain. This includes not only knowledge of language but also knowledge of the world – all the reader has gleaned over the years from going to school, observing, socializing, reading watching television and the like. All this is the basis for the jumble of beliefs assumptions values and conceptions that we rely on in reading. ... The external aspect of context also includes more specialized knowledge that particular readers might have of the genre being used, the subject being discussed, the identity of the author, the circumstances of the writing, the purposes sought and the like.

Despite this apparently relative knowledge, it is submitted, however, that it is possible to establish an objective ordinary meaning which is based upon the overall limits of mutual comprehensibility of speakers of a particular human language.[13] Part of the

10. R Sullivan, *Sullivan and Driedger on the Construction of Statutes* (Vancouver, Butterworths, 2002) at 21-22, *supra*.
11. *Ibid.*, at 20.
12. *Ibid.*, at 21-22.
13. E Paunio & S Lindross-Hovinheimo, 'Taking Language Seriously: An Analysis of Linguistics Reasoning and Its Implications in EU Law' (2010) *ELJ* (16) (4) 395 at 398 argue that 'This article argues that no unambiguous 'meaning of a word' can be found. In fact whenever words are given definitions they are not discovered but rather they are invented. Pinning down the meaning of words involves choice and is not a completely value free process. The possibility

attempt to define the ordinary meaning of words will involve the separation of the overall semantic components thereof which occur consistently in the language as a whole from the individual and personal values and perceptions which will be brought by the individual speaker when using and interpreting the language. Arguably one of the general limits[14] which may be imposed upon the departure from the ordinary meaning of words notably when seeking to rely upon the purpose of the text or the legislative intent is that the interpretation adopted must be one which the words can reasonably bear. That is, the interpretation must be plausible. Sullivan[15] observes:

> In principle, the plausibility requirement is an important constraint on judicial interpretation. The range of meanings that can plausibly be attributed to a text creates the limits within which interpretation can legitimately occur. ... A strained interpretation is one that departs from the ordinary meaning of the text to a noticeable extent but is nonetheless judged to be plausible: it is an interpretation which the text can bear as opposed to one that amends it. The jurisdiction to adopt a strained interpretation is frequently exercised although it is somewhat less frequently acknowledged. When judges decline to adopt a strained interpretation they emphasize than any departure from ordinary meaning must be plausible from a linguistic and not just a legal point of view. The problem with this approach is that it is impossible to say how strained interpretation may become before it must be rejected as implausible. In practice however, there is less to this constraint than meets the eye. The first problem is that the concept of plausible meaning is largely unexplored and undefined. The courts rely on a standard rhetoric as exemplified in the passages quoted above but little effort is made to explain why sometimes adding words to the text is considered permissible paraphrase but at other times it is an impermissible amendment. Judicial assessment of plausibility remains a matter of personal linguistic intuition.

It is submitted however, that just as an objective factor can be said to exist as regards the ordinary meaning of words which arises from the overall semantic limits imposed by the need for mutual comprehension so it is that such mutual comprehension can also play a role in establishing functionally objective limits as regards norms of plausibility. It is in this sense that the aforementioned statement of Sullivan is to be

always exists of the exercise of power involved in defining words and imposing on them a specific meaning. In fact defining concepts or leaving them undefined are not neutral speech acts. Subjective elements are related to interpretation are present in all situations where concepts are defined. In other words definitions are not neutral.' Having set forth this view of what might be termed a relative and non-objective aspect to establishing the ordinary meaning of works, Paunio and Lindross-Hovinheimo then recognise at p. 398 that an objective element does attach to the ordinary meaning of words which is independent of a particular speaker of a human language: 'All language users be it a court or a private person speaking or writing are partly controlled by language and the rules of the linguistic community. However they also partly control language. In this sense language has a two-fold role in communication: it includes forms and structures that cannot be determined by the person using language. In other words language contains both objective and subjective elements. Therefore, a language contains both objective and subjective elements. Therefore a language user is never completely free in using language since all linguistics communication is conditioned by the structure and grammar of language.'

14. R Sullivan, *Sullivan and Driedger on the Construction of Statutes* (Vancouver, Butterworths, 2002), *supra*, at 125.
15. *Ibid.*, at 125.

interpreted: namely, that 'judicial assessment of plausibility remains a matter of personal linguistics intuition' signifies in reality personal perception of a semantic norm which is objective in the sense that it is functionally required to ensure mutual comprehension of the native speakers of a particular human language. There is in addition to the norms of plausibility a further restriction upon interpretations which deviate from the ordinary meaning of words: that is, that the legislature, as observed in the previous chapter, does not intend its legislation to have absurd consequences. Accordingly, at least for Sullivan,[16] absurd consequences are not limited to logical contractions or internal incoherence but include violations of established legal norms such as rule of law; they also include violations of widely accepted standards of justice and reasonableness. Whenever possible an interpretation that leads to absurd consequences is rejected in favour of one that avoids absurdity. The more compelling the absurdity, the greater the departure from ordinary meaning which is tolerated. Therefore, whenever possible an interpretation that leads to absurd consequences is rejected in favour of one which avoids absurdity.

It is perhaps useful to note in passing, that in so far as at least Sullivan establishes a relationship between reasonableness and limits to the departure from the ordinary meaning such as the need to avoid absurdity, it may be possible to establish an additional relationship: namely, the limit to statutory interpretation recognized by the ECtHR as in the case of SW and *CR v UK*:[17] that is, 'In a common law system therefore,

16. *Ibid.*, at 236.
17. *SW and CR v UK* (1996) 21 *EHRR* 363 at paras 46-49. Art. 7 (1) of the ECHR Convention; 'No one shall be held guilty of any criminal offence on account of any act or omission which did not constitute a criminal offence under national or international law at the time when it was committed .... .'

    Opinion her Commission ... .

    45 In the context of 'prescribed by law' the Court set the standard of foreseeability to that of reasonable certainty; ... . (*Sunday Times v UK*, para. 49) ... a norm cannot be regarded as a 'law' unless it is formulated with sufficient precision to enable the citizen to regulated his conduct; he must be able – if need be with appropriate advice – to foresee to a degree that is reasonable in the circumstances the consequences which a given action may entail. Those consequences need not be foreseeable with absolute certainty: experience shows this to be unattainable. Again whilst certainty is highly desirable it may bring in its train excessive rigidity and the law must be able to keep pace with changing circumstances. Accordingly many laws are inevitably couched in terms which to a greater or lesser extent are vague and whose interpretation and application are questions of practice.

    46 In a common law system not only written statutes but also rules of common or other customary law may provide sufficient legal basis for the criminal convictions envisaged in Article 7 of the Convention.

    47 Where law is developed by application and interpretation of courts in a common law system their law making function must remain within reasonable limits. Article 7 (1) excludes that any acts not previously punishable should be held by the courts to entail criminal liability or that existing offences should be extended to cover facts which previously did not clearly constitute a criminal offence.

    48 It is however compatible with the requirements of Article 7 (1) for the existing elements of an offence to be clarified or adapted to new circumstances or developments in society in so far as this can reasonably be brought under the original concept of the offence. The constituent elements of an offence may not however be essentially changed to the detriment of an accused

the courts may exercise their customary role of developing the law through cases but in doing so may not exceed the bounds of reasonably foreseeable change.' One of the primary objectives in this regard is legal certainty. The essential difficulty here, however, is that what appears to be an objective limit on the departure from the ordinary meaning of word can potentially be transformed into a limit which is relative to the perceptions of a particular speaker.[18] This consequence would however be avoided if, as submitted earlier, a form of functional objectivity is imposed by the demands of mutual comprehension on the part of native speakers of a particular language.

[B] Intentional or Original Meaning

The concerns which arise from this method of interpretation are based upon the observation that over time, the meaning, in particular, ordinary meaning may and indeed does change. In such a situation the court must decide whether to utilize the original meaning of the words, that is, the original ordinary meaning or use the current meaning of thereof. 'The original or intention meaning rule has been criticized primarily on two grounds. First as a matter of fairness readers of legislation should be entitled to rely on the current ordinary meaning of words. Bowers writes 'The fact that an utterance might be interpreted years after it is made does not remove the reader's interpretive right to expect that words have been conventionally used'.[19] Similarly as Cross[20] observes the courts should respect 'the view point of the ordinary legal interpreter of today who expects to apply ordinary current meanings to legal texts rather than to embark on research and linguistics cultural and political history'.[21] According to Sullivan[22] the second criticism of the original meaning rule focuses on the importance of adapting law to social change. As a rule the public acts of a legislature are not meant to operate as historical documents. They are written with an eye to the indefinite future on the assumption that they will be applied not only to facts in existence at the time they come into force but also to conditions and circumstances arising from time to time. Bennion[23] makes the point that the parliament or legislature cannot engage in continuous monitoring and adaptation of legislation:

---

and any progressive development by way of interpretation must be reasonably foreseeable to him with the assistance of appropriate legal advice if necessary.

49 In a common law system therefore, the courts may exercise their customary role of developing the law through cases but in doing so may not exceed the bounds of reasonably foreseeable change.

18. My thanks to Dr E Bates, Solicitor, *The Evolution of the European Convention on Human Rights* (Oxford, OUP, 2010), *supra*, for a helpful discussion of this point. The usual disclaimers.
19. F Bowers, *Linguistic Aspects of Legislative Expression* (Vancouver, UBC Press, 1989), 64.
20. J Bell & G Engle, *Cross on Statutory Interpretation*, 2nd edn (London, Butterworth, 1987), 50.
21. R Sullivan, *Sullivan and Driedger on the Construction of Statutes* (Vancouver, Butterworths, 2002), *supra*, at 106-107.
22. *Ibid.*, at 107.
23. F Bennion, *Statutory Interpretation*, 2nd edn (London, Butterworths, 1992), 618.

> Each generation lives under the law it inherits. Constant formal updating is not practical so an Act takes on a life of its own. What the original framers intended sinks gradually into history. While their language may endure as law its current subjects are likely to find that law more and more ill fitting.

It is clear that one of the restrictions here just as with the teleological method is that the courts must take care not to exceed their institutional rule. Their mandate is to interpret legislation not to amend or repeal it. However, as Bennion and other indicate it is essential that legislation be adapted to changing social and material circumstances. It is unrealistic to expect the legislature to engage in this continuous monitoring and adaptation for which role the courts are admirably adapted.[24]

[C] Teleological or Purposive Method of Interpretation

The third general method of interpretation used by the Community Courts may be described as teleological or purposive in nature. According to Sullivan,[25] such an analysis of legislation is based upon the following propositions: firstly, that all legislation is presumed to have a purpose: it is possible for courts to discover or adequately reconstruct this purpose through interpretation; secondly, that legislative purpose should be taken into account in every case and at every stage of interpretation including the determination of a text's meaning; and thirdly, in so far as the language of the text permits, interpretation that are consistent with or promote the legislation purpose should be adopted while interpretations that a defeat or undermine legislation purpose should be avoided. Once again, this method can be expressed as a presumption related to the presumed intention: namely that the interpretation which is consistent with or promotes the purpose of the legislation is to be preferred over that which does not. Under a purposive approach the purpose or mix of purposes identified by the interpreter is the primary concern, and other indicators of legislative intent including the words of the text are subordinate. However, it is clear that the actual establishment of the purpose will depend upon the interpretation of the legislative text which in turn will depend at least in first instance upon the ordinary meaning of the words which compose the text and disclose the intention of the legislature: namely the purpose. In reality, the limitations upon the purposive or teleological method are twofold: first, identification of the purpose may not solve the interpretative problem which confronts the court. That is, the object or purpose may not suffice to identify the overall meaning of the statute or of certain of the individual words: that is both narrow and wide interpretations may be consistent with the objectives.[26] In addition, descriptions of legislative purpose tend to be vague and incomplete while inferences of legislative purposes are subjective and prone to error. In order to go from the words of the text to the possible reasons for those words interpreters must rely on norms of plausibility. These consist of relevance, coherence, causation, probability, desirability,

24. R Sullivan, *Sullivan and Driedger on the Construction of Statutes* (Vancouver, Butterworths, 2002), *supra*, at 108.
25. *Ibid.*, at 195.
26. *R v Heywood* (1994) 3 *SCR* 761 at 812 per Gonthier J.

etc. Norms of plausibility resemble the conventions of language in that they are shared by members of a community. The more widely they are shared the more evidence they appear to be to those who accepts them. However, the degree of assent or importance attaching to such norms may vary sharply among persons or groups of persons within society. Persons who do not share the same norms are unlikely to draw the same inferences. This is a significant source of indeterminacy. In short, by making outcomes dependent on the purpose of legislation courts do not avoid the problem of indeterminacy. Legislative purpose is as much an interpretive construction as the ordinary meaning of words. There is no avoiding the creative dimension of interpretation nor is there any reason to do so. Constructing meaning out the conventions of language and the norms of plausibility which judges share with other members of the community including the legislature is what interpretation consists of. There is no other way to do it.[27]

[D] Technical Meaning of Words

Finally, it is proposed to consider what might be termed a supplementary category to that of ordinary meaning, namely that of technical meaning. Technical meaning as opposed to ordinary meaning is defined by Sullivan[28] in the following manner:

> Technical or scientific terms are words or expressions that have not common or popular meaning: their only meaning derives from the specialized use by a distinct portion of the community. When technical or scientific terms are used in legislation there is no possibility of confusion: such terms automatically receive their technical or scientific meaning.
> Technical meanings are helpful because they permit insiders to refer to aspects of their activity in a precise and functional way. To other insiders technical meanings are clear and present little interpretative challenge; they facilitate accurate efficient communication. Because technical meanings are not familiar to the average speaker of the language used they do not meet the test for judicial notice. They must be proven through the testimony of expert witnesses. ... Whether a term has a technical meaning and what that meaning is are both questions of fact which must be established in a legally acceptable way. When a technical or specialized meaning is not something that everybody knows it cannot be judicially noticed but must be established through evidence normally expert evidence. Such evidence is required to establish both that a term has a technical meaning and the content of that meaning. The expert may introduce specialized dictionaries or encyclopedias. Textbooks, publications of regulatory authorities or even legislation to support his or her testimony.

A more difficult problem arises when legislation contains words that have both a technical and an ordinary meaning. In such cases a court must decide which meaning should prevail. In addition to the usual techniques for resolving ambiguity such as purposive and consequential analysis the courts draw on two special rules. The first is

27. R Sullivan, *Sullivan and Driedger on the Construction of Statutes* (Vancouver, Butterworths, 2002) *supra*, at 230.
28. *Ibid.*, at 40.

a presumption in favour of the meaning that would be understood by the audience to which the legislation is addressed given the matter dealt with. Where legislation is addressed to the public at large these presumptions complement one another but where legislation is addressed to a specialized audience they may be at odds.

In reality, it is submitted that the various methods of interpretation described notably by Fitzmaurice[29] and Jacobs[30] all contain one aspect in common: conspicuously, the interpretation of the words in at least two senses: namely that of the ordinary meaning and that of the technical meaning. It is clear that the identification of the purpose or of the intention of a particular article of the ECHR or the TFEU or of secondary legislation such as a regulation or a directive requires consideration of the meaning both ordinary and technical of the words which compose them. Therefore, whilst the referent of the teleological or the intentional methods may vary, necessarily the identification thereof requires analysis of the meaning of the words considered at least from two different points of view: the ordinary and the technical meaning. According to Paunio and Lindroos-Hovinheimo:[31]

> ... the model for interpreting Community law adopted by the ECJ can be traced back to the Vienna Convention on the Law of the Treaties. Article 31 of the Convention gives the general rule for interpreting of the Convention gives the general rule for interpreting international treaties. The starting point is the ordinary meaning of the treaty text followed by context and other interpretative methods. It should however, that the ECJ has never explicitly referred to the Convention. And in any even the ECJ inversed the order of interpretative methods provided in the Convention in the Van Gend en Loos case (Case 26/62 Van Gend en Loos (1963) ECR I)

In addition to the preceding discussion, it may be of heuristic value to set forth some of the principles of interpretation of EU law as expressed in the case law as presented by authors such as Lasok[32] in relation to Article 31 (1) of the Vienna Convention:

> Article 31
>
> General rule of interpretation
>
> 1. A treaty shall be interpreted in good faith in accordance with the ordinary meaning to be given to the terms of the treaty in their context and in the light of its object and purpose.

---

29. GG Fitzmaurice,' The Law and Procedure of the International Court of Justice: Treaty Interpretation and Certain Other Treaty Points' (1951) *BYBIL* (28) 1; *supra*, at 1-2; A Carty & RA Smith, *Fitzmaruice and the World Crisis 1939-1945* (The Hague Martinus Nijhoff, 2000), *supra*; JG Merrills, *Judge Sir Gerald Fitzmaurice and the Discipline of International Law* (The Hague, Kluwer Law Books, 1998), *supra*.
30. FG Jacobs, 'Varieties of Approach to Treaty Interpretation: With Special Reference to the draft Convention of the Law of Treaties Before the Vienna Diplomatic Conference' (1969) *ICLQ* (18) 318, *supra* at 319.
31. E Paunio & S Kindroos-Hovinheimo, 'Taking Language Seriously: An Analysis of Linguistic Reasoning and Its Implications in EU Law' (2010) *ELJ* (10) (4) 395; R Sullivan, *Sullivan and Driedger on the Constitution of Statutes*, 4th edn (Vancouver, Butterworths, 2002), Ch. 3.
32. P Lasok QC, T Millett & A Howard, *Judicial Control in the EU: Procedures and Principles* (Richmond, Richmond Law and Tax Ltd, 2004) at 375-376.

2. The context for the purpose of the interpretation of a treaty shall comprise, in addition to the text, including its preamble and annexes:
   (a) any agreement relating to the treaty which was made between all the parties in connection with the conclusion of the treaty;
   (b) any instrument which was made by one or more parties in connection with the conclusion of the treaty and accepted by the other parties as an instrument related to the treaty.
3. There shall be taken into account, together with the context:
   (a) any subsequent agreement between the parties regarding the interpretation of the treaty or the application of its provisions;
   (b) any subsequent practice in the application of the treaty which establishes the agreement of the parties regarding its interpretation;
   (c) any relevant rules of international law applicable in the relations between the parties.
4. A special meaning shall be given to a term if it is established that the parties so intended.

The operative words as regards Article 31 of the Vienna Convention which refer to the text to be interpreted as opposed to the manner in which it is to be interpreted – namely in good faith are as follows:

(i) a treaty shall be interpreted in accordance with the ordinary meaning to be given to the terms of the treaty;
(ii) in their context; and
(iii) in the light of its object and purpose.

The only provision for deviation from the ordinary meaning is provided in subsection (4) namely 'special meaning' if it is established that the parties so intended.

As can be readily seen in contrast to the more general principles of statutory interpretation, there is no specific mention of technical terms in the sense noted by Sullivan:

> Technical or scientific terms are words or expressions that have no common or popular meaning; their only meaning derives from their specialized use by a distinct portion of the community. When technical or scientific terms are used in legislation here is no possibility of confusion. Such terms automatically receive their technical or scientific meaning. When words are ambiguous in the sense that they could bear either a technical or a non-technical meaning in the context in which they appear he courts presume that the ordinary non-technical meaning was intended. As explained by Pollock B in *Grenfell v Commissioners of Inland Revenue* (1876) 1 *Ex D* 242 at 248 if a statute contains language that is capable of being construed in a popular sense it 'is not to be construed according to the strict or technical meaning of the language contained in it but ... is to be construed in its popular sense: meaning of course by the words 'popular sense' that sense which people conversant with the subject matter with which the statute is dealing would attribute to it.[33]

33. R Sullivan, *Sullivan and Driedger on the Construction of Statutes*, 4th edn (Vancouver, Butterworths, 2002), *supra*; at 24: 'How Ordinary Meaning is Proven; Judicial Notice: Courts are entitled to take judicial notice of facts that in their opinion are indisputable. This includes (a) fact as that are notorious in the senses that everyone knows and accepts them; they belong to the store of information that every educated member of the society takes for granted and (b) facts

Arguably, the scope for technical words is rather limited: first, at most if such words are recognized then they would be absorbed by the category of special meaning and second, this category will only be accepted if it is deemed that such technical meaning was intended by the parties. Nevertheless, it would appear that provision has been made in the Vienna Treaty for both ordinary meaning and technical or special meaning at least when the latter can be established as being intended by the parties which is more restrictive than the manner which appears to operate in the non EU principles:

> that is, in those cases where there is not a word which has both an ordinary meaning and a technical meaning the judge categorises it on the basis of his own knowledge of the language unless there is a presumption to the contrary. Overall, it is not clear whether Art 31 (4) Vienna Treaty would preclude or at least discourage the use of technical meanings notably in the case where a judge wishes to rely upon his or her own knowledge of the language.

The other significant consideration with regard to Article 31 Vienna Treaty is that it specifically establishes that the meaning of a Treaty provision is to be determined arguably in relation to firstly the ordinary meaning of the words (unless it is established that the intention of the parties is otherwise) and then secondly on the basis of the object and purpose.

As regards, specifically, EU law, it is useful to consider the case based summary of principles of EU law interpretation by Lasok and Millett[34] in the context of Article 31 of the Vienna Convention. However, one should bear in mind that the Community Courts (now EU Courts) rendered decisions prior to its adoption in 1969 and second, they appear not to have made reference expressly to the Vienna Convention in their judgments post-1969; and third, it will be useful to bear these EU principles of interpretation in mind in relation to the non-EU principles of statutory interpretation as presented by authors such as Sullivan.[35] The following general paragraph of Lasok and Millett[36] is helpful in that it explains why there is perhaps some uncertainty as to the exact method of interpretation used in EU law:

> When interpreting a provision of EU law, the function of the Court of Justice is to ensure that the law is observed (Note 2778 EC Treaty Art 220 (ex 164). .... The case law and writings on the subject occasionally refer to particular methods of interpretation such as the literal and teleological (or purposive) methods. The majority of cases in which a legal provision is construed contain no statement of the principle of construction sued by the Court. (note 2782 For example in Cases C 46/93 Brasserie du Pêcheur and Factortame (1996) ECR I 1029 at para 27 the ECJ

---

that can be demonstrated to be true by resorting to sources that are easily accessible and whose authority and accuracy are accepted by all. See *R V Williams* (199) 1 *SCR* 1128 at 114 where a majority of the court took judicial notice of the history of discrimination face by disadvantaged groups in Canadian society.)"

34. KP Lasok QC, T Millett & A Howard, *Judicial Control in the EU: Procedures and Principles* (Richmond, Richmond Law and Tax Ltd, 2004), at 582-689.
35. R Sullivan, *Sullivan and Driedger on the Construction of Statutes*, 4th edn (Vancouver, Butterworths, 2002), *supra*; J Bell & G Engle, *Cross on Statutory Interpretation* (Butterworths, London, 1995).
36. KP Lasok QC, T Millett & A Howard, *Judicial Control in the EU: Procedures and Principles* (Richmond, Richmond Law and Tax Ltd, 2004), at 582-689.

> referred to 'generally accepted methods of interpretation' without stating what they are. ...

A careful search through the bases is therefore capable of dredging up all manner of dicta or apparent statements of principle that can be used to support the most diverse approaches to the problem of construction of legislative texts and may appear to be mutually inconsistent.

Thus, in order to avoid the inconsistencies to which Lasok and Millet advert, it is no doubt useful to consider elements of statutory interpretation of non-EU law: such an approach may not only explain at least in part the inconsistency to which Lasok and Millett advert but also the violations of the principle of rectitude of decision of Bentham and Article 6 (1) ECHR coupled with the principle of legal certainty in the context of the rule of law which is the foundation of the Convention.

The most obvious omission is perhaps lack of clarity as regards the category of ordinary words and secondly, the absence of any mention of technical words. While certainly there can exist indeterminacy as regards ordinary words notably as Paunio and Lindroos-Hovinheimo[37] point out, this problem will not be necessarily clarified by resorting to the purposive or teleological approach. As Sullivan observes:

> By making outcome dependent not the purpose of legislation courts do not avoid the problem of indeterminacy. Legislative purpose is as much an interpretative construction as the ordinary meaning of words. Here is no avoiding the creative dimension of interpretation nor is there any reason to do so. Constructing meaning out of the conventions of language and the norms of plausibility which judges share with other members of the linguistic community including the legislature is of what interpretation consists. There is no other way to do it.[38]

The cases which will be considered in later sections of this study from both the CJ, GC and the ECtHR arguably, provide examples of where effectively words with technical meaning which require expert evidence have been interpreted by judges as if they were words with an ordinary meaning. As a result of the failure by the aforementioned courts to clearly identify the technical words, there are various consequences: firstly, the interpretation of the purpose of the legislation expressed with words which bear a technical meaning will be obscured by reason of the fact that the latter is unrelated to the ordinary meaning; secondly, the failure to replace the ordinary meaning by the technical meaning particularly in the interpretation of the purpose which consists of technical words results from a failure on the part of the court to use existing procedural rules which permit the court to appoint its own expert and thereby obtain where necessary additional expert and to also use concepts.[39] This may extend even to the

37. E Paunio & S Kindroos-Hovinheimo, 'Taking Language Seriously: An Analysis of Linguistic Reasoning and its Implications in EU Law' (2010) *ELJ* (10) (4) 395.
38. R Sullivan, *Sullivan and Driedger on the Constitution of Statutes*, 4th edn (Vancouver, Butterworths, 2002), *supra*, at 43.
39. I Solanke 'Stop the ECJ: An Empirical Analysis of Activism at the Court' (2011) *ELJ* (17) 6 at 764 dealt with an extremely difficult matter empirically: namely, how the decisions of the CJ and GC are taken given that the process is secretive. The study while interesting does not per se deal with the structure of the statutory interpretation demonstrated in the published judgments of the CJ and GC which reveal an evidentiary deficit at the level of empirical expert evidence. It is clear

interpretation of the ordinary meaning of certain words where what is required is the most reliable meaning available. Further, this process may involve the use of reliable sources such as dictionaries but also of experts who may be called to given their opinions albeit not under oath but in so doing would provide an indisputable answer to the judge thereby dispensing with the normal method of cross examined proof.[40]

Further, the meaning of technical words will also be considered in light of the principles of Bentham's procedural concept of rectitude of decision as well as ECHR Article 6 (1). As noted in the previous chapter, the working hypothesis of the instant analysis is that the failure on the part of the EU judiciary and the ECtHR to utilize in certain circumstances expert opinion produces an interpretation of the meaning of technical words contained within the TFEU and subordinate legislation as well as the ECHR which is inaccurate. This inaccurate statutory interpretation of the technical meaning of words in turn impinges upon notably the teleological method of interpretation which necessarily depends upon both the ordinary and technical meaning of the ECHR, TFEU and subordinate EU legislation. Finally, and as noted in earlier sections of this book, the deficit of expert information leads not only to inaccurate or incomplete definitions of technical words but errors which contravene the following: the principle of rectitude of decision;[41] the EU principle of effective

that if one were to equate evidentiary deficiency with the method by means judicial activism is implemented - which is not the thesis of this analysis - then the conclusions of Solanke in her study - namely, the absence of judicial activism as purported displayed in answers to questions submitted by her to Advocates General and Referendaires, would not be valid: that is the focus of the study of Solanke was the replies to the questions which she devised and not the public judgments containing evidentiary deficits which serve as a basis for a violation of ECHR Art 6 (1) and the principle of rectitude of decision in the sense of failing to provide a technically accurate statutory interpretation of the law which is then applied accurately to the correct facts.

40. P Roberts & A Zuckerman, *Criminal Evidence*, 2nd edn (Oxford, OUP, 2010) at 170 'The test of indisputability is therefore the key to identifying when a judge may properly dispense with the normal requirements of proof. However "indisputability' can be understood in two different senses. The first sense corresponds to facts that 'everybody knows". For example, judicial notice has been taken of the fact that human gestation takes longer than two weeks .... Indisputability in a second sense covers facts that can be ascertained definitively without necessarily being universally or even widely known. Verification by reference to indisputable sources occurs where for example, he court needs to know he day of the week on which 1 January 2010 fell ... To summarize, facts may be indisputable either because they are generally accepted by the community at large or because they may be ascertained by consulting reliable and trusted sources.'

41. A Zuckerman (ed), *Civil Justice in Crisis: Comparative Perspectives of Civil Procedure* (Oxford, OUP, 1999) at 4-5 'In Bentham's terminology the purpose of procedure is rectitude of decision which requires the correct application of the law to the true facts.' (note 1, 4: Principles of Procedure in Collected Works of J Bentham, ed. Bowring (1938-43) Vol. ii) '... 'Most if not all procedural requirements are concerned to secure rectitude of decision including the requirements of procedural justice. Measures such as the right to be heard or the right to an impartial tribunal are dictated by the desire for rectitude of decisions. Of course the appearance of justice is also important but it does not alter the fact that at the foundation of procedure lies the objective getting at the truth. This objective lies behind the entire procedural organisation. Rules such as those dealing with notice of commencement of proceedings with the definition of the issues between the parties with the obtaining of evidence and with the calling of witnesses are all designed to facilitate the correct determination of fact and law. (Note 4, 5 Rectitude of decision will dictate these measures regardless of whether or not they may be regarded as justified independently of the objective of arriving at the truth. Or instance the right to be heard may be considered as deserving the respect regardless of whether it leads to more factually

judicial protection;[42] as well as and above all, the principle of due process, as noted earlier, provided by ECHR Article 6 (1). However, whilst a panoply of violations may result from the evidentiary deficit in statutory interpretation as practised by both the EU courts and the ECtHR, the study will focus on those which sound in a breach of ECHR Article 6 (1).

§1.02 TECHNICAL MEANING OF WORDS, EXPERT EVIDENCE AND A COURT APPOINTED EXPERT

It is appropriate in order to investigate the working hypothesis of a deficit of expert information in the statutory interpretation carried out by the CJ, the GC and the ECtHR, to consider the following two matters: first, as previously noted, the concept of technical meaning of words; second, expert evidence as utilized in the interpretation of the TFEU and the ECHR by the respective courts. For heuristic reasons, the consideration of the scope and nature of expert evidence in EU and ECHR law can be more easily presented by using as a background reference expert evidence in English law; third, the procedural introduction of expert evidence so defined into statutory interpretation as well as its use within litigation in the context of the various direct actions as well as the references made to the GC, the CJ and the ECtHR.

[A] Technical Meaning of Words

As noted earlier according to Sullivan,[43] the technical meaning of words requires proof by means of an expert for the following reasons and in the following manner:

---

correct judgments. But the fact remains that the right to be heard is a requirement of rectitude too because without hearing the parties affected the court is less likely to arrive at the truth'.

42. AG Sharpston, *Unibet*, C 432/05 (2007) *ECR* I 2271 at para: '38. That approach reflects the fact that the principle of effective legal protection itself reflects a general principle of law which underlies the constitutional traditions common to the Member States. That principle, the right to a fair trial, is enshrined in Art. 6 (1) of the European Convention on Human Rights and is now recognised as a general principle of Community law by virtue of Art. 6 (2) EU. In embodying the 'right to a court', of which the non-absolute right of access is one aspect, Art. 6 (1) of the Convention impliedly requires access for the purpose of review in the context of a specific case. Limitations to such access are compatible with Art. 6 (1) only where they do not impair the essence of that right, where they pursue a legitimate aim, and where a reasonable relationship of proportionality exists between the means employed and the aim sought to be achieved.' CJ at para. 37 'It is to be noted at the outset that, according to settled case-law, the principle of effective judicial protection is a general principle of Community law stemming from the constitutional traditions common to the Member States, which has been enshrined in Arts 6 and 13 of the European Convention for the Protection of Human Rights and Fundamental Freedoms (Case 222/'84 *Johnston* [1986] *ECR* 1651, paras 18 and 19; Case 222/86 *Heylens and Others* [1987] *ECR* 4097, para. 14; Case C-424/99 *Commission v Austria* [2001] *ECR* I-9285, para. 45; Case C-50/00 P *Unión de Pequeños Agricultores v Council* [2002] *ECR* I-6677, para. 39; and Case C-467/01 *Eribrand* [2003] *ECR* I-6471, para. 61) and which has also been reaffirmed by Art. 47 of the Charter of fundamental rights of the European Union, proclaimed on 7 December 2000 in Nice (OJ 2000 C 364, 1).' DJ Rhee, 'The Principle of Effective Judicial Protection' BEG/ALBA Conference 2011, www.adminlaw.org.uk, last date for consultation was 14 October 2013.

43. R Sullivan, *Sullivan and Driedger on the Construction of Statutes* (Vancouver, Butterworths, 2002), *supra*, at 40.

(1) Because technical meanings are not familiar to the average speaker of the language used they do not meet the test for judicial notice.
(2) Therefore, they must be proven through the testimony of expert witnesses. When a technical or specialized meaning is not something that everybody knows it cannot be judicially noticed but must be established through evidence normally expert evidence. Such evidence is required to establish both that a term has a technical meaning and the content of that meaning.
(3) Whether a term has a technical meaning and what that meaning is are both questions of fact which must be established in a legally acceptable way. The expert may introduce specialized dictionaries or encyclopaedias. Textbooks, publications of regulatory authorities or even legislation to support his or her testimony.

It is submitted that some of the types of experts would include linguistics[44] in addition to economists, sociologists among others.[45]

44. RH Robins, *General Linguistics*, 4th edn (London, Longmans, 1990), *supra*, at 1 'General Linguistics may be defined as the science of language' and at p. 7 'In say that Linguistics is a science in a stricter sense one is saying that it deals with a specific body of material, namely, spoken and written language and that it proceeds by operations which can be publicly communicated and described and justified by reference to stateable principles and to a theory capable of formulation. Its purpose in this proceeding is that analysis of the material and the making of general statements that summarize and as far as possible relate to rules and regularities the infinite variety of phenomenon (utterances in speech or writing) that fall within its scope.'
45. R Sullivan, *Sullivan and Driedger on the Construction of Statutes* (Vancouver, Butterworths, 2002), *supra*, at 38. 'In particular the courts should be willing to receive expert opinion evidence tendered by professional linguistics; whether based on their own expert knowledge of language or on empirical studies. The assumption that lawyers and judges are in as good a position as linguistics to identify the ordinary meaning of words is false. Because of their training professional linguists are better placed to appreciate the nature of the interpretative problem created by a text and the possible ways of resolving the problem. They are also better placed to appreciate the nature of the interpretative problem created by a text and the possible ways of resolving the problem. They are also better placed to make judgments about the relative clarity of a text and the relative plausibility of a proposed interpretation. Further in recent years linguists have developed techniques which permit them to study word combinations instead of words in isolation and to determine how impressions of meaning are actually formed. (Biber Conrad & Reppen, *Corpus Linguistics: Investigating Language Structure and Use* (Cambridge CUP,1989); A Linguistics Analysis of the Meanings of 'Search' in the Fourth Amendment: a Search for Common Sense' (1988) 73 *Iowa Law Rev* 541; L Sola *The Language of Judges* (Chicago UCP, 1993) Clark Cunningham, Levi and Green 'Plain Meaning and Hard Cases (1994) *Yale LJ* (103) 1561; The authors conclude at 1561-62 'In each case [the linguists'] analysis demonstrates that the disputed text is ambiguous and reveals that the lower courts' efforts to resolve the ambiguity are seriously flawed as a matter of ordinary language interpretation. The linguists' analysis of the textual ambiguity however ... narrows the field of possible interpretations in ways that are both linguistically and intuitively sensible make the court's decision more coherent and understandable to the various audiences the court must address. ... [C]ompared to analysis of a particular textual problem by a trained linguist, dictionaries are a crude and frequently unreliable aid to work meaning and usage'.

[1] Proof of Technical Meaning by an Expert

Normally[46] courts do not admit evidence of the meaning of words. Judges are deemed to have what might be termed common knowledge of the meaning of the words at least in their native language. This possession of a common knowledge of the meaning of ordinary words in ordinary language permits the use of the concept of Judicial Notice. As noted previously, it is normally only where a technical as opposed the ordinary meaning that evidence thereof is admissible.

The significance of the use of expert opinion in the interpretation of technical words in this analysis is that it may be employed to ascertain the appropriate scope of technical words when used in particular circumstances: namely, in the context of the teleological method of interpretation notably of the TFEU and subordinate legislation such as regulations and directives and the ECHR. Here, what might be termed the appropriate scope of the technical words contained within the TFEU and subordinate legislation and the ECHR may be considered to correspond completely to the accurate statutory interpretation of the technical meaning of words achievable by means of expert evidence, ipso facto by reason of the words possessing a technical meaning which is known only to experts. It is submitted that the use of statutory interpretation involving technical meaning which requires expert evidence may conveniently subsume the concerns of the incorrect scope of interpretation of what now constitutes the TFEU[47] by such scholars as among others, Rasmussen,[48] Hartley,[49] Arnull,[50]

46. J Bell & G Engle, *Cross On Statutory Interpretation*, 3rd edn (London, Butterworths, 1995) at 59-60 'Except as regards the meaning of non-legal technical terms the courts do not admit evidence as to the meaning of words. Judges are deemed to have common knowledge of ordinary language derived from 'the ordinary experience of those who read newspapers at the present day' (Note 17 *Lord Fraser Mandla v Dowell Lell* (1983) 1 All ER 1062 at 1066). Even though the meaning of ordinary words may thus sometimes be treated as a question of fact it is far from being an ordinary question of fact for legal purposes. In the first place it is usual to think of questions of fact as something upon which evidence can be called on each side. But this is not so in the case of statutory interpretation. Only where a technical term is used or where technical background information is needed to form a judgment will evidence be admissible. That cases illustrates the way in which the characterization of a question of interpretation as one of fact rather than law is in many cases used to limit the reviewing powers of a superior court or to define the role of judge and jury in criminal cases. The second reason why the meaning of ordinary words is no ordinary question of fact is that it is the subject of judicial notice. The first is that although the direct evidence of witness concerning the ordinary meaning of statutory words is inadmissible recourse may be had to all the other sources of information which a judge may tap when considering a fact is one of which judicial notice should be taken. These include dictionaries.'
47. In contradistinction to the Treaty of Rome, officially the Treaty establishing the European Economic Community (TEEC), is an international agreement that led to the founding of the European Economic Community (EEC) on 1 January 1958. It was signed on 25 March 1957 by Belgium, France, Italy, Luxembourg, the Netherlands and West Germany.
48. H Rasmussen, *On Law and Policy in the European Court of Justice* (Dordrecht, Martinus Nijhoff Publishers, 1986).
49. TC Hartley, 'The European Court, Judicial Objectivity and the Constitution of the European Union' (1996) *LQR* (112) 95.
50. A Arnull, 'The European Court and Judicial Objectivity: A Reply to Professor Hartley' (1996) *LQR* (112) 411.

Bengoetxea,[51] Dougan,[52] and Hailbronner.[53] The analysis of the scope of the interpretation of the TFEU and the ECHR as being, at least partially, a function of deficits of expert information in the context of statutory interpretation of the technical meaning of words permits the possibility of evaluating the following consequences: namely, as information deficits which attract the application of the principles of rectitude of decision, proportionality and legal certainty particularly in the context of ECHR Article 6 (1). In short, as noted earlier, some judgments of the EU Courts and the ECtHR may be too wide as regards the application of TFEU and the ECHR by reason of procedural difficulties notably, disproportionate and unjustifiable restrictions upon the scope of the procedural rules which concern the appointment of an expert. Accordingly, by placing the matter of the scope of the TFEU and the ECHR within the context of statutory interpretation of technical words it is possible to simplify at least at first instance, the analysis of the application of the TFEU and the ECHR including categories of linguistics.[54] It is submitted that such an analysis facilitates a later intervention which involves consideration of statutory interpretation in the context of the political

51. J Bengoetxea, *The Legal Reasoning of the European Court of Justice* (Oxford, Clarendon Press 1993).
52. M Dougan, 'Fees Grants Loans and Dole Cheques: Who Covers the Costs of Migrant Education within the EU' (2005) *CMLRev* (42) 943.
53. K Hailbronner, 'Union Citizenship and Access to Social Benefits' (2005) *CMLRev* (42) 1245.
54. See in contra: E Paunio & S Lindroos-Hovenheimo, 'Taking Language Seriously: An Analysis of Linguistics Reasoning and its Implications in EU Law' (2010) *ELJ* (16) 4, 395 at 416 'Conclusion: In this article we have critically assessed the conceptions related to linguistic argumentation and legal reasoning at the ECJ. Based on this analysis we have further argued that legal certainty cannot be assured by means of linguistic argumentation. This is particularly so in relation to the specific problems of multilingualism in EU law. The official EU policy of linguistic equality requires that legislative texts are available in all official language and that they are used in legal interpretation. Additionally the ECJ seems to aim at more predictability in legal decision making by referring to linguistics arguments although neither of these objectives – linguistic equality and predictability – can be fulfilled by means of linguistic arguments. For this reason this article suggests an alternative way for conceptualising the issue of legal reasoning and the principle of legal certainty in EU law. In essence we argue that instead of hiding behind the meaning of words the focus should shift to open and transparent argumentation based on a purposive approach not only because of the requirement of legal certainty but also because this approach better conforms to the aim of uniform interpretation and application of EU law throughout the Union.' The analysis of Paunio and Lindroos-Hovenheimo is predicated upon a complete separation of textual analysis based upon the ordinary meaning of words and the teleological method of interpretation. They do not however demonstrate that interpretation of the purpose of legislation can be completely separated from the interpretation both of the ordinary and the technical meaning of the words which are contained within the purpose. Rather, it is submitted that the contrary is true: in order to ascertain the meaning of the purpose it is necessary to consider the signification of its component ordinary and technical words as a minimum bearing in mind the fact that as Paunio and Lindroos-Hevenheimo do point out, that meaning does change. Therefore the meaning attributed will to use the expression of Sullivan in *Sullivan and Driedger on the Construction of Statutes*, 4th edn (Vancouver, Butterworths (2002) 123-125, a plausible meaning, that is, one which is acceptable to the ordinary speakers of a language and as regards the technical meaning, one which is acceptable to the smaller group of experts which forms part of the larger group of the ordinary speakers of the language. Further, Paunio and Lindroos-Hevenheimo do not indicate why in their discussion of the ordinary meaning of words they have not included a discussion of the technical meaning of words.

function of the EU courts.[55] Such an intervention involving the political function of the EC courts will not be considered here.[56] In this regard and as just noted it is instructive and useful to place in the context of the failure of EU Courts to utilize expert evidence in the statutory interpretation of technical words the objection raised by Rasmussen:[57] that is, the failure of the CJ, the GC as well as the ECtHR to utilize expert socio-economic evidence in the rendering of judgments with the result that the 'transparency' and the 'consequences of judicial choices':

> Adjudicative facts pertain to the outbreak of a concrete conflict between two or more parties. Socio-economic fact pertains to the validity of a certain legislative action now under attack for its alleged incompatibility with the Treaty. A national legislative act which on the surface appears to constitute an infringement of the free flow of goods in intra-Community trade might nonetheless be fully justified by the demonstration of the existence of an overriding legitimate local public policy need embedded in the statute. The primary function of socio-economic fact is to prove and make credible the existence of such a putative local policy worth of survival in the face of a constitutional attack on its validity. My hypothesis is that EC judicial access to socio-economic fact will enhance the quality of EC judicial decisions whereby some existing EC Member State tensions will tend to de-escalate. In the following I shall substantiate that hypothesis in two ways. One is to draw on the American experience. The other consists in demonstrating how socio-economic fact sporadically in operation in EC judicial decision-making greatly contributed to enhancing the quality of the Court's rulings. On this background I will conclude that a more generalized socio-economic fact briefing is desirable... Acquiring access to and actually integrating socio-economic fact in the court's decision making is paramount to achieving greater transparency of issues and consequences of judicial choices. Judicial outcomes will become more practical in the sense that basis for performing a balancing or weighing of the opposing central parochial values will be made as optimal as possible within the framework of what basically remains a judicial process.

55. T Horsley, 'Reflections on the Role of the Court of Justice as the 'Motor' of European Integration: Legal Limits to Judicial Lawmaking' (2013) CMLRev (50) (4) 931.
56. B Bix, *Law, Language and Legal Determinacy* (Oxford, Clarendon Press, 1993) draws a clear distinction between the limits of the operation of law from a linguistic point of view and the operation thereof as a system within a political context. At pp. 178-179: ... I believe that language has for the most part been a false focus for legal theory. Language and theories of language have been used as an excuse for decisions that are more properly attributable to political or at least policy decisions about how we want the various institutions in our legal system to interact. What do we want judges to ignore or to override legislative intent? Are there times when rules should be overruled altered or ignored due to the apparent absurdity or injustice of their application. And how much attention should be given to the more abstract aspects of the rule-maker's intentions? I believe that it is at best misleading to claim that the problems of resolving disputes in the context of a legal system would be resolved if only we had a better theory of language or if only judges would follow the proper theory of language that we already have. A theory about language and communication is likely to consider various elements: what ideas the speaker meant to convey, how words are conventionally understood how context affects intention, meaning or understanding and the role of dialects and idiolects. However one arranges these elements in constructing a theory of meaning it could be still argued that different factors should be emphasized in the special context of drafting, interpreting and enforcing legal rules (the argument emphasizing the special features of rule application or the special features of law or both).
57. H Rasmussen, *On Law and Policy in the European Court of Justice* (Dordrecht, Martinus Nijhoff Publishers, 1986), *supra*, 432-33.

It is submitted that there is a slight difference in the current analysis in relation to that which was undertaken by Rasmussen[58] and his critics: that is, in the instant analysis,

58. H Rasmussen, *On Law and Policy in the European Court of Justice* (Dordrecht, Martinus Nijhoff Publishers, 1986), *supra*, at 432 'Adjudicative facts pertain to the outbreak of a concrete conflict between two or more parties. Socio-economic fact pertains to the validity of a certain legislative action now under attack for its alleged incompatibility with the Treaty. A national legislative act which on the surface appears to constitute an infringement of the free flow of goods in intra-Community trade might nonetheless be fully justified by the demonstration of the existence of an overriding legitimate local public policy need embedded in the statute. The primary function of socio-economic fact is to prove and make credible the existence of such a putative local policy worth of survival in the face of a constitutional attack on its validity. My hypothesis is that EC judicial access to socio-economic fact will enhance the quality of EC judicial decisions whereby some existing EC Member State tensions will tend to de-escalate. In the following I shall substantiate that hypothesis in two ways. One is to draw on the American experience. The other consists in demonstrating how socio-economic fact sporadically in operation in EC judicial decision-making greatly contributed to enhancing the quality of the Court's rulings. On this background I will conclude that a more generalized socio-economic fact briefing is desirable.' At p. 433 'Acquiring access to and actually integrating socio-economic fact in the court's decision making is paramount to achieving greater transparency of issues and consequences of judicial choices. Judicial outcomes will become more practical in the sense that basis for performing a balancing or weighing of the opposing neutral parochial values will be made as optimal as possible within the framework of what basically remains a judicial process. .... It would be erroneous not because the resemblance is always an altogether false impression but because it must emphatically be concluded that performing that task is part of the judicial duty of the Court of Justice. For the Court in controversies arising under Articles 30, 36 48 (3) to refuse to perform the balancing would amount to a deni de justice.' At p. 433 'Let me anticipate another objection based equally on tradition to judicial processing of comprehensive and complex socio-economic facts. It would be that courts and judges including the ECJ and its members are unequipped and not educated for doing that kind of business. Indeed, judicial constitutional legacy may be cited in favour of this. The changing character of judicial involvement in political government which in particular is associated with federalism constitutionalism and constitutional review in the second half of the 20th century makes however the tenor of that legacy obsolete in the Community. In the following I purport to show how Judges of the ECJ in a number of important cases have performed the necessary balancing with considerable success. What is more while performing more traditional judicial tasks for example in the handling of anti-trust cases courts and judges s have become acquainted with complex factual settings.' Page 434 'Assuming that the ECJ enjoys a similar discretion it might take judicial notice of the existence of an economic depression and of encompassing and rising unemployment in Member States throughout the 1970s.' J Bengoetxea, *The Legal Reasoning of the European Court of Justice* (Oxford, OUP (1993) at page 102: 'In relation to the ECJ the analysis of that environment has been carried out by Rasumussen. He argues that the major cost of too much political jurisprudence is the predictable loss of judicial authority and legitimacy. Judicial policy making must remain within socially acceptable boundaries. But the problem lies in how to fix those boundaries how to model a test for judicial activism. He thinks that they can be fixed by examining the negative policy inputs i.e. reaction of the Court's countervailing powers namely the Member States courts and legislatures and executive branches of government and the Council of Ministers. Pescatore's argument is that activism may be legitimate if it develops in order to compensate society for the social consequences of legislative deficit but Rasumussen replies that the judiciary cannot expand its activities beyond some point where it stops enjoying the tolerance of the countervailing political branch because it has not developed techniques and methods of functioning fully adequate to that role; it is isolated from socio-economic fact and has failed to develop docket controlled mechanisms in line with its policy involvement. Rasmussen has criticized the Court's activism party on the ground that the Court has drawn much inspiration from the Preamble and the Foundations of the Treaties. He thinks these are made for political not judicial consumption. I do not subscribe to this point of view.'

the expert evidence is to be utilized by the judge in order to the prove, as a matter of fact, the meaning of a technical word contained in the TFEU or, the ECHR.

§1.03 CONCLUSION

The objective of this method of presentation has been to present statutory interpretation notably as regards the construction of the TFEU and the ECHR in a wider context than is normally the case: that is, specifically through in the inclusion of the semantic and grammatical components of statutory interpretation, namely, words . This consideration is, it is a submitted, a prerequisite to the use of any principles of statutory interpretation such as the teleological or strict methods of interpretation. Such principles or methods of interpretation presuppose the consideration of whether the word is one which possesses an ordinary meaning or whether, on the contrary, the word or expression is one which comports a technical meaning. In turn, both types of meaning but, in particular, the technical meaning will require proof but proof of a specific kind: conspicuously, proof by means of an expert. In this wider context of the operation of statutory interpretation based upon the correct linguistic components, namely, words viewed primarily from a semantic point of view the matter of proof and in particular procedural methods of proof become of great importance. It is for this reason that expert evidence in terms of use within the process of statutory interpretation must be considered as extremely important particularly in terms of compliance with Article 6 (1) ECHR as interpreted by the ECtHR in *Kraska v Switzerland*.[59] Accordingly, consideration was given to the use of expert evidence in the context of a form of proof - namely an indisputable source - which permits the utilization of judicial notice. Technically, this method of interpretation does not use proof per se given that the information used by the judge to form his interpretation of the ordinary meaning of words is not tested sworn evidence. Rather, it is considered to be part of the general knowledge which the judge as a competent speaker of the language of the case possesses albeit obtained from an expert. By contrast, proof of technical words the meaning of which is not within the normal semantic capacities of the judge require formal proof in the sense of sworn witnesses who may be cross examined. It is only once the basic meaning of the word, either ordinary or technical that such principles such as strict or teleologically can cogently proceed and notably in a way which is compliant with the express right to a fair trial as guaranteed by Article 6 (1) ECHR notably as interpreted by *Kraska v Switzerland*.[60]

59. *Kraska v Switzerland* (1994) *EHRR* (18) 188.
60. *Kraska v Switzerland* (1994) *EHRR* (18) 188 *ibid*.

CHAPTER 2

Scope of Expert Evidence as Regards the Court of Justice of the European Union, the General Court and the European Court of Human Rights

Having considered the importance of expert evidence in the process of statutory interpretation notably in order to ensure conformity with Article 6 (1) ECHR, it is appropriate to consider the various procedures available for the introduction of such evidence.

With respect to expert evidence[1] and the legal scope thereof, one might observe firstly that the CJ, the GC and the ECtHR are frequently asked to pass judgment on

1. P Lasok, *European Court of Justice: Practice and Procedure*, 2nd edn (London, Butterworths, 1994), 401: 'The function of an expert is basically to give an opinion on questions of fact but on occasion and depending on the scope of his remit he may be called to examine questions of mixed fact and law. His conclusions do not constitute a decision on matters submitted for his consideration but evidence of how they are to be resolved. It remains for the Court to decide the questions taking account of all the evidence including the expert's report and whether or not the expert has followed the right approach in law (*Commission v Codemi* (1985) *ECR* 3693 at 3701). The Court is not bound by his conclusions and may review them (Cases 24 & 34/58, *Chambre Syndicale* (1960) *ECR* 281 at 310).' Concerning the utility of considering the principles of the law of evidence of a Member State such as the UK and more particularly of one of its constituents, England, N Emiliou, *The Principle of Proportionality in European Law: A Comparative Study* (The Hague, Kluwer, 1996), Ch. 4, 127 comments upon the use of general principles of law which the ECJ draws from the Member States as for example with the formation of the principle of proportionality as follows: 'General principles of law as unwritten principles of Community law are derived mainly if not exclusively from principles and conceptions which are common to the legal systems of the member States and the origins of which may very often be traced back to Roman law (Case 25/68, *Klomp* (1969) *ECR* 43, 50: 'In accordance with a principle common to the legal systems of the Member States the origins of which may be traced back to Roman law when legislation is amended unless the legislature expresses a contrary intention continuity of the legal system must be ensured'). ... Nevertheless with the enlargement of the Communities the concept of legal principles is liable to become broader so as to take account of the laws of acceding

matters composed of complex scientific and technical matters. Cases[2] which are brought before notably the CJ and the GC may raise questions concerning *inter alia* the hazards of pharmaceutical substances, market analysis in competition law, the accuracy of tariff classifications or the reality of an occupation disease. These are all fields of law which may require expert knowledge in the form of an opinion. As will be seen, however, the mere fact that the matter may involve complex scientific and technical matters requiring the opinion of an expert in reality does not lead automatically to the GC the CJ or the ECtHR appointing an expert pursuant to the rules which will be considered shortly. The difficulty arises not so much from the failure of the GC, the CJ and the ECtHR to accept the report of the court-appointed expert as opposed to a failure to appoint an expert under their rules of procedure. This failure to appoint experts is attributable to what is arguably, the operation of either a restriction on the admissibility or more particularly, the threshold of admissibility which is unjustifiable or if it is justifiable, then it is disproportionate in its operation. In short, this failure to appoint a court expert in order to make expert opinion evidence available to the court, at least in some cases, as previously argued herein, may lead to a violation of Article 6 (1) ECHR as well as secondarily in terms of the priorities of this instant analysis, the principles of rectitude of decision and the EU principle of effective judicial protection.[3] Paradoxically, understanding the matter of the infringements caused by the restrictions upon the appointment by the court of the expert presupposes the ability to identify in what circumstances an expert opinion may be or ought to be utilized. Compliance with the principles involved in rectitude of decision, Article 6 (1) ECHR and the EU principle of effective judicial protection[4] must first be determined in relation to the normal scope of expert evidence in order to then be able to ascertain and explain why certain restrictions upon the appointment of experts developed by the European courts may be said to constitute infringements thereof particularly in the sense of being either unreasonable or disproportionate.

As to the general scope of expert evidence in terms of what might be considered to be an appropriate subject of an expert opinion Barbier and Sibony[5] observe:

Member States and with them of the principles of the common law system While it is clear that these laws cannot be relevant to the solution of a problem that arose before accession the principles of common law have from the early days of the UK's access to the Communities started to make their impact upon the Community legal system thus contributing to its development through the concept of general principles of law [note 54 in text see in particular the adoption of the principle of audi alteram partem following AG Warner's strong plea in Case 17/74, *Transocean Marine* (1974) *ECR* 1063, pp. 1079-1080. Also the principle of legal professional privilege established by the *AM&S* (1982) *ECR* 1575, 1648 per AG Slynne].' D Dwyer, *The Judicial Assessment of Expert Evidence* (Cambridge CUP 2009); DM Dwyer, 'The Future of Assessors under the CPR' (2006) *CJQ* 219; L Blom-Cooper 'Experts and Assessors: Past, Present and Future' (2002) *CJQ* 341.

2. P Lasok, *European Court of Justice: Practice and Procedure*, 2nd edn (London, Butterworths, 1994), Ch. 13 passim, case 155/79.
3. S Prechal, *Directives in EC Law* (Oxford, OUP, 2005), p. 142; Case C-432/05, *UNIBET* (2007) *ECR* I-2271, paras 42 and 43; and A-G Sharpston, Opinion, Case C-432/05, *UNIBET* (2007) *ECR* I-2271, para. 38.
4. *Unibet* C 432/05 (2007) *ECR* I 2271, *supra*: A-G Sharpston, para. 38 and the CJ at para. 37.
5. E Barbier de la Serre & A-L Sibony, 'Expert Evidence before the EC Courts' (2008) *CMLRev* 941 at 941-942.

> These issues can indeed be so complex that one may legitimately wonder how the EC courts manage to cope with them. After all the EC Treaty does not require members of the courts to prove technical skills other than those 5.2.1. necessary to be appointed to judicial office. (Note 4: see arts 223, 224 and 225 a EC. ...) While some judges may possess expertise in certain fields they certainly cannot be omniscient: on their own they cannot solve all the intricate issues raised by economics, chemistry or engineering. However judges are precisely not on their own: in order to apprehend complex technical issues the EC courts may like any other courts rely on expert evidence.[6]

In principle, therefore, it is submitted that the scope for expert evidence is relatively wide certainly in the enforcement of the both the TFEU and the ECHR;[7] that is, the substantive scope is sufficiently wide that technically complicated opinion evidence may be admitted before the court notably as regards competition law. However, in such an instance the problem is that the judges of the GC, CJ and ECtHR do not have specific knowledge, training or expertise in the particular field of expertise necessary to understand and to evaluate the evidence, notably economics. Moreover, there is an additional problem: arguably whilst the substantive scope of evidence and notably expert evidence in the enforcement of the TFEU and the ECHR by the aforementioned courts may be wide, nevertheless its actual availability or use is constrained as a result of the following: the limitations which the CJ and the GC have placed upon the exercise of discretion pursuant to the Measures of Inquiry,[8] and specifically the commissioning of an expert's opinion. Arguably, the same remarks can be made as regards the scope of evidence for the ECtHR: namely, that the actual scope of what may be considered to constitute expert opinion evidence would seem to be quite wide. It is submitted that admissibility is in reality determined by the scope of the substantive law of the

6. *Ibid.*, at 941-942. Certainly in English law there exists procedurally pursuant to CPR 35.15 the possibility of appointing an assessor who is effectively a type of exert appointed by the court to assist the court in understanding the '... the proper technical inferences to be drawn from proved fact or as to the apparently contradictory conclusions in the expert field' per Viscount Simon LC in *Richardson v Redpath Brown & Co.* (1944) AC 62, 70 but which is unsworn. Certainly Sir L Blom-Cooper proposes that in order to ensure conformity with ECHR Art 6.1 that modifications be made to the system of assessors which he describes in the following manner at 351 &' The assessor system being advice by an expert not under oath given to the court on matters not disclosable for cross examination by either party before judgment and not qualifying as evidence would be regarded today as being incompatible ... with Art 6 of the ECHR. ... The tentative view is that the assessor's report consisting of written evidence not subject to questioning but no doubt highly influential in the court's adjudication on the expert issue falls foul of Art 6. The fact that unlike the pre-1999 practice the parties see the assessor's report (if there is one at the court's discretion) and may comment on it does not suffice in my view to escape the precept of Art 6. Parties are entitled to be heard on all important issues including a challenged directly of the expert witness.' At p. 356 'Perhaps the one significant shift towards the inquisitorial approach of European legal systems lies in the modified form of the assessor system hitherto almost exclusively restricted to the Admirably jurisdiction. Although Part 35.15 will not permit any questioning of the assessor any pre-trial report will be disclosed to the parties. Should the modified assessor system in Part 35.15 become Convention compatible and be brought into use by the judiciary? If so the mish mash of English and European procedural laws will be complete.'
7. P Lasok, *European Court of Justice: Practice and Procedure*, 2nd edn (London, Butterworths, 1994).
8. Council Regulation (EC) No 139/2004 of 20 January 2004 on the control of concentrations between undertakings (the EC Merger Regulation) Official Journal L 24, 29.01.2004, 1-22.

operation of the case management rules which ultimately concern the role of the court itself. That is, the availability and use of the evidence is determined by the procedural constraints which the CJ and the GC have placed upon the exercise of the discretion pursuant to Article 64 (2) (d)[9] CJ:

> Article 64 '1. The Court, after hearing the Advocate General, shall prescribe the measures of inquiry that it considers appropriate by means of an order setting out the facts to be proved.
>
> 2. Without prejudice to Articles 24 and 25 of the Statute, the following measures of inquiry may be adopted:
>
> ....
>
> (d) the commissioning of an expert's report.

Article 65 (d)[10] of the GC rules provides as follows:

> Without prejudice to Articles 24 and 25 of the Statute, the following measures of inquiry may be adopted:
>
> ....
>
> (d) the commissioning of an expert's report;
>
> For the ECtHR, the rule, as is recalled, which appear to deal with evidence and case management is Art A 1 in the Annex.[11]
>
> Rule A1 - Investigative measures 1. The Chamber may, at the request of a party or of its own motion, adopt any investigative measure which it considers capable of clarifying the facts of the case. The Chamber may, *inter alia*, invite the parties to produce documentary evidence and decide to hear as a witness or expert or in any other capacity any person whose evidence or statements seem likely to assist it in carrying out its tasks...

It is clear that without considering the scope of what might be termed expert evidence as contained notably within an expert's report, all three courts, namely, the CJ, the GC and the ECtHR possess, procedurally, the ability not only to permit the use of expert evidence but indeed to order of their own motion the production of expert evidence. It is submitted therefore, that this brief consideration of the rules of procedure establish that there is no procedural impediment in the three courts as regards the introduction and use of expert evidence in statutory construction, if necessary on the motion of the courts themselves.

According to Mulcahy,[12] Article 6 (1) ECHR does not specify any particular rules of evidence in civil proceedings:

9. Rules of Procedure of the Court of Justice of the European Union: Determination of measures of inquiry www.curia.europa.eu.
10. Rules of Procedure of the General Court: Section 2 - Measures of inquiry Article 65.
11. Rules of Procedure of the European Court of Human Rights: Annex 1: www.echr.coe.int, 29.10.2013.
12. LA Mulcahy (ed) *Human Rights and Civil Practice* (London, Sweet and Maxwell, 2001), *supra*, at 402-403.

> Issues of admissibility and the probative value to be attached to the evidence are in principle a matter for the domestic courts. Nonetheless, the European Court is concerned about the extent to which rules of evidence may affect the right to a fair trial as a whole and whether the rights of the parties were adequately respected: Miailhe v France (No 2).[13] Accordingly, any evidential unfairness will be looked at in light of the fairness of the proceedings taken in the round. The way in which both oral and written evidence is admitted or excluded may prejudice the fairness of the hearing particularly in relation to the ability of a litigant to participate effectively in the proceedings. ... It is for the national court to determine the weight to be given to any evidence: Bernard v France.[14] If however the national court has drawn arbitrary or unfair conclusions from the evidence before it the European Court is prepared to interfere: Edwards v UK.[15]

As was noted earlier, it would appear that a case such as *Kraska v Switzerland*[16] requires effectively an active case management obligation which will in turn lead the court to diligently appoint pursuant to Annex 1 Rule A1 'The Chamber may, ... of its motion, adopt any investigative measures which it consider capable of clarifying the facts of the case' that is the degree of discretion which it is submitted, the CJ, GC and ECtHR enjoy as regards the appointment of an expert under the aforementioned procedural rules is effectively diminished in proportion to the technical complexity of the case. Therefore, arguably, the more technically complex the case is the more that the judges will require expert evidence in order to fulfil their obligations pursuant to *Kraska v Switzerland*,[17] namely, that they are 'under a duty to conduct a proper examination of the submission, arguments and evidence'.

---

13. (1993) 23 EHRR 491 at para. 43 'It is not for the Court to substitute its view for that of the national courts which are primarily competent to determine the admissibility of evidence. It must nevertheless, satisfy itself that the proceedings as a whole were fair having regard to any possible irregularities before the case was brought before the courts of trial and appeal and checking that those courts before the courts of trial and appeal and checking.'
14. *Bernard v France* (2000) *EHRR* 30 at 808 para. 37 '... It will accordingly consider the applicant's complaints from the standpoint of these two provisions taken together. In so doing it must consider the criminal proceedings as a whole. It is admittedly not the Court's task to substitute its own assessment of the facts and the evidence for that of the domestic courts and as a general rule it is for these courts to assess the evidence before them. The Court's task is to ascertain whether the proceedings considered as a whole, including the way in which the evidence was taken were fair.'
15. *Edwards v UK* (A/247B) (1993) 15 *EHRR* 417, para. 34. 'In so doing the Court must consider the proceedings [complaint that criminal proceedings violated Art 6.3 (d) ECHR)] as a whole including the decisions of the appellate courts. Moreover it is not within the province of the European Court to substitute its own assessment of the facts for that of the domestic courts and as a general rule it is for these courts to assess the evidence before them. The Court's task is to ascertain whether the proceedings in their entirety including the way in which evidence was taken were fair.'
16. *Kraska v Switzerland* (1994) *EHRR* (18) 188, *supra*.
17. *Kraska v Switzerland* (1994) *EHRR* (18) 188 para. 30. 'It falls to the Court to decide whether the contested proceedings considered as a whole were fair within the meaning of the Convention. The effect of Article 6 para. 1 (Article 6-1) is, inter alia, to place the 'tribunal' under a duty to conduct a proper examination of the submissions, arguments and evidence adduced by the parties, without prejudice to its assessment of whether they are relevant to its decision (see, among other authorities, mutatis mutandis, the Barberà, Messegué and Jabardo v Spain judgment of 6 December 1988, Series A no. 146, 31, para. 68). It has to be determined whether this condition was satisfied in the instant case.'

It is, therefore, submitted that overall the scope of the substantive law on evidence would appear to be sufficiently wide so as to provide for the admission of, notably, economic expert evidence in matters involving the Articles 101 and 102 TFEU as well as the Merger Control Regulation.[18] Further, it is submitted that the procedural rules of all three courts herein examined permit the introduction of expert evidence commensurate with the wide scope of admissible expert evidence. In truth, therefore, the evidentiary deficits arise from what appear to be various restrictions which the aforementioned courts and in particular the CJ, have developed and which has been analysed in particular by Barbier and Sibony.[19] It is these judge developed restrictions which may lead to the breach Article 6 (1) ECHR in addition to the principles of effective judicial protection and rectitude of decision as opposed to either the substantive rules of evidence or the rules of procedure themselves.

Notwithstanding, it will arguably be of assistance to consider in further detail the scope of the general rules on evidence as regards the GC, CJ and the ECtHR but in relation to the English substantive law on expert evidence given that from a heuristic point of view, the abundance of detailed commentaries thereon may help to understand more clearly the substantive scope of the rules on evidence as used by the aforementioned courts.[20] Generally, at least in English law, it is said that[21] opinion evidence is inadmissible: a witness may only speak of facts which he has personally perceived, not of inferences drawn from those facts. To this general rule there are two exceptions: (i) an appropriately qualified expert may state his opinion on a matter which calls for the expertise which he possesses; and (ii) a non-expert witness may

18. Rules of Procedure of the General Court; Art 65 Without prejudice to Articles 24 and 25 of the Statute, the following measures of inquiry may be adopted: (a) the personal appearance of the parties; (b) a request for information and production of documents; (c) oral testimony; (d) the commissioning of an expert's report; (e) an inspection of the place or thing in question, www.curia.europa.eu.
19. E Barbier de La Serre and A-L Sibony 'Expert Evidence before the EC Courts' (2008) *CMLRev* (45) 4, 941, *supra*.
20. The scope of expert evidence in EU law would appear to be wide. See *infra* footnote and E Barbier de la Serre & A-L Sibony, 'Expert Evidence before the Courts' (2008) CMLRev (45) 941, *ibid.*, at 974: 'There are very few rules on the admissibility of evidence before the EC courts let alone rules on the admissibility of expert evidence. In the Polypropylene cases, Judge Vesterdorf acting as AG state that 'the activity of the ECJ and ... the CFI is governed by the principle of unfettered evaluation of evidence unconstrained by the various rules laid down in the national legal systems. Apart from the exceptions laid down in the Communities' own legal order it is only the reliability of the evidence before the Court which is decisive when it comes to its evaluation.' P Lasok, *The European Court of Justice: Practice and Procedure*, 2nd edn (London, Butterworths, 1994), observes at p. 431: 'The laws of the member state contain many rules excluding relevant evidence (e.g. the rule of hearsay) or which comes to much the same defining what may constitute proof of a fact (the necessity for written evidence in certain matters under Article 1341 of the French Civil Code). With the exception of the limited circumstances in which relevant evidence may be excluded from the proceedings (because it lacks probative value for the purposes of the proceedings or has been improperly obtained) or must be excluded from consideration (because it is legally irrelevant) the Court does not apply such artificial rules of proof: the only criterion, the golden rule, is the credibility of evidence) Case T-1/89, *Rhône-Poulenc SA v Commission*, (1991) *ECR* II-867 at 954.' For this reason, it is considered to be heuristically useful to consider briefly the scope of evidence in English law in order to be able to understand more clearly the scope of expert evidence in EC law.'
21. A Keane, *Modern Law of Evidence* (Oxford, OUP, 2006), at 528.

state his opinion on a matter not calling for any particular expertise as a way of convening the facts which he personally perceived. There are, it is claimed, two main reasons for the general rule which restricts the use of opinion evidence which includes expert evidence: first, it has been said that whereas any fact that a witness can prove is relevant his opinion is not; second, the general exclusionary rule prevents witnesses from usurping the role of the tribunal of fact. The latter although free to reject any opinions proffered might be tempted simply to accept those opinions rather than draw its own inferences from the facts of the case.

§2.01 PURPOSE OR REASON FOR THE USE OF EXPERT EVIDENCE

In order to understand more clearly the scope and the purpose of expert opinion in the GC CJ and the ECtHR it is, as just observed, heuristically of value to relate it to that of another legal system, namely the English legal system, and in particular the substantive law of expert evidence. No attempt will be made to compare or contrast the use of expert evidence in the systems. It is simply that from an analytical point of view there may be some value in considering certain aspects of the English system in order to better comprehend expert evidence as used in the aforementioned courts. In terms of the English law of evidence, some authors, such as Keane,[22] observe that what might be termed the first exception to the general rule concerning the exclusion of opinion evidence stems from an acknowledgement that in some cases the tribunal of fact in the absence of opinion evidence may be unable to reach a conclusion properly. Therefore, expert opinion evidence is admitted because the drawing of certain inferences calls for expertise which the tribunal of fact simply does not possess.[23] Accordingly, the use of expert evidence or more, particularly, opinion evidence becomes virtually necessary in such circumstances so as to provide the knowledge of the technical issues at hand which the court would not otherwise possess. It is submitted that this particular form of reasoning as regards the use of expert opinion evidence in general may also be applied as regards the elucidation and explanation of the technical meaning of words. However, as already noted, there is a danger that the tribunal of fact may blindly defer to the opinion given. This eventuality is particularly acute in the case of opinions expressed by expert witnesses who proffer views on subjects in respect of which scientific knowledge may be limited or incomplete, such as economics, resulting thereby in miscarriages of justice. This apprehension, therefore, of deference by the non-expert judges to the opinion given by the expert may serve to counterbalance the use of expert evidence even in those circumstances. This could be the case for example when its use appears necessary as where specifically the opinion of the expert, as noted earlier, is required in order to draw certain inferences which would be impossible for non-expert judges.

Further, the second exception stems from a recognition that the fundamental assumption upon which the general rule is based, namely, that it is possible to

22. *Ibid.*, at 528.
23. *Ibid.*, 529.

distinguish between fact and opinion, is false. ('In a sense all testimony to matter of fact is opinion evidence; i.e. it is a conclusion formed from phenomena and mental impressions'. Thayer A Preliminary Treatise on Evidence at the Common Law Boston (1898) 524.) The words of a witness testifying as to perceived facts are always coloured to some extent by his opinion as to what he perceived. The separation of an inference or value judgment form the facts on which it is based is often extremely difficult and sometimes impossible.

As previously noted, certain authors, such as Keane,[24] state that the reason for the use and, therefore, the introduction of opinion evidence given by the expert is because 'the drawing of certain inferences calls for an expertise which the tribunal of fact simply does not possess'. This formulation would appear to indicate that the scope for the introduction of evidence is both wide and not subject to any particular restriction; that is, as observed, expert evidence is, as it were, obligatorily used in all circumstances in which the tribunal of fact does not possess the competence to draw certain inferences which require expertise. In contrast, Zuckerman[25] presents the scope of the use of expert evidence in a narrower fashion when he observes as follows:

> The greater part of the case law is concerned not with the fact-opinion distinction but with a different question altogether: the scope for expert evidence.[26] English law, it seems, has always been prepared to accept the opinions and conclusions of experts in matters which requires specialized knowledge or training and which the judge and the jury cannot be expected to possess.[27] An expert may be asked to draw conclusions from facts that he himself has observed. A pathologist who has examined a corpse may testify as to the likely cause of death. Alternatively, an expert may be required to form a view on the basis of facts supplied by others. A pathologist may be asked for his opinion about the cause of death given that a body was found to bear certain marks. While the employment of experts is both necessary and desirable it is nevertheless fraught with risks which the courts strive to minimize. In our adversarial system the parties themselves employ experts and

---

24. *Ibid.*, passim.
25. A Zuckerman, *The Principles of Criminal Evidence* (Oxford, OUP, 1989), 62.
26. A Keane, *Modern Law of Evidence* (Oxford, OUP, 2006), passim; T Hodgkinson, *Expert Evidence: Law and Practice* (London, Sweet & Maxwell, 1990), Ch. 18, Specific Commercial Jurisdictions: The Restrictive Practices Court; also OECD, *Judicial enforcement of Competition Law* (Paris, OECD, 1997) in particular the contributions of D Bellamy & D Dwyer, *The Judicial Assessment of Expert Evidence* (Cambridge, CUP, 2008); L Hand, 'Historical and Practical Considerations Regarding Expert Testimony' (1901) *Harvard Law Rev* 15(40); B Vesterdorf, 'Economics in Court: Reflections on the Role of Judges in Assessing Economic Theories and Evidence in the Modernised Competition Regime', in M Johansson, N Wahl & U Bernitz (eds), *Liber Amicorum in Honour of Sven Norbert: A European for All Seasons* (Bruxelles, Bruylant, 2006); B Vesterdorf, 'Standard of Proof in Merger Cases: Reflections in the Light of Recent Case Law of the Community Courts' (2005) *European Competition Journal* 1 at 3; I Lianos, *La Transformation du droit de la concurrence par le recours à l'analyse économique* (Bruxelles, Bruylant/Sakkoulas, 2007); S Brewer, 'Scientific Expert Testimony and Intellectual Due Process' (1998) *Yale L J* (107) 1535, 1586.
27. *Buckley v Rice-Thomas* (1554) 1 *Plowd* 118; *Folkes v Chadd* (1782) 3 *Doug KB* 157; WM Best, in S.L. Phipson (ed), *The Principles of the Law of Evidence*, 12th edn (London, Sweet & Maxwell, 1922); HA Hammelmann, 'Expert Evidence' (1947) 10 MLR 32).

naturally pay their fees. Consequently, the scope for bias conscious and unconscious is considerable.[28] These difficulties are augmented by a further factor. When the determination of an issue requires specialized knowledge, neither the jury nor the judge is likely to be able to subject the testimony of the expert to searching scrutiny. In theory Lord President Cooper may have been right to say of expert that:

[t]heir duty is to furnish the judge or jury with the necessary scientific criteria for testing the accuracy of their conclusions so as to enable the judge or jury to form their own independent judgment by the application of these criteria to the facts provide in evidence.

However, in practice this is rather unrealistic. As Learned Hand observed, we call experts because the trier of fact is not competent to judge on the matter. How can we then expect the trier of fact to adjudicate between conflicting expert opinions? (Basten, 'The Court Expert in Civil Trials' (1977) 40 MLR 174.) There is, therefore, a risk that a jury's decision may be influenced less by the merits of the opinions advanced than by the self-confidence and apparent respectability of those who advance them. For these reasons, the courts try to limit the scope for expert evidence to issues which the court feels incompetent to judge.[29]

---

28. I Lianos 'Judging Economists: Economic Expertise in Competition Law Litigation: A European View', in I Lianos & I Kokkoris (eds), *Towards an Optimal Competition Law System* (The Hague, Kluwer International, 2009) argues that 'bias' serves to distort the accuracy of evaluation of expert opinion evidence where given in EC competition proceedings in what he terms 'the European legal system': 'The paper will conclude that the possible adverse effects of the epistemic asymmetry and expert bias between judges and experts raise important concerns that the legal systems should tackle. The current procedural institutional and substantive legal framework governing economic expertise does not however take sufficiently into account important concerns that are specific to economics and other social sciences such as the preservation of the scientific 'competition' in the supply of economic theory and consequently methodological assumptions related pluralism in economic thought. In particular I will argue against adopting specific standards of admissibility of economic expertise in Europe. This is a US context specific solution which does not necessarily fit with the specific characteristics of the European legal system. It is also an approach that represents an outdated and partial view of the scientific as well as of the judicial adjudication process. But impartiality and independence are relationship concepts: they should not be confused with the requirement of objectivity. The requirement of objectively which is important for the legitimacy and social acceptability of the judicial decision-making process is profoundly interlinked with the development of objective knowledge in the antitrust field. However this study will argue that notwithstanding the problem of expert bias, the conception of economics as a source of objective knowledge does not hold.' As regards bias D Dwyer, *The Judicial Assessment of Expert Evidence* (Cambridge, CUP 2008), observes at p. 363: 'The procedural devices that one might employ to address expert bias depend very much on two things: the role that one expects the expert to play in civil litigation and the types of bias that one considers most damaging to the court's ability to determine the facts accurately. The second of these may in turn depend on the type of question that the expert is addressing. This is an example of an occasion when the obvious answer is not wrong. If we expect the expert to act alone or in a team as a direct or indirect servant of the court then discussion of litigation privilege is inappropriate and inadmissibility rules are probably misplaced. Conversely it would be difficult to justify simultaneously saying that the expert is part of the party's advocacy teams in the US or Italy and the discussion the use of single experts recusal or even realistically the expert's duty to the court. Courts in the US may express the view that an expert's professional duty is not to the party that pays her but to the court and to the truth finding process of the trial but this norm is lost behind the much more pervasive and powerfully pursued norm of litigation pugnacity.'
29. A Zuckerman, *The Principles of Criminal Evidence* (Oxford, OUP, 1989), *supra*, passim.

In short, there would appear to be a potential void: that is, a particular matter may well exceed the competence of a judge. However, he may well choose at least in civil trials to rely upon his own layman's opinion to avoid the difficulties involved in endeavouring to assess the opinion of an expert. Others, such as Lawton LJ, explained the limitation on the use of expert evidence, that is the scope thereof, and its reasons in the case of Turner:

> If on the proven facts a judge or jury can form their own conclusions without [expert] help then the opinion of an expert is unnecessary. In such a case if it is given dressed up in scientific jargon it may make judgment more difficult. The fact that an expert witness has impressive scientific qualifications does not by that fact alone make his opinion on matters of human nature and behaviour within the limits of normality any more helpful than that of the jurors themselves; but there is a danger that they may think it does (*Turner* (1975) 1 All ER 70, 74).

This would seem to narrow the scope of the expert. However, it would appear that the honourable judge did not refer specifically to another factor; that is, the social acceptance of a particular type of expert knowledge must exist in addition to the inherent complexity of the subject before arguably a strong case can be made for its inclusion within the field of expert evidence. In any event, Lawson LJ makes no reference between a possible disparity with respect to a judgment rendered on a particular subject with expert evidence and one made without and the inconsistencies which could arise on a long-term basis. It may, therefore, be that Lawson LJ was referring either to matters which were not inherently complicated or if they were the view of experts had not yet achieved currency or unanimity socially as it were. It is submitted for reasons which will be developed subsequently that once the three elements of scientific complexity, consistency and social acceptance of an opinion thereon exist, then the matter would seem to fall within the scope of an expert witness. This categorization is therefore likely to override the reasons for the restrictions upon the use of an expert evidence and notably that produced by an expert appointed by the court. This inherent scope and purpose, so to speak, form the basis upon which to decide matters involving the use of expert evidence, restrictions thereupon and compliance with the legal principles contained within the concept of rectitude of decision, due process and access to courts contained with Article 6 (1) ECHR and effective legal protection.

§2.02 POSSIBLE CONSTRAINTS UPON THE USE OF EXPERT EVIDENCE

In reality, the scope of the use of expert evidence creates an additional problem; that is, following Zuckerman,[30] judgments which vary in degrees of accuracy in the sense of the difference between a judgment based upon an expert opinion and a judgment which is not. This eventuality which is apparently the most significant consequence of the decision as to whether or not to use expert evidence may impact upon the principle of rectitude of decision; that is, in those fields where a consensus exists that a particular

30. A Zuckerman, *The Principles of Criminal Evidence* (Oxford, OUP, 1989), *supra*, 65-66.

type of opinion evidence such as for example that of an economist is more appropriate than are lay opinions notably those of judges, as would be the case in EU competition law.[31] Furthermore, there should be consistency as to those areas in which the standard of the expert is required and those areas where it is not so as to avoid double standards of accuracy or rectitude of decision. Zuckerman observes that there are in reality at least three matters to consider with respect to the use of expert evidence by the court: first, the admissibility of expert evidence is a function of the degree or extent to which it can contribute to supplying understanding in a field in which the judge does not possess such knowledge and as such is clearly related to the fundamental purpose of expert evidence; second, the difference between the standard of the judgment rendered with expert evidence and that which is given without such evidence; and third, the availability of such expert evidence to the court in last instance depends upon prior recognition by the community of the discipline in question being appropriate and suitable for the legal domain or area. Zuckerman[32] makes the following observation:

> The different outcome in these two cases is not necessarily objectionable. Admissibility depends as we have seen on probative usefulness. If a decision on the admissibility of particular expert evidence were binding, future courts would be obliged to admit expert evidence even where expertise has turned out to be unreliable. There is however, another dimension to the problem of expert evidence and on this one might expect some judicial consistency. The decision to admit or reject expert evidence on a certain issue is not only a function of whether it can contribute to the determination of truth by supplying knowledge which the judge and the jury do not possess. A much more important and troublesome question is whether it is proper to bring to bear on an issue which is not strictly an issue of fact an expert body of opinion rather than to leave the matter to be determined by lay standard. The fact that psychiatry is a study of mental processes does not of itself dictate that psychiatric evidence must be admissible on an issue of provocation. This issue requires a decision whether the accused had lost control over himself as a result of provocation. But there are degrees of loss of control and it is possible that the ordinary man's standards of what amounts to loss of control are different from those of psychiatrists. Hence the question whether to accept psychiatric evidence on provocation may involve a choice between different standards of judgment.[33]

As noted earlier, Zuckerman argues effectively, that the use of expert evidence is also subject not just to the condition that it be capable of improving the quality of the judgment which is the purpose but in addition there is a requirement that the field in which the expert provides his opinion has been already publicly recognized as one which is appropriate for that type of expertise in addition to the third criterion of consistency. Once such recognition has been achieved, then the courts must be

31. A Christiansen, 'The Reform of Merger Control – Fundamental Reversal or Mere Refinement' <www.papers.ssrn.com> (2005) Abstract 898845.
32. A Zuckerman, *The Principles of Criminal Evidence* (Oxford, OUP, 1989), *supra*, 65.
33. *Ibid.*, footnote 18: 'Lawton LJ made it clear in Turner that he was rejecting psychiatric standards as a matter of principle and preferring the application of popular standards to the issue (1975) 1 All ER 70 at 75.'

consistent in their approach involving the use of expert evidence in that field. Zuckerman[34] observes as follows:

> A judge deciding whether expert opinion should be accepted as an arbiter of a certain matter has to consider the state of public opinion on the point. If the community has come to defer to professional standards on the matters in question the courts will normally follow suit. Medical evidence is admissible on matters of health because we accept the authority of the medical profession in this regard. Psychiatry has not yet attained a like acceptance. Psychiatric evidence is admissible on the issue of insanity but not as we have seen on the mental state of a normal person. It is arguable that the distinction is irrational; for to understand abnormality psychiatry has first to master the normal mental processes. However as long as the community does not defer to psychiatry on matters such as intention and credibility the scope for expert evidence on such matters must remain limited and judicial difference of opinion of the kind we came across in Turner and Lowery are to be expected. Only when public opinion is clear one way or another can we demand consistency from the courts.

Therefore, in summary, for Zuckerman[35] the matter of the use of expert evidence consists of three elements: first, '... whether it can contribute to the determination of truth by supplying knowledge which the judge and the jury do not possess'; second, as noted earlier the public recognition of the utility and value of such expert knowledge and opinion in a specific domain: 'A judge deciding whether expert opinion should be accepted as an arbiter of a certain matter has to consider public opinion on the point. If the community has come to defer to professional standards on the matters in question the courts will normally follow suit'; third, in addition, the requirement of consistency that is necessary in order to avoid a discrepancy between a judgment rendered with an expert opinion and that which is not. In terms of the present circumstances of proceedings involving the Merger Regulation[36] and the application of Articles 101 and 102 TFEU, it is perhaps the first element discussed by Zuckerman which most clearly requires the use of expert evidence as regards proceedings under both of the aforementioned for the following reason: '... whether it can contribute to the determination of truth by supplying knowledge which the judge and the jury do not possess'. Further, it is submitted that the second of the requirements is fulfilled: specifically, that there exists both public and at least indirectly judicial acceptance that economic expert evidence as being appropriate in the field of the application of not only EU competition law and in particular of the merger control regulation. Indeed, with respect to the latter, the position of the CJ has consistently been that the application of the merger control regulation involves the use of complex economic theory at least by the Commission.[37] The third requirement depends upon the application in the facts of the case as it is most strongly related to the rectitude of decision.

---

34. A Zuckerman, *The Principles of Criminal Evidence* (Oxford, OUP, 1989), 67.
35. *Ibid.*, 67.
36. Council Regulation (EC) No. 139/2004 of 20 January 2004 on the Control of Concentrations between Undertakings.
37. See, A Christiansen, 'The Reform of Merger Control – Fundamental Reversal or Mere Refinement' <www.papers.ssm.com> (2005) Abstract 898845; DJ Gerber, 'Courts as Economic

§2.03 OVERVIEW OF THE SCOPE OF EXPERT EVIDENCE FOR THE CJ, GC AND ECTHR

Insofar as the principles underlying the substantive law of expert evidence in England may be of use to define more clearly the scope of expert evidence as used by the CJ, the GC and the ECtHR, it would seem that overall they are wide;[38] that is, first, overall the purpose of opinion evidence is clearly to provide information to judges on technical issues upon which they, as non-experts, have no information or understanding either of the concepts or of the terminology; second, following Zuckerman,[39] at least in English law there must exist an element of public acceptance of the type of expertise involved. There is nothing to indicate that either the GC, CJ or the ECtHR approaches matters differently in this respect. As regards specifically economic expert opinions as in the case of damages actions for non-contractual liability pursuant to Article 340 (2) TFEU for erroneous Commission decisions made under the Merger Control Regulation[40] it is submitted that the public acceptance recognizes, therefore, that economics is the type of evidence which is appropriate for the adjudication of issues involving anti-trust issues generally and in particular mergers. Further, the recognition that economic issues in anti-trust law particularly involving mergers and damages is such that it falls not only within the scope of a subject the technical nature of which is such as to require expert evidence but also that coupled with the recognition that economic expertise is socially acceptable would seem to preclude any problem with consistency. Therefore, the parameters of expert evidence as recognized by the GC, CJ and the ECtHR particularly when analysed in more detail by means of the constructs used in the substantive law of English expert evidence, which may even be slightly narrower than for the aforementioned courts, is confirmed as being wide. These parameters, as so analysed, will certainly accommodate the application of the Merger Regulation Control[41] and Articles 101 and 102 TFEU. The real difficulty arises at the level of the application of this wide substantive concept of expert evidence by means of the rules of procedure embodied within the Measures of Inquiry of the GC and the CJ. It is submitted that the real sheet anchor of the utilization of expert evidence in the aforementioned courts, however, is the judicial recognition that a particular issue

---

Experts in European Merger Law', in *Annual Proceedings of the Fordham Corporate Law Institute*, Fordham University, School of Law (2004).

38. As noted earlier, the scope of expert evidence in EU law would appear to be wide: see E Barbier de la Serre & A-L Sibony, 'Expert Evidence before the Courts' (2008) *CMLRev* (45) 941, *supra*, at 974; P Lasok, *The European Court of Justice: Practice and Procedure*, 2nd edn (London, Butterworths, 1994), *supra*, 431.
39. A Zuckerman, *The Principles of Criminal Evidence* (Oxford, OUP, 1989), *supra*, 67.
40. Council Regulation (EC) No. 139/2004 of 20 January 2004 on the Control of Concentrations between Undertakings. *My Travel v Commission* T 212/03 (2008) *ECR* II 1967 www.curia.europa.eu.
41. Council Regulation (EC) No. 139/2004 of 20 January 2004 on the Control of Concentrations between Undertakings. *My Travel v Commission* T 212/03 (2008) *ECR* II 1967 www.curia.europa.eu, *ibid*.

requires expert evidence because of its inherent technical nature.[42] Here, it is submitted that what is required by this aspect of the substantive definition of expert evidence by the CG, GC and the ECtHR is as follows: that compliance with certain principles such as Article 6 (1) ECHR,[43] effective judicial protection and rectitude of decision, contingent upon the circumstances of the case, may well require by reason of the nature of the material the following: the appointment by the Court pursuant to Article 65 (d) GC and Article 45 (2) (d) CJ of an expert economist notably in the instant field of the application of Merger Control Regulation[44] and Articles 101 and 102 TFEU. As regards the ECtHR, the appropriate rule of procedure would be as noted previously, Article A (1) (Annex). However, such a characteristic of the scope of expert evidence, or more particularly the commissioning of an expert's report in the context of a Measures of Inquiry would not require that the judges follow the decision of the expert, notably, expert economist in anti-trust matters or merger matters. The only requirement would be for the judges, once they have commissioned the export report, to evaluate the report properly.

§2.04 ESSENTIAL PROBLEM

As noted earlier, the consequences of the failure to utilize the expert evidence for the interpretation of the meaning of a technical word can lead to a breach of ECHR Article 6 (1) (breach of the right to a fair trial) breach of the EU principle of effective judicial protection[45] and breach of the procedural principle of rectitude of decision, i.e.,

42. R Sullivan, *Sullivan and Driedger on the Construction of Statutes*, 4th edn (Vancouver, Butterworths, 2002), *supra*, at 43: 'Baron Pollock in the Grenfell case makes audience understanding the key. He assumes that most statutes are addressed to the general public and therefore the common understanding of the words used should prevail. Lord Esher in Unwin v Hanson makes a statute's subject matter the key. He assumes that a statute dealing with a specialized subject is addressed to a specialized audience and therefore the relevant technical meanings should prevail'; at 46 'In deciding whether to adopt the ordinary or the technical meaning of words courts look to the usual range of factors: the purpose, the scheme of legislation, the consequences of preferring one meaning over the other, relevant common law principles etc. ... Whether a term has a technical meaning and what that meaning is are both questions of fact which must be established in a legally acceptable way. When a technical or specialized meaning is not something that everybody knows it cannot be judicially noticed but must be established through evidence, normally expert opinion evidence. Such evidence is required to establish both that a term has a technical meaning and the content of that meaning.'
43. *Kraska v Switzerland* (1993) 18 *EHRR* 188, para. 30.
44. Council Regulation (EC) No. 139/2004 of 20 January 2004 on the Control of Concentrations between Undertakings.
45. *Unibet v Justitiekanslern* at Case 432/05(2007) *ECR* I 2271 para. 37 'It is to be noted at the outset that, according to settled case-law, the principle of effective judicial protection is a general principle of Community law stemming from the constitutional traditions common to the Member States, which has been enshrined in Articles 6 and 13 of the European Convention for the Protection of Human Rights and Fundamental Freedoms (Case 222/84 *Johnston* [1986] *ECR* 1651, paragraphs 18 and 19; Case 222/86 *Heylens and Others* [1987] *ECR* 4097, paragraph 14; Case C-424/99 *Commission v Austria* [2001] *ECR* I-9285, paragraph 45; Case C-50/00 P *Unión de Pequeños Agricultores v Council* [2002] *ECR* I-6677, paragraph 39; and Case C-467/01 *Eribrand* [2003] *ECR* I-6471, paragraph 61) and which has also been reaffirmed by Article 47 of the Charter of fundamental rights of the European Union, proclaimed on 7 December 2000 in Nice' (OJ 2000 C 364, 1).

an inaccurate judgment which does not correspond to the true facts. As previously noted by Barbier and Sibony[46] various possible restrictions upon the use of expert evidence which appear in the judgments of the CJ and GC. Certainly, one method which can assist the aforementioned courts and the ECtHR would be the appointment of an assessor or expert for the court itself in order to assist in explaining, arguably through judicial notice, the meaning of technical terms in expert evidence.

[A] Evaluation of Expert Evidence by Means of an Assessor

As just noted, a possible method for assisting judges to evaluate expert evidence and thereby increasing the use of expert evidence is to be found in the appointment of a court expert referred to as an assessor.[47] The procedural example considered will be taken from the English CPR.[48] The nature of the intervention of the assessor, however, is restricted to giving advice to the judge as part of the court concerning technical information but not evidence. Accordingly, the assessor cannot be cross examined as no evidence is presented and the assessor intervenes as part of the court in order to assist the judge in his judicial functions. Blom-Cooper,[49] however, argues that this system of providing advice to a judge which is not subject to cross-examination is likely to contravene Article 6 (1) ECHR. He writes:

> The assessor system being advice by an expert not under oath given to the court on matters not disclosable for cross examination by either party would be regarded today as being incompatible under S 3(1) of the Human Rights Act 1988 as a violation of Art 6.1 ECHR.

---

46. E Barbier de La Serre & A-L Simony, 'Expert Evidence before the EC Courts' (2008) *CMLRev* (45) (4) 941, *supra*, at 951-961.
47. The English CPR 35 provides for the appointment of an assessor in the following manner and circumstances: (2). Assessors CPR 35 (15) provides as follows: This rule applies when the court appoints one or more persons (an assessor) under S 70 of the Supreme Court Act (1981) or S 63 of the County Courts Act (1984) (1) The assessor shall assist the court in dealing with a matter in which the assessor has skill and experience (2) An assessor shall take such part in the proceedings as the court may direct and in particular may – a) direct the assessor to prepare a report for the court on any issue in the proceedings b) direct the assessor to attend the whole or any part of the trial to advise the court on any such matter (3) If the assessor prepares a report for the court before the trial has begun – (a) the court will send a copy to each of the parties; and (b)the parties may use it at the trial (4) The remuneration to be paid to the assessor for his services shall be determined by the court and shall form part of the costs of the proceedings; The Practise Direction for CPR 35.15 provides: 7. 1 An assessor may be appointed to assist the court under rule 35.15. Not less than 21 days before making such an appointment the court will notify each party in writing of the name of the proposed assessor of the matter in respect of which the assistance of the assessor will be sought and of the qualification to the assessor to give that assistance. 7.2 Where any person has been proposed for appointment as an assessor objection to him, either personally or in respect of his qualification may be taken by any party. 7.3 Any such objection must be make in writing and filed with the court within 7 days of receipt of the notification referred to in para. 6.1 and will be taken into account by the court in deciding whether or not to make the appointment. 7. 4 Copies of any report prepared by the assessor will be sent to each of the parties but the assessor will not give oral evidence or be open to cross-examination or questioning.
48. *Civil Procedure Rules*, www.justice.gov.gov.uk/courts/procedure-rules/civil/.
49. Sir Louis Blom-Cooper QC, 'Experts and Assessors' (2002)(21) *CJQ* pg. 345, at 348.

Notwithstanding, it is submitted that this analysis may possibly not apply in the following situations: first, where the assessor provides information which the court uses in order to take judicial notice of non-controversial matters:[50] second, in those circumstances where the rights of the defence do not require cross examination, the proposition being that defence rights do not require in all situations the right to cross examination in order to be upheld notably when they are accompanied by an effective system of appeal.

Etymologically, assessor signifies a person who is authorized to sit with others in order to assist directly in the taking of decisions. In practice, the role of the assessor may vary widely. Indeed, for some, such as Viscount Simon LC,[51] an assessor may intervene exclusively on matters which require an explanation of the meaning of technical terms. Moreover, an assessor, being unsworn may not give evidence. Others, such as Viscount Dunedin,[52] believe that an assessor may provide a source of facts beyond simply the meaning of words. For Zuckerman,[53] the assessor in providing either the information concerning the meaning of words or more generally, facts, assists the judge in his judicial capacity. Therefore, the assessor cannot be cross examined. Dwyer[54] observes that 'it is settled law that an assessor acting in a normal civil capacity or under a particularly statutory form of proceedings is not an evidentiary source and almost certain constitutes part of the tribunal as scientific adviser under S 70 (3) of the Supreme Court act (1981) and CPR 35.15.'

One method of analysing the function of the assessor is to relate it to the process of judicial notice. Indeed, Lord Denning[55] observed that a judge in using the advice of the assessor 'equips himself in order to take judicial notice'. In terms of a definition judicial notice may be defined as a compendious method of proof. Further, the facts which may be noticed judicially vary between those the veracity of which is indisputable to those which require some type of proof. Restricting judicial notice to the category of indisputable facts entails a procedural advantage: it explains both why an assessor cannot be cross examined and why such absence of cross-examination cannot violate the rights of the defence:[56] namely, that the veracity of the facts noticed

50. AAS Zuckerman, *Civil Procedure* (London, Lexis Nexis, 2003), *supra*; at 640 'Assessors fulfil a different role from that of expert witnesses. Assessors sit with the judge and assist the court in its deliberations both during the presentation of evidence and argument and after they have been concluded. Since an assessor assists the court in its judicial role, an assessor cannot be cross-examined.'
51. *Richardson v Redpath Brown & Co Ltd* (1944) *AC* 67, speech of Viscount Simon LC at 70.
52. SS *Australia v SS Nautilus (Cargo Owners) The Australia* (1927) *AC* 145 at 150.
53. AAS Zuckerman, *Civil Procedure* (Lexis Nexis, London, 2003), *supra*, at 640.
54. D Dwyer, 'The Future of Assessors under the CPR' (2006) (25) *CJQ* 219 at 230 refers to *The White Book Service* (Sweet & Maxwell, London, 2006) at 962: 'The assessor assists the judge in discharging his judicial role. His function is to educate the judge and to enable him to reach a properly informed decision' contrary to Sir Louis Blom-Cooper QC who observes at 350: 'There has been significant uncertainty as to the status of the advice given to judges by assessors'.
55. *Baldwin & Francis v Patents Appeal Tribunal* (1959) *AC* 663 at 691 where Lord Denning explains that the purpose of the appointment of assessors is '... the court is equipping itself for its task by taking judicial notice of all such things as it ought to know in order to do its work properly'.
56. AAS. Zuckerman, *Principles of Criminal Evidence* (Oxford University Press, Oxford, 1989) at 98 'Where there can be no reasonable dispute between parties it is wasteful to insist on a full trial of fact. The doctrine of judicial notice relieves the parties of the burden of proving facts which

judicially is indisputable. If, on the other hand, the concept of judicial notice is expanded so as to include not only indisputable but also disputable matters as, for example, the meaning of economic terms in EC competition law expert evidence then the rights of the defence may be ensured in two ways: first, by means of appeal and second, by the right of the parties to respond in some way before judgment to the information given to the judge by the assessor through judicial notice.[57] With regard to the type of facts which may be judicially noticed, the distinction is sometimes made between adjudicative facts which are not disputable and legislative facts which are disputable. Indeed, Davis[58] includes both types of facts, legislative and adjudicative, within the concept of judicial notice. Accordingly, it will be argued here that a judge when sitting with the assessor takes judicial notice by means of the information which the assessor provides him of facts some of which are indisputable and others which are disputable.

In order to ensure that the functions of the assessor correspond to the notion of the judge taking judicial notice, it may be that compliance with Article 6 (1) EHCR will require certain changes to the structure of CPR 35. 15. One may consider the following:

> First, it is submitted that CPR 35. 15 (3) and (4) may be ultra vires of the enabling states.

The editor of the White Book[59] observes:

> CPR 35 (15) (3) provides that an assessor may take part 'in the proceedings as the Court may direct'. This seems wider than the former provisions and without the statutory provision. S 70 (1) of the 1981 Act says that the Court 'may hear and dispose' of the case 'with their assistance' and S 63 (1) of the 1984 Acts states that the assessor 'may sit with the judge'.[60]

In short, a court can only direct assessors to '... take part in the proceedings' as in conformity with the Supreme Court Act (1981)(SCA) and the County Court Act (1984)(CCA). More particularly, it would seem that CPR 35.15 (3) and (4) permit the

---

are not reasonably disputable and thereby solves the problems when an indisputable fact is taken for granted it clearly cannot be said that one of the parties has been deprived of the opportunity to present his case.'

57. KC Davis, 'Judicial Notice' (1955) (55) *Columbia Law Review* 945 at 978.
58. KC Davis, 'Judicial Notice' (1955) (55) *Columbia Law Review* 945, *supra*, at 976.
59. Rt Hon Lord Justice Jackson (Editor in Chief) *Civil Procedure*, vol. 1 White Book Service (London, Sweet and Maxwell, 2013) at 1109.
60. Supreme Court Act (1981) S 70 provides: (1) In any cause or matter before the High Court the court may, if it thinks it expedient to do so, call in the aid of one or more assess specially qualified and hear and dispose of the cause or matter wholly or partially with their assistance; (2) The remuneration, if any, to be paid to an assessor for his services under subsection (1) in connection with any proceedings shall be determined by the court and shall form part of the costs of the proceedings;
(3) Rules of Court shall make provision for the appointment of scientific advisors to assist the Patents Court in proceedings under the Patents Act 1949 and Patents Act 1977 and for regulating the functions of such advisors;
(4) The remuneration of any such adviser shall be determined by the Lord Chancellor with the concurrence of the Minister for the Civil Service and shall be defrayed out of the money provided by Parliament.'

assessor to provide what could be construed as evidence in so far as the report can be relied upon by the parties. Accordingly, this possibility arguably exceeds the scope of both the SCA (1981) and the CCA (1984) but also tends to obliterate the distinctions as to the appropriate function of a court expert: that is an expert appointed ex officio by the court in contrast to the current single expert provided by CPR 35. This would approximate the former court expert under the RSC 40 r 1.[61]

It would seem, therefore, that the elimination of CPR 35. 15 (3) and (4) may be required in order to ensure compliance with Article 6 (1) ECHR for the following reason: first, to ensure that the operation of the assessor for the enforcement of TFEU 101 and 102 comes squarely within the ambit of SCA (1981)[62] and CCC (1984).[63] Following this analysis above, the restriction of CPR 35.15 to the parameters of the enabling statutes ensures, thereby, that the role of the assessor is in turn limited to one of assisting the judge to take judicial notice of the meaning of technical words. It is submitted that this restriction of the role of the assessor ensures, thereby, the incorporation of its functions into those of the tribunal. Accordingly, it is apparent that the assessor operating in this manner may contribute to ensuring that TFEU 101 and 102 are effectively enforced in the sense of adequate enforcement by the ordinary court in conformity with the EU principle of effective judicial protection and above all, ECHR Article 6 (1).

One might note in addition that in order to ensure more fully the reduction in the scope of the assessor which would result from the removal of CPR 35.15 (3) and (4), arguably, conformity with the rights of defence in ECHR Article 6 (1) may require an amendment of Practice Direction 7.4:[64] specifically, the words 'copies of any report prepared by the assessor will be sent to each of the parties' would be removed in order to more effectively prevent the production of evidence by an assessor. In the event that

61. Sir Louis Blom-Cooper 'Experts and Assessors: Past Present and Future' (2002) *CJQ* 341 at 347 notes that RSC Or 40 r. 1 which is now replaced by CPR 35 provided:

> 1. In any cause or matter which is to be tried without a jury and in which any question for an expert witness arises, the Court may at any time; on the application of any party, appoint an independent expert of if more than once question arises, two or more such experts, to enquire and report on any question of fact or opinion involving questions of law or of construction. An expert appointed under this paragraph is referred to as a court expert.
> 2.Any court expert in a cause or matter shall, if possible be a person agreed between the parties and failing agreement, shall be nominated by the court.
> 3. The question to be submitted to the court expert and the restrictions (if any) given to him shall, failing agreement between the parties, be settled by the court.
> 4. In this rule 'expert' in relation to any question arising in a cause or matter means any person who has such knowledge or experience of or in connection with the question that his opinion on it would be admissible in evidence.
> RSC 40 r 1 (2) is the germ of the idea for the single joint expert provision in CPR 35.7 and one wonders why the court appointed expert provision was dropped.

62. *Supreme Court Act* (1981).
63. *County Court Act* (1984).
64. Sir Louis Blom-Cooper 'Experts and Assessors: Past Present and Future' (2002) *CJQ* 341 *ibid.*, at 352 (footnote 11 *supra*) argues that the 'advice' which the assessor may provide to the judge pursuant to CPR 35.15 in fact is evidence: 'Under r 35.15 the 'advice' will qualify as evidence (35.15 (4)(b) and Practice Direction 7.4 and to the extent that a pre-trail report from the assessor is directed by the court, the parties will have sight and the facility to make use of its contents.'

the judge feels that his judgment is likely to be influenced by the advice of the assessor with respect to the meaning of particular words then it may be appropriate that he indicate to the parties the nature of this advice before judgment.[65] This will more easily enable the parties to exercise their rights of defence in the following manner: first, they are indirectly able to respond to the assessor's advice by commenting thereupon to the judge before judgment despite the exclusion of oral cross-examination of the assessor by S 7.4 of the Practice Direction: and second, the parties are able to use this information given by the judge in order to assist in forming eventual grounds of appeal from the judgment.[66] Therefore, the rights of the defence would appear to be adequately protected by a combination of the aforementioned two provisions: namely, the possibility for the parties to respond directly although not through oral cross examination of the assessor to the information contained in his written report prior to the entry of judgment:[67] and additionally, the opportunity of using the judge's written comments to assist in making an appeal against the judgment where he relied upon the information provided by the assessor in making his judgment.

65. *Richardson v Redpath* (1944) *AC* 62 at 71, Viscount Simon, 'It would seem desirable in cases where the assessor's advice, within its proper limits, is likely to affect the judge's conclusion for the latter to inform the parties before him of the advice which he has received from the assessor.'
66. Sir Louis Blom-Cooper QC 'Experts and Assessors, Past Present and Future': (2002) 21 *CJQ* 350, *supra*, and footnote 11 *supra*: 'The assessor system being advice by an expert no under oath given to the court on matters not discloseable for cross examination by either party before judgement and qualifying as evidence would be regarded today as being incompatible under S 3 (1) of the Human Rights Act 1998 as a violation of Art 6 (1) of the European Convention of Human Rights.' Clearly, this view is based upon an interpretation of EHRC Art 6 (1) as providing a right to direct oral cross examination as the only method of ensuring the rights of the parties to respond to the case being made against as provided by *van Orshoven v Belgium* (1997) (26) EHRR 55. However, it is not absolutely clear that Art 6 (1), and such cases such van Orshoven require that that the right to respond is coterminous with the right to direct oral examination as opposed to the right to respond indirectly coupled with written notice of the information which in turn forms the basis for an eventual appeal. D Dwyer, in 'The Future of Assessors under the CPR' (2006) 25 *CJQ* Vol at 219, *supra*, argues at 225 that 'Four distinct functions can be identified for assessors within the current scope of CPR 35.15: tribunal member, court expert, court officer and scientific adviser. .. The assessor as scientific adviser would seek to clarify technical points of evidence for the judge and might suggest to the judge possible areas for further questioning in relation to a CPR r 35.2 expert's opinion. This appears to be the type of assessor Mackay J. had in mind in *XYZ v Schering Health Care (XYZ v Schering Health Care* (2002) *EWCA* 1420 (QB) at 148-49) when consider expert evidence involving algebra'; It would seem the Dwyer feels that the function of scientific adviser which would under her analysis characterize the manner in which an assessor could intervene in enforcement proceedings for EC Arts 81 and 82 may not require cross-examination: she notes at 229 'The final point in applying Art – (1) to the use of assessors is that one must have regard to the extent to which a particular practice might affect the substantive fairness of the process taken as a whole rather than in isolation. Thus the use of assessors to give opinions on the acceptability of the conduct of the parties might reasonably be considered to have a significant effect on the trial and so procedure surrounding such a use should be subject to Art 6 (1) scrutiny. On the other hand, the use of assessors to advise the judge in general terms or to suggest further lines of question might be see has having significantly less impact on the case as a whole.' See generally D Dwyer, 'Changing Approaches to Expert Evidence in England and Italy' (2003) *Intl. Commentary on Evidence*: www.law.qub.ac.uk/ice/papers/expert2pdf, *supra*.
67. It is useful to note that the CAT Rules restrict the availability of cross examination: the CAT Guidelines (2005) provide at 3.4 (IV) The Tribunal will pay close attention to the probative value of documentary evidence. When there are essential evidential issues that cannot be resolved without cross examination, the Tribunal may permit oral examination of the witness.'

Overall, it may be said that the general procedural principle of rectitude of decision coupled with ECHR Article 6 (1) apply so as to favour the use of the assessor notably in enforcement of the TFEU and the ECHR for the following reasons: recourse to the assessor will ensure first, that justice be done particularly in competition law cases in the sense that the decision would be accurate as possible in relation to the true facts properly understood by the judge; and second, that the decision be taken with a minimum of expense. Indeed, it may be that the use of an assessor is proportionately cheaper and quicker than would be the case if an additional expert were appointed. This reflects what appears to be the historic advantages of the use of the assessor and of judicial notice.[68] Accordingly, in conclusion it is difficult to see why a priori the use of the assessor coupled with judicial notice as operated in the English system of procedure could not be replicated by the current rules of procedure of the CJ, the GC and notably in the ECtHR: that is, taking account of the fact that the rules of procedure of the three aforementioned courts permit these courts to appoint of their own motion an expert who can then through judicial notice provide explanations of the technical meaning to the judge. The expert could be subject to cross examination notably in those situations where the explanations involve meanings of a disputable nature as opposed to indisputable nature where the cross examination could be eliminated. Similarly, the scope of expert evidence as regards the CJ, the GC and the ECtHR is sufficiently wide such that relevant expert evidence can be introduced. Therefore, the restrictions upon the use of expert evidence by the three courts does not involve impediments in the rules of procedure but are entirely of judicial origin as effectively demonstrated by Barbier and Sibony.[69]

§2.05 EVIDENCE BOTH EXPERT AND NON-EXPERT, FACTS AND STATUTORY INTERPRETATION

In noting the factors which the court may consider in order to form the contemporaneous context according to Sullivan[70] it is necessary to focus upon the cogency of the expert or non-expert evidence or legislative facts if one uses the concept of judicial notice developed by Davis.[71] In truth, it must be added that the justification for a dynamic as opposed to a static interpretation is in first instance decided upon the basis of the cogency of the evidence either expert or non-expert or legislative facts which are used. In addition, it is submitted that the probative value of the evidence or the facts used to establish the necessity of using either the dynamic or the static change in large measure determines the limits to the dynamic as opposed to static approach. In short, the establishment of whether a particular interpretation can be said to exceed the role of the judiciary notably as regards the dynamic interpretation is most profitably and

68. KK Davis (1955) (55) *Columbia Law Review, supra*, 945 at 983 and J Dickey, 'Assessors' (1970) *MLR* 494 at 501.
69. E Barbier de La Serre and A-L Simony 'Expert Evidence before the EC Courts' (2008) *CMLRev* (45) (4) 941, at 951-961.
70. R Sullivan. *Sullivan and Driedger on the Construction of Statutes*, 4th edn (Vancouver, Butterworth, 2002), *supra*, at 112.
71. KC Davis 'Judicial Notice' (1955) *C L Rev* (55) (7) 945.

succinctly to be considered in terms of a question of evidence or facts particularly if judicial notice is used: namely, whether the evidence or the facts led either expert or non-expert to establish the contemporaneous context in which the legislation is to be interpreted.[72] Arguably, failure to establish as a matter of evidence or facts if one uses the judicial notice of Davis[73] certain elements within the contemporaneous context would lead to the conclusion that the limits upon the use of the dynamic interpretation had been exceeded.

[A] Procedural Introduction of Evidence and Proof of the Ordinary Meaning of Words

Normally, as previously noted, a court does not admit evidence in order to prove the ordinary meaning of words. Rather[74] the ordinary meaning of language used in legislation is considered to constitute a fact which every competent speaker either knows or knows how to look up. In reality, the concept[75] of judicial notice can be used a method for determining the ordinary meaning of words: that is, under the doctrine of judicial notice it is permissible for judges to declare the ordinary meaning of a word or expression without explaining how they arrived at their conclusion. In short, courts are entitled to take judicial notice[76] of facts, that is, the meaning of ordinary words, that in their opinion are indisputable. This includes first, facts that are notorious in the sense that everyone knows and accepts them; they belong to the store of information that every educated member of the society takes for granted and second, facts that can be

72. This is effectively the argument of 'vires' dealt with in the previous chapter wherein it is submitted that it is extremely difficult if not impossible to establish what the legal limits or the vires involved in the TFEU and also the ECHR without obtaining first of all a proper pursuant to *Kraska v Switzerland* (1993) 18 *EHRR*, *supra*, at para. 30 evaluation of the technical meaning of certain of the words through an expert opinion presented in some manner, possibly through judicial notice and an assessor, to the court.
73. KC Davis 'Judicial Notice' (1955) *C L Rev* (55) (7) 945.
74. R Sullivan, *Sullivan and Driedger on the Construction of Statutes*, 4th edn (Vancouver, Butterworth, 2002), *supra*, at 24-25.
75. There will be considered in this section two different concepts of judicial notice.
76. H Rasmussen, *On law and policy in the European Court of Justice: a Comparative Study in Judicial Policymaking* (Dordrecht, M. Nijhoff, 1986), *supra*, observes at p. 434 Judicial Notice. The facts which a judge needs in order to be informed sufficiently before making a decision which involves broad issues of public policy may be supplied to some degree by what is usually called judicial notice. The inadequacies of the information of the Court of Justice about facts highlights however the narrow confines of a 'judicial notice' doctrine in Community law. Nowhere in that law is it spelled out in clear language what that of which the Court may take notice. It may in the absence of pertinent provisions be recalled that the Model Code of Evidence of the American Law institute states that a judge may on his own motion take notice inter alia of specific facts so notorious as to not be the suspect of reasonable dispute and ... specific facts and propositions of generalized knowledge which are capable of immediate and accurate demonstration by resort to easily accessible sources of indisputable accuracy. Assuming that the Court of Justice enjoys a similar discretion it might take judicial notice of the existence of an economic depression and of encompassing and rising unemployment in the Member States throughout most of the 1970's. It might probably without requiring specific proof take notice that non-tariff barriers to intra Community trade have been sharply on the increase during that economic depression. The precise scope of downward economic and social curve would however have to be demonstrated by evidence.

demonstrated to be true by restoring to sources that are easily accessible and whose authority and accuracy are accepted by all. Nevertheless, there are some difficulties with judicial notice: namely the element of personal relativity involved: in short, what is indisputable to one person may not be indisputable to another. Ironically, this difficulty may justify the introduction of evidence: that is in order to minimize the danger of judicial notice it is appropriate to let in sworn testimony or other evidence for the purpose of establishing the ordinary meaning of words or challenging judicially noticed facts. According to Sullivan:[77]

> Such evidence might be introduced through expert testimony or in the form of a Brandeis brief. This differs from the evidence of meaning that could be offered by an expert with knowledge of the matters to which the legislation applies. Without necessarily attempting to establish a technical meaning for the words the witness explains how persons engaged in that activity understand the language in question. Such evidence has proved useful in cases where the court has been asked to interpret a word or expression not defined in a dictionary or where the dictionary definition was too vague or contradictory to be helpful. Arguably, evidence respecting the meaning of words should be admissible in o so far as it is relevant and reliable.

[B] Judicial Notice as a Method of Proof

In reality, the concept of judicial notice has at least two different forms: the first, is one whereby the concept extends only to matters the veracity of which is not disputable: the truth of the proposition is accepted generally. Accordingly, formal proof is not required. For this reason, Zuckerman[78] argues:

77. R Sullivan, *Sullivan and Driedger on the Construction of Statutes*, 4th edn (Vancouver, Butterworth, 2002), *supra*, at 31.
78. P Robert & A Zuckerman, *Criminal Evidence*, 2nd (Oxford, OUP, 2010) at 169: 'The theoretically strict test of indisputability in practice has proved ambiguous and malleable precipitating judicial over reaching. It seems plausible enough in this day of age that a court might take judicial notice of wide spread knowledge that computer use can be reconstructed from the hard drive even after files have been wiped off the computer and that passengers flying economy 'have to accept relatively cramped conditions which bring them into close proximity with their neighbours. It may even be indisputable in certain social milieu that by mid 1996 the style of restaurants in London had greatly changed. Apart from a few established and very tradition restaurants such as Simpsons and perhaps Rules the era of minimalist decorations and almost minimalist cuisine had begun. For the purposes of taking judicial notice general knowledge may be assessed by reference to a particular locality or specialist group of litigants. Proceeding by way of judicial notice is unobjectionable provided that the noticed facts are truly indisputable between the parties and everybody knows where they stand. In certain cases however judges have proposed to notice facts which are far from indisputable including facts which were actually disputed in the proceedings. In these scenarios judicial notice becomes an illegitimate pretext for short circuiting adversarial argument and proof.' and at 175 'Logically a fact is either open to dispute amongst reasonable people or it is not. If not, then by hypothesis no dispute can arise once that fact has been judicially noticed and rebuttal evidence is precluded. If on the other hand the point can reasonably be disputed the test for judicial notice is not satisfied and the matter remains open to proof by admissible evidence in the ordinary way. Argument should therefore concentrate on whether a particular fact is amenable to being noticed and once that question is settled there is no room for further evidence to unseat noticed facts though of course

In theory the doctrine of judicial notice answers all of the standard objections to settling questions of fact by judicial fiat because only indisputable facts can be judicially noticed. When a genuinely indisputable fact[79] is taken for granted it cannot be said that either part has been deprived of a fair opportunity to advance his case. Not even the appearance of unfairness is given since ex hypotheses there is no real dispute to be had. Nor is there need for matters beyond dispute to be regulated by admissibility requirements at least to the extent that rules of admissibility safeguard against time wasting confusions or misapprehensions. And the test of indisputability also pre-empts jurisdictional qualms in the absence of a genuine dispute for the jury's determination there can be no objection to settling factual questions on the trial judge's directions. Conversely it would be gratuitous to insist on a full trial of fact in such circumstances. Requiring a party to prove a matter which is patently a foregone conclusion would saddle him with an excessive and unnecessary probative burden. The test of indisputability is therefore the key to identifying when a judge may properly dispense with the normal requirements of proof. However 'indisputability' can be understood in two different senses. The first sense corresponds to facts that 'everybody knows'. For example judicial notice has been taken of the fact that human gestation takes longer than two weeks that the University of Oxford exists for the advancement of learning and that a postcard is likely to be read by people other than the addressee. Indisputability in a second sense covers facts that can be ascertained definitively

---

the nature of any further inferences which might be drawn from a noticed fact remains fully contestable. Though rebuttal evidence cannot be adduced to dispute a noticed fact it remains entirely legitimate for the opposing party to adduce evidence to show that particular facts are not indisputable and consequently are not amenable to judicial notice in the first place. Suppose that the timing of tidal flows at a particular coastal location on a certain day become relevant in a criminal trial. The approximate times of high and low tide are not really disputable and judicial notice may be taken. For that purpose the trial judge would normally consult a tide table or receive expert advice. But what if the parties want to challenge the authenticity of the table or the reliability of the expert? Authenticity and reliability are clearly questions of fact. However, the parties' objection is not to an already noticed fact but goes to the prior question of whether notice should be taken in reliance on those particular sources of information. Only if that collateral question can be answered satisfactorily in our hypothetical evidence or agreement that a certain tide table or expert is authoritative may judicial notice be taken. But at that point the noticed fact is conclusively settled for the purposes of the trial.'

79. C Manchester, 'Judicial Notice and Personal Knowledge' (1979) *MLR* (42) 22 -23 'The concept of judicial notice is then that the judge can make use of his general knowledge where some fact has to be established and take notice of the existence of that fact without requiring it to be formally proved. In fact, it is evident that judges frequently to make use of their general knowledge. Indeed as Thayer (A Preliminary Treatise on Evidence (1889), 279) quite rightly points out 'in conducting a process of judicial reasoning as of other reasoning not a step can be taken without assuming something which has not been proved'. However, neither judge nor jury can make use of their personal knowledge. The principle laid down then allows a judge or jury to make use of their general knowledge but not their personal knowledge. The meaning of 'general knowledge' in this context initially seemed to have encompassed only knowledge which was common to the whole community – the court in Rosser referred to general knowledge 'which any many can bring to the subject' while in Ernest Jones it was what the jury know of the state of the country and of society generally (which presumably would be what was known universally throughout the country). Thus it would seem that in its initially development the principle only allowed judicial notice to be taken of matters which were common knowledge throughout the country and not it is submitted of matters which were common knowledge within the locality of the court. It seems to have been a later extension whereby notorious local matters were regarded as matters of general knowledge.' Therefore, arguably an indisputable fact is one which forms part of the general knowledge of either the larger community or of a specific locality which is what Zuckerman terms above 'what everybody knows'.

> without necessarily being universally or even widely known. Verification by reference to indispensable sources occurs where for example the court needs to know the date of the week on which 1 January 2010 fell, or to ascertain historical facts that can be ascertained definitively without necessarily being universally or even widely known. For the purpose of informing itself of such matters the court may have access not only to reliable documentary sources but also to experts. To summarize, facts may be indisputable either because they are generally accepted by the community at large or because they may be ascertained by consulting reliable and trusted source.

It is clear that the concept of judicial notice as proposed by Zuckerman[80] may be described as the narrow view in that it is restricted to indisputable facts either in the sense of something the veracity of which is accepted by the whole community or something the truth of which can be ascertained through an indisputable source such as a dictionary. This indisputability precludes the use of notably cross examination. Further Zuckerman[81] makes a difference between a fact which once recognized as being indisputable in either of the two aforementioned precludes any challenge on the basis of facts and the separate or prior question of whether a particular fact is disputable. On these questions evidence may be led. Quere to what extent the introduction of evidence as suggested by Sullivan[82] as just described herein fall within the category provided by Zuckerman who foresees the introduction of evidence to challenge the fact of indisputability of a particular meaning on the basis following Sullivan, that the meaning given is relative to the judge but not the majority in the majority of native speakers of the language. Furthermore Zuckerman[83] rejects the

80. P Robert & A Zuckerman, *Criminal Evidence* 2nd (Oxford, OUP, 2010), *supra*, at 169.
81. *Ibid.*, at 170-71.
82. R Sullivan, *Sullivan and Driedger on the Construction of Statutes*, 4th edn (Vancouver, Butterworth, 2002), *supra*, at 31.
83. P Robert & A Zuckerman, *Criminal Evidence*, 2nd (Oxford, OUP, 2010) *supra*, at 172 'Thus it is said that judicial notice is taken of the law of the land or a close analogue that courts are presumed to know the law dispensing in either case with the need for proof in accordance with the ordinary rules of evidence (Note 179 *Cross on Evidence*, 5th edn (London, Butterworths, 1979). But this is to confuse matters of evidence and proof with judicial interpretation and development of the law. Legal argument may need to be addressed to disputable points of law but judicial notice as a proxy for proof by admissible evidence is confined to indisputable questions of fact.... When the Court of Appeal declared in Simpson (note 180: *R v Simpson* (1983) 1 WLR 1494 CA that a flick knife qualified as an offensive weapon within the legislative definition and that future courts may take judicial notice of this fact the court was stretching the concept of notice beyond the point at which it ceases to be useful. ...Whereas jurors make normative choices as part of their fact finding responsibilities however judicial classifications settle questions of law. (Note 183: 'Cf. The distinction between 'adjudicative facts' and 'legislative facts' suggested by KC Davis (1942) 55 Harvard LR 364; 'Judicial Notice (1955) 55 Columbia LR 945; and 'Facts in Lawmaking' (1980) 80 Columbia LR 931. According to this taxonomy adjudicative facts relate to a particular event in litigation e.g. the date on which an offence took place whereas legislative facts concern general states of affairs relevant to interpreting and developing the law. In determining whether flick knives are offensive weapons for example it is relevant to know how often flick knives are used offensively and there they might have other legitimate uses, etc.) When courts are engaged in law making they are not noticing facts or concerning themselves with any other aspect of evidence or proof but simply discharging their constitutional mandate to maintain and where necessary to develop and repair the law. Judicial law making should be openly acknowledged for what it is free from consumed and confusing appeals. To bring this activity under the umbrella of judicial notice serves only to

application of the concept of judicial notice being applied to knowledge of the law by the courts. Rather judicial notice is to be restricted to indisputable facts. It is to be noted that Zuckerman rejects the notion that judicial notice of facts is binding. Rather, he asserts that the indisputability depends upon the state of knowledge at the time and place of the trial and therefore is subject to change:

> Whether or not a fact may be regarded as indisputable depends upon the state of knowledge at the time and place of trial. What may reasonably be disputed today may cease to be controversial as time and progress march on. It follows that a decision to take judicial notice of a certain fact cannot conclude the matter once and for all. If it did judicial notice of fact X would effectively create an irrebuttable legal presumption that X is the case. .... As long as a fact is genuinely indisputable on the other hand it should be noticed consistently by different courts in successive proceedings. Indeed it may verge on abuse of process for a party to attempt to re-litigate a previously noticed matter which is not reasonably open to dispute. This still of course leaves open the possibility that scientific or other advances will continuously reconfigure the shifting boundary between what is and what is not reasonably open to dispute ... .[84]

Having considered the concept of judicial notice as presented by such authors as Zuckerman, it is appropriate to consider a model thereof which is substantially different: namely, that of KC Davis[85] which is much wider conceptually than that of

---

obscure the test of indisputability and imperil the values of open justice and fair procedure which that test aims to preserve. Judges are not the only culprits. There term judicial notice appears in a number of English statutes in the over extended sense in which it was used in Simpson'. It is submitted exclusion by Zuckerman of judicial notice from the development of the law by judges need not entail its exclusion from the interpretation of the law in the sense of statutory interpretation based in first instance upon the determination of the ordinary or technical meaning of words contained within statutes where the meaning thereof can be considered a fact which may or may not require formal proof. In the event that formal proof is not required as is normally the case with the ordinary meaning of words, because the meaning may be taken as indisputable within the speakers of a language, then judicial notice may apply so as to dispense with proof of such meaning. This may possibly approximate the 'legislative facts' of KC Davis mentioned in the instant footnote.

84. P Robert & A Zuckerman, *Criminal Evidence*, 2nd (Oxford, OUP, 2010) *ibid.*, at 172-173.
85. The distinction between 'adjudicative facts' and 'legislative facts' suggested by KC Davis (1942) 55 Harvard LR 364; 'Judicial Notice (1955) 55 Columbia LR 945; and "Facts in Lawmaking" (1980) 80 Columbia LR 931. Arguably the observations concerning socio-economic facts as developed by Rasmussen falls within the category of legislative facts for which judicial notice is possible following KC Davis. H Rasmussen, *On Law and Policy in the European Court of Justice* at 432; 'Adjudicative facts pertain to the outbreak of a concrete conflict between two or more parties. Socio-economic fact pertains to the validity of a certain legislative action now under attack for its alleged incompatibility with the Treaty. A national legislative act which on the surface appears to constitute an infringement of the free flow of goods in intra-Community trade might nonetheless be fully justified by the demonstration of the existence of an overriding legitimate local public policy need embedded in the statute. The primary function of socio-economic fact is to prove and make credible the existence of such a putative local policy worth of survival in the face of a constitutional attack on its validity. My hypothesis is that EC judicial access to socio-economic fact will enhance the quality of EC judicial decisions whereby some existing EC Member State tensions will tend to de-escalate. In the following I shall substantiate that hypothesis in two ways. One way is to draw on the American experience. The other consists in demonstrating how socio-economic fact sporadically in operation in EC judicial decision-making greatly contributed to enhancing the quality of the Court's rulings. On this background I will conclude that a more generalized socio-economic fact briefing is desirable.' And at p. 433:

Zuckerman. In short, it encompasses both indisputable as well as disputable facts as well as depending upon the overall importance of the fact, and its categorization, legislation or adjudicative. Significantly, a major difference is that contradiction of the veracity of the judicially noticed fact is possible in order to ensure the rights of the defence in certain circumstances. Overall, one of the primary differences between what might be termed the standard concept as presented by Zuckerman[86] and that of Davis,[87] is that the concept of the latter provides for a much wider input of data or information in that it is not restricted to that which is indisputable. However, the inclusion of both indisputable and disputable facts contained within general knowledge or ascertainable through indisputable sources may in certain circumstances be subject to contraction by means of contradictory evidence. According to Davis,[88] the advantage of such a wider concept of judicial notice is that it describes much more accurately than that of the standard model which contains indisputable evidence is that it more accurately describes the actual method by which courts ensure judicial

---

'Acquiring access to and actually integrating socio-economic fact in the court's decision making is paramount to achieving greater transparency of issues and consequences of judicial choices. Judicial outcomes will become more practical in the sense that basis for performing a balancing or weighing of the opposing central parochial values will be made as optimal as possible within the framework of what basically remains a judicial process. .... It would be erroneous not because the resemblance is always an altogether false impression but because it must emphatically be concluded that performing that task is part of the judicial duty of the Court of Justice. For the Court in controversies arising under articles 30, 36 48 (3) to refuse to perform the balancing would amount to a deni de justice. .... Let me anticipate another objection based equally on tradition to judicial processing of comprehensive and complex socio-economic facts. It would be that courts and judges including the ECJ and its members are unequipped and not educated for doing that kind of business. Indeed judicial constitutional legacy may be cited in favour of this. The changing character of judicial involvement in political government which in particular is associated with federalism constitutionalism and constitutional review in the second half of the 20th century makes however the tenor of that legacy obsolete in the Community. In the following I purport to show how Judges of the ECJ in a number of important cases have performed the necessary balancing with considerable success. What is more while performing more traditional judicial tasks for example in the handling of anti-trust cases courts and judges have become acquainted with complex factual settings' at 434 Judicial Notice. 'The facts which a judge needs in order to be informed sufficiently before making a decision which involves broad issues of public policy may be supplied to some degree by what is usually called judicial notice. The inadequacies of the information of the Court of Justice about facts highlights however the narrow confines of a 'judicial notice' doctrine in Community law. Nowhere in that law is it spelled out in clear language what that of which the Court may take notice. It may in the absence of pertinent provisions be recalled that the Model Code of Evidence of the American Law institute states that a judge may on his own motion take notice inter alia of specific facts so notorious as to not be the suspect of reasonable dispute and ... specific facts and propositions of generalized knowledge which are capable of immediate and accurate demonstration by resort to easily accessible sources of indisputable accuracy. Assuming that the Court of Justice enjoys a similar discretion it might take judicial notice of the existence of an economic depression and of encompassing and rising unemployment in the Member States throughout most of the 1970's. It might probably without requiring specific proof take notice that non-tariff barriers to intra Community trade have been sharply on the increase during that economic depression. The precise scope of downward economic and social curve would however have to be demonstrated by evidence.

86. P Robert & A Zuckerman, *Criminal Evidence*, 2nd edn (Oxford, OUP, 2010) *supra*, at 172.
87. KC Davis (1942) 55 *Harvard LR* 364; 'Judicial Notice' (1955) 55 *Columbia LR* 945, *supra*, 952, passim.
88. 'Judicial Notice' (1955) 55 *Columbia LR* 945, 952.

interpretation of statutes: that is the more restricted concept of judicial notice based upon indisputable facts fail 'to recognize that courts go beyond the record for facts bearing upon law and policy to a much greater extent than they do for facts about the parties and their activities'.[89] Davis[90] observes as follows:

> When a court or an agency finds facts concerning the immediate parties – who did what where when how and with what motive or intent – the court or agency is performing an adjudicative function and the facts so determined are conveniently called adjudicative facts. When a court or an agency develops law or policy it is acting legislatively; the courts have created the common law through judicial legislation and the facts which inform the tribunal's legislative judgment are called legislative facts. Stated in other terms the adjudicative facts are those to which the law is applied in the process of adjudication. They are the facts that normally go to the jury in a jury case. They relate to the parties their activities their properties their businesses. Legislative facts are those which help the tribunal determine the content of law and policy and to exercise its judgment or discretion in determining what course of action to take.

Davis[91] then goes on to compare what he regards as the advantages of his wider system of judicial notice:

> The exceedingly practical difference between legislative and adjudicative facts is that apart from facts properly noticed the tribunal's findings of adjudicative facts must be supported by evidence but findings or assumptions of legislative facts need not, frequently are not and sometimes cannot be supported by evidence. The formulation of law and policy both in the judicial process and in the administrative process obviously gains strength to the extent that information replaces guesswork or ignorance or intuition or general impressions. Questions of law and policy often yield to comprehensive factual study as the magnificent leadership of Justice Brandeis in that direction so eloquently testifies. But the present development of the social sciences unfortunately brings us no more than to the threshold of ability to solve our basic problems of law and policy through a full-bodied factual technique. The result is an uneven mixture of a priori conjectures and partially informed guesses with occasional factual investigations of varying depth.

As noted earlier, Davis[92] focuses upon what he terms legislative facts as opposed to adjudicative facts which are involved in the actual facts in the pleadings for the litigation. In this regard, Davis observes that the legislative facts according to normal court practise are not proved. They are simply noticed. That is they are, as noted previously: the 'findings or assumptions of legislative facts frequently are not and sometimes cannot be supported by evidence. The formulation of law and policy both in the judicial process and in the administrative process obviously gains strength to the extent that information replaces guesswork or ignorance or intuition or general impressions.'

---

89. 'Judicial Notice' (1955) 55 *Columbia LR* 945, 952.
90. *Ibid.*, 946.
91. *Ibid.*, 946.
92. *Ibid.*, 946.

Davis[93] describes in the following terms the justification for increasing the scope of judicial notice so as to include words with uncertain meanings:

> Courts do not and cannot so limit their use of extra record facts for all thinking processes whether about finding facts or making law or declaring policy or exercising discretion necessarily involve reliance upon facts that have not been proved and the facts that enter into thinking processes are frequently highly disputable or inseparable fused with questionable or uncertain judgment. The courts often take judicial notice of legislative facts in circumstances in which they would not take judicial notice of adjudicative facts but the Model Code and the Uniform Rules apply in the same way to all facts without drawing the cardinal distinction between legislative and adjudicative facts. The provisions of the Model Code and of the Uniform Rules also fail to reflect the customary judicial practice of using extra record facts embodied in rules of law which declare factual propositions even when the facts are debatable. Relatively incidental and probably inadvertent is the failure of the Model Code and the Uniform Rules to permit judicial notice of all the legal materials that courts customarily notice.

Dealing with the need for contradiction of the facts which have been noticed, Davis[94] observes:

> The principle is not that all facts used should be in the record unless they are indisputable or contained in sources of indisputable accuracy. Nor is it that all facts used should be subject to cross-examination and rebuttal evidence. Nor is what the Supreme Court has said several times it is- that 'nothing can be treated as evidence which is not introduced as such'. The fundamental principle is that parties should have the opportunity to meet in the appropriate fashion all facts that influence the disposition of the case. What is the appropriate fashion depends upon three main variables – how far the facts are from the centre of the controversy between the parties, the extent to which the facts are adjudicative facts about the parties or legislative facts of a general character and the degree of certainty or doubt about the facts. Nothing short of bringing the facts into the record so that an unabridged opportunity is allowed for cross-examination and for presentation of rebuttal evidence will suffice for disputed adjudicative facts at the centre of controversy. Debatable and critical legislative facts probably need not always be brought into the records but such facts usually should be subject to challenge through briefs and arguments and the court should have a discretionary power to determine whether cross- examination is appropriate in the circumstances. The most obvious facts often may be used without even stating that judicial notice is being taken; the less obvious or the more critical or debatable the facts may be the more the reason for mention. The ultimate problem of judicial notice is the highly practical one of accomplishing two purposes that are often difficult to reconcile with each other – facilitating a tribunal's access to the facts and assuring that parties are given an appropriate opportunity to apply their testing processes to the facts that influence either the findings or the decision.

It is submitted that the practical thrust of the concept of Judicial Notice developed by Davis[95] is that, as noted earlier, it clearly connects the process of law and policy making with a larger body of facts, that is, those which are disputable in addition to those

93. 'Judicial Notice' (1955) 55 *Columbia LR* 945, 983-84.
94. *Ibid.*, 983-84.
95. *Ibid.*

which are indisputable in contradistinction to the model of judicial notice based exclusively on undisputable facts. The disputable facts can be subject to cross-examination in so far as they may affect or influence the findings or the decision, and therefore the interest of the parties. Once again this is in contrast to the model of judicial notice which being based upon exclusively undisputable facts excludes by definition cross-examination of the facts except as in the dimension accepted earlier by Zuckerman.[96] It is proposed that this more open model is more appropriate for dealing with constitutional interpretation such as that[97] involving Roper as well as the CJ. At this point, it is of use to consider the type of facts as opposed to evidence which used according to Davis in the US courts when judges take judicial notice of facts, particularly of legislative facts following Davis in carrying out statutory interpretation and the application of the law. Davis[98] observes as follows as regards the facts:

96. A Zuckerman & P Roberts, *Criminal Evidence*, 2nd edition (Oxford, OUP, 2010) 172-73 who confines judicial notice to indisputable questions of fact. 'Judges have sometimes declared themselves to be taking notice of matters which on more careful examination have nothing whatever to do either with factual indisputability or an appropriately circumscribed doctrine of judicial notice. Thus it is said that judicial notice is taken of the law of the land or a close analogue that courts are presumed to know the law dispensing in either case with the need for proof in accordance with the ordinary rules of evidence. But this is to confuse matters of evidence and proof with judicial interpretation and development of the law. Legal argument may need to be addressed to disputable points of law but judicial notice as a proxy for proof by admissible evidence is confined to indisputable questions of fact. When courts are engaged in law-making they are not noticing facts or concerning themselves with any other aspect of evidence or proof but simply discharging their constitutional mandate to maintain and where necessary develop and repair the law. Judicial law making should be openly acknowledge for what it is free from confused and confusing appeals to evidentiary doctrines. To bring this activity under the umbrella of judicial notice serves only to obscure the test of indisputability and imperil the values of open justice and faire procedure which that tests aims to preserve.' Zuckerman also notes at p. 171 that 'In certain cases however judges have purported to 'notice' facts which were far from indisputable including facts which were actually disputed in the proceedings. In these scenarios judicial notice becomes an illegitimate pretext for short circuiting adversarial argument and proof. A different even more troubling type of judicial overreaching occurs when adjudicators rely on their personal knowledge to supplement the evidence and settle factual issues contested in the trial. In *Wetheral v Harrison* (1976) QB 773 DC) the prosecution's medical expert testified that the accused had no good clinical reason for refusing. Lord WIdgery CJ rationalized this manoeuvre by saying that whilst magistrates may not contradict factual evidence given in court individual magistrates are permitted to draw on their personal knowledge when assessing the evidence in order to arrive at factual conclusions as the doctor-magistrate had done in this case. Unfortunately Lord Widgery's suggested distinction between supplying and evaluating evidence is insufficiently determinate and robust to keep judicial notice within acceptable bounds.' Clearly one of the essential difficulties of the rather more open ended concept of judicial notice which accepts disputable information as regards legislative facts is the danger that the disputable information which is untested by cross-examination constitutes effectively unreliable or false information thereby undermining the probative value as regards statutory interpretation of the meaning of ordinary words It is submitted that in so far a statutory meaning may involve as indisputable facts the ordinary meaning of words, judicial notice restricted to indisputable facts would apply. Statutory meaning which involved disputable meaning would arguably attract proof through cross examination and evidence. Given that the distinction between disputable and indisputable may not be clear the rights of the defence will protection which in certain circumstances may take the form of cross examination.
97. *Roper v Simmons* (2005) 543 *US* 551, *supra*.
98. KC Davis (1942) 55 *Harvard LR* 364; 'Judicial Notice (1955) 55 *Columbia LR* 945, *supra*, 947 at 949.

> Above all, judges and administrative officers should make their policy choices on the basis of all relevant facts even though the kind of facts that usually influence policy choices are often too elusive to be captured and penned up within a formal record. The wisdom we seek in judges and in administrative officers is made up of multifarious ingredients that often defy identification and usually defy separation from other ingredients knowledge of specific facts, prior experience in trying to solve similar problems mental processes such as logic or reasoning and mental processes such as appraising or estimating or guessing formulation and application of notions of policy imagination inventiveness and intuition emotional reactions and emotional control. The idea that facts can be found and that law and policy can be either found or created in complex cases without using any extra-record facts except those that are either indisputable or contained in sources indisputable accuracy seems contrary to the necessary behaviour of all judges and offices who are engage in adjudication. Thayer was clearly rights when he wrote in 1898 'In conducting a process of judicial reasoning as of other reasoning not a step can be taken without assuming something which has not been proved (Note 7 Thayer, A preliminary Treatise on Evidence 279 (1898)

Davis[99] adds:

> McCormick (Note 16 McCormick Evidence 712 (1954)) after writing a masterful summary of the law of judicial notice concluded that 'judicial notice is not merely a substitute for formal proof by witnesses but is itself another method of proof of certain kinds of facts, namely the method of research into professionally authoritative books and reports in the particular field'. He added that certain directions of growth must be looked for if judicial notice is to attain full usefulness and that among these is 'the provision for the judges of expert and impartial assistants who can evaluate the data from the viewpoint of the particular science in cases when such evaluation is beyond the competence of the judges'. Of course if 'research into the professionally authoritative books and reports' is appropriate its effectiveness will be destroyed if the research is limited to the indisputable or if the facts discovered are never mixed with uncertain judgment.

It is appropriate to place the concept of judicial notice in the context in which Davis developed it which is described by Monahan and Walker[100] in the following manner:

> Davis (Approach to Problems of Evidence in the Administrative Process 55 Harv L Rev 364 (1942)) originally focused upon the problem of developing appropriate techniques for managing evidence in the administrative process. He argued that the then burgeoning federal administrative agencies should not indiscriminately apply rules of evidence developed for common law jury trials to their decision making tasks. He suggested a number of principles for the development of evidentiary practises in administrative decision making that take into account the needs of the agencies, the differences between agencies and courts and the fact that many administrative proceedings are non adversarial and are conducted by experts. Many of Davis' principles rest on the distinction he made between adjudicative and legislative facts a distinction he still maintains is valid and useful.

99. KC Davis (1942) 55 *Harvard LR* 364; 'Judicial Notice (1955) 55 *Columbia LR* 945, *supra*, at 947-951.
100. J Monahan & L Walker 'Social Authority: Obtaining Evaluating and Establishing Social Science in Law' (1986) *U of Penn LRev* (134) (3) 477 at 482 Footnote 18.

That being said, according to Monahan and Walker,[101] the primary problem of judicial notice of legislative facts as conceived by Davis is as follows:

> The procedural ramifications emanating from Davis' tacit acceptance of the manner in which classical jurisprudence separated fact and law have been limited to the largely negative proposal that facts used to create a rule of law are not to be treated as other facts are treated in court. This view fails to provide clear direction regarding how courts should obtain social science date and contains no information about how courts should evaluate what they have obtained or what effect they should give to the evaluation of other courts.

Ultimately according to Monahan and Walker[102] the matter turns on how one will present the expert social science material, that is as untested facts through judicial notice of legislative facts or whether the facts should be presented with experts and expert evidence subject to cross-examination coupled with perhaps assessors who may assist the judges to understand the expert testimony:

> The general and established rule is that questions of law are answered by the judge and questions of fact are answered by the jury (or trier of fact). If the interpretation of scientific research is considered a question of fact it seems apparent that the research should be introduced as other facts are introduced by oral testimony (here the oral testimony of experts) for consideration by the jury. As Davis recognized however presenting facts to a jury is 'wholly inappropriate' when those facts are used to determine the content of law and policy. (Note 28 To present such facts to a jury would allow the jury to create law a task universally regarded as reserved do the legislature and the judiciary) Legislative facts in contrast should be presented to the court in its capacity as lawmaker. But how should the parties present legislative facts for the court's consideration? Here Davis and the Federal Rules of Evidence which incorporate his distinction are not conclusive. The parties appear to be free either to present legislative facts via expert witnesses at a hearing or to include them in briefs as Brandeis did in Muller. No positive guidance is provided although the theoretical and practical differences between the two techniques are great. In short how could Brandeis briefs be submitted initially to the Supreme Court without having the facts first tested by the confrontation procedures of a trial court.? Finally, he argued that the traditional evidentiary rulers of fact gathering to legislative facts would preclude the courts from making independent investigations of the facts at issue in a case applying only to adjudicative facts.

It is submitted that the primary matter is the balancing of the procedural rights of defence in the context of due process against the procedural imperatives of fair trial pursuant ECHR Article 6 within a proper period: in the context of cost and time of a trial: that is a trial where judicial notice involving disputable legislative facts with the possibility for the parties, following Davis[103] to meet 'in appropriate fashion all the facts

101. J Monahan & L Walker 'Social Authority: Obtaining Evaluating and Establishing Social Science in Law' (1986) *U of Penn LRev* (134) (3) 477 at 485.
102. J Monahan & L Walker 'Social Authority: Obtaining Evaluating and Establishing Social Science in Law' (1986) *U of Penn LRev* (134) (3) 477 *ibid.*, at 485.
103. KC Davis (1942) 55 *Harvard LR* 364; 'Judicial Notice (1955) 55 *Columbia LR* 945, *supra*, at 947, 983.

which influence the disposition of the case ' as opposed straightforward cross-examination. An additional problem however remains: namely, that of the evaluation of the facts and or the evidence whether or not judicial notice is utilized.

Of interest here in the observations made by McCormick as cited by Davis is the concept of 'assistants' to assist the judges in comprehending and evaluating 'who can evaluate the data from the view point of the particular science in cases when such evaluation is beyond the competence of the judges.' This would seem to involve what is termed in English law an assessor which was discussed earlier within this chapter.

§2.06 APPOINTMENT OF A COURT EXPERT

Having being briefly alluded to in the previous chapter, this section will contain a short analysis of the rules for the appointment of a court expert in the context of Measures of Inquiry as provided by the rules of procedure[104] of both the CJ, GC and the ECtHR.

[A] The Rules of Procedure Dealing with Expert Evidence

The rules which provide for the appointment of an expert by the court in the ECJ and the GC are as follows:

> Article 25 of the Statute of the Court of Justice of the European Union.
>
> The Court of Justice may at any time entrust any individual, body, authority, committee or other organization it chooses with the task of giving an expert opinion.
>
> 2.1 Rules of the CJ
>
> Measures of inquiry[105]
>
> Article 63
>
> Decision on measures of inquiry
>
> 1. The Court shall decide in its general meeting whether a measure of inquiry is necessary.
>
> 2. Where the case has already been assigned to a formation of the Court, the decision shall be taken by that formation.
>
> Article 64
>
> Determination of measures of inquiry
>
> 1. The Court, after hearing the Advocate General, shall prescribe the measures of inquiry that it considers appropriate by means of an order setting out the facts to be proved.

104. The commissioning of an expert by the court is carried out in the context of Measures of Inquiry as provided by ECJ (Consolidated Version of the Rules of Procedure of the Court of Justice 2010/C 177/01) Article 45.2. (d) and EGC (Consolidated Version of the Rules of Procedure of the General Court 2010/C 177/02; www.cura.europa.eu) Article 65(d).
105. www.curia.europa.eu, 29.9.2012, *Official Journal of the European Union* L 265/21.

2. Without prejudice to Articles 24 and 25 of the Statute, the following measures of inquiry may be adopted:

(a) the personal appearance of the parties;
(b) a request for information and production of documents;
(c) oral testimony;
(d) the commissioning of an expert's report;
(e) an inspection of the place or thing in question.

3. Evidence may be submitted in rebuttal and previous evidence may be amplified.

Article 70

Expert's report

1. The Court may order that an expert's report be obtained. The order appointing the expert shall define his task and set a time-limit within which he is to submit his report.

2. After the expert has submitted his report and that report has been served on the parties, the Court may order that the expert be examined, the parties having been given notice to attend. At the request of one of the parties or of his own motion, the President may put questions to the expert.

3. The other Judges and the Advocate General may do likewise.

4. Subject to the control of the President, questions may be put to the expert by the representatives of the parties.

2. 2 Rules of the GC[106]

Section 2 — Measures of inquiry

Article 65

Without prejudice to Articles 24 and 25 of the Statute, the following measures of inquiry may be adopted:

(a) the personal appearance of the parties;
(b) a request for information and production of documents;
(c) oral testimony;
(d) the commissioning of an expert's report;
(e) an inspection of the place or thing in question.

Article 66

1. The General Court, after hearing the Advocate General, shall prescribe the measures of inquiry that it considers appropriate by means of an order setting out the facts to be proved. Before the General Court decides on the measures of inquiry referred to in Article 65(c), (d) and (e) the parties shall be heard. The order shall be served on the parties.

2. Evidence may be submitted in rebuttal and previous evidence may be amplified.

106. The Rules of the General Court are included primarily because the judgment analysed in this case was rendered by the GC in Case T-212/03 *My Travel Group plc v Commission* (2008) *ECR* II-1967, *supra*, as a direct action for damages for non-contractual liability and not a reference.

Article 70

1. The General Court may order that an expert's report be obtained. The order appointing the expert shall define his task and set a time-limit within which he is to make his report. ....

2. 3 ECtHR
Concerning the appointment of experts the rules of procedure of the ECtHR provide for the following:[107]

1. The Chamber may, at the request of a party or of its own motion, adopt any investigative measure which it considers capable of clarifying the facts of the case. The Chamber may, *inter alia*, invite the parties to produce documentary evidence and decide to hear as a witness or expert or in any other capacity any person whose evidence or statements seem likely to assist it in carrying out its tasks.

2. The Chamber may also ask any person or institution of its choice to express an opinion or make a written report on any matter considered by it to be relevant to the case.

3. After a case has been declared admissible or, exceptionally, before the decision on admissibility, the Chamber may appoint one or more of its members or of the other judges of the Court, as its delegate or delegates, to conduct an inquiry, carry out an onsite investigation or take evidence in some other manner. The Chamber may also appoint any person or institution of its choice to assist the delegation in such manner as it sees fit.

4. The provisions of this Chapter concerning investigative measures by a delegation shall apply, *mutatis mutandis*, to any such proceedings conducted by the Chamber itself.

5. Proceedings forming part of any investigation by a Chamber or its delegation shall be held in camera, save in so far as the President of the Chamber or the head of the delegation decides otherwise.

6. The President of the Chamber may, as he or she considers appropriate, invite, or grant leave to, any third party to participate in an investigative measure. The President shall lay down the conditions of any such participation and may limit that participation if those conditions are not complied with.

It is submitted that there are, in addition to *Kraska v Switzerland*,[108] at least two other cases which are of significance as regards the application of the above rules for the appointment of an expert:

first, H v France[109] and second, Mantavanelli v France.[110] H v France arguably stands for the proposition that unless there is a prima facie case for the expert information to be relevant to the pleaded case and in particular the cause of action, the expert evidence is not admissible. Mantavanelli reaffirmed the necessity of respecting the rights of the defence when a court expert notably in the form of an

107. Rules of Court – 1 July 2013 Annex to the Rules1 (concerning investigations) Rule A1 – Investigative measures, www.echr.coe.int.
108. *Kraska v Switzerland* (1994) *EHRR* (18) 188, *supra*, at para. 33.
109. *H v France* (1990) *EHRR* (12) 74.
110. *Mantavanelli v France* (1997) *EHRR* (24) 370.

> assessor is appointed which may involve a duty on the part of the court to ensure these rights by means of adversarial proceedings.

The essential procedural point here is that the above Rules of Procedure[111] authorize the CJ to appoint an expert on its own initiative. This is in the context of the Court exercising its powers of inquiry and specifically, of obtaining facts evidence and opinions. Indeed Judge Versterdorf[112] observes the following with respect to the rules of procedure in the GC and impliedly the CJ:

> The Rules of Procedure of the CFI contain adequate tools for the production of sufficient economic evidence before the CFI. The review and the use of this evidence can be improved through two main ways: first, better presentation of such evidence by the parties and second, more specialisation of the judiciary so that it is more capable of understanding and using this evidence.

Arguably, the powers contained within the aforementioned articles coupled with the statute are sufficiently wide in relation to their purpose which is arguably to ensure the effective application of the TFEU pursuant to Article 19 TEU.[113] Specifically, it is submitted that the CJ may appoint an expert either at the request of the parties or more particularly upon its own initiative once it has heard the Advocate General. Further, it would appear that the CJ pursuant to the aforementioned rules may appoint not only one expert in the aforementioned circumstances but also several experts whose tasks may include among other things, giving an expert opinion on a specific subject in issue; or intervening to explain in the context of Judicial Notice and as an assessor as discussed earlier, the meaning of technical words being used by the expert or experts appointed by the Court.

The essence of the legal analysis in this book is that the exercise by the CJ and the GC to appoint an expert is pre-eminently judicial. In the case of the CJ, no appeal mechanism exists against its exercise of its discretion to appoint an expert. Similarly with the ECtHR. As noted earlier, the exercise as regards the CJ and the GC, therefore, is subject not only to EU legal principles as recognized by the court but since the adoption of the Treaty of Lisbon it is or will be in some way subject to the jurisprudence of the ECtHR and its interpretation of the ECHR. With respect to the ECtHR it is subject to the ECHR and in particular Article 6 (1) thereof. The examination of the rules of procedure establish that there is no procedural deficit at the level of the rules in themselves. Any non-compliance with notably ECHR Article 6 (1) which results from failure to apply one of the aforementioned rules is to be attributed to a defective exercise of the discretion by the CJ, GC and or the ECtHR. Certainly, it is possible to argue for example, that the failure on the part of the three courts to exercise their

---

111. Notes for The Guidance of Counsel in Written and Oral Proceedings before the Court of Justice of the European Communities, www.curia.europa.eu.
112. B Vesterdorf 'Economics in Court' in M Johansson, N Wahl and U Bernitz (eds) *Liber Amicorum in Honour of Sven Norberg* (Brussels, Bruylant, 2006) 511 at 527; J MacClennan 'Evidence, Standard and Burden of Proof and the Use of Experts in Procedure before the Luxembourg Courts' in F Weiss (ed) *Improving WTO Dispute Settlement Procedures* (London, Cameron May, 2000).
113. Article 19 TEU provides that the role of the European Court of Justice (ECJ) is '(...) to ensure that in the interpretation and application of the Treaties the law is observed.

discretion to appoint an expert by means of the above rules arises from a defective use of the concept of judicial notice in the interpretation of ordinary meaning of words: that is, in such instances as noted in the cases considered in this analysis, it is clear that interpretation was made both of the ordinary meaning but above all the technical meaning of words without the use of experts. As regards the interpretation of the ordinary meaning of words, failure on the part of court to utilize an expert is a manifestation that the three courts feel individually and collectively as judges that they understand the ordinary meaning sufficiently well as native speakers of at least their own languages. This raises of course the problems of translation identified by Schilling[114] as leading to a possible breach of ECHR Article 6.2 at least as regards the TFEU and secondary EU legislation.[115]

However, the problem of utilizing less than certain sources for the ascertainment of the ordinary meaning is exacerbated when the same method of what can only be described as defective statutory interpretation is utilized as will be seen in the specific cases examined when the meaning of technical words is involved. It is clear that the real problem is what may be described objectively as defective interpretation of both the ordinary and technical meaning by both the CJ the GC and the ECtHR, in two senses: first, an inappropriate use of the concept of judicial notice whereby the three courts fail to ensure that an indisputable source is used in order to provide the ordinary meaning of a word, namely, either a dictionary or more likely an expert; the second, perhaps more visible example of the expert evidentiary deficit concerns the failure of the aforementioned courts to use the discretion provided by their respective rules of procedure so as to appoint an expert to deal with the technical meaning of words. It is submitted that procedurally this defective method of statutory interpretation can be sanctioned as a procedural error by making recourse to the case of *Kraska v Switzerland*[116] in the context of the application of Article 6 (1) ECHR:[117] that is, the duty of court to ensure a proper assessment of the factual and evidentiary merits of a case by notably utilizing the rules of procedure which exist with respect to obtain expert opinion evidence specifically as regards both the technical meaning of words in translation but also the ordinary meaning in the context of judicial notice. It must also be added that it is difficult to comprehend the objections raised against the analysis undertaken by Rasmussen:[118] that is, in essence, Rasmussen correctly identified the essential problem with judgments involving socio economic factors as examples of in

114. T Schilling, 'Beyond Multilingualism: On Different Approaches to the Handling of Diverging Language Versions of a Community Law' (2010) *ELJ* (16) (1) 47, *supra*, passim.
115. *Ibid.*, passim.
116. *Kraska v Switzerland* (1994) *EHRR* (18) 188, *supra*, at para. 33.
117. The European Convention on Human Rights, Rome 4 November 1950 Art 6 (1) In the determination of his civil rights and obligations or of any criminal charge against him, everyone is entitled to a fair and public hearing within a reasonable time by an independent and impartial tribunal established by law. Judgment shall be pronounced publicly by the press and public may be excluded from all or part of the trial in the interest of morals, public order or national security in a democratic society, where the interests of juveniles or the protection of the private life of the parties so require, or the extent strictly necessary in the opinion of the court in special circumstances where publicity would prejudice the interests of justice. www.hri.org.
118. H Rasmussen, *On Law and Policy in the European Court of Justice* (Martinus Nijhoff, Dordrecht, 1986), *supra*, passim.

truth examples of where the statutory interpretation was not based upon facts or evidence. Rasmussen[119] Gerber[120] and Barbier de La Serrre - Sibony[121] fundamentally assert what appears to be a plausible conclusion: the incontestable observation is that the three courts in the cases examined herein and in the cases cited by the aforementioned four authors, simply do not use any expert evidence. The plausible conclusion drawn from that is that the Courts must have relied upon their own personal information. The next conclusion is that while it is completely normal for judges to rely upon information which they possess in certain specific circumstances, that information is insufficiently legally to ensure procedural compliance with the duty of the Court[122] notably pursuant to Article 6 (1) ECHR. This regretfully is also politically unacceptable when various of the judgments involve ultimately financial consequences of considerable magnitude for tax payers in the Member States - both of the EU and the signatories of the ECHR.

§2.07 PROBLEMS: CJ, GC AND THE ECTHR, JUDICIAL NOTICE AND EXPERT EVIDENCE

In short, it is submitted that the CJ, the GC and the ECtHR utilize Judicial Notice. However, there exists various major problems with the manner in which the court uses judicial notice. Overall, the courts appear to utilize their own knowledge of facts as a basis for interpreting technical words as well as certain words with ordinary meaning. In so doing, the three courts, as was noted, create the following problems: first, by taking judicial notice of disputable facts based upon their own personal knowledge the court undermines the rights of the defence. In short, following Davis[123] by using its own personal as opposed to public knowledge of notably legislative facts the court thereby prevents the parties from having the 'opportunity to meeting in the appropriate fashion all facts which influence the disposition of the case'. According to the narrow definition of judicial notice proposed by Zuckerman[124] who restricts the concept to the use of indisputable facts, the problem is as follows: that the judge notices facts which are disputable and the source is his personal as opposed to general knowledge: 'Judicial notice refers to facts which a judge can be called upon to receive and to act upon either from his general knowledge of them or from inquiries to be made by himself from his own initiative from sources which it is proper for him to use. In certain

119. DJ Gerber, 'Courts as Economic Experts in European Merger Law' in BE Hawk (ed) *Annual Proceedings for the Thirtieth Fordham Corporate Law institute: International Law and Policy* (Huntington NY Juris Publishing, 2004), 47, passim.
120. H Rasmussen, *On Law and Policy in the European Court of Justice* (Martinus Nijhoff, Dordrecht, 1986), *supra*, passim.
121. E Barbier de La Serrer & A-L Sibony, 'Expert Evidence before the EC Courts' (2008) *ECLRev* (45) 4 941, *supra*, passim.
122. Article 19 TEU (ex. Article 164 EEC / Article 220 EC)) provides that the function of the *Court of Justice of the European Union* ('ECJ') is to 'ensure that in the interpretation and application of the Treaties the law is observed.'
123. KC Davis 'Judicial Notice' (1955) C L Rev' (35) (7) 945 at 983, *supra*.
124. P Roberts and A Zuckerman Criminal Evidence (Oxford, OUP, 2010) at 176 note 167, *supra*.

cases, however, judges have purported to 'notice' facts which were far from indisputable including facts which were actually disputed in the proceedings. In these cases judicial notice becomes an illegitimate pretext for short circuiting adversarial argument and proof.' Arguably however, the consequences of the substitution by the judge of his own knowledge of the facts exceeds simply the misuse of what might be termed the wide scope of the concept of judicial notice as developed by Davis.[125] Regretfully, it would appear that by using facts which are derived from his personal knowledge the judge thereby prevents in all cases involving legislative facts the parties from exercising their rights of defence thereby leading among other things to a breach of ECHR Article 6 (1):

> that parties should have an opportunity to meet in the appropriate fashion all facts that influence the disposition of the case. What is the appropriate fashion depends upon three main variables: how far the facts are from the centre of the controversy between the parties the extent to which the facts are adjudicative facts about the parties or legislative facts of a general character and the degree of certainty or doubt about the facts.

Further, one notes that although Roberts and Zuckerman[126] define judicial notice narrowly by linking it to the concept of indisputability, they use a wide category of indisputable sources which a judge may use in ascertaining both ordinary and technical meaning of words in statutes. Accordingly, indisputable sources for Roberts and Zuckerman includes not only encyclopaedias, documents but also experts.[127]

In short, the cases to be examined in the course of this analysis will disclose that the judge in taking judicial notice of legislative facts based upon his personal knowledge does not provide the parties with the possibility of meeting these facts in so far as they may have influenced the disposition of the case. Thereby, the judge exceeded the limits established by Davis[128] as regards his model of judicial notice. In addition as noted earlier, it would appear that in addition, the use of the private knowledge by the use sounds as a violation of Article 6 (1) ECHR in so far as it conspicuously deprives the party or parties of the possibility of meeting 'in appropriate fashion all facts that influence the disposition of the case'. Concerning the use of personal knowledge by the judge in attempting to take judicial notice Manchester[129] observes:

125. KC Davis 'Judicial Notice' (1955) C L Rev' (35) (7) 945 at 983, *supra*.
126. P Roberts & A Zuckerman *Criminal Evidence*, 2nd edn (Oxford, OUP, 2010), *supra*.
127. *Ibid.*, 170: 'The test of indisputability if therefore the key to identifying when a judge may properly dispense with the normal requirements of proof. However 'indisputability' can be understood in two different senses. The first sense corresponds to facts that 'everybody knows'. ... Indisputability in a second sense covers facts that can be ascertained definitively without necessarily being universally or even widely known. ... For the purpose of informing itself of such matters the court may have access not only to reliable documentary sources but also to experts. To summarize facts may be indisputable either because they are generally accepted by the community at large or because they may be ascertained by consulting reliable and trusted sources.'
128. KC Davis, 'Judicial Notice' (1955) *C L Rev*' (35) (7) 945 at 983, *supra*.
129. C Manchester, 'Judicial Notice and Personal Knowledge' (1979) *MLR* (42) 22 at 22-23.

> The concept of judicial notice is then that the judge may make use of his general knowledge where some fact has to be established and take notice of the existence of that fact without requiring it to be formally proved. In fact, it is evident that judges frequently to make use of their general knowledge. Indeed as Thayer (A Preliminary Treatise on Evidence (1889) p 279) quite rightly points out ' in conducting a process of judicial reasoning as of other reasoning not a step can be taken without assuming something which has not been proved'. However, neither judge nor jury can make use of their personal knowledge. The principle laid down then allows a judge or jury to make use of their general knowledge but not their personal knowledge. The meaning of 'general knowledge' in this context initially seemed to have encompassed only knowledge which was common to the whole community – the court in Rosser referred to general knowledge 'which any many can bring to the subject' while in Ernest Jones it was what the jury know of the state of the country and of society generally (which presumably would be what was known universally throughout the country). Thus it would seem that in its initial development the principle only allowed judicial notice to be taken of matters which were common knowledge throughout the country and not it is submitted of matters which were common knowledge within the locality of the court. It seems to have been a later extension whereby notorious local matters were regarded as matters of general knowledge.

As regards the use of judicial notice and statutory interpretation, Sullivan[130] observes:

> When judges take judicial notice of ordinary meaning with or without the assistance of dictionaries they necessarily depend on their own knowledge of language and the world to make sense of what they are reading. Their assumption s about what is plausible coherent relevant or worthwhile enter the interpretative process without comment and usually without awareness because these things operate at a subconscious level; they are like the air we breathe too basic to obvious to notice. This points to the danger of judicial notice. What is indisputable fact to one person may be nonsense or distortion to another. Yet once a fact is judicially notice it does not have to be justified or event mentioned by a judge regardless of its impact on this or her decisions. One way of minimising the danger of judicial notice is to let in sworn testimony or other evidence of the purposes of establishing the ordinary meaning of words or challenging judicially noticed facts. Such evidence might be introduced through expert testimony or in the form of a Brandeis brief. Further, it is submitted that by seeking to interpret technical meaning without the assistance of either an expert through cross examination or by means of judicial notice involving expert opinion, the judge also fails to provide a fair trial.

Overall, the problems noted with respect to judicial notice would appear to breach in particular ECHR Article 6 (1), the right to a fair trial notably as regards the rights of the defence for the following reasons: ': first, following Krcmar[131] a breach of the right to a fair trial takes place by depriving a party of the possibility of challenging facts or evidence even obtained by the court itself and used in a decision which affects the rights a party; and second, the use of the personal knowledge rather than seeking an expert opinion may also lead to a breach of the rights of the defence for two reasons:

130. R Sullivan, *Sullivan and Driedger on the Construction of Statutes*, 4th edn (Vancouver, Butterworths, 2002), *supra*, at 31.
131. Case of *Krcmar and others v The Czech Republic* (Application no. 35376/97).

on the one hand, for the reason just noted pursuant to Krcmar; and on the other for the reason utilized by the ECtHR in Kraska:[132] namely the contravention of the right to a proper evaluation of the substantive merits of the case as disclosed on the facts, evidence and documents. It is submitted that an evaluation in certain circumstances may require an expert opinion in order to be following Kraska, proper: that is, that the court may require an expert in order to assist it to either understand the expert evidence which has been presented by one of the parties or may require an expert because the statute contains words with a technical meaning.

[A] Duty to Properly Examine the Merits

The thrust of the instant analysis consists in the observation that the misuse of the concept of judicial notice and, notably, the extended form involving disputable legislative facts may lead to a breach of ECHR Article 6 (1), the right to a fair trial. This arises from both the use by the judge of private knowledge in the process of statutory assessment to the failure of judges to under the wide concept of judicial knowledge to use the opinion of experts as regards judicial facts, in particular, technical words or making recourse to assessors to assist in understanding expert evidence involving technical words. Therefore, at this point it is useful to consider the principle of the duty to properly examine the merits as expressed notably in Kraska[133] wherein the Court held as noted earlier that:

> 30. It falls to the Court to decide whether the contested proceedings considered as a whole were fair within the meaning of the Convention. The effect of Article 6 para. 1 (art. 6-1) is, inter alia, to place the 'tribunal' under a duty to conduct a proper examination of the submissions, arguments and evidence adduced by the parties, without prejudice to its assessment of whether they are relevant to its decision (see, among other authorities, mutatis mutandis, the Barberà, Messegué and Jabardo **v.** Spain judgment of 6 December 1988, Series A no. 146, p. 31, para. 68). It has to be determined whether this condition was satisfied in the instant case.

This case clearly establishes that there exists overall a duty on the part of the court to ensure a fair trial. A decision as to the fairness of a hearing is based on an assessment of the course of the proceedings as a whole in the sense of the totality of the rules of in particular procedure and notably their provision for appeal. Kraska[134] establishes that the duty to ensure a fair trial involves an obligation on the part of the court or tribunal to examine properly the evidence which is submitted by the parties. This is notably so in a reference which involves the statutory interpretation of both ordinary and technical words. Further, and depending upon the nature of the rules of civil procedure, the duty to ensure a fair trial may oblige the court to use its own procedural powers on its own initiative to obtain expert evidence in order to properly evaluate the evidence which has been tendered by the parties. Moreover, the judgments of

132. *Kraska v Switzerland* (1994) 18 *EHRR* 188 at para. 30.
133. *Ibid.*, at para. 30.
134. *Ibid.*, at para. 30.

Kraska[135] and Krcmar[136] may require a court or tribunal to make recourse to assessors capable of assisting the judges to understand expert evidence so as to ensure that overall the evidence tendered by the parties is properly considered. However, once again the application of these obligations depends very much upon the national rules of civil procedure considered in their entirety and the proceedings as a whole and in particular, the availability of appeal and its scope.

§2.08 CONCLUSION

In the course of this chapter, the emphasis has been placed upon clearly linking the judicial use of the rules of procedure of the CJ, the GC and the ECtHR which serve to introduce expert evidence to the duty placed upon the three courts by the case of Kraska[137] and Article 6 (1) ECHR as well as Bentham's procedural principle of rectitude of decision, to carefully examine the merits of each case. This involves proper analysis of the evidence which in the circumstances of statutory interpretation will require, it is submitted, the appointment of experts by the respective courts of experts if necessary on their own initiative to provide expert opinion to assist in the interpretation of words with technical and or ordinary meaning. It is clear that a failure on the part of the respective courts to use the relevant judicial discretion so as to appoint an expert if necessary upon their own motion may sound as a breach of Article 6 (1) ECHR. It is also clear that not only do the requisite rules of procedure exist in the three courts for the appointment of an expert: in addition the procedural concept of an assessor and the evidential concept of judicial notice may be used so as to facilitate the introduction and use of exert evidence in order to ensure an accurate statutory interpretation in conformity with both Article 6 (1) ECHR and also the principle of rectitude of decision. Further, it is submitted that the CJ, the GC and the ECtHR already make use of the concept of judicial notice as regards the interpretation of the ordinary meaning of certain words. However, the use which is made thereof is erroneous in that all three courts as will be observed in a later examination of the relevant judges commit the following errors: the judges in the courts endeavour to take notice by relying entirely upon their own understanding of a particular human language when in truth an indisputable and technical accurate opinion is required, either from a dictionary or from an expert called as a witness. In so far as the scope of judicial notice, particular as advocated by Davis,[138] may include both non-disputable and disputable matters, certainly provision must be made for cross examination of the expert as regards the former.

135. *Ibid.*, at para. 30.
136. *Krcmar v Czech Republic Application* No 3376/97.
137. *Kraska v Switzerland* (1994) 18 *EHRR* 188, at para. 30.
138. KC Davis 'Judicial Notice' (1955) *C L Rev* (55) (7) 945.

CHAPTER 3

Use of Expert Evidence in Selected Judgments of the United States' Supreme Court (USSC), the Supreme Court of Canada (SCC) and the Supreme Court of British Columbia (Canada) (BCSC)

§3.01 INTRODUCTION

In this chapter, judgments from the USSC, the SCC and the BCSC, which are common law inspired courts, will be considered. This is in part because all three judgments deal with subject matters which involve fields of expertise which are less formalized than is the case of economics involved in one of the EU judgments considered earlier, namely, My Travel.[1] In truth, the judgments of the aforementioned North American courts concern in large measure political values as studied notably by political scientists, criminologists and political philosophers in the context of Human Rights legislation. As regards the right to vote of common law prisoners, it is submitted that it is useful to consider the use of expert evidence in the SCC and notably the judgment of the Learned Minority and that of the judgments of the ECtHR. Reflections upon the use of comparative law will be set forth in the concluding chapter of this book. In the case of the SCC court, the case is on appeal from the Court of First Instance,[2] which heard the sworn expert witnesses. Notwithstanding, the SCC examined the expert evidence carefully and referred to it specifically in its judgment. Similarly with the USSC. The judgment of the BCSC constitutes a constitutional reference to the court emanating from the Government of the Province of British Columbia. The purpose in examining

1. *My Travel Group v Commission*, Case T 212/035 (2008) *ECR* II 1967.
2. Federal Court, Trial Division (1996) 1 FC 857, Wetston, J; appealed to Federal Court of Appeal (2000) 2 FC 117; 180 DLR (4th) 385.

these judgments is to see how these courts utilize expert evidence in terms of scope and methods of analysis thereof in a legal setting which approximates as will be seen the legal setting which surrounds the judgments of the CJ, the GC and the ECtHR which will be examined in subsequent chapters.

§3.02 EXAMINATION OF CASES

The first case will be that of *Roper v Simmons*[3] from the USSC. In short, *Roper v Simmons*[4] involved an appeal which challenged the constitutionality of capital punishment for persons who were juveniles – less than 18 years of age – when their crimes were committed. The case focused upon the Eighth Amendment to the US Constitution which proscribes cruel and unusual punishment.

[A] Brief Factual Summary of *Roper v Simmons*[5]

In this case, Christopher Simmons (CS) who, in 1993 at the age of 17, murdered Shirley Crook, by involving two younger friends, Charles Benjamin (CB) and John Tessmer (JT). The plan was to commit burglary and murder by breaking and entering, tying up a victim who would later be thrown off a bridge. The two juveniles CS and CB, the third having withdrawn, broke into Mrs. Crook's home, bound her hands and covered her eyes. They drove her to a state park and threw her off a bridge.

Once the case was brought to trial, the evidence was overwhelming. CS confessed to the murder, performed a videotaped re-enactment at the crime scene. JT testified such that premeditation was established. The jury returned a guilty verdict. Even considering mitigating factors (no criminal history and his age), the jury recommended a death sentence, which the trial court imposed. CS appealed the convention and sentence of the first court which was rejected. The case ultimately advanced to the US Supreme Court (USSC). However, by reasons of a 2002 USSC judgment, in *Atkins v Virginia*, 536 U.S. 304 (2002) which overturned the death penalty for the mentally retarded, the Supreme Court of Missouri ultimately concluded that a national consensus has developed against the execution of the mentally ill. As such the Supreme Court of Missouri held that such punishment as imposed upon CS now violates the US Eighth Amendment prohibition of cruel and unusual punishment. Thus, they sentenced Simmons to life imprisonment without parole.

3. *Roper v Simmons* 543 US 551 (2005).
4. DZ Denno, 'The Scientific Shortcomings of Roper v Simmons' (2006) *Ohio State Journal of Criminal Law* (3) 379. This Article contends that some of the case law and social science research that form the basis for the United States Supreme Court's decision in Roper (*Roper v Simmons* 543 *US* 551 (2005) *ibid.*) are insufficient and outdated. The Court also relies heavily upon briefs submitted by the respondent and his amici, in lieu of providing more pertinent citations and analysis that could have enhanced and modernized the Court's arguments. The sparse and sometimes archaic sources for Roper potentially limit the opinion's precedential value.
5. *Roper v Simmons* 543 *US* 551 (2005), *supra*.

The State of Missouri appealed the decision to the USSC: it challenged the constitutionality of capital punishment for persons who were juveniles when their crimes were committed, citing the US Eighth Amendment protection against cruel and unusual punishment.

Under the 'evolving standards of decency' test, the USSC held that it was cruel and unusual punishment to execute a person who was under the age of 18 at the time of the murder. Writing for the majority, Kennedy CJ cited a corpus of sociological and scientific research which found that juveniles have a lack of maturity and sense of responsibility compared to adults. Adolescents were found to be overrepresented statistically in virtually every category of reckless behaviour. The USSC noted that in recognition of the comparative immaturity and irresponsibility of juveniles, almost every state prohibited those under age 18 from voting, serving on juries, or marrying without parental consent. The studies also found that juveniles are also more vulnerable to negative influences and outside pressures, including peer pressure. They have less control, or experience with control, over their own environment.

In support of the 'national consensus' position, the USSC noted the increasing infrequency with which states were applying capital punishment for juvenile offenders. At the time of the decision, twenty states had the juvenile death penalty on the books, but only six states had executed prisoners for crimes committed as juveniles since 1989. Only three states had done so in the past ten years: Oklahoma, Texas, and Virginia. Furthermore, five of the states that allowed the juvenile death penalty at the time of the 1989 case had since abolished it.

The USSC also looked to practices in other countries to support the holding: Iran, Pakistan, Saudi Arabia, Yemen, Nigeria, the Democratic Republic of the Congo, and China. Justice Kennedy noted that since 1990 each of those countries had either abolished the death penalty for juveniles or made public disavowal of the practice, and that the United States stood alone in allowing execution of juvenile offenders. Accordingly, the appeal of the State of Missouri was rejected and a finding was made which established the violation of the Eight Amendment of the US Constitution: that is, the imposition of the death penalty upon a minor constituted unfair and unusual punishment.

[B] Analysis of the Judgment

Kennedy C.J. who wrote the majority opinion, cited sociological and scientific research which found that juveniles lack maturity and sense of responsibility compared to adults. Adolescents were found to be overrepresented statistically in virtually every category of reckless behaviour. The USSC noted that in recognition of the comparative immaturity and irresponsibility of juveniles, almost every state prohibited those under age 18 from voting, serving on juries, or marrying without parental consent. The studies cited also found that juveniles are also more vulnerable to negative influences and outside pressures, including peer pressure. They have less control, or experience with control, over their own environment. In support of what was termed 'national consensus' position, the USSC noted the increasing infrequency with which states within the USA applied capital punishment for juvenile offenders. At the time of the decision, twenty US states had the juvenile death penalty on the books, but since 1989 only six states had executed prisoners for crimes committed as juveniles. Only three states had done so in the previous ten years: Oklahoma, Texas, and Virginia. Furthermore, five of the states which applied the juvenile death penalty at the time of the 1989 case had since abolished it. The USSC also looked to practices in other countries to support the holding. Between 1990 and the time of the case, the court said, 'only seven countries other than the United States ha[d] executed juvenile offenders ...: Iran, Pakistan, Saudi Arabia, Yemen, Nigeria, the Democratic Republic of Congo, and China.' Kennedy C.J. also noted that since 1990 each of those countries had either abolished the death penalty for juveniles or made public disavowal of the practice, and that the United States stood alone in allowing execution of juvenile offenders. The USSC also observed that only the United States and Somalia had not ratified Article 37 of the United Nations Convention on the Rights of the Child (2 September 1990), which expressly prohibits capital punishment for crimes committed by juveniles. In conclusion, the USSC held notably in application of what is termed the 'evolving standards of decency' test that the Eighth Amendment was breached in that it was cruel and unusual punishment to execute a person who was under the age of 18 at the time of the murder.

Of substantial interest is the position of the minority as expressed in particular by Scalia J. The learned judge and those who concurred in the minority opinion with respect to the assessment of the expert evidence carried out by the majority held in short, that the burden of proof had not been discharged. Therefore, according to Scalia J. the judgment being devoid of any factual basis represented nothing more than the factually unsubstantiated opinion of the members of the majority. As such, in holding that the state legislation involving capital punishment for those less than 18 years of age contravened the eighth Amendment the Court had usurped the powers of the legislature by substituting its own unsubstantiated view on the morality of capital punishment of adolescents. Scalia J.[6] observed as follows:

> Of course, the real force driving today's decision is not the actions of four state legislatures, but the Court's 'own judgment' that murderers younger than 18 can never be as morally culpable as older counterparts. Ante, at 9 (quoting Atkins, 536 U.S., at 312 (in turn quoting Coker, 433 U.S., at 597 (plurality opinion)). The Court claims that this usurpation of the role of moral arbiter is simply a 'retur[n] to the rul[e] established in decisions predating Stanford,' ante, at 9... If the Eighth Amendment set forth an ordinary rule of law, it would indeed be the role of this Court to say what the law is. But the Court having pronounced that the Eighth Amendment is an ever-changing reflection of 'the evolving standards of decency' of our society, it makes no sense for the Justices then to prescribe those standards rather than discern them from the practices of our people. On the evolving-standards hypothesis, the only legitimate function of this Court is to identify a moral consensus of the American people. By what conceivable warrant can nine lawyers presume to be the authoritative conscience of the Nation? ... The reason for insistence on legislative primacy is obvious and fundamental: '[I]n a democratic society legislatures, not courts, are constituted to respond to the will and consequently the moral values of the people.' Gregg v. Georgia, 428 U.S. 153,

6. *Ibid.*

> 175-176 (1976) (joint opinion of Stewart, Powell, and Stevens, JJ.) (quoting Furman v. Georgia, 408 U.S. 238, 383 (1972) (Burger, C. J., dissenting)). ....Today's opinion provides a perfect example of why judges are ill equipped to make the type of legislative judgments the Court insists on making here. To support its opinion that States should be prohibited from imposing the death penalty on anyone who committed murder before age 18, the Court looks to scientific and sociological studies, picking and choosing those that support its position. It never explains why those particular studies are methodologically sound; none was ever entered into evidence or tested in an adversarial proceeding. As the Chief Justice has explained: '[M]ethodological and other errors can affect the reliability and validity of estimates about the opinions and attitudes of a population derived from various sampling techniques. Everything from variations in the survey methodology, such as the choice of the target population, the sampling design used, the questions asked, and the statistical analyses used to interpret the data can skew the results.' Atkins, supra, at 326-327 (dissenting opinion) (citing R. Groves, Survey Errors and Survey Costs (1989); 1 C. Turner & E. Martin, Surveying Subjective Phenomena (1984)). In other words, all the Court has done today, to borrow from another context, is to look over the heads of the crowd and pick out its friends. Cf. Conroy v. Aniskoff, 507 U.S. 511, 519 (1993) (Scalia, J., concurring in judgment).

Dealing specifically with the quality of the expert evidence Scalia J.[7] observed as follows:

> We need not look far to find studies contradicting the Court's conclusions. As the petitioner points out, the American Psychological Association (APA), which claims in this case that scientific evidence shows persons under 18 lack the ability to take moral responsibility for their decisions, has previously taken precisely the opposite position before this very Court. In its brief in Hodgson v. Minnesota, 497 U.S. 417 (1990), the APA found a 'rich body of research' showing that juveniles are mature enough to decide whether to obtain an abortion without parental involvement. Brief for APA as Amicus Curiae, O. T. 1989, No. 88-805 etc., p. 18. The APA brief, citing psychology treatises and studies too numerous to list here, asserted: '[B]y middle adolescence (age 14-15) young people develop abilities similar to adults in reasoning about moral dilemmas, understanding social rules and laws, [and] reasoning about interpersonal relationships and interpersonal problems.' Id., at 19-20 (citations omitted). Given the nuances of scientific methodology and conflicting views, courts – which can only consider the limited evidence on the record before them – are ill equipped to determine which view of science is the right one. Legislatures 'are better qualified to weigh and 'evaluate the results of statistical studies in terms of their own local conditions and with a flexibility of approach that is not available to the courts.' McCleskey v. Kemp, 481 U.S. 279, 319 (1987) (quoting Gregg, supra, at 186). Even putting aside questions of methodology, the studies cited by the Court offer scant support for a categorical prohibition of the death penalty for murderers under 18. At most, these studies conclude that, on average, or in most cases, persons under 18 are unable to take moral responsibility for their actions. Not one of the cited studies opines that all individuals under 18 are unable to appreciate the nature of their crimes.

7. *Ibid.*

Scalia J.[8] then goes on to examine further deficiencies of the expert evidence and then concludes that these deficiencies undermine the constitutional value of the court's judgment:

> Moreover, the cited studies describe only adolescents who engage in risky or antisocial behaviour, as many young people do. Murder, however, is more than just risky or antisocial behaviour. It is entirely consistent to believe that young people often act impetuously and lack judgment, but, at the same time, to believe that those who commit premeditated murder are – at least sometimes – just as culpable as adults. Christopher Simmons, who was only seven months shy of his 18th birthday when he murdered Shirley Crook, described to his friends beforehand – '[i]n chilling, callous terms,' as the Court puts it, ante, at 1 – the murder he planned to commit. He then broke into the home of an innocent woman, bound her with duct tape and electrical wire, and threw her off a bridge alive and conscious. Ante, at 2. ...Though these cases are assuredly the exception rather than the rule, the studies the Court cites in no way justify a constitutional imperative that prevents legislatures and juries from treating exceptional cases in an exceptional way – by determining that some murders are not just the acts of happy-go-lucky teenagers, but heinous crimes deserving of death.

Once again Scalia[9] J. relates what he describes as the insufficiency of the evidence to justify preventing the application of the state legislation providing for application of the death penalty for those less than 18 years of age by the application of the eighth Amendment applied in a teleological manner. Clearly, for Scalia J., the deficiency of the expert evidence undermined the constitutional legitimacy of the Majority of the Supreme Court: that is, holding that the state legislation which provided for the execution of persons less than 18 years convicted for murder by reason of violation of the Eighth Amendment as cruel and unusual punishment. The essential difficulty with Roper[10] from the point of view of statutory interpretation is the adequacy of both expert and non-expert evidence utilized by the US Supreme Court in the statutory interpretation of the eighth Amendment of the US Constitution in the context of a teleological or purposive method of construction: specifically, whether the Amendment and in particular the words 'cruel and unusual punishment' could apply legislation adopted in certain States: the legislation provided for the application of the death penalty to those under the age of 18. Notwithstanding, it is appropriate to examine briefly the method of the statutory interpretation from two points of view: first, from the point of view of the majority and second, from the point of view of the minority. Overall it can be said that the judgment of Roper[11] represents an application of notion of dynamic or teleological as opposed to static meaning.[12] Arguably, the learned majority in the Supreme Court sought to give what might be termed a dynamic interpretation of the words contained within the Eighth Amendment: specifically, to alter what had been an interpretation of the eighth Amendment where the scope of the words contained

8. *Ibid.*
9. *Ibid.*
10. *Ibid.*
11. *Ibid.*
12. R Sullivan, *Sullivan and Driedger on the Construction of Statutes*, 4th edn (Vancouver, Butterworth, 2002), *supra*, at 110.

therein was too narrow to one which was much wider: the expansion of the scope of the meaning of the ordinary words contained within the Eighth Amendment through taking into account among other things, expert evidence. In terms of the operation of statutory interpretation, normally, according to Sullivan,[13] judges do not admit proof of the meaning of ordinary words. Rather, they proceed by means of judicial notice which will be described subsequently notably in the context of assessors. However, as Sullivan observes, in some circumstances, notably when it is clear that interpretation of the ordinary meaning based effected without evidence and in particular expert evidence may produce an implausible or otherwise inacceptable meaning. This would appear to be the case as regards the introduction of evidence and notably expert evidence to ensure the movement from a static interpretation to a dynamic interpretation notably of the Eighth Amendment. Sullivan[14] observes:

> When ordinary meaning is not binding: although there are good reasons for courts to prefer the ordinary meaning of a legislative text that meaning is often unhelpful. Even with the benefit of the immediate context words are often ambiguous or uncertain in scope or are otherwise unclear. In such cases the courts have no choice but to look elsewhere for assistance. Ordinary meaning is apt to be unhelpful when the language in which the legislation is drafted is vague abstract or requires the interpreter to apply a standard rather than a rule. Standards are provisions that set out principles or policies to be applied or goals to be sought by the official interpreter of the legislation. Provisions that incorporate normative concepts like 'just' and 'reasonable' or 'appropriate' or relatives terms like 'undue exploitation' or abstract concepts like 'discrimination' 'wrongful ' or 'obscene' are all examples of standards. (M Kelman A guide to Critical Legal Studies) Cambridge, Harvard University Press 1987 p 155.) Although it would be possible to look up words like these in a dictionary the result would not be helpful because what is called for is a judgment based on principle or policy rather than an interpretation based on the shared conventions of language. Even when the language is relative concrete and descriptive it may not lend itself to the ordinary meaning rule. ... The presumption in favour of ordinary meaning is rebutted by evidence that another meaning was intended or is more appropriate in the circumstances.

In the instant case, following Sullivan, the Eighth Amendment, as a constitutional document, involves the application of standards or political policies the interpretation of which does not depend exclusively upon the ordinary meaning of the words. Accordingly, it is appropriate for the court to consider evidence and notably expert evidence of the ordinary words in the Eighth Amendment. Even though the words contained within the Eighth Amendment are not considered to be technical words Sullivan envisages, nevertheless, the utilization in some circumstances of expert evidence:

> Without necessarily attempting to establish a technical meaning for the words, the witness explains how persons engage in that activity understand the language in question. Such evidence has proved useful in cases where the court has been asked to interpret a word or expression not defined in a dictionary or where the

13. *Ibid.*, 36.
14. *Ibid.*, at 110.

> dictionary definition was too vague or contradictory to be helpful. Arguably evidence respecting the meaning of words should be admissible in so far as it is relevant and reliable. In particular, the courts should be willing to receive expert opinion evidence tendered by professional linguists whether based on their own expert knowledge of language or on empirical studies. The assumption that lawyers and judges are in as good a position as linguists to identify the ordinary meaning of words is false. Because of their training professional linguists are better placed to appreciate the nature of the interpretive problem created by a text and the possible ways of resolving the problem. They are also better placed to make judgments about the relative clarity of a text and the relative plausibility of a proposed interpretation. Further in recent years linguists have developed techniques which permit them to study word combinations instead of words in isolation and to determine how impression of meaning are actually formed.[15]

Therefore, Sullivan advocates overall what might be used a lower threshold for the use of expert evidence notably as regards the establishment of the ordinary meaning of words. The analysis of the words within the Eight Amendment as one which involves the interpretation of the ordinary meaning but with the use of evidence and in particular expert evidence would appear to conform most easily with the normal framework of statutory interpretation as provided notably by authors such as Sullivan: that is the categories of ordinary and technical words, with historical intention and teleological purpose necessarily based initially upon the ordinary or technical meaning of the words. In the instant case of Roper,[16] it is submitted that as regards the statutory interpretation the primary issue turns on the adequacy of evidence both non expert and expert to establish the meaning of the Eighth Amendment and whether or not it would apply so as to prevent the application of the death penalty to convicted criminal younger than 18 years of age. For the majority of the Supreme Court, the first category of evidence was the practice of States which applied the death penalty. Here the controversial matter was the manner in which this information which could have been noticed judicially. The second type of evidence was expert opinion evidence provided by an amicus curiae, the American Psychological Association. Here the overall opinion held that those under the age of 18 in general were not capable of possessing the requisite ability to form an intention to kill and therefore, application of the death penalty would not be justified. Thus, the conclusion would be, that such punishment would violate the Eight Amendment. The third category of evidence was existence of various laws outside the jurisdiction of the United States which excluded those younger than 18 years of age from the death penalty. The primary criticism of the Minority can be analysed at least for the purposes of statutory interpretation in terms of the insufficiency of the probative value of the expert evidence: first, the evidence as to the number of States which did not permit the application of the death penalty to those younger than 18 years could not be established solely on the figures given; second, an insufficiency of the expert evidence presented which did not establish that in the instant case the applicants for certiorari did not have the ability to form the requisite attention: at most the expert evidence presented established only that generally such

15. *Ibid.*, at 31-32.
16. *Roper v Simmons* 543 *US* 551 (2005), *supra*.

individuals may not have the ability to form such an intention and not that all individuals including therefore the applicants could not form such an intention. Finally, as to the legislative position of countries outside the US jurisdiction, such evidence was not irrelevant. For the Minority, the absence of evidence both expert and non-expert, resulted in the following: namely, that the wide or dynamic interpretation of the Eight Amendment could not be justified on the basis of the evidence both expert and non-expert. As a consequence, the failure to adduce sufficient expert and non-expert led to not only an evidentially unjustifiable interpretation but one which impinged upon the legislative functions. In short, the insufficiency of the evidence led to the contravention of the limits which form part of the dynamic method of interpretation thereby constituting an usurpation by the court of the functions of the legislature. It is instructive at this point to consider what might be termed the limits or constraints upon the dynamic method of interpretation as applied in the instant case taking into consideration notably the probative value of the evidence both expert and not expert to prove the ordinary meaning of the words contained in the Eighth Amendment. In large measure, the primary restraint is of a political order as regards the role and objective to be pursued by the dynamic interpretation. In this regard, Sullivan[17] observes:

> In dealing with the problem of change two concerns must be addressed. These concerns are not easily reconciled. On the one hand the courts must take care not to exceed their institutional role. Their mandate is to interpret legislation not to amend or repeal it. The political choices expressed in legislation should be made by the democratically elected legislature.

However, as Bennion[18] points out, it is essential that legislation be adapted to changing social and material circumstances:

> It is unrealistic to expect the legislature to engage in this continuous monitoring and adaptation. The courts on the other hand are well suited to this role. ... Law reform initiatives involving political choice are left to the legislature but simple adaptations in which the original purposes and policies of the legislature are applied to new facts are regularly undertaken by the courts.[19]

---

17. R Sullivan, *Sullivan and Driedger on the Construction of Statutes*, 4th edn (Vancouver, Butterworth, 2002), *supra*, at 108.
18. FAR Bennion, *Bennion on Statutory Interpretation* (London, Lexis, 2008), *supra*, at 154.
19. According to R Sullivan, *Sullivan and Driedger on the Construction of Statutes*, 4th edn (Vancouver, Butterworth, 2002), *supra*, at 105 effectively the political structure of the institutions in the context of which the statutory interpretation takes place coupled with the nature of the document and of course the wording, namely, generally as opposed to specifically worded technically words very much establishes the scope and the scope of dynamic as opposed to statutory interpretation; '105 It is presumed that the meaning of words used in legislation is stable. Unless there is reason to suppose that a change in meaning has occurred the current and the contemporaneous understandings of a provision are assumed to be the same. However this assumption is open to challenge and when it is successfully challenged the courts has a decision to make: should it insist on the original meaning of the legislation which presumably was the meaning 'intended' by the legislature or should it adopt the current meaning which is likely to be relied on by those whose conduct or interests are currently affected by the legislation. In response to the problem Canadian courts draw a sharp distinction between ordinary legislation and constitutional text. With respect to the Charter and other constitutional documents the

Notwithstanding the cogency of this distinction articulated by Sullivan[20] based upon adaptations of legislation to new facts which constitute the province of the courts as opposed to law reform initiatives with distinct policy and political choices which are the prerogative of the legislature there remains an additional factor: namely the cogency of the evidence both expert and non-expert which establish the need to change, notably, the change in social circumstances or the change in the meaning of a word or the modification of its application. Sullivan[21] describes these factors in the following manner but without referring to the effect of the probative value of the evidence:

> In practice the courts are free to take into account as much or as little of the contemporaneous context as seems appropriate in the circumstances. In exercising their discretion courts are influenced by a number of factors which favour either a dynamic or a static approach. These include (1) the legislature's own intention respecting the dynamic or static character of the legislation; (2) the character of the legislative language (3) the degree of discretion conferred on the interpreter and (4) the kind of choice the interpreter is called on to make.

Thus in the case of Roper,[22] an incorrect application or violation of the limits on the use of the dynamic method of interpretation can be established where there was a failure

---

courts adopt a dynamic approach. Under this approach meaning is not tied to the framer's original understanding but is permitted to evolve in respect to both linguistic and social change. With respect to ordinary legislation however the original meaning rule prevails. It assumes that the meaning of legislation is fixed when the legislation is first enacted and once fixed nothing short of amendment or repeal can change it. The reason underlying the distinction between constitutional texts and ordinary legislation is explained by Carceau JA in *Canaa v Vossop* (1991) 1 *FC* 18. In that case the court refused to take a dynamic approach to interpreting the words 'family status' in the Canadian Human Rights Act. Marceau JA wrote: '... the main reason why the Charter is interpreted in a very special way and particularly without the same deference to the historical intentions of the drafters and legislators is that the difficulties of amending the Constitution could cause its provisions to fall behind changes in society's conception of basic society values and thereby render them inadequate and unable to fulfil its very roe ... If the courts were to adopt in interpreting human rights acts a 'living tree' approach towards discerning new grounds of discrimination for proscriptions or re-defining past meanings given to existing rounds they would step outside the scope of their constitutional responsibilities and usurp the function of Parliament (at 376). Although human rights legislation is quasi constitutional legislation it is not entrenched; it can be amended by a simple majority of the legislature in the usual way. For this reasons it has been suggested that the interpretation of human rights legislation although liberal and purposive should not be 'organic'. That is the language should not be reinterpreted from time to time to reflect changing social and political thought '... There are of course important difference between entrenched constitutional instruments and ordinary legislation. When it comes to interpreting these texts however, the significance of the differences is easily overstated. A text that is written in general or abstract language invites an organic approach, regardless of whether the instrument would be easy or difficult to amend. In so far as an 'organic' approach consists of adapting legislation to evolving conceptions of society and its basic values it is normal and appropriate part of interpretation. Courts are bound to respect the meaning of the words used by the legislature but given the plastic character of language especially the general language typically found in human rights codes, this constraint does not prevent the courts from taking a flexible and adaptive approach.'

20. R Sullivan, *Sullivan and Driedger on the Construction of Statutes*, 4th edn (Vancouver, Butterworth, 2002), *supra*, at 112.
21. *Ibid.*
22. *Roper v Simmons* 543 *US* 551 (2005), *supra*.

to lead expert probative evidence dealing with the following aspects of the contemporary context of that case: namely, a failure to establish by means of probative evidence that the majority of states currently do not apply the death penalty to those under 18; second, that expert evidence establishes or does not establish that the claimant Roper[23] belongs to a category of young people who do not have sufficient stability of judgment to form the required intention to kill; third, that the majority of jurisdictional instances do not apply the death penalty to those under 18. It is clear that the evidence must be analysed within the context of the normal parameters of the law of evidence such as relevance of evidence, and strength or cogency of evidence as well as standard of proof. It is submitted that one of consequences of the failure to prove either by means of expert or non-expert evidence certain elements such as the social factors may be that the interpretation has no justification in fact. Therefore, following Scalia, J., the judiciary in rendering such a decision which has no basis in fact usurps the function of the legislature exceeding therefore the limits of the dynamic interpretation.

§3.03 RE: POLYGAMY[24]

The next case is that of a reference to the British Columbia Supreme Court (Canada) (BCSC) which concerns the conformity of S 293 of the Criminal Code of Canada (CCC) with Article 2 of the Charter of Fundamental Rights and Freedoms (CFRF).

[A] Summary

On 23 November 2011, the BCSC issued its decision in the polygamy reference case, stating that Canada's anti-polygamy law, S 293 CCC, should be upheld. Bauman CJBC found that the Attorneys General had demonstrated a reasoned basis for the apprehension that polygamy (especially polygyny) is inherently harmful to the participants, to their offspring and to society generally. The judgment notes a number of harms affecting women and children which involve CFRF rights arguments. The BCSC found that the anti-polygamy law is consistent with the CFRF except to the extent that it includes within its terms, children between the ages of 12 and 17 who marry into polygamy or a conjugal union with more than one person at the same time. Specifically, it ruled that the law does not breach the Article 2 (b) right to freedom of expression nor the Article 2 (c) right to freedom of association. The BCSC also found the law does not breach equality rights under Article 15 (a) CCRF. While the ruling agreed the law does infringe on the Article 2 (a) right to freedom of religion, and the section right to liberty and security of the person, it found these infringements to be within the 'reasonable limits prescribed by law as can be demonstrably justified in a free and democratic society,' the measure defined in Article 1 CFRF.

The essence of the instant judgment turns upon proving by means of expert and non-expert evidence that even if S 293 CCC violates Article 2 of the CFRF then it is

23. *Ibid.*
24. *Reference re: section 239 Criminal Code of Canada* 2011 BCSC 1588, www.courts.gov.bc.

saved by the operation of Article 1 CFRF thereof in so far as the restriction upon freedom of religion is reasonable and proportionate. In short, the aforementioned evidence establishes on the balance of probabilities that polygamy interpreted in the sense of polygyny is sufficiently harmful both innately and as applied notably by the Mormons to women, children and young men that the restriction of Article 2 CRFR conforms with Article 1: in short, S 293 CCC constitutes a proportionate attempt to prevent the harm.

The relevant article of the CCC provides as follows:

> Section 293 provides:
> 293(1) Everyone who
> (a) practises or enters into or in any manner agrees or consents to practise or enter into
> (i) any form of polygamy, or
> (ii) any kind of conjugal union with more than one person at the same time, whether or not it is by law recognized as a binding form of marriage; or
> (b) celebrates, assists or is a party to a rite, ceremony, contract or consent that purports to sanction a relationship mentioned in subparagraph (a)(i) or (ii),
> is guilty of an indictable offence and liable to imprisonment for a term not exceeding five years.
> (2) Where an accused is charged with an offence under this section, no averment or proof of the method by which the alleged relationship was entered into, agreed to or consented to is necessary in the indictment or upon the trial of the accused, nor is it necessary on the trial to prove that the persons who are alleged to have entered into the relationship had or intended to have sexual intercourse.

The CRFR provides as follows:

> Guarantee of Rights and Freedoms
> 1. The Canadian Charter of Rights and Freedoms guarantees the rights and freedoms set out in it subject only to such reasonable limits prescribed by law as can be demonstrably justified in a free and democratic society.
> Fundamental Freedoms
> 2. Everyone has the following fundamental freedoms:
> (a) freedom of conscience and religion.

The focus here is upon the use of expert and non-expert evidence in order to establish the existence of the harm the prevention of which is the object of S 293 (1) CCC. It is submitted that, overall, the use of the very substantial quantity of both expert and not expert evidence led to a relatively moderate interpretation of the scope of the purpose of S 293 (1) CCC, namely, its objective is the restriction of polygamy which includes polygyny; second, the interpretation of proportionality as contained within Article 1 of the CRFR was profoundly rooted in facts some of which had been admitted into the record by two methods: first, by means of the process of Judicial Notice without proof on the basis of being incontestable, and second by means of cross-examination of sworn witnesses both expert and non-expert.

An attempt was made to strengthen the probative quality of the evidence in the adjudication of the matter by means of the use of a reference procedure created by Constitution Question Act:[25] this system of reference provides not only for the use of evidence but also for the use of expert evidence and its evaluation through cross-examination. Despite the emphasis upon the procedural capacity to cross-examine expert witnesses notably by means of the Amicus Curiae, no attempt was made by the BCSC to utilize court experts appointed on its own initiative pursuant to Rule 11-5[26] to assist in the explanation of the meaning of technical terms by means of information given in the context of either judicial notice or through information which in turn could be cross-examined. It may well be that the quality of the cross-examination of certain of the witnesses by counsel could have been improved to ensure his immediate understanding of the experts research if the court had appointed an expert in order to explain the methodology being used by certain of the experts. This is arguably an expert appointed by the court under its own rules to intervene as an assessor or court adviser under the existing Rules of Procedure of the Supreme Court of British Columbia in a manner somewhat akin to an assessor under English procedure[27] would have improved the evaluation of the expert evidence given generally and where the experts

25. By Order in Council dated 22 October 2009, the Lieutenant Governor in Council referred two questions to this Court for hearing and consideration pursuant to the *Constitutional Question Act*, R.S.B.C. 1996, c. 68, s. 1 [*CQA*]: a) Is section 293 of the *Criminal Code of Canada* consistent with the *Canadian Charter of Rights and Freedoms*? If not, in what particular or particulars and to what extent? b) What are the necessary elements of the offence in section 293 of the *Criminal Code of Canada*? Without limiting this question, does section 293 require that the polygamy or conjugal union in question involved a minor, or occurred in a context of dependence, exploitation, abuse of authority, a gross imbalance of power, or undue influence?
26. Rule 11-5 – Appointment of Court's Own Expert (1) Subject to this rule, the court may, on its own initiative at any stage of an action, appoint an expert if it considers that expert opinion evidence may help the court in resolving an issue in the action. (2) In deciding whether to appoint an expert under this rule in relation to an issue in an action, the court may (a) ask each party of record to name one or more persons who (i) are qualified to give expert opinion evidence on the issue, and (ii) have been made aware of the content of this Part and consent to being appointed(b) require each party of record to state any connection between an expert named under paragraph (a) and a party to the action, and (c) receive other material and make other inquiries to help decide which expert to appoint. (3) The court may appoint an expert under this rule whether or not that expert was named by a party under subrule (2) (a). (4) The court may appoint an expert under this rule if the expert consents to the appointment after he or she has been made aware of the content of this Part.
27. Civil Procedure Rules, Assessors '35.15 (1) This rule applies where the court appoints one or more persons under section 70 of the Senior Courts Act 19811 or section 63 of the County Courts Act 19842 as an assessor. (2) An assessor will assist the court in dealing with a matter in which the assessor has skill and experience. (3) An assessor will take such part in the proceedings as the court may direct and in particular the court may direct an assessor to – (a) prepare a report for the court on any matter at issue in the proceedings; and (b) attend the whole or any part of the trial to advise the court on any such matter. (4) If an assessor prepares a report for the court before the trial has begun – (a) the court will send a copy to each of the parties; and (b) the parties may use it at trial. (5) The remuneration to be paid to an assessor is to be determined by the court and will form part of the costs of the proceedings. (6) The court may order any party to deposit in the court office a specified sum in respect of an assessor's fees and, where it does so, the assessor will not be asked to act until the sum has been deposited. (7) Paragraphs (5) and (6) do not apply where the remuneration of the assessor is to be paid out of money provided by Parliament.' www.justice.gov.uk/courts/procedures-rules/civil.

were cross-examined by lawyers who were not experts in the field. The omission arguably to appoint a court expert to assist not only the judge but counsel such as the Amicus Curiae to understand the methodology of the experts constitutes perhaps a weak point of the judgment. It underlines the difficulty of presentation but above all examination of expert opinion by means of cross-examination where the examining lawyer is not an expert in the field of the expert witness and therefore approaches the expert's opinion from the point of view of an amateur or non-expert which undermines effectively the rights of the defence. That being said, arguably certain of the witnesses provided summaries of the research carried out by other experts in a manner approximating the type of information which would be given by a court appointed expert or assessor.

Given that the interest of the judgment for the present purposes lies in the evidence rather more than the actual statutory interpretation of the questions referred, it is useful to consider the following matters: the reason for the use of evidence and in particular expert evidence in the statutory interpretation of the matter referred in the instant case; second, method by which the evidence was introduced; third, the type of evidence used; fourth, the standard of proof utilized by the court; finally, whether or not the interpretation of the scope of Article 1[28] and in particular Article 2 of the CCRF was related to the strength or weakness of the evidence presented. Perhaps rather more than the actual method by which the evidence was introduced, the reason for the use of thereof, both expert and non-expert, can serve to fundamentally distinguish the method of statutory interpretation of certain of the Canadian courts from the CJ, GC as well as the ECtHR. It is submitted that despite the difference of the judicial function and status of the TFEU and the ECHR on the one hand and the CRFR on the other, a descriptive comparison is at a minimum possible of the manner by which statutory interpretation is carried out. This possibility arises because the process of statutory interpretation constitutes a discrete judicial function and process as opposed to the operation and purpose of the documents which are interpreted in the instant case. Bauman CJBC[29] observes as follows concerning the use if not necessity of introducing evidence with regard to a reference involving in particular a restriction of a Charter right and an attempt at justification pursuant to Article 1 CFRF on the basis of proportionality in the sense of reasonableness:

> [46] ' I have taken a liberal approach to admissibility in this proceeding, admitting all the evidence tendered. This approach accords with the Supreme Court of Canada's emphasis on the importance of a proper evidentiary foundation in

28. CONSTITUTION ACT, 1982 PART I CANADIAN CHARTER OF RIGHTS AND FREEDOMS Guarantee of Rights and Freedoms: 1. The Canadian Charter of Rights and Freedoms guarantees the rights and freedoms set out in it subject only to such reasonable limits prescribed by law as can be demonstrably justified in a free and democratic society.

    2. Everyone has the following fundamental freedoms: (a) freedom of conscience and religion;(b) freedom of thought, belief, opinion and expression, including freedom of the press and other media of communication; (c) freedom of peaceful assembly; and (d) freedom of association, www.laws-lois.justice.gc.ca.
29. *Reference re: section 239 Criminal Code of Canada* 2011 BCSC 1588, *supra*, paras 46-51, www.courts.gov.bc.

Charter litigation. It also maximizes the trial reference's potential in terms of creating an evidentiary record.

1. The Importance of Evidence in Charter Litigation

[47] Since the earliest days of Charter jurisprudence, the Supreme Court of Canada has consistently emphasized the importance of evidence in Charter litigation.

[48] In the very first Charter case to reach the Court, Law Society of Upper Canada v. Skapinker, [1984] 1 S.C.R. 357, Mr. Justice Estey criticized the thinness of the evidentiary record, particularly noting the importance of evidence to the s. 1 analysis (at 384):

May it only be said here, in the cause of being helpful to those who come forward in similar proceedings, that the record on the s. 1 issue was indeed minimal, and without more, would have made it difficult for a court to determine the issue as to whether a reasonable limit on a prescribed right had been demonstrably justified. Such are the problems of the pioneer and such is the clarity of hindsight.

[49] Chief Justice Dickson emphasized the importance of evidence to the s. 1 analysis in R. v. Oakes, [1986] 1 S.C.R. 103 (at 138):

Where evidence is required in order to prove the constituent elements of a s. 1 inquiry, and this will generally be the case, it should be cogent and persuasive and make clear to the Court the consequences of imposing or not imposing the limit.

[50] It is implicit in the analytical framework for s. 1 established in that decision that compelling evidence will generally be necessary, given that much of the analysis is focused on the effects of the legislation in question. Determining the actual salutary and deleterious effects of an infringement of a Charter right, for example, calls for more than a hypothetical or theoretical analysis.

[51] The importance of a proper evidentiary record in Charter litigation was further emphasized by Mr. Justice Cory in MacKay v. Manitoba, [1989] 2 S.C.R. 357, a constitutional challenge to Manitoba's election funding scheme (at 361-62):

Charter cases will frequently be concerned with concepts and principles that are of fundamental importance to Canadian society. For example, issues pertaining to freedom of religion, freedom of expression and the right to life, liberty and the security of the individual will have to be considered by the courts. Decisions on these issues must be carefully considered as they will profoundly affect the lives of Canadians and all residents of Canada. In light of the importance and the impact that these decisions may have in the future, the courts have every right to expect and indeed to insist upon the careful preparation and presentation of a factual basis in most Charter cases. The relevant facts put forward may cover a wide spectrum dealing with scientific, social, economic and political aspects. Often expert opinion as to the future impact of the impugned legislation and the result of the possible decisions pertaining to it may be of great assistance to the courts.

Charter decisions should not and must not be made in a factual vacuum. To attempt to do so would trivialize the Charter and inevitably result in ill-considered opinions. The presentation of facts is not, as stated by the respondent, a mere technicality; rather, it is essential to a proper consideration of Charter issues. A respondent cannot, by simply consenting to dispense with the factual background, require or expect a court to deal with an issue such as this in a factual void. Charter decisions cannot be based upon the unsupported hypotheses of enthusiastic counsel.

[Emphasis added.]'[30]

Arguably the essence of the position of Bauman CJBC is expressed in the following sentence in para 50 above:

> ... Determining the actual salutary and deleterious effects of an infringement of a Charter right, for example, calls for more than a hypothetical or theoretical analysis.

In short, theoretical and hypothetical analysis devoid of facts and evidence will be insufficient to establish not only the breach of a charter right in the form of a restriction but also the justification thereof through Article 1 of the Charter. The statutory interpretation notably must be grounded in evidence both expert and non-expert. This is further detailed in the citation of the judgment of Cory J[31] in terms of the actual reason or need for the evidence:

> Decisions on these issues must be carefully considered as they will profoundly affect the lives of Canadians and all residents of Canada. In light of the importance and the impact that these decisions may have in the future, the courts have every right to expect and indeed to insist upon the careful preparation and presentation of a factual basis in most Charter cases. The relevant facts put forward may cover a wide spectrum dealing with scientific, social, economic and political aspects. Often expert opinion as to the future impact of the impugned legislation and the result of the possible decisions pertaining to it may be of great assistance to the courts. Charter decisions should not and must not be made in a factual vacuum. To attempt to do so would trivialize the Charter and inevitably result in ill-considered opinions. The presentation of facts is not, as stated by the respondent, a mere technicality; rather, it is essential to a proper consideration of Charter issues.

Arguably Corey J[32] in using the expression 'ill-considered opinions in the sentence' in 'To attempt to do so would trivialize the Charter and inevitably result in ill-considered opinions' refers to effectively a breach of Article 6 (1) ECHR as regards the ECtHR and the CJ: namely, the duty of the court to respect due process and notably to ensure that where necessary evidence is not only evaluated correctly but is indeed present to ensure that the merits claims and arguments of the parties are correctly evaluated following *Kraska v Switzerland*.[33]

The type of evidence introduced consisted in a very wide range of expert evidence as well as evidence from notably the individuals who had been members of the Mormons, specifically, women, children and young men:

> [26][34] 'British Columbia is unusual in authorizing the Lieutenant Governor in Council to refer questions to the trial court. In most other provinces, the Court of

30. *Reference re: section 239 Criminal Code of Canada* 2011 BCSC 1588, 'www.courts.gov.bc', *supra*, paras 46-51.
31. In *MacKay v Manitoba*, [1989] 2 *S.C.R.* 357, *supra*.
32. *Ibid.*
33. *Kraska v Switzerland* (1994) *EHRR* (18) 188, *supra*, para. 30.
34. *Reference re: section 239 Criminal Code of Canada* 2011 BCSC 1588, www.courts.gov.bc, *supra*, paras 26-32.

> Appeal alone can provide reference opinions. As far as I am aware, a reference of this significance in a trial court is a first.
>
> [27] A reference in this forum enables the participants to create an evidentiary record impossible in the typical appellate reference. The participants in the present proceeding embraced that opportunity and compiled a record that is remarkable not only for its size, but also for the breadth and diversity of its contents. Indeed, it is no exaggeration to say that the record embodies the bulk of contemporary academic research into polygamy.
>
> [28] Much of the evidence comprises affidavits and expert reports. Over 90 such are before me. In large measure, these were exchanged and filed with the Court in advance of the hearing according to a schedule directed by the Court. Approximately 22 of the experts were then examined and cross-examined during the hearing phase of the proceeding.
>
> [29] The expert witnesses represent a broad range of disciplines including anthropology, psychology, sociology, law, economics, family demography, history and theology. The caliber and breadth of knowledge of these experts is impressive. Some undertook original research specifically for this reference. Others are clinical experts who offer case study observations from their practices. Yet others have studied aspects of polygamy relevant to their particular disciplines for years.
>
> [30] The lay witnesses are largely individuals who have lived – and in some cases continue to live – in polygamous families in both Canada and the United States. Most have experience with polygamy in the context of fundamentalist Mormonism, and they spoke of those experiences, both positive and negative. Other witnesses described their involvement with polyamory.
>
> [31] Unusually, most of the FLDS's lay witnesses gave their evidence, both written and viva voce, under cover of anonymity pursuant to an order I granted earlier in the proceeding (indexed at 2010 BCSC 1351). Also somewhat unusually, the AGBC tendered the evidence of many of his lay witnesses by video affidavits which were played in Court during the hearing.
>
> [32] In addition to the affidavits and expert reports, the participants also filed and exchanged an extensive collection of Brandeis Brief materials. These comprise several hundred legal and social science articles, books and DVDs. An index of these materials is attached as Appendix A to these reasons.

As regards expert witnesses the following criterion for admission were used[35] as noted by Bauman CJBC:[36]

35. The significant parts of the judgment for the purposes of the instant book deal with effectively the manner in which the court uses expert evidence to decide the questions which were referred to it and which deal with statutory interpretation of a constitutional document. The nature of the reference which as a procedural mechanism permits the interpretation of both the Canadian Charter of Fundamental Rights and Art. 293 of the Criminal Code of Canada. Para. 26: British Columbia is unusual in authorizing the Lieutenant Governor in Council to refer questions to the trial court. In most other provinces, the Court of Appeal alone can provide reference opinions. As far as I am aware, a reference of this significance in a trial court is a first'. Para. 27 'A reference in this forum enables the participants to create an evidentiary record impossible in the typical appellate reference. The participants in the present proceeding embraced that opportunity and compiled a record that is remarkable not only for its size, but also for the breadth and diversity of its contents. Indeed, it is no exaggeration to say that the record embodies the bulk of contemporary academic research into polygamy.' [28] 'Much of the evidence comprises

C. Expert Evidence

[71] The basic test for the admissibility of expert opinion evidence was established in R. v. Mohan, [1994] 2 S.C.R. 9 (at para. 17). To be admissible, expert evidence must satisfy each of these four familiar criteria:

(a) relevance;
(b) necessity in assisting the trier of fact;

---

affidavits and expert reports. Over 90 such are before me. In large measure, these were exchanged and filed with the Court in advance of the hearing according to a schedule directed by the Court. Approximately 22 of the affiants and experts were then examined and cross-examined during the hearing phase of the proceeding'. [29] The expert witnesses represent a broad range of disciplines including anthropology, psychology, sociology, law, economics, family demography, history and theology. The caliber and breadth of knowledge of these experts is impressive. Some undertook original research specifically for this reference. Others are clinical experts who offer case study observations from their practices. Yet others have studied aspects of polygamy relevant to their particular disciplines for years'. It is submitted that the essential matter here is that the reference system wherein there is no permanent disposition of rights but where evidence is introduce notably by means of judicial notice. In using the mechanism of judicial notice the learned judge taking into consideration the procedural imperatives of time and expense makes recourse to unsworn information which does not have the status of sworn evidence on the basis that the source therefore, namely an expert in relation to the subject of polygamy is uncontestable. The learned justice notes in his presentation of the evidence that he has chosen to use this method of introducing expert opinion because the statutory interpretation involved in answering the questions deal with what Davies (KC Davis, 'Judicial Notice' (1955) *C L Rev*' (35) (7) 945 at 983, *supra*,) calls legislative facts: that is, issues which are not involved in adjudication but in terms of law making which is the function of the court. On those matters where the judge feels that the sources are disputable he allows for cross examination and indeed proceeds by traditional cross-examination. Bauer J admits expert evidence by two methods: on the one hand, by means of judicial notice as regards what Davis terms legislative as opposed to adjudicative facts; and, on the other, by means of cross examination. As regards the use of judicial notice as pertaining to the statutory interpretation of the two statutes involved Sullivan observes as follows: Courts are entitled to take judicial notice of facts that in their opinion are indisputable. This includes (a) facts that are notorious in the sense that everyone knows and accepts them; they belong to the store of information that every educated member of the society takes for granted and (b) facts that can be demonstrated to be true by resorting to sources that are easily accessible and whose authority and accuracy are accepted by all. As is recalled Roberts and Zuckerman (P Roberts & A Zuckerman *Criminal Evidence*, 2nd edn (Oxford, OUP, 2010), *supra*, 170) include within the scope of indisputable sources experts. Consequently, the use of judicial notice may lead to the introduction of unsworn expert evidence for the establishment of the ordinary meaning. However, following Sullivan (*Sullivan and Driedger on the Construction of Statutes*, 4th edn (Vancouver, Butterworths, 2002), *supra*, 46) sworn expert evidence may be used to prove the meaning of technical words: 'Whether a term has a technical meaning and what that meaning is are both questions of fact which must be established in a legally acceptable way. When a technical or specialized meaning is not something that everybody knows it cannot be judicial noticed but must be judicially noticed but must be established through evidence normally expert opinion evidence. Such evidence is required to establish both that a term has a technical meaning and the content of that meaning. The expert may introduce specialized dictionaries or encyclopedias textbooks publications of regulatory authorities or eve legislation to support his or her testimony.' One recalls that the scope for the use of judicial evidence and the introduction of unsworn evidence thereby is larger under the definition provided by Roberts and Zuckerman as compared to that of Sullivan: Roberts and Zuckerman specifically include experts as constituting indisputable sources which may be consulted by judges even as regards subjects which are not widely known.

36. *Reference re: section 239 Criminal Code of Canada* 2011 BCSC 1588, www.courts.gov.bc, '*supra*, paras 71-79.

(c) the absence of any exclusionary rule; and
(d) a properly qualified expert.

[72] This test applies to constitutional cases as it does in other areas. The burden of proof lies with the party tendering the proposed expert.

[73] Mr. Justice Doherty of the Ontario Court of Appeal recently suggested a helpful approach to assessing the admissibility of expert evidence in R. v. Abbey, 2009 ONCA 624, leave to appeal refused [2010] S.C.C.A. No. 125. This approach does not purport to alter the principles expressed in Mohan, but, as Doherty J.A. explained it, the approach seeks to 'facilitate the admissibility analysis and the application of the Mohan criteria' (at para. 77).

[74] Justice Doherty's innovation in Abbey was to divide the admissibility inquiry into a two-step process, as he described at para. 76:
Using these criteria, I suggest a two-step process for determining admissibility. First, the party proffering the evidence must demonstrate the existence of certain preconditions to the admissibility of expert evidence. For example, that party must show that the proposed witness is qualified to give the relevant opinion. Second, the trial judge must decide whether expert evidence that meets the preconditions to admissibility is sufficiently beneficial to the trial process to warrant its admission despite the potential harm to the trial process that may flow from the admission of the expert evidence. This 'gatekeeper' component of the admissibility inquiry lies at the heart of the present evidentiary regime governing the admissibility of expert opinion evidence.

[75] He explained his rationale for doing so at paras. 78-79:
It is helpful to distinguish between what I describe as the preconditions to admissibility of expert opinion evidence and the performance of the 'gatekeeper' function because the two are very different. The inquiry into compliance with the preconditions to admissibility is a rules-based analysis that will yield 'yes' or 'no' answers. Evidence that does not meet all of the preconditions to admissibility must be excluded and the trial judge need not address the more difficult and subtle considerations that arise in the 'gatekeeper' phase of the admissibility inquiry.
The 'gatekeeper' inquiry does not involve the application of bright line rules, but instead requires an exercise of judicial discretion. The trial judge must identify and weigh competing considerations to decide whether on balance those considerations favour the admissibility of the evidence. This cost-benefit analysis is case-specific and, unlike the first phase of the admissibility inquiry, often does not admit of a straightforward 'yes' or 'no' answer. Different trial judges, properly applying the relevant principles in the exercise of their discretion, could in some situations come to different conclusions on admissibility.

[76] This analytical approach is particularly helpful in the present case since separating the rules-based preconditions from the discretionary 'gatekeeper' inquiry makes it easier to factor the unique context of a reference into the admissibility analysis.

It is recalled from the above extracts that the evidence particularly the expert evidence was introduced by two methods: firstly, by means of judicial notice which involved the use of the so called Brandeis brief and the second was by means of cross examination of sworn witness, particularly non-experts. The concept of judicial notice discussed earlier is utilised but in the restrictive sense: that is matters which are not disputable or can be readily determined from an indisputable source ranging from a dictionary to an expert. In the view of the court the quality of the evidence is lower than is the case where the evidence is cross examined. One might question this given that effectively the veracity is said to be incontestable thereby not depriving the defence of the right to an adversarial trial. This is an instance arguably where the procedural principles of economy and time constitute the reason for dispensing with the normal formal proof which involves swearing the witness coupled with cross examination. The concept of legislative facts as developed by Davis[37] is utilised as opposed to that of adjudicative facts. The learned Bauman CJBC opines that absence of proof for legislative facts is appropriate for legislative as opposed to adjudicative facts because they are not dispositive. Unlike Davis[38] who extends the scope of judicial notice to include not only indisputable facts but also disputable facts providing also for the possibility in certain circumstances according to the importance of the facts in relations to the subject pleaded for cross examination Bauman CJBC as noted restricts the scope of judicial notice: that is to indisputable non-dispositive facts which are said to be legislative facts.

> [59][39] The nature of the evidence on this reference as legislative fact further allows an expansive approach to admissibility.
>
> 1. Legislative and Adjudicative Facts
>
> [60] The admissibility requirements for evidence in constitutional litigation are partially determined by whether the evidence in question is legislative fact or adjudicative fact. The difference between these two categories was explained by Mr. Justice Sopinka in Danson v. Ontario (Attorney General), [1990] 2 S.C.R. 1086 (at 1099):
> It is necessary to draw a distinction at the outset between two categories of facts in constitutional litigation: 'adjudicative facts' and 'legislative facts'. These terms derive from Davis, Administrative Law Treatise (1958), vol. 2, para. 15.03, p. 353. (See also Morgan, 'Proof of Facts in Charter Litigation', in Sharpe, ed., Charter Litigation (1987).) Adjudicative facts are those that concern the immediate parties: in Davis's words, 'who did what, where, when, how and with what motive or intent . ...' Such facts are specific, and must be proved by admissible evidence. Legislative facts are those that establish the purpose and background of legislation, including its social, economic and cultural context. Such facts are of a more general nature, and are subject to less stringent admissibility requirements: see e.g., Re Anti-Inflation Act, [1976] 2 S.C.R. 373, per Laskin C.J., at p. 391; Re Residential Tenancies Act, 1979, [1981] 1 S.C.R. 714, per Dickson J. (as he then was), at p. 723; and Reference re Upper Churchill Water Rights Reversion Act, [1984] 1 S.C.R. 297, per McIntyre J., at p. 318.
>
> [61] There are no 'immediate parties' in a constitutional reference, which means there are no adjudicative facts; that is, there is no specific 'who' that did 'what, where, when, how and with what motive or intent'.
>
> [62] As such, all the evidence on this reference is properly categorized as legislative fact. This is no less the case for the witnesses who described their experiences with polygamy, notwithstanding the intensely personal nature of

37. KC Davis, *Judicial Notice* (1995) *Col Law Rev* (55) (7) at 945, *supra*, passim.
38. *Ibid.*, passim.
39. *Reference re: section 239 Criminal Code of Canada* 2011 BCSC 1588, 'www.courts.gov.bc, '*supra*, paras 59-70.

some of this evidence. These legislative facts assist in developing 'the social, economic and cultural context' of s. 293. The less stringent admissibility requirements for legislative facts described in Danson have allowed me to receive much of the evidence on this reference.

2. Judicial Notice

[63] Judicial notice is one vehicle through which the less stringent admissibility requirements for legislative facts are put into effect.

[64] Chief Justice McLachlin summarized the process of judicial notice in R. v. Find, 2001 SCC 32 (at para. 48):
Judicial notice dispenses with the need for proof of facts that are clearly uncontroversial or beyond reasonable dispute. Facts judicially noticed are not proved by evidence under oath. Nor are they tested by cross-examination. Therefore, the threshold for judicial notice is strict: a court may properly take judicial notice of facts that are either: (1) so notorious or generally accepted as not to be the subject of debate among reasonable persons; or (2) capable of immediate and accurate demonstration by resort to readily accessible sources of indisputable accuracy: R. v. Potts (1982), 66 C.C.C. (2d) 219 (Ont. C.A.); J. Sopinka, S. N. Lederman and A. W. Bryant, The Law of Evidence in Canada (2nd ed. 1999), at p. 1055.

[65] Judicial notice is an exception to the usual requirement of proof by evidence given under oath, which accounts for the strict approach taken by McLachlin C.J.C. in Find.

[66] This definition of judicial notice, and the circumstances in which it may be applied, is based on the work of Professor E.M. Morgan in 'Judicial Notice' (1943-1944), 57 Harv. L. Rev. 269. Professor Morgan argued that a strict formulation of judicial notice was necessary as he considered any fact properly subjected to judicial notice irrebuttable (at 273). Any broader formulation of judicial notice would allow the court to make too much use of unreliable out-of-court information.

[67] In Spence, Binnie J. explained how the approach to judicial notice differs for adjudicative and legislative facts. He referred to the Morgan criteria adopted by McLachlin C.J.C. in Find as the 'gold standard' for judicial notice (at para. 61) and summarized their application to adjudicative facts (at para. 62):
If the Morgan criteria are not satisfied, and the fact is 'adjudicative' in nature, the fact will not be judicially recognized, and that too is the end of the matter.

[68] For legislative facts, the Morgan criteria are the starting point of the court's analysis, but how strictly they are applied will depend on the nature of the facts presented and whether the information may be dispositive of a case. Justice Binnie explained (at para. 63):
It is when dealing with social facts and legislative facts that the Morgan criteria, while relevant, are not necessarily conclusive. There are levels of notoriety and indisputability. Some legislative 'facts' are necessarily laced with supposition, prediction, presumption, perception and wishful thinking. Outside the realm of adjudicative fact, the limits of judicial notice are inevitably somewhat elastic. Still, the Morgan criteria will have great weight when the legislative fact or social fact approaches the dispositive issue.
Therefore, judicial notice will more easily be taken of legislative facts than adjudicative facts, especially where the evidence does not border on dispositive.

> [69] Although the participants in this proceeding have been able to present much of their evidence under oath and many of the witnesses were cross-examined, a significant portion of the materials before me has not been subjected to these protections. In particular, all of the materials in the Brandeis Brief are unproven in the traditional sense.
>
> [70] This will require a consideration not only of the basis upon which such materials are admitted, but also of the weight they may be given and the uses to which they may be put.

Further, the concept of the Brandeis Brief is utilized within the category of judicial notice: that is, information particularly expert which is introduced from reliable sources which is not proved:

> E. The Brandeis Brief[40]
>
> [106] Much of the evidence in this reference has been presented in the form of 'Brandeis Brief' materials. The Brandeis Brief is named after Louis D. Brandeis (later Brandeis J. of the Supreme Court of the United States) who, as counsel for the state of Oregon in Muller v. Oregon (1908), 208 U.S. 412, filed a brief that included a range of social science materials which supported the constitutionality of a restriction on the weekly hours of female labour. These materials were not presented through a witness at trial, but were merely attached to the written brief filed with the Supreme Court.
>
> [107] The participants in this reference have submitted a wide range of Brandeis Brief materials, as reflected in Appendix A to these reasons. The materials have not been sworn to under oath by their creators, and may therefore only be received as legislative facts through judicial notice.
>
> [108] None of the participants objected to the admissibility of any of the Brandeis Brief materials.
>
> 1. Canadian Use of Brandeis Brief Materials
>
> [109] The use of unsworn evidence in a brief is relatively common in American constitutional litigation but developed much later in this country. Until the 1970s, extrinsic evidence of the surrounding social context that led to the enactment of legislation or the effects of its implementation was generally inadmissible in constitutional cases. The analysis in such cases tended to take an abstract and strictly legalistic form that focused predominantly on the text of the legislation.
>
> [110] The Supreme Court of Canada began to develop a more liberal approach to the use of extrinsic evidence in Reference re: Anti-Inflation Act, [1976] 2 S.C.R. 373, and Reference re: Residential Tenancies Act (Ontario), [1981] 1 S.C.R. 714.
>
> [111] In Reference re: Anti-Inflation Act, the parties included a variety of extrinsic materials, including the federal government's White Paper on inflation, a Statistics Canada bulletin, a study by an economics professor, a critique of that study, and the transcript of a speech from the Governor of the Bank of Canada. In each of the three judgments issued in the reference this evidence was accepted. In his concurring judgment Chief Justice Laskin ruled that (at 391):
> The present case is likewise one in which federal legislation is challenged as involving unconstitutional regulation, and I am of the opinion that extrinsic

40. *Ibid.*, paras 106-113.

> material, bearing on the circumstances in which the legislation was passed, may be considered by the Court in determining whether the legislation rests on a valid constitutional base. ... As will appear from what follows, the arguments of the proponents and the opponents of the Anti-Inflation Act turn substantially on whether the social and economic circumstances upon which Parliament can be said to have proceeded in passing the Act were such as to provide support for the Act in the power of Parliament to legislate for the peace, order and good government of Canada. The extrinsic material proffered in this case was directed to this question and may, hence, be properly considered thereon.
>
> [112] Justice Dickson (as he then was) took a similar approach to the admissibility of extrinsic evidence in Reference re: Residential Tenancies Act, where he held that the Court (at 722-23):
> should be loathe, it seems to me, to enunciate any inflexible rule governing the admissibility of extrinsic materials in constitutional references. The effect of such a rule might well be to exclude logically relevant and highly probative evidence. It is preferable, I think, to follow the practice adopted in the Anti-Inflation Reference and give timely directions establishing the evidence or extraneous materials to be admitted to serve the ends of the Court in the particular reference.
>
> [113] In justifying the admissibility of such materials, Dickson J. made reference to the 'living tree' doctrine of progressive constitutional interpretation (at 723):
> A constitutional reference is not a barren exercise in statutory interpretation. What is involved is an attempt to determine and give effect to the broad objectives and purpose of the Constitution, viewed as a 'living tree', in the expressive words of Lord Sankey in Edwards and Others v. Attorney-General for Canada and Others. Material relevant to the issues before the court, and not inherently unreliable or offending against public policy should be admissible ...
> One notes here in paragraphs 111-113 the use of the Brandeis brief coupled with judicial notice in order to produce the most accurate interpretation possible which would require taking into consideration of factors both directly and indirectly related to the words being interpreted.

Bauman CJBC[41] then goes on to enumerate the limited scope of the Brandeis Brief in the context of judicial notice: namely, it is restricted to non-dispositive facts.

> [120] The judgment of Binnie J. in Spence is the Supreme Court's last word on this topic. Justice Binnie explained the proper approach to legislative facts that are not dispositive (at para. 65):
> When asked to take judicial notice of matters falling between the high end already discussed where the Morgan criteria will be insisted upon, and the low end of background facts where the court will likely proceed (consciously or unconsciously) on the basis that the matter is beyond serious controversy, I believe a court ought to ask itself whether such 'fact' would be accepted by reasonable people who have taken the trouble to inform themselves on the topic as not being the subject of reasonable dispute for the particular purpose for which it is to be used, keeping in mind that the need for reliability and trustworthiness increases directly with the centrality of the 'fact' to the disposition of the controversy.

41. *Ibid.*, paras 120-127.

> [121] None of the materials in the Brandeis Brief are dispositive of any points in issue. Accordingly, a less stringent approach to judicial notice is appropriate, consistent with Binnie J.'s comments in Spence.
>
> [126] I have drawn a substantial amount of the historical evidence regarding polygamy in 19th century United States and Canada from books and articles in the Brandeis Brief. I do not understand this history to be seriously in dispute.
>
> [127] I have used the non-academic books and articles, such as journalistic and autobiographical descriptions of polygamy, for limited purposes. In many cases, there is a significant overlap between these materials and the testimony of personal witnesses. Several of the journalistic books recount the life stories of witnesses who appeared before me. Two of the personal witnesses have also written books that were attached as exhibits to their affidavits. Where sworn and unsworn evidence overlapped in this manner, I have relied upon the sworn evidence.

In addition other witnesses, in particular the non-expert witnesses, gave their evidence under oath and were subject to cross-examination:

> Lay Witnesses
>
> [104][42] In addition to the expert witnesses, the participants tendered the evidence of a number of lay witnesses by way of affidavit, both written and video, and viva voce testimony. Some of these witnesses provided intensely personal evidence regarding their experiences with polygamy. Others provided statistics and documents relating to the community in Bountiful, as well as the FLDS more generally.
>
> [105] In both cases, these witnesses provided legislative fact evidence only.

[B] Standard of Proof

The standard of proof is apparently that of the civil standard, namely, the balance of probabilities:

> [1336][43] The government need only show that 'it is reasonable to suppose that the limit [on the right] may further the goal, not that it will do so' (Hutterian Brethren at para. 48). It is certainly reasonable to suppose that the limits on religious liberty that s. 293 imposes may further the objectives of the provision. The evidence that the incidence of polygamy would plausibly increase in a non-trivial way if not criminalized certainly makes this point.

The standard of proof appears to be the normal civil standard at least in English courts of the balance of probabilities however expressed in the following manner: that Parliament must justify to that standard a 'reasonable apprehension of harm' but 'not scientific proof based on concrete evidence':

42. *Ibid.*, paras 104-105.
43. *Ibid.*, para. 1336.

> [1043][44] When I examined the alleged harms associated with polygamy, I discussed the burden on government to justify criminalizing an activity in an exercise of the criminal law power. Parliament must demonstrate a reasoned apprehension of harm, not scientific proof based on concrete evidence: Sharpe. It need only demonstrate that the harm is not de minimus, not insignificant or trivial. Absent gross disproportionality, the precise weighing and calculation of the nature and extent of the harm is Parliament's job: Malmo-Levine. As I also discussed, a reasoned apprehension of harm is relevant to the justification analysis under s. 1 of the Charter.
>
> [1044] On the whole of the evidence here, I conclude that the Attorneys General have certainly demonstrated a reasoned apprehension of harm associated with polygyny. Indeed, they have cleared the higher bar: they have demonstrated 'concrete evidence' of harm. I have detailed that evidence at length. I have discussed the varied nature of the harms associated with polygyny and highlighted their coincidence across nations, cultures and socio-economic units.
>
> [1045] The evidence, in particular that of Drs. Heinrich and McDermott, supports the reasoned view that the harms associated with the practice are endemic; they are inherent. This conclusion is critical because it supports the view that the harms found in polygynous societies are not simply the product of individual misconduct; they arise inevitably out of the practice. And many of these harms could arise in polyandrous or same sex polygamous relationships, rare as those appear to be. Here I mention, without limitation, harm to children (for example, from divided parental investment or as a result of less genetic-relatedness of family members), to the psychological health of the spouses, and to the institution of monogamous marriage.

[C] Essence of the Judgment

Arguably one of the most significant parts of the analysis of Bauman CJBC deals with the matter of whether the criminal restriction provided by S 293 CCC as regards the freedom of religion provided by S 2 (a) CHRF was proportionate to the harm caused by polygamy and in particular polygamy: that is in the sense of constituting a response that was both reasonable and proportionate to the harm it caused.

The analysis of Bauman CJBC is cogent in the sense that he appropriate uses the evidence both expert and non-expert of the harm which polygamy creates as it were ab initio: that is under all circumstances. Bauman CJBC holds that the evidence discloses that there are no instances of non-harmful polygamy. Further, this analysis of harm is buttressed with the finding that the Government of Canada has established by means of reasonable apprehension that failure to criminalize polygamy would lead to its propagation in Canada with a particularly catastrophic result for women, children and young men. It is upon these findings of fact based upon the expert and non-expert opinion that the learned judge concludes that the entire criminalization of polygamy is proportionate to the harm which it causes or may cause. Bauman CJBC holds as follows in this regard:

44. *Ibid.*, paras 1043-1045.

> [1329][45] Having found s. 293 to infringe both s. 2(a) and s. 7 of the Charter, I advance to apply the Oakes test to each infringement.
>
> a) Section 2(a)
>
> [1330] To constitute a justifiable limit on a right or a freedom, the objective of the impugned measure must advance concerns that are pressing and substantial in a free and democratic society.
>
> [1331] As I have concluded, s. 293 has as its objective the prevention of harm to women, to children and to society. The prevention of these collective harms associated with polygamy is clearly an objective that is pressing and substantial.
>
> [1332] The positive side of the prohibition which I have discussed – the preservation of monogamous marriage – similarly represents a pressing and substantial objective for all of the reasons that have seen the ascendance of monogamous marriage as a norm in the West.
>
> [1333] I reject the Amicus' concentration on, and rather dismissive critique of, the harms associated with the so-called 'cruel arithmetic' of polygamy. The existence of these harms has been demonstrated by the defenders.

Therefore, Bauman CJBC holds that the Federal and Provincial governments have established to the requisite level that the harms which are caused by polygamy. He then goes on to establish the rational connection. It is here that the Government need only demonstrate that criminalization is one method which is likely in a rational sense to prevent polygamy:

> [1334] At the next stage of the analysis, the Court turns to determine whether there is a rational connection between the criminal prohibition of polygamy and Parliament's pressing and substantial objective.
>
> [1335] Having found a reasoned apprehension that polygamy is associated with numerous harms, it follows that criminalizing the practice is one way of limiting those harms. As Chief Justice Lamer observed in the Prostitution Reference (at 1195):
> Regulating or prohibiting the cause is at least one method of controlling its effects. A piece of legislation that proceeds upon such a premise does, in my view, exhibit a rational connection between the measures and the objective.
>
> [1336] The government need only show that 'it is reasonable to suppose that the limit [on the right] may further the goal, not that it will do so' (Hutterian Brethren at para. 48). It is certainly reasonable to suppose that the limits on religious liberty that s. 293 imposes may further the objectives of the provision. The evidence that the incidence of polygamy would plausibly increase in a non-trivial way if not criminalized certainly makes this point.
>
> [1337] The Amicus suggests that s. 293 has not been effective, and points to the miniscule number of prosecutions over the provision's 120 year history. The Supreme Court answered this submission in R. v. Lucas, [1998] 1 S.C.R. 439, where it rejected a similar argument with respect to s. 300 of the Criminal Code, the prohibition of defamatory libel (at 466):
> The appellants argued that the provisions cannot be an effective way of achieving the objective. They contended that this was apparent from the fact that

45. *Ibid.*, paras 1329-1339.

criminal prosecutions for defamation are rare in comparison to civil suits. However, it has been held that '[t]he paucity of prosecutions does not necessarily reflect on the seriousness of the problem', rather it 'might be affected by a number of factors such as the priority which is given to enforcement by the police and the Crown' (R. v. Laba, [1994] 3 S.C.R. 965, at p. 1007 (emphasis added)). There are numerous provisions in the Code which are rarely invoked, such as theft from oyster beds provided for in s. 323 or high treason in s. 46. Yet, the infrequency of prosecutions under these provisions does not render them unconstitutional or ineffective. I agree that the small number of prosecutions under s. 300 may well be due to its effectiveness in deterring the publication of defamatory libel (Stevens, supra, at p. 310).

[1338] The Amicus also maintains that s. 293 is not an effective deterrent since those who are religiously motivated to practice polygamy will do so regardless of its criminalization. Again, the Supreme Court answered this submission in Malmo-Levine (at paras. 177-178):

This Court has exercised caution in accepting arguments about the alleged ineffectiveness of legal measures: see Reference re Firearms Act (Can.), supra, where the Court held that '[t]he efficacy of a law, or lack thereof, is not relevant to Parliament's ability to enact it under the division of powers analysis' (para. 57). While somewhat different considerations come into play under a Charter analysis, it remains important that some deference be accorded to Parliament in assessing the utility of its chosen responses to perceived social ills.

Questions about which types of measures and associated sanctions are best able to deter conduct that Parliament considers undesirable is a matter of legitimate ongoing debate. The so-called 'ineffectiveness' is simply another way of characterizing the refusal of people in the appellants' position to comply with the law. It is difficult to see how that refusal can be elevated to a constitutional argument against validity based on the invocation of fundamental principles of justice. Indeed, it would be inconsistent with the rule of law to allow compliance with a criminal prohibition to be determined by each individual's personal discretion and taste. [Emphasis added]

[1339] While the Supreme Court made these comments in the context of s. 7 of the Charter, in my view they have equal application to the rational connection analysis under s. 1.

[D] Principle of Proportionality

Bauman CJBC then deals with proportionality in the sense of the necessity for the restriction of the right to be minimal. The learned judge holds that the blanket restriction of polygamy in the circumstances constitutes a minimal restriction. Here once again the analysis is predicated upon the evidence having established that polygamy is per se harmful irrespective of its method of application and accordingly only a wide prohibition such as that provided by S 293CCC would be capable of preventing the reasonably apprehended harm:

[1341][46] Moving to minimal impairment, it is my view that s. 293 minimally impairs religious freedom.

[1342] In addressing the harms reasonably believed to be associated with polygamy - inherently I add - Parliament is entitled to some deference. This is a complex social issue. Parliament is better positioned than the Court to choose among a range of alternatives to address the harms [1343] When one accepts that there is a reasoned apprehension that polygamy is inevitably associated with sundry harms, and that these harms are not simply isolated to criminal adherents like Warren Jeffs but inhere in the institution itself, the Amicus' complaint that there are less sweeping means of achieving the government's objective falls away. And it most certainly does when one considers the positive objective of the measure, the protection and preservation of monogamous marriage. For that, there can be no alternative to the outright prohibition of that which is fundamentally anathema to the institution. In the context of this objective, there is no such thing as so-called 'good polygamy'.

[1344] It is therefore my opinion that s. 293 is 'carefully tailored so that rights are impaired no more than necessary' (RJR-MacDonald, at para. 160).

[1345] Finally, I find s. 293 to be proportional in its effects.

[1346] As Aharon Barak, former president of the Supreme Court of Israel, explained (in turn adopted by McLachlin C.J.C. in Hutterarian Brethren):

... the test of proportionality (stricto sensu) examines whether realization of this proper objective is commensurate with the deleterious effect upon the human right ... It requires placing colliding values and interests side by side and balancing them according to their weight.

[1347] I start with the deleterious effects.

[1348] I accept that for some, especially fundamentalist Mormons, the interference with a sincerely held belief represented by the prohibition in s. 293 is very significant. Still, I acknowledge the point made by the Attorneys General that some fundamentalist Mormons do choose to live monogamously without sacrificing their religious beliefs. And as we have seen, polygamy in Islam is not mandated, although it is permitted by the Qu-ran.

[1349] Further, I accept that the prohibition tends for some to encourage isolationism and insularity.

[1350] But, in my view, the salutary effects of the prohibition far outweigh the deleterious. The law seeks to advance the institution of monogamous marriage, a fundamental value in Western society from the earliest of times. It seeks to protect against the many harms which are reasonably apprehended to arise out of the practice of polygamy.

[1351] Finally, and not insignificantly, the prohibition is consistent with, and furthers, Canada's international human rights obligations. In my view, this adds very significant weight to the salutary effects side of the balance.

[1352] To the extent that s. 293 breaches the right guaranteed by s. 2(a) of the Charter, the Attorneys General have clearly met the burden of demonstrating that it is demonstrably justified in a free and democratic society.

46. *Ibid.*, paras 1341-1352.

[E] Concluding Remarks as Regards Re: Polygamy

Over all, it is clear that this analysis of proportionality of the restriction is determined by the evidence which the BCSC considered in the form of both expert and non-expert evidence and in this sense followed the injunction of Cory J cited earlier, namely that the statutory interpretation of the CRFR must be found upon fact and in particular expert opinion. It is to be recalled that the evidence notably expert evidence was admitted by two methods: first, by means of sworn witnesses who were subject to cross-examination by the parties; second as regards what are referred to as legislative fact, by means of judicial notice in the form of Brandeis Brief. The latter which were restricted to issues which were either indisputable or where the indisputability could be determined from an indisputable source and which dealt with legislative facts, namely, those which were not related to the adjudication of the case, arguably were introduced in this manner in order to comply with other procedural imperatives: namely, to reduce costs and time which would be expended unnecessarily on the introduction and the cross-examination of witnesses by the parties.

Perhaps most significantly, the concept which facilitates the evaluation of what is presented as evidence is basically that proof utilized in statutory interpretation which emanates from social sciences is not to be evaluated in the same manner as proof emanating from the empirical or hard sciences. There is less precision as regards the former. Notwithstanding the lack of precision as factual matrix as noted by Corey[47] J, is required in order to ensure a substantively accurate interpretation. It is here that one notes the fundamental difference in the manner whereby interpretation qua interpretation as carried out by these two Canadian courts fundamentally differs from that of both the ECtHR and the CJ notably in the context of references. Overall, the two judgments, rather more the minority judgment than that of the majority as regards *Sauvé v Canada*[48] and the single judgment in the Re: Polygamy Reference[49] more fully comply with the procedural rights of the defence: evidence, particularly expert evidence is used in order to give the most accurate statutory interpretation possible so as to ensure in turn, an accurate interpretation of the law to the facts. Further, the two judgments rendered by the Canadian courts possess by reason of the basis in facts which have either been tested through cross-examination or admitted because they are non-contentious without such a guarantee a certain credibility. The judgment is founded upon certain facts. This is in contrast to the interpretations rendered by certainly in the cases considered herein by the CJ and the ECtHR where the lack of a factual context arguably undermines the credibility and the technical quality of the statutory interpretations. The paucity of facts and notably expert evidence as noted earlier can also through lack of information lead to inaccurate interpretations notably of both the TFEU and the ECHR where the scope of certain rights is interpreted too widely and the derogation too narrowly. As noted earlier in the section dealing with EU Competition Law the effect of the distorted statutory interpretations of TFEU Article

47. *MacKay v Manitoba*, [1989] 2 *S.C.R.* 357, *supra*.
48. *Sauvé v Canada (Attorney General)*, [2002] 3 *S.C.R.* 519.
49. *Reference re: section 239 Criminal Code of Canada* 2011 BCSC 1588, 'www.courts.gov.bc, *supra*.

101 (ex EEC Article 85) which were based upon little or no expert economic opinion led to a fundamentally inaccurate application of that article by not only the European Commission but also and perhaps above all by the CJ. Similarly it is submitted that the failure upon the part of the ECtHR to provide a factual nexus based in particular upon expert opinion leads to interpretations where the scope of the rights involved has little or no objective justification. This inaccuracy is particularly grave in the context restriction of national powers and legislation where particular judgments of an international court require firstly factual accuracy and secondly credibility. The interpretations provided must be accurate but above all be plausible.[50] They become linguistically plausible and therefore credible in large measure because of the factual linguistics context in which they are used which must be detailed in terms of specific facts and often time expert opinions notably where the meaning of technical words is involved. As regards the evidentiary deficits particularly of an expert nature, once again it is submitted that this results not only in inaccurate judgments but as regards the ECtHR and the CJ violation of Article 6 (1) of due process in so far as it sounds in a breach of duty to examine the merits of the proceedings following *Kraska v Switzerland*.[51]

50. R Sullivan, *Sullivan and Driedger on the Construction of Statutes*, 4th edn (Vancouver, Butterworths, 2002), *supra*, at 125 'In principle, the plausibility requirement is an important constraint on judicial interpretation. The range of meanings that can be attributed to a text creates the limited within which interpretation can legitimately occur.' A different way of looking at the limit of the range of interpretations involved in the statutory interpretation of a piece of legislation or a treaty document is to consider whether the context is such that the words or a word can depending upon its purpose and the audience to whom it was directed be said to possess a technical meaning which will require expert opinion introduced either through judicial notice or through sworn witnesses appointed by the court either of its own initiative or on the request of parties. An error of interpretation which arises from a failure to introduce expert evidence may be analysed in various ways: firstly, as a breach of the duty to correctly analyse the facts involved in the meaning of the words which arguably would fall within the parameter of *Kraska v Switzerland* (1994) *EHRR* (18) 188, *supra*, at para. 33 and therefore as a breach of Art. 6 (1) ECHR and also as a straightforward error of law; similarly a refusal to permit expert evidence by the court despite a recognition that the matter is appropriate for expert evidence whereby the judges substitute their opinion for that of experts would sound simultaneously as a procedural error under *Kraska v Switzerland* and therefore as a breach of Art. 6 (1) ECHR and also necessarily as an error of law and possibly as intention abuse of process as a ground of substantive review or appeal. It would seem that there would be a difference between an accidental or negligent error of interpretation based upon a failure to consider the technical meaning of a term and to introduce expert evidence and an intentional refusal to use expert evidence on the basis that the terminology of the expert is too complicated to understand. Ultimately, the bottom line is, as noted in previous chapters herein, that technical meanings requiring expert evidence will be generally narrower in scope being addressed to specialists rather than the layman which is ultimately the result of the use of expert evidence on such a wide scale through judicial notice and through sworn witnesses as was the case with the two judgments of the Canadian courts. The narrower scope given the circumstances dealing with the technical nature of the words gives therefore greater plausibility to the interpretation and simultaneously greater credibility.
51. *Kraska v Switzerland* (1993) 18 *EHRR* at para. 30.

§3.04 *SAUVÉ V CANADA*[52]

It is appropriate now to consider now the last of the judgments by the North American Courts, namely, *Sauvé v Canada.*[53]

In *Sauvé v The Attorney General of Canada,*[54] the Chief Electoral Officer of Canada and the Solicitor General of Canada, Richard Sauvé, an ex-inmate, challenged the section of the Canada Elections Act that prohibited voting by inmates serving a sentence of two years or more. In this case, the Attorney General of Canada did not dispute that the law infringed upon the right of inmates to vote. However, the government did argue that denying this right was justifiable under the Charter as it served several purposes best determined by Parliament. Those purposes included the goal of promoting civic responsibility and respect for the law and that denial of the vote was a reasonable punishment in addition to that specified by the court. However, in a five-four (5-4) ruling, the Supreme Court of Canada (SCC) ruled against the government for, according to the learned Majority, the following reasons:

> first, the SCC found that as voting was a fundamental right in a democracy, any attempt made to restrict that right had to be made on the basis of a compelling reason that fulfilled specific legal criterion. In particular the restriction had to be justified on the basis of necessity: it could not be arbitrary, and further, the objectives of the ban could not be achieved through other measures. In dismissing the arguments formulated by the Government, the majority rejected the argument that denying the vote would assist in achieving the objective of 'promoting civic responsibility and respect for the law.' In fact, the SCC in the form of the learned majority found that:
>
> denying penitentiary inmates the right to vote is more likely to send messages that undermine respect for the law and democracy than messages that enhance those values. The legitimacy of the law and the obligation to obey the law arise directly from the right of every citizen to vote. Denial to the inmates of the right to vote is to ignore an important means of teaching them democratic values and social responsibility. Further, according to the learned majority, the government's political theory that would permit elected representatives to disenfranchise a segment of the population is inappropriate in a democracy which include necessarily, principles of inclusiveness, equality, and citizen participation; second, the SCC found that denying a fundamental right is arbitrary because it is applied to all offenders regardless of the circumstances relating to the offender or his/her offence. In short, according to the learned majority, blanket punitive measures are arbitrary. Finally, the SCC asserted that the negative aspects outweigh the positive benefits that may come from denying this right. According to the learned majority of the SCC denying inmates the right to vote imposes negative costs on inmates and on the penal system. It removes a method of social development and undermines correctional law and policy directed towards rehabilitation and integration. In light of the disproportionate number of Aboriginal people in penitentiaries, the negative effects of (this law) upon inmates have a disproportionate impact on Canada's already disadvantage Aboriginal population.

52. *Sauvé v Canada (Attorney General)*, [2002] 3 *S.C.R.* 519.
53. *Ibid.*
54. *Ibid.*

In short, in the view of the learned majority, the federal government did not have sufficient reason to deny inmates the right to vote.

[A] Analysis of *Sauvé v Canada*[55] for the Instant Purposes

Given that the interest of the judgment, for the present purposes, lies in the evidence rather more than the actual statutory interpretation alone of the questions referred, it is useful to consider the following matters: the reason for the use of evidence and in particular expert evidence in the statutory interpretation of the matter referred in the instant case; second, the method by which the evidence was introduced; third, the type of evidence used; fourth, the standard of proof utilized by the court; finally, whether or not the interpretation of the scope of Article 1 and in particular Article 2 of the CCRF was related to the strength or weakness of the evidence presented.

McLachlin[56] CJ provides the following summary of the learned Majority for which she spoke:

> Para 1: The right of every citizen to vote, guaranteed by s. 3 of the Canadian Charter of Rights and Freedoms, lies at the heart of Canadian democracy. The law at stake in this appeal denies the right to vote to a certain class of people – those serving sentences of two years or more in a correctional institution. The question is whether the government has established that this denial of the right to vote is allowed under s. 1 of the Charter as a 'reasonable limi[t] ... demonstrably justified in a free and democratic society'. I conclude that it is not. The right to vote, which lies at the heart of Canadian democracy, can only be trammeled for good reason. Here, the reasons offered do not suffice.

The relevant sections of the Canadian Charter of Rights and Freedoms[57] are:

> 1. The Canadian Charter of Rights and Freedoms guarantees the rights and freedoms set out in it subject only to such reasonable limits prescribed by law as can be demonstrably justified in a free and democratic society.
> 3. Every citizen of Canada has the right to vote in an election of members of the House of Commons or of a legislative assembly and to be qualified for membership therein.

Further the Canada Elections Act (1985)[58] provides as follows:

> Disqualifications
> 51. The following persons are not qualified to vote at an election and shall not vote at an election:
> (e) every person who is imprisoned in a correctional institution serving a sentence of two years or more.

55. *Ibid.*
56. *Ibid.*, at para. 1.
57. Constitution Act (1982) Part I Canadian Charter of Rights and Freedoms, http://laws-lois.justice.gc.ca/eng/const/page-15.html, date at which last consulted: 1.11.2013.
58. Canada Elections Act, R.S.C. 1985, c. E-2, s. 51(e).

[B] Position of the Learned Chief Justice

The essential objection of the learned Chief Justice and the majority is that the disenfranchisement is disproportionate and is therefore not rationally linked to the objectives presented and therefore breaches Article 3 of the CCRF but cannot be saved by Article 1 CCRF because it is disproportionate: the disenfranchisement is applied irrespective of the length of the sentence and further, it does not fulfil a legitimate penal function. Specifically, there is no proof that the disenfranchisement serves to reduce or to deter criminal behaviour. Nor logically according to authors such as JS Mill, could that be the case given that enfranchisement serves to teach 'democratic values and civil responsibility'. Further, in so far as disenfranchisement constitutes denunciation such must be individually adapted in order to be proportional to the criminal behaviour. By reason of this lack of proportionality, the restriction on the right of freedom to vote cannot be said to achieve a rational objective and thereby becomes irrational and disproportionate. McLachlin CJ[59] sets out these reasons in more detail as follows:

> 48 The second flaw in the argument that s. 51(e) furthers legitimate punishment is that it does not meet the dual requirements that punishment must not be arbitrary and must serve a valid criminal law purpose. Absence of arbitrariness requires that punishment be tailored to the acts and circumstances of the individual offender: R. v. Smith, [1987] 1 S.C.R. 1045, at p. 1073. In the immortal words of Gilbert and Sullivan, the punishment should fit the crime. Section 51(e) qua punishment bears little relation to the offender's particular crime. It makes no attempt to differentiate among inmates serving sentences of two years and those serving sentences of twenty. It is true that those serving shorter sentences will be deprived of the right to vote for a shorter time. Yet the correlation of the denial with the crime remains weak. It is not only the violent felon who is told he is an unworthy outcast; a person imprisoned for a non-violent or negligent act, or an Aboriginal person suffering from social displacement receives the same message. They are not targeted, but they are caught all the same. For them the message is doubly invidious – not that they are cast out for their apparently voluntary rejection of society's norms, but that they are cast out arbitrarily, in ways that bear no necessary relation to their actual situation or attitude towards state authority.
> 49 Punishment must also fulfill a legitimate penal purpose: see Smith, supra, at p. 1068. These include deterrence, rehabilitation, retribution, and denunciation: R. v. M. (C.A.), [1996] 1 S.C.R. 500, at para. 82. Neither the record nor common sense supports the claim that disenfranchisement deters crime or rehabilitates criminals. On the contrary, as Mill recognized long ago, participation in the political process offers a valuable means of teaching democratic values and civic responsibility.

The fundamental objection is to be found in the following two paragraphs.[60] This objection turns on the fact that the duration of the disenfranchisement is not calculated according to the gravity of offence and the character and conduct of the accused and the circumstances in which the crime was committed.

> 50 This leaves retribution and denunciation. Parliament may denounce unlawful conduct. But it must do so in a way that closely reflects the moral culpability of the

59. *Sauvé v Canada (Attorney General),* [2002] 3 *S.C.R.* 519 *supra* at para. 1.
60. *Ibid.*, at paras 49-51.

> offender and his or her circumstances. As Lamer C.J. indicated in M. (C.A.), supra, at para. 80:
> Retribution in a criminal context, by contrast [to vengeance], represents an objective, reasoned and measured determination of an appropriate punishment which properly reflects the moral culpability of the offender, having regard to the intentional risk-taking of the offender, the consequential harm caused by the offender, and the normative character of the offender's conduct. [Emphasis in original.]

Denunciation as a symbolic expression of community values must be individually tailored in order to fulfil the legitimate penal purpose of condemning a particular offender's conduct (see M. (C.A.), *supra*, at para. 81) and to send an appropriate 'educative message' about the importance of law-abiding behaviour.

> 51 Section 51(e) imposes blanket punishment on all penitentiary inmates regardless of the particular crimes they committed, the harm they caused, or the normative character of their conduct. It is not individually tailored to the particular offender's act. It does not, in short, meet the requirements of denunciatory, retributive punishment. It follows that it is not rationally connected to the goal of imposing legitimate punishment.

Perhaps most significantly McLachlin CJ provides a wide definition of the scope of beneficiary for the class of rights known as electoral rights. According the learned Chief Justice the jurisprudence of the court must be followed so that the rights are defined as follows:[61]

> 11 At the first stage, which involves defining the right, we must follow this Court's consistent view that rights shall be defined broadly and liberally: Hunter v. Southam Inc., [1984] 2 S.C.R. 145, at p. 156; R. v. Big M Drug Mart Ltd., [1985] 1 S.C.R. 295, at p. 344; Eldridge v. British Columbia (Attorney General), [1997] 3 S.C.R. 624, at para. 53. A broad and purposive interpretation of the right is particularly critical in the case of the right to vote. The framers of the Charter signaled the special importance of this right not only by its broad, untrammeled language, but by exempting it from legislative override under s. 33's notwithstanding clause. I conclude that s. 3 must be construed as it reads, and its ambit should not be limited by countervailing collective concerns, as the government appears to argue. These concerns are for the government to raise under s. 1 in justifying the limits it has imposed on the right.

It is necessary, however, to note a caveat with respect to the use of cases such as Hunter,[62] which concern a specific method of statutory interpretation: namely, that it cannot be applied in a manner which would lead to absurd results or consequences,[63] notably as discussed in an earlier chapter herein. In this regard, one recalls the definition of religion in Re Polygamy[64] where the jurisprudence apparently requires a

61. *Ibid.*, at para. 11.
62. *Hunter v Southam Inc.*, [1984] 2 *S.C.R.* 145, at 156; *R. v Big M Drug Mart Ltd.*, [1985] 1 *S.C.R.* 295, at 344; *Eldridge v British Columbia (Attorney General)*, [1997] 3 *S.C.R.* 624, at para. 53.
63. R Sullivan, *Sullivan and Driedger on the Construction of Statutes*, 4th edn (Vancouver, Butterworths, 2002), *supra*, Chapter 9, Consequential Analysis, 235-257.
64. 2011 *BCSC* 1588 Re: S 293 CCC, passim.

broad purposive interpretation which was best restricted pursuant to Article 1 CCRF[65] in that case, freedom of religion. This wide interpretation could then be restricted pursuant to Article 1 CCRF as opposed to giving a more restrictive interpretation under the definition of religious freedom pursuant to Article 2 (a) CCRF[66] such as a right to freedom of religion which causes harm as is the case of polygamy. Interpreting the right of freedom of religion very broadly so that it could only be restricted pursuant to Article 1 CCRF might lead to the conclusion that there exists a right to religion even where such causes harm which contravenes other jurisprudence which arguably is absurd. On the contrary, the interpretation must proceed so as to achieve rational results. Accordingly, the jurisprudence cited by the learned McLachlin CJ must be interpreted and applied in such a manner as to deal with the fact that it is it is both rational and conceivable to argue that convicted prisoners be excluded on the basis of a rational decision from the category of enfranchised persons for the period of their incarceration. In short, as the members of the learned Minority argue, it is both rational and conceivable to restrict the category of beneficiaries of the right to vote ab initio so as to exclude prisoners for the duration of their incarceration provided that it is based upon accurate proof and or reasoning. In truth, it is as the level of proof or more particularly the deficiency of proof that the wide definition of the right to vote proposed by McLachlin CJ falters. Indeed, the essential weakness of the statutory interpretation proposed by the learned majority on behalf of whom the Chief Justice speaks is that it relies upon evidence, notably that of political theorists such as JS Mill as well as logical reasoning. However, this reasoning, although certainly cogent, does not suffice to undermine what might be termed the equal credibility of the evidence of social scientists produced on behalf of the Canadian Government in the Federal Court[67] which considered the evidence and heard the witnesses, including the experts cross-examined. In short, the statutory interpretation proposed by the learned majority suffers from an evidentiary deficit. The evidence used by McLachin CJ does not undermine the cogency of the evidence proposed by the opponents. This arguably also describes a fortiori the statutory

65. 'Constitution Act 1982, PART I, Canadian Charter of Rights and Freedoms, Whereas Canada is founded upon principles that recognize the supremacy of God and the rule of law: GUARANTEE OF RIGHTS AND FREEDOMS 1. The *Canadian Charter of Rights and Freedoms* guarantees the rights and freedoms set out in it subject only to such reasonable limits prescribed by law as can be demonstrably justified in a free and democratic society. FUNDAMENTAL FREEDOMS: 2. Everyone has the following fundamental freedoms: (*a*) freedom of conscience and religion; (*b*) freedom of thought, belief, opinion and expression, including freedom of the press and other media of communication; (*c*) freedom of peaceful assembly; and (*d*) freedom of association. DEMOCRATIC RIGHTS 3. Every citizen of Canada has the right to vote in an election of members of the House of Commons or of a legislative assembly and to be qualified for membership therein. http://laws-lois.justice.gc.ca/eng/const/page-15.html http: Date on which last consulted: 1.11. 2013.
66. See text in above footnote of the Constitution Act (1982), Canadian Charter of Rights and Freedoms.
67. APPEAL from a judgment of the Federal Court of Appeal, [2000] 2 F.C. 117, 180 D.L.R. (4th) 385, 248 N.R. 267, 29 C.R. (5th) 242, 69 C.R.R. (2d) 106, [1999] F.C.J. No. 1577 (QL), allowing the respondents' appeal and dismissing the appellants' cross-appeal from a decision of the Trial Division, [1996] 1 F.C. 857, 106 F.T.R. 241, 132 D.L.R. (4th) 136, [1995] F.C.J. No. 1735 (QL). Therefore, the original judgment was that of Wetston J. Federal Court, Trial Division (1996) 1 FC 857.

position of the ECtHR particularly in the Hirst[68] judgment which will be considered in the following chapter herein. By marked contrast however with Sauvé,[69] and both the opinions of the Majority and the Minority, the Hirst[70] judgment will be analysed by reason of its complete reliance upon pure reasoning which was and is devoid of any facts or expert opinions. The opinion of Gonthier J. on behalf of the learned Minority in Sauvé[71] will be analysed later in this section. The primary finding however of the Majority as expressed in the opinion of McLachlin C.J. concerns what the learned justice describes succinctly in paragraph 51, cited again herein for convenience, as a disproportionality of the system of disenfranchisement based, solely, upon the sentence received by incarcerated prisoner:

> Para 51[72] Section 51(e) imposes blanket punishment on all penitentiary inmates regardless of the particular crimes they committed, the harm they caused, or the normative character of their conduct. It is not individually tailored to the particular offender's act. It does not, in short, meet the requirements of denunciatory, retributive punishment. It follows that it is not rationally connected to the goal of imposing legitimate punishment.

According to the learned Chief Justice, the application of the temporary disenfranchisement of an incarcerated convict based solely upon the type of sentence he or she has received from the court which has considered various factors involving the personal characteristic, is arbitrary. By reason of its arbitrary quality the measure becomes irrational and therefore disproportionate in the following manner according to McLachlin C.J.:

> Para 48[73] It makes no attempt to differentiate among inmates serving sentences of two years and those serving sentences of twenty. It is true that those serving shorter sentences will be deprived of the right to vote for a shorter time. Yet the correlation of the denial with the crime remains weak. It is not only the violent felon who is told he is an unworthy outcast; a person imprisoned for a non-violent or negligent act, or an Aboriginal person suffering from social displacement receives the same message. They are not targeted, but they are caught all the same. For them the message is doubly invidious – not that they are cast out for their apparently voluntary rejection of society's norms, but that they are cast out arbitrarily, in ways that bear no necessary relation to their actual situation or attitude towards state authority.

Arguably, however, this analysis of McLachlin C.J. is entirely dependent upon interpreting the category of beneficiaries of the right to vote in a very wide fashion so as to include, ab initio, incarcerated prisoners with a sentence of two years or more. Accordingly, this wide interpretation of the right appears to lead to a limited or restricted interpretation of Article 1 CCRF[74] which exempts reasonable restrictions. The

68. *Hirst v UK (No 2)* (2005) *ECR* 681, *supra*.
69. *Sauvé v Canada* (2002) 3 *SCR* 519, *supra*.
70. Hirst *v UK (No 2)* (2005) *ECR* 681, *supra*.
71. *Sauvé v Canada* (2002) 3 *SCR* 519, *supra*.
72. *Ibid*., para. 51.
73. *Ibid*., para. 48.
74. See above footnote for the text of Art. 1 CCRF.

difficulty here of course is that the original wide interpretation of the right to vote in Article 3 CCRF[75] was not established in a cogent manner in terms of the evidence which was led. Similarly, the restrictive interpretation of Article 1 CCRF whereby the use of a court imposed sentence to operate a system of temporary disenfranchisement is equated with being arbitrary and, therefore, irrational which leads to disproportionality, has not be motivated by a clear logical and factual (based upon expert opinion) explanation. This is of course the essence of the rejection by the learned Majority of the argument led by the Minority, as expressed by Gonthier, J. which will now be considered.

One could commence by saying that it may be the case that Gonthier J. may have envisaged the category of beneficiaries of the right to vote as being narrower than that of the McLachlin C.J. in that the learned judge regrets that the lawyer for the Government of Canada immediate admitted violation of Article 3 CCRF[76] as noted in the following:

> Para 78[77] The respondents conceded that s. 3 of the Charter has been infringed by s. 51(e) of the Act. I would like to sound a cautionary note regarding the appropriateness of concessions of infringement. The specific problem with such a concession is that it may deprive the courts of the benefit of the fruitful argument which most often occurs at that initial phase of the analysis, in defining the scope of the right, particularly with regard to historical and philosophical context. The development of contextual factors examined with regard to the scope of the right is of great importance since they clearly 'animate' the later stages of the test elaborated in R. v. Oakes, [1986] 1 S.C.R. 103: see McLachlin J. (as she then was) in Reference re Provincial Electoral Boundaries (Sask.), [1991] 2 S.C.R. 158, at p. 182. The following comment, which I shared with L'Heureux-Dubé and Bastarache JJ. in Sharpe, supra, at para. 151, is equally apposite here: 'it is unfortunate that the Crown conceded that the right to free expression was violated in this appeal in all respects, thereby depriving the Court of the opportunity to fully explore the content and scope of s. 2(b) as it applies in this case'.

The first point is what has been described herein as the narrow interpretation of the justifying provision of Article 1 CCRF[78] whereby effectively, the justification was analysed exclusively in terms of punishment and the prisoner. No consideration was given to the general context in which the temporary disenfranchisement took place: namely, subsequent to a conviction in which the sentence first, was imposed by the Canadian court in light of the individual circumstances of the case involving the condemned; however second, in the context of the effect of the commission of the crime on the public and third, in light of the operation of the system of voting for parliamentary elections and their relationship with those who have contravened democratically adopted laws. Arguably, the narrow interpretation of Article 1 CCRF[79]

75. See above footnote for the text of Art. 3 CCRF.
76. *Ibid.*
77. *Sauvé v Canada* (2002) 3 *SCR* 519, *ibid.*, paras 78.
78. See above footnote for the text of Art. 1 CCRF.
79. For convenience the text is cited again: 'Constitution Act 1982, PART I, Canadian Charter of Rights and Freedoms, Whereas Canada is founded upon principles that recognize the supremacy of God and the rule of law: GUARANTEE OF RIGHTS AND FREEDOMS 1. The *Canadian Charter of Rights*

which arises from the wide interpretation of the class of beneficiaries of the right to vote is not justified on the facts and leads to an incompletely proved and argued judgment by the learned Majority in that it apparently excludes the following: first, the general context of the sentencing as just noted and in particular the effects upon society; second, the specific context in the sense of the type of data and information which is being examined wherein proof involving the social sciences is less precise and less determinative than in the physical sciences which thereby would appear to prevent conclusions such as those of the learned Majority notably on the point of disproportionality. It is clear that the description by the learned Majority of a temporary disenfranchisement based exclusively upon and coterminous with the length of the sentence as being either by definition or by proof, arbitrary and irrational and therefore disproportional, is devoid of any cogent proof or logical analysis. Specifically, concerning therefore the method of proof to be used under the justifying provision of Article 1 CCRF,[80] Gonthier J. observes as follows:[81]

> C) Justification Under Section 1 Where the Context Involves Competing Social or Political Philosophies
>
> Para 90 Generally, the result of a concession of a breach of a right is that the burden for justifying the infringement falls to the Crown. With regard to the standard of proof for s. 1 analysis, the civil standard of the balance of probabilities applies, and it is important to stress that this standard does not require scientific proof: Libman v. Quebec (Attorney General), [1997] 3 S.C.R. 569, at para. 39. The application of common sense to what is known will suffice, even if this falls short of a scientific standard: McLachlin J. at para. 137 of RJR-MacDonald Inc. v. Canada (Attorney General), [1995] 3 S.C.R. 199. Justification can be based upon reason, logic, common sense, and knowledge of human nature: see R. v. Butler, [1992] 1 S.C.R. 452, at p. 524, referring to Irwin Toy Ltd. v. Quebec (Attorney General), [1989] 1 S.C.R. 927, and Keegstra, supra. In the case at bar, there is very little quantitative or empirical evidence either way. In such cases, the task of justification relates to the analysis of human motivation, the determination of values, and the understanding of underlying social or political philosophies – it truly is justification rather than measurement. (Libman v Quebec – para 39 The AG must show that the statutory restrictions can be justified under s1 of the Canadian Charter. The standard of proof to be used is the civil standard namely proof on the balance of probabilities. Scientific proof is not required to meet this standard: the balance of probabilities may be established by the application of common sense to what is known even though what is known may be deficient from a scientific point of view. Referendum campaigns fall within the realm of social science which does not lend itself to precise proof.)

---

and Freedoms guarantees the rights and freedoms set out in it subject only to such reasonable limits prescribed by law as can be demonstrably justified in a free and democratic society. FUNDAMENTAL FREEDOMS: 2. Everyone has the following fundamental freedoms: (*a*) freedom of conscience and religion; (*b*) freedom of thought, belief, opinion and expression, including freedom of the press and other media of communication; (*c*) freedom of peaceful assembly; and (*d*) freedom of association. DEMOCRATIC RIGHTS 3. Every citizen of Canada has the right to vote in an election of members of the House of Commons or of a legislative assembly and to be qualified for membership therein. http://laws-lois.justice.gc.ca/eng/const/page-15.html, date on which last consulted: 1.11.2013.

80. *Ibid.*
81. *Sauvé v Canada* (2002) 3 *SCR* 519, *ibid.*, paras 90-91.

> Para 91 Justifying, therefore, is not a matter of one value clearly prevailing over the other, but is rather a matter of developing the significance of the values being dealt with and asking whether Parliament, in its attempt to reconcile competing interests, has achieved a rational and reasonable balance. Proportionality, in the context of Charter analysis, does not mean a perfect solution, as any balance arising from competing interests will involve preferring one value over the other to some extent.

Gonthier J. refers as follows to the difference of the interpretation as regards to category of beneficiaries of the right to vote:[82]

> Para 92 As emerges from the submissions before this Court, there seem generally to be two options available for dealing with the issue at hand. The first, that chosen by the Chief Justice, is to prefer an inclusive approach to democratic participation for serious criminal offenders incarcerated for two years or more. This view locates democratic participation as a central dimension of rehabilitation, insofar as the incarcerated offenders remain citizens with the fullest exercise of their democratic rights. By the same token, the unrestricted franchise enhances democratic legitimacy of government, and confirms or enhances the citizenship or standing of prisoners in society. To do otherwise, it is suggested, undermines the 'dignity' or 'worth' of prisoners. The alternative view, adopted by Parliament, considers that the temporary suspension of the prisoner's right to vote, in fact, enhances the general purposes of the criminal sanction, including rehabilitation. It does so by underlining the importance of civic responsibility and the rule of law. This approach sees the temporary removal of the vote as a deterrent to offending or re-offending and the return of the vote as an inducement to reject further criminal conduct. In withdrawing for a time one expression of political participation concurrently with personal freedom, the significance of both are enhanced. Rather than undermine the dignity or worth of prisoners, the removal of their vote takes seriously the notion that they are free actors and attaches consequences to actions that violate certain core values as expressed in the Criminal Code.

Gonthier J. deals with the influence that the particular theory of political science which is used in order to define the category of beneficiaries of the right to vote will ultimately exercise upon the particular view as regards the justification and the operation of Article 1 CCRF[83] in relation to eventual restriction under Article 3 CCRF.[84] More significant, however, is the use of what might be termed 'competing' political or social theories in the context of proof of concepts in litigation involving the social sciences and notably political theories as rendering almost impossible proof beyond the determination that they are or may be reasonable and have been articulated in a rational manner. Beyond that point, it is impossible to affirm the superiority of one such theory over another or as the learned Chief Justice endeavours to do, reject a competing theory which is reasonable and rational simply as being incorrect because it is different or competing as she does with the position of the Minority. Gonthier J. observes in this regard as follows:[85]

82. *Ibid.*, para. 92.
83. See above footnote for the text of Art. 1 CCRF.
84. See above footnote for the text of Art. 3 CCRF.
85. *Sauvé v Canada* (2002) 3 *SCR* 519, *ibid.*, paras 93, 97 and 98.

Para 93 Both of these approaches, however, entail accepting logically prior political or social philosophies about the nature and content of the right to vote. The former approach, that accepted by the reasons of the Chief Justice, entails accepting a philosophy that preventing criminals from voting does damage to both society and the individual, and undermines prisoners' inherent worth and dignity. The latter approach also entails accepting a philosophy, that not permitting serious incarcerated criminals to vote is a social rejection of serious crime which reflects a moral line which safeguards the social contract and the rule of law and bolsters the importance of the nexus between individuals and the community. Both of these social or political philosophies, however, are aimed at the same goal: that of supporting the fundamental importance of the right to vote itself. Further, both of these social or political philosophies are supported by the practices of the various Canadian provinces, the practices of other liberal democracies, and academic writings. Finally, neither position can be proven empirically – rather, the selection of one over the other is largely a matter of philosophical preference. What is key to my approach is that the acceptance of one or the other of these social or political philosophies dictates much of the constitutional analysis which ensues, since the reasonableness of any limitation upon the right to vote and the appropriateness of particular penal theories and their relation to the right to vote will logically be related to whether or not the justification for that limitation is based upon an 'acceptable' social or political philosophy.

...

Para 97 There is a flaw in an analysis which suggests that because one social or political philosophy can be justified, it necessarily means that another social or political philosophy is not justified: in other words, where two social or political philosophies exist, it is not by approving one that you disprove the other. Differences in social or political philosophy, which result in different justifications for limitations upon rights, are perhaps inevitable in a pluralist society. That having been said, it is only those limitations which are not reasonable or demonstrably justified in a free and democratic society which are unconstitutional. Therefore, the most significant analysis in this case is the examination of the social or political philosophy underpinning the justification advanced by the Crown. This is because it will indicate whether the limitation of the right to vote is reasonable and is based upon a justification which is capable of being demonstrated in a free and democratic society. If the choice made by Parliament is such, then it ought to be respected. The range of choices made by different legislatures in different jurisdictions, which I will review below, supports the view that there are many resolutions to the particular issue at bar which are reasonable; it demonstrates that there are many possible rational balances.

Para 98 The role of this Court, when faced with competing social or political philosophies and justifications dependent on them, is therefore to define the parameters within which the acceptable reconciliation of competing values lies. The decision before this Court is therefore not whether or not Parliament has made a proper policy decision, but whether or not the policy position chosen is an acceptable choice amongst those permitted under the Charter. This was the view advanced by Linden J.A. for the Court of Appeal ([2000] 2 F.C. 117, at para. 60).

In the following passages Gonthier J. clearly indicates that there is more than one aspect, namely, that of punishment, which is involved in the temporary disenfranchisement which effectively must be considered under Article 1 CCRF:[86] this is, in the

86. For convenience the text is cited again: 'Constitution Act 1982, Part I, Canadian Charter of Rights and Freedoms, Whereas Canada is founded upon principles that recognize the supremacy

instant case, 'the promotion of civic responsibility' through the sending of a message to the prisoners from the population generally by means of temporary disenfranchisement.[87]

> Para 180 The salutary effects in the case at bar are particularly difficult to demonstrate by empirical evidence given their largely symbolic nature. On this point, I note that it would be difficult for the Crown to justify all penal sanctions, if scientific proof was the standard which was required. I discussed this above, and would like to reiterate that many core values of the Canadian community might suffer if put to such a test. In such cases, the weighty merit of the objectives themselves must be considered with the social, legislative and factual context in mind. In this case, a central dimension of the context is Parliament's choice of a particular social or political philosophy on which the justification for the limitation of the right is based. As Bastarache J. noted in Thomson Newspapers, supra, at para. 125, this third phase of the proportionality prong of the Oakes test is unique in that it provides an opportunity to assess, in light of the practical and contextual details which are elucidated in the first and second stages, whether the benefits which accrue from the limitation are proportional to its deleterious effects as measured by the values underlying the Charter.
> 181 Linden J.A. found that the primary salutary effect was that the legislation, intrinsically, expresses societal values in relation to serious criminal behaviour and the right to vote in our society. He thus concluded, at para. 137, that it has more than symbolic effect: This legislation sends a message signalling Canadian values, to the effect that those people who are found guilty of the most serious crimes will, while separated from society, lose access to one of the levers of electoral power. This is an extremely important message, one which is not sent by incarceration alone. Incarceration is essentially separation from the community. Incarceration alone signals a denunciation of the offender's anti-societal behaviour and indicates society's hope for rehabilitation through separation from the community. Incarceration by itself, however, leaves those convicted of serious crimes free to exercise all the levers of electoral power open to all law-abiding citizens. This maintains a political parity between those convicted of society's worst crimes and their victims. Disqualification from voting, however, signals a denunciation of the criminal's anti-societal behaviour and sends the message that those people convicted of causing the worst forms of indignity to others will be deprived of one aspect of the political equality of citizens – the right to vote. It can be said that, in this context, 'kindness toward the criminal can be an act of cruelty toward his victims, and the larger community'. [Footnotes omitted; emphasis in original.]

---

of God and the rule of law: GUARANTEE OF RIGHTS AND FREEDOMS 1. The *Canadian Charter of Rights and Freedoms* guarantees the rights and freedoms set out in it subject only to such reasonable limits prescribed by law as can be demonstrably justified in a free and democratic society. FUNDAMENTAL FREEDOMS: 2. Everyone has the following fundamental freedoms: (*a*) freedom of conscience and religion; (*b*) freedom of thought, belief, opinion and expression, including freedom of the press and other media of communication; (*c*) freedom of peaceful assembly; and (*d*) freedom of association. DEMOCRATIC RIGHTS 3. Every citizen of Canada has the right to vote in an election of members of the House of Commons or of a legislative assembly and to be qualified for membership therein. http://laws-lois.justice.gc.ca/eng/const/page-15.html http, date on which last consulted: 1.11.2013.

87. *Sauvé v Canada* (2002) 3 *SCR* 519, paras 180-182.

Linden J.A. suggested that value emerges from the signal or message that those who commit serious crimes will temporarily lose one aspect of the political equality of citizens. Therefore, 'the enactment of the measure is itself a salutary effect' (para. 138). I agree. As can be drawn out from the overview of the arguments which were placed before this Court, one is forced to either accept the objectives, and consequently grant them weight at this stage of the analysis, or discount them. I am of the view that the salutary effects and objectives must be granted the respect of this Court:

> 182 The signalling function of s. 51(e) is highly important. Linden J.A., below, noted at paras. 139 and 141 of his reasons, that: 'The signal itself is a double signal, a message about the community's view of crime and a repudiation of the indignity perpetrated on victims of crime. Where someone, by committing a serious crime, evinces contempt for our basic societal values, their right to vote may be properly suspended. Indeed, not to do so undermines our democratic values ...' In context, this legislation puts forward a statement of principles by which Canadians live. That is a valid role which Parliament may play. The formal enactment of these principles itself is as important as any tangible effects that the law may have. [Footnotes omitted.] This view is supported by the Crown's experts, Professors Pangle and Manfredi. Professor Pangle emphasized that the provision in question reflects a signal to society and to offenders that the commission of serious criminal acts will result in the loss of a dimension of political participation. Professor Manfredi developed the argument, employed above, that there is something important about the nexus between the exercise of the vote by citizens and the responsibilities and duties inherent in citizenship. Also as reflected upon above, the provision reflects society's desire to promote the rule of law and civic responsibility, which are inherent in and required by the rule of law and the notion of the social contract. This provision draws a line which sends a strong and beneficial moral message to society as a whole, the message that crime will not be tolerated. As was said in Sharpe, supra, by L'Heureux-Dubé and Bastarache JJ. and myself, at para. 191: 'The Court should be particularly sensitive to the legitimate role of government in legislating with respect to our social values'.

As regards the matter of whether or not the method of applying the temporary disenfranchisement, namely, based solely upon the length of the sentence is irrational and therefore disproportionate Gonthier J. observes that as a matter of evidence given that one is dealing with matters involving social behaviour and the social sciences the standards used to evaluate evidence in the precise 'hard' sciences cannot be utilized in matters involving the social sciences. The rational connection necessary to establish proportionality must be considered in the following manner as well be seen from the paragraph below from the judgment of Gonthier J.:

> [r]ational connection is to be established, upon a civil standard, through reason, logic or simply common sense.

The learned judge observes as follows:

> Para 150[88] In the case at bar, as discussed above, a causal relationship between disenfranchising prisoners and this Court has unanimously agreed that '[r]ational connection is to be established, upon a civil standard, through reason, logic or

88. *Ibid.*, para. 150.

> simply common sense': RJR-MacDonald, supra, per La Forest J., at para. 86, McLachlin J., at paras. 156-58, and Iacobucci J., at para. 184; referred to in Thomson Newspapers, supra, at para. 39. The existence of scientific proof is simply of probative value in supporting this reason, logic or common sense. The objectives approved of above is not empirically demonstrable. However, this Court has clearly stated that Parliament must be afforded a margin of appreciation in regard to legitimate objectives which may, nonetheless, be based upon somewhat inconclusive social science evidence: Sopinka J. in Butler, supra, at pp. 502-3. I offer two examples: in Butler, Sopinka J. found, at p. 502, that it was 'reasonable to presume' that there was a causal relationship between obscenity and harm to society, and in Ross v. New Brunswick School District No. 15, [1996] 1 S.C.R. 825, at para. 101, La Forest J. stated that it was 'reasonable to anticipate' that there was a causal link between anti-Semitic activity by school teachers outside school and discriminatory attitudes within school. Thus, it is clear that this Court's approach to this dimension of the test demands not the strongest connection, the most convincing rational connection, but a logical or rational connection.

Dealing more precisely with the nature of the evidence which can be tendered and as to whether symbolic and abstract ideas can be legitimately utilized in establishing the rational connection, Gonthier J. replies in the affirmative: namely that such ideas would be presented in the context of expert evidence and that at the end of the day the evaluation must take into account the notion that there can, subsequent to establishment of a rational connection, several competing ideas which are equally valid:

> Para 99[89] A subject that is related to and follows from the above discussion concerning the evaluation of competing social or political philosophies is the role of symbolic arguments in Charter adjudication. In the context of the Charter analysis, it is important not to downplay the importance of symbolic or abstract arguments. Symbolic or abstract arguments cannot be dismissed outright by virtue of their symbolism: many of the great principles, the values upon which society rests, could be said to be symbolic. In fact, one of the more important dimensions of s. 3[90] of the Charter is clearly its symbolism: the affirmation of political equality reflected in all citizens being guaranteed the right to vote, subject only to reasonable limits prescribed by law that can be demonstrably justified in a free and democratic society. The case at bar concerns debates about symbolism, as the arguments involved relate to abstract concepts such as democracy, rights, punishment, the rule of law and civic responsibility. To choose a narrow reading of rights over the objectives advanced by Parliament is to choose one set of symbols over another.
>
> 100 In her reasons, the Chief Justice claims at para. 16 that Parliament is relying on 'lofty objectives', and suggests at para. 23 that the presence of 'symbolic and abstract' objectives is problematic. However, the reasons of the Chief Justice have the very same objective – to protect the value of the right to vote and the rule of law – and rely on equally vague concepts. Breaking down the meaning and value of the right to vote, one is unavoidably led to abstract and symbolic concepts such as the rule of law, the legitimacy of law and government, and the meaning of democracy. The Chief Justice discusses these concepts at length, along with theories of individual motivation. For instance, relying on the philosopher J. S. Mill, she suggests at para. 38 that '[t]o deny prisoners the right to vote is to lose an

89. *Ibid.*, paras 99-101.
90. See above footnote for the text of Art. 3 CCRF.

> important means of teaching them democratic values and social responsibility'. This type of statement is as symbolic, abstract and philosophical as the government's claim that denying serious incarcerated criminals the right to vote will strengthen democratic values and social responsibility.
> 101 Most of the evidence in this case is that of expert opinions on the matters of political theory, moral philosophy, philosophy of law, criminology, correctional policy, and penal theory. I would suggest distinguishing between two kinds of expert evidence in this case. First, there is very limited social scientific evidence, e.g. in the field of criminology, that seeks to establish the practical or empirical consequences of maintaining or lifting the ban on prisoner voting. Second, there is copious expert testimony in the nature of legal and political philosophy. I do not think that the Court need necessarily defer to this second type of expertise, or take into account the 'skill' and 'reputation' of the experts in weighing this evidence (as the trial judge purported to do at [1996] 1 F.C. 857, at pp. 865-66). First, most if not all of the philosophers or theorists on which these experts rely never in fact even addressed the specific issue of prisoner enfranchisement or disenfranchisement. Second, legal theory expert testimony in this context essentially purports to justify axiomatic principles. Therefore, these arguments are either persuasive or not. In this context, it is appropriate for courts to look not only to such theoretical arguments but also beyond, to factors such as the extent of public debate on an issue, the practices of other liberal democracies and, most especially, to the reasoned view of our democratically elected Parliament.

Gonthier J. then seeks to establish that 'serious crime reflects contempt for the rule of law and a rejection of the basis for the operation of a free and democratic society. This, if it is symbolic or abstract, reflects a core value of the community, a value that is reflected throughout the Criminal Code and in the provision before us today. As will be argued below, this value is based on a reasonable social or political philosophy.' Once again, for Gonthier J., the bottom line is that:

> Para 103[91] Aforementioned philosophy is an entirely rational and reasonable social philosophy and that it should be considered as a competing philosophy to that presented by the learned Chief Justice. A key justification before this Court, to be analysed in depth below, is that serious crime reflects contempt for the rule of law and a rejection of the basis for the operation of a free and democratic society. This, if it is symbolic or abstract, reflects a core value of the community, a value that is reflected throughout the Criminal Code and in the provision before us today. As will be argued below, this value is based on a reasonable social or political philosophy. Temporarily removing the vote from serious criminal offenders while they are incarcerated is both symbolic and concrete in effect. Returning it on being released from prison is the same.

In large measure it is necessary to conceive of the disenfranchisement as representing not per se punishment but rather the expression of public obloquy which attaches to those who have violated the canons of good citizenship which is necessary to sustain a democratic society. The civil expression of obloquy, the temporary disenfranchisement, attaches to the penal sentence of incarceration which itself is calculated on an individual case by basis to any grave cases of penal violation. In the course of his evaluation the learned judge specifically adverts to the use of evidence and more

91. *Sauvé v Canada* (2002) 3 *SCR* 519, *supra*, para. 105.

specifically to the type of evidence required in the instant situation given that precise scientific measurement is impossible but such does not prevent nevertheless the use of rational arguments to establish a link notably of proportionality of the attachment of this civil expression of societal disapproval to all those cases of grave criminal breach where the sentences had been necessarily individually decided and calculated.

Gonthier J. then observes, overall, that the restriction, contrary to the learned McLachlin C.J. of temporary disenfranchisement is proportionate in that the temporary disenfranchisement is related to the sentences which are, themselves, individually imposed in relation to each prisoner:

> Para 171[92] The approach taken by Linden J.A. for the majority of the Federal Court of Appeal below is sound. He held that the current provision was minimally impairing for a number of reasons: only 'serious offenders', as determined by Parliament, are subject to disenfranchisement; accused persons and those convicted but out on bail are permitted to vote; those out on parole are permitted to vote; and the provision acts proportionately since it is individualized insofar as those with longer sentences will be disenfranchised longer. The provision is reasonably tailored insofar as disenfranchisement reflects the length of the sentence and actual incarceration, which, in turn, reflects the seriousness of the crime perpetrated and the intended progress towards the ultimate goals of rehabilitation and reintegration.

Gonthier J. Concludes, finally, that the temporary disenfranchisement which is visited upon incarcerated prisoners of two or more years is effectively reasonable and therefore proportional in relation to Article 1 CCRF:[93]

> Para 188[94] When the objectives and the salutary effects are viewed in the totality of the context, they outweigh the temporary disenfranchisement of the serious criminal offender which mirrors the fact of his or her incarceration. In my view, Parliament has enacted a law which is reasonable, and which is justified in a free and democratic society.

§3.05 CONCLUSION

Overall, it is submitted that the judgment and particularly that of the learned Minority, is based upon evidence as regards the reasonability of the application of temporary disenfranchisement which potentially undermines the construction of Article 3 CCRF[95] at least as argued by the Majority. Arguably, the excessively wide interpretation of the category of beneficiaries of the right to vote led to difficulties as regards the operation of Article 1 CCRF[96] which regularizes breaches of the rights contained in the Charter. As specifically noted by Gonthier J. the unjustified greater importance given by McLachlin C.J. to the right to vote appears to have affected the operation of Article 1

92. *Ibid.*, para. 171.
93. See above footnote for the text of Art. 1 CCRF.
94. *Sauvé v Canada* (2002) 3 *SCR* 519, *ibid.*, para. 188.
95. See above footnote for the text of Art. 3 CCRF.
96. See above footnote for the text of Art. 1 CCRF.

CCRF[97] specifically in the sense of the type of evidence which was or is acceptable in the interpretation thereof. The learned Chief Justice having admitted that empirical evidence is not the sole type of evidence which is acceptable, then went on to reject the evidence recognized by the Minority and tendered as regards the proportionality of the temporary disenfranchisement, on the basis that it was symbolic and vague. This is inconsistent with the actual type of evidence used by the learned Chief Justice in order to advance the position of the learned Majority which is based upon an unproved special importance allegedly possessed by the right of enfranchisement. Ultimately, by its consistency to the method and scope of proof agreed by both sides, the judgment of the learned Minority written by Gonthier J. is to be preferred to that of the learned Majority wherein the scope of the right to vote remains unproved. Significantly, the position of the learned Minority permitted a wide interpretation of Article 1 CCRF[98] so as to include as the objective of Article 53 (e) of the Canada Elections Act (RSC 1985)[99] the following: namely, that the disenfranchisement can be conceived of in the context of several factors as endeavouring to achieve several functions: not only punishment and retribution but declaratory and denunciatory the latter perceived as being ultimately a civil expression of obloquy in the form of disenfranchisement. The civil deprivation of the citizen's right to vote is designed, arguably, to achieve the need of society at large to express its moral opprobrium as regards the failure of those incarcerated to have displayed good citizenship. Rather, the prisoners have violated the rules adopted by the Parliament and undermined the operation of democracy. It is therefore, reasonable, in those circumstances, argues the learned Minority in the speech of Gonthier J., to attach this civil expression of disapproval expressed collectively through an automatic attachment to any criminal sentence resulting in

97. *Ibid.*

98. For convenience the text is cited again: 'Constitution Act 1982, PART I, Canadian Charter of Rights and Freedoms, Whereas Canada is founded upon principles that recognize the supremacy of God and the rule of law: GUARANTEE OF RIGHTS AND FREEDOMS 1. The *Canadian Charter of Rights and Freedoms* guarantees the rights and freedoms set out in it subject only to such reasonable limits prescribed by law as can be demonstrably justified in a free and democratic society. FUNDAMENTAL FREEDOMS: 2. Everyone has the following fundamental freedoms: (*a*) freedom of conscience and religion; (*b*) freedom of thought, belief, opinion and expression, including freedom of the press and other media of communication; (*c*) freedom of peaceful assembly; and (*d*) freedom of association. DEMOCRATIC RIGHTS 3. Every citizen of Canada has the right to vote in an election of members of the House of Commons or of a legislative assembly and to be qualified for membership therein. 'http://laws-lois.justice.gc.ca/eng/const/page-15.html, date on which last consulted: 1.11.2013.

99. Prior to amendment Art.53 (e) Canada Elections Act (1985) provided: Section 51(*e*) of the *Canada Elections Act* denies the right to vote to '[e]very person who is imprisoned in a correctional institution serving a sentence of two years or more.' The constitutionality of s. 51(*e*) was challenged on the grounds that it contravenes ss. 3 and 15 (1) of the *Canadian Charter of Rights and Freedoms* and is not demonstrably justified under s. 1. In the Federal Court, Trial Division, the Crown conceded that s. 51(*e*) infringes the right to vote guaranteed by s. 3 of the *Charter* and the trial judge found that the infringement was not justified under s. 1 of the *Charter*. The majority of the Federal Court of Appeal set aside the decision and upheld the constitutionality of s. 51 (*e*). The court held that the infringement of s. 3 was justifiable in a free and democratic society and that s. 51(*e*) did not infringe the equality rights guaranteed by s. 15 (1) of the *Charter*. *Held* (L'Heureux-Dubé, Gonthier, Major and Bastarache JJ. dissenting): The appeal should be allowed.

incarceration for two or more years. This is, of course, in the procedural context where the criminal sentence involving incarceration which itself is calculated entirely on an individual basis. The incarceration and the temporary disenfranchisement serve different purposes which are reasonable. Therefore, it is equally reasonable to apply them differently: the criminal incarceration is imposed subsequent to an individual assessment and the expression of societal obloquy attaches automatically to only those sentences where two or more years have been imposed by the court on the prisoner. This aforementioned analysis has been proved by logical analysis and political theories to the level of the balance of probabilities but not by means of empirical data which in the instant case is impossible given that the matters concerned, involve the social science and measurements are difficult therein. Accordingly, in so far as the civil obloquy attaches only to the most grave of the sentences which have been imposed subsequent to individual determination of the prisoners by the Court and is removed automatically upon release in those circumstances the disenfranchisement can be said to be proportionate and therefore a reasonable restriction upon the right to vote as provided within Article 1 CCRF[100] and Article 3 CCRF.[101] Once again, the most important matter for the purposes of this analysis is the degree of proof considered by the SCC notably at the hearing of Federal Court[102] not formally considered herein.

At this point it is appropriate to commence an examination of certain judgments which have been given by the CJ, the GC and the ECtHR. The choice of the judgments has been made primarily on their ability to demonstrate the operation of the respective courts as regards their failure to use expert evidence in specific legal areas: student rights, competition law and prisoner voting rights. It is felt that there is a difference between the types of expert evidence which can be used by the courts in the following sense: perhaps the use of expert economic evidence has become potentially more acceptable during the past two decades as regards European Competition law.[103] It is submitted however, that the field involving student rights under the TFEU can and should equally be considered an area appropriate for the use of expert evidence given that much of the EU legislation[104] is in truth, contains words, at least in English, which may have an technical meaning[105] in addition to ordinary meaning appropriate for the opinion of experts. Further, the judgments of the USSC, the SCC and the BCSC indicate that notably in the field of human rights and in particular prisoner voting rights, expert evidence is considered by those respective courts both as tendered by sworn witnesses and through the form of judicial notice. This is, as will be seen, in stark contrast to the

100. See above footnote for the text of Art. 1 CCRF.
101. See above footnote for the text of Art. 3 CCRF.
102. Wetston J. Federal Court, Trial Division (1996) 1 FC 857.
103. This would be attributable to the writings, in particular, of Judge R. Joliet and Prof V Korah whose work will be examined in a subsequent chapter herein.
104. S Prechal, *Directives in EC Law*, 2nd edn (Oxford, OUP, 2005) provides a thorough and sound discussion of the interpretation of directives in EU law.
105. R Sullivan, *Sullivan and Driedger on the Construction of Statutes*, 4th edn (Vancouver, Butterworths, 2002), *supra*, Chapter 3, 39-72.

judgments in those fields involving the CJ, the GC and above all the ECtHR. Given that, as has been observed earlier in this analysis, the rules of civil procedure of the CJ, the GC and the ECtHR do permit these courts to introduce expert evidence[106] the scope of which is, as has been noted earlier herein, appropriately wide, in the same fields as those in which the Canadian and US courts made their judgments the following conclusion may be drawn: that in truth, by failing to use the rules to introduce expert evidence the aforementioned CJ, GC[107] and ECtHR have failed to carry out their duty as established by *Kraska v Switzerland*[108] which was discussed earlier.

106. B Vesterdorf 'Economics in Court' in M Johansson, N Wahl and U Bernitz (eds) *Liber Amicorum in Honour of Sven Norberg* (Brussels, Bruylant, 2006), *supra*.
107. E Barbier de La Serre and A-L Sibony, 'Expert Evidence before the EC Courts' (2008) *CMLRev* (45) 4, *supra*, at 941.
108. *Kraska v Switzerland* (1993) *EHRR* (18) 188, *supra*, para. 30.

CHAPTER 4

The CJ and GC Involving Primarily pursuant to Article 267 TFEU References Citizenship and Competition Law and One Direct Action for Non-contractual Liability against the Commission

§4.01 INTRODUCTION

At this point, it is useful to consider certain judgments, not necessarily the most recent, rendered by the CJ and the GC during the past forty years. The EU substantive law areas of these judgments range from education and citizen rights to economic rights which are involved in competition, the prohibition of antitrust agreements and the abuse of dominant position. Overall, the primary procedural element which differentiates all of the herein considered judgments of the CJ and the GC from those of the USSC, SCC and the BCSC analysed in the previous chapter is the following: namely, the overall absence of any use of expert evidence in the interpretation of the TFEU despite the fact the rules of procedure, as examined earlier, demonstrate the capacity of the CJ and the GC to appoint experts if necessary of their own initiative. It is submitted that the absence of expert evidence as regards the interpretation of the technical and ordinary meaning of words which compose the TFEU (and the ECHR as will be seen in the subsequent chapter) overall appears to have the following effect: namely, the complete violation of the procedural principle of rectitude of decision established by Bentham considered in earlier chapters herein. This is in the sense that by reason of the evidential situation the scope of the meaning of the words which compose the aforementioned treaties is incorrectly interpreted. The violation of this principle sounds in a contravention of

Article 6 (1) ECHR as interpreted in Kraska[1] which encompasses, it is submitted, the underlying principle of the Rule of Law. In short, most frequently the scope of the rights enunciated by the TFEU (and the ECHR as will be seen subsequently) is too widely interpreted and any restrictions thereupon are, as previously noted, by reason of the deficit in expert evidence, interpreted, too narrowly. In brief, interpretative principles such as the teleological method coupled with a narrow interpretation of the derogations necessarily lead to profoundly unjustifiable and incorrect interpretations and, therefore, to catastrophic results. This of course led to the iconic misinterpretation by the CJ, the GC and the European Commission of, notably, Article 101 TFEU (ex Article 85 EEC): that is, an unjustifiably wide interpretation devoid of any basis in economic expert evidence of the prohibition contained in ex Article 85 (1) EEC. In truth, this evidentially defective statutory interpretation led on the one hand, to the voiding of an excessively large number of business agreements pursuant to ex Article 85 (2) EEC and on the other, to very limited derogations pursuant to ex Article 85 (3). This particular violation of the principle of rectitude of decision and, therefore, of ECHR Article 6 (1) was ultimately at least in part, corrected as a result of vigorous academic criticism.[2] Nevertheless, it is appropriate to commence the instant analysis with a judgment of the CJ drawn from the field of education as provided by the TFEU.

§4.02 BIDAR[3] SUMMARY

The first preliminary reference to the CJ from a national court (UK) to be considered, herewith, is that of Bidar.[4] This case involved the financing of education expenses incurred by an EU student, Bidar, in the UK, pursuant to interpretations of Article 18 TFEU (ex Article 12 EC) and Article 21 TFEU (ex Article 18 EC)[5] coupled with Directives 1993/96, 90/365, 90/364 and 2004/38. The facts of the case briefly stated were as follows: Bidar, a French national, entered the territory of the UK, accompanying his mother who was to undergo medical treatment there. In the UK, he lived with his grandmother, as her dependent, and pursued and completed his secondary education without ever having recourse to social assistance. He then started a course in economics at the University College London. While Bidar received assistance with

1. *Kraska v Switzerland*, Application No. 13942/88, Judgement of 19 April 1993 (1993) *EHRR* (18) 188 at para. 30. 'It falls to the Court to decide whether the contested proceedings considered as a whole were fair within the meaning of the Convention. The effect of Article 6 para. 1 (Article 6-1) is, inter alia, to place the 'tribunal' under a duty to conduct a proper examination of the submissions, arguments and evidence adduced by the parties, without prejudice to its assessment of whether they are relevant to its decision (see, among other authorities, mutatis mutandis, the *Barberà, Messegué and Jabardo v Spain* judgment of 6 December 1988, Series A no. 146, 31, para. 68). It has to be determined whether this condition was satisfied in the instant case.'
2. See in particular V Korah 'EEC Competition – Legal Form or Economic Efficiency' (1986) *Current Legal Problems* (39) 85-109.
3. *Bidar v London Borough of Ealing*, Case C-209/03 (2005) *ECR* I 2119.
4. *Ibid.*
5. It is to be noted that the quotations from the various authors cited in this section and separate analysis afferent thereto retain the original EC numbering which was converted by the TFEU into the following equivalences: Art 18-25 TFEU absorb ex Art 12-22 EC; Art 18 TFEU = Art 12 EC; Art 20-21 TFEU = ex Art 17-18 EC.

respect to tuition fees, his application for financial assistance to cover his maintenance costs, in the form of a student loan, was fused on the ground that he was not settled in the UK. He brought proceedings against that refusal.

Hailbronner[6] observes the following as regards the legal context of the judgment in Bidar:

> The law of the European Community was based on the distinction between economically active Union citizens and non-economically active citizens. The latter category not covered by the freedom of movement provisions of the Treaty until the introduction of Union citizenship into the Treaty did not have an independent right to entry and residence. The extension of free movement rights to non-economically active Union citizens was one of the major conditions to 'liberate' the Community from its economic preoccupation and to prepare the way for a community of citizens. Only after more than ten years of protracted negotiations among the members States shortly before the introduction of Union citizenship into the Maastricht Treaty could agreement be reached on the extension of freedom of movement for students retired persons and other Union citizens by the directives of 1991 and 1992. However all three directives took great care to provide residence rights only for those who could support themselves in order to exclude risks for the social systems in the Member States as a result of immigration of persons who might become a burden on the social assistance systems of their host Member States. Effectively, all three directives took great care to provide residence rights only for those who could support themselves in order to exclude risks for the social systems in the Member States as a result of immigration of persons who might become a burden on the social assistance systems of their host Member States. The debate was clearly focussed on the concern of some Member States hat due to the substantial differences in the social systems of Member States the extension of the free movement without additional requirements might create problems and provoke a social welfare immigration.

Hailbronner[7] specifically makes the following observations as to the extension of jurisprudence through statutory interpretation of the economic rights available to non-economically independent citizens:

> The pattern changed however fundamentally with the Court's use of the concept of Union citizenship enshrined in Art 17-21 of the EC Treaty establishing the

6. K Hailbronner, 'Union Citizenship and Access to Social Benefits' (2005) *CMLRev* (42)1245 at 1245; M Dougan, 'Fees, Grants, Loans and Dole Cheques: Who Covers the Costs of Migrant Education within the EU' (2005) *CMLRev* (42) 943; C Tomuschat 'Sala' (2000) *CMLRev* (37) 449; H Wallace & M Pollak (eds) *Policy Making in the European* Union (Oxford, OUP, 2000); T Hartley 'La libre circulation des Etudiants en droit communatuaire' (1989) *CDE* 325; S O'Leary 'The principle of equal treatment on grounds of nationality in Art 12 EC: A Lucrative Source of Rights for Member State nationals?' in A Dashwood & S O'Leary (Eds), *The Principle of Equal Treatment in EC Law* (Sweet & Maxwell, London, 1997); M Dougan & E Spaventa 'Educating Rudy and the (Non) English Patient: A Double Bill on Residency Rights under Art 18 EC' (2003) *ELR* (28) 699; European Commission, *The Role of Universities in the Europe of Knowledge*, COM (2003) 58 Final; European Commission, Commission Staff Working Paper, Progress Towards the Lisbon Objectives in Education and Training (2005 Report) SEC (2005) 419 SEC (2005) 419; C Barnard 'EU Citizenship and the Principle of Solidarity', in M Dougan & E Spaventa (Eds), *Social Welfare and EU Law* (Oxford, Hart Publishing, 2005).
7. K Hailbronner, 'Union Citizenship and Access to Social Benefits' (2005) *CMLRev* (42)1245, *supra*, at 1247.

European Community in combination with Art 12 EC. Although Art 18 EC provided a right of Union citizens only ' subject to the limitation and conditions' laid down in this and by measures adopted to give it effect; the Court made clear that it was determined to use Union citizenship as an instrument to overcome the existing basic distinction between economically active and non economically active Union citizens. In Sala (Note 8 Case C-85/96 (1998) Maria Martina Sala (1998) ECR I 2691) the Court for the first time used the Community citizenship in order to circumvent the specific limitations in secondary Community law on access to social benefits although such conditions and limitations had been recognized by Art 18 EC. In Sala a Spanish national who had for some time worked and resided in Germany and subsequently lost her job and become permanently dependent upon social assistance claimed child care allowance. Until the Sala case certain conditions for the application of the regulations were applied in order to find out whether an individual in relying upon the equal treatment clause could be considered as a worker/employee. If this was not the case union citizen could not rely upon the general principle of non discrimination to grant unlimited equal treatment with regard to social benefits. The Court departing from its previous jurisprudence decided that social benefits fall within the scope of application of the treat. Therefore, the mere fact of establishing a lawful residence in the Court's view entitled Mrs Sala to claim equal access to a child raising allowance.......the major legal instrument used by the Court to overcome the restrictive attitude of EU Member States as to residence rights of non-economically active Union citizens who might become dependent on social welfare payments is a combination of Union citizenship and equal treatment even though however according to Art 12 the latter is granted only 'within the scope of application of this treaty.'

As regards specifically Bidar,[8] in this reference made by the High Court of England pursuant to Article 267 TFEU (ex Article 234 EC), the CJ (ex ECJ) was asked to answer, in particular, the following questions:

Question 1
Para 28 By its first question, the national court asks essentially whether, in the present state of Community law, assistance to students in higher education intended to cover their maintenance costs, in the form of a subsidised loan or a grant, falls outside the scope of the Treaty, in particular the first paragraph of Article 12 EC.

Question 2
By its second question, the national court seeks to know the criteria which a national court must apply to determine whether the conditions of granting assistance to cover the maintenance costs of students are based on objective considerations independent of nationality.

With respect in particular to Question 1, the Community legislation which required statutory interpretation was as follows:

Firstly, the first paragraph of Article 12 EC provides:
Within the scope of application of this Treaty, and without prejudice to any special provisions contained therein, any discrimination on grounds of nationality shall be prohibited.

8. *Bidar v London Borough of Ealing*, Case C-209/03 (2005) *ECR* I 2119, *supra*.

> Secondly, Article 18(1) EC which reads as follows:
> Every citizen of the Union shall have the right to move and reside freely within the territory of the Member States, subject to the limitations and conditions laid down in this Treaty and by the measures adopted to give it effect.
>
> Thirdly, Article 149 EC which provides:
> 1. The Community shall contribute to the development of quality education by encouraging cooperation between Member States and, if necessary, by supporting and supplementing their action, while fully respecting the responsibility of the Member States for the content of teaching and the organisation of education systems and their cultural and linguistic diversity.
> 2. Community action shall be aimed at:
> - developing the European dimension in education, particularly through the teaching and dissemination of the languages of the Member States,
> - encouraging mobility of students and teachers, by encouraging inter alia, the academic recognition of diplomas and periods of study,
> - promoting cooperation between educational establishments,
> - developing exchanges of information and experience on issues common to the education systems of the Member States,
> - encouraging the development of youth exchanges and of exchanges of socio-educational instructors,
> - encouraging the development of distance education.
> 4. In order to contribute to the achievement of the objectives referred to in this Article, the Council:
> - acting in accordance with the procedure referred to in Article 251, after consulting the Economic and Social Committee and the Committee of the Regions, shall adopt incentive measures, excluding any harmonisation of the laws and regulations of the Member States,
> - acting by a qualified majority on a proposal from the Commission, shall adopt recommendations.

In particular, the relevant legislation to be interpreted included the following restrictions:

> Article 3 of Directive 93/96[9] provides:
> This Directive shall not establish any entitlement to the payment of maintenance grants by the host Member State on the part of students benefiting from the right of residence.

The national legislation[10] established that in short, a student who could not establish that he was 'settled' in the United Kingdom within the meaning of the Immigration Act

9. Council Directive 93/96/EEC of the Council of 29 October 1993 on the right of residence for students. Repealed by: Directive 2004/38/EC of the European Parliament and of the Council of 29 April 2004 on the right of citizens of the Union and their family members to move and reside freely within the territory of the Member States amending Regulation (EEC) 1612/68 and repealing Directives 64/221/EEC, 68/360/EEC, 72/194/EEC, 73/148/EEC, 75/34/EEC, 75/35/EEC, 90/364/EEC, 90/365/EEC and 93/96/EEC.
10. The ECJ notes in *Bidar v London Borough of Ealing*. Case C-209/03 (2005) *ECR* I 2119, *supra*, paras 13-19. 'In England and Wales, financial assistance for students to cover maintenance costs is, under the Education (Student Support) Regulations 2001 ('the Student Support Regulations'),

would not be eligible for a student loan. The applicant Bidar was unable to comply with these requirements.

Following the text of the judgment, the essence of the submissions of the parties, commencing with Mr Bidar, was as follows:

> Para 23: In the proceedings brought by him against that refusal, Mr Bidar submits that, by making the grant of a student loan to a national of a Member State conditional on his being settled in the United Kingdom, the Student Support Regulations introduced discrimination prohibited under Article 12 EC. He submits, in the alternative, that, even if it were accepted that the provision of a grant falls outside the scope of the Treaty, that is not the case with an application for assistance in the form of a subsidised loan.[11]

With respect to the defendant, namely, the United Kingdom the position was as follows:

> Para 24: The Secretary of State for Education and Skills, who is the responsible authority for making the Student Support Regulations, contends, on the other hand, that the provision of assistance for maintenance costs, whether in the form of a grant or a loan, does not fall within the scope of Article 12 EC, as the Court acknowledged in Case 39/86 *Lair* [1988] ECR 3161 and Case 197/86 *Brown* [1988] ECR 3205. Even if such assistance were to fall within the scope of the Treaty, the

provided essentially by means of loans. Para. 13: Under the Student Support Regulations, students who are recipients of a loan receive 75% of the maximum amount of the loan, while the remaining 25% is granted on the basis of the financial position of the student and of his parents or partner. The loan is provided at an interest rate which is linked to the rate of inflation and is therefore below the normal rate for a commercial loan. The loan is repayable after the student completes his studies, provided that he is earning in excess of GBP 10 000. If that is the case, he pays an annual amount equivalent to 9% of the income earned above GBP 10 000, until the loan is repaid in full. Para. 14: Under regulation 4 of the Student Support Regulations, a person is eligible for a student loan for a designated course if he falls within one of the situations mentioned in Schedule 1 to those regulations. Para. 15: Under paragraph 1 of that schedule, a person is eligible to receive a student loan if he is settled in the United Kingdom within the meaning of the Immigration Act 1971 and meets the residence conditions referred to in paragraph 8 of the schedule, namely: (a) he is ordinarily resident in England and Wales on the first day of the first academic year of the course; (b) he has been ordinarily resident throughout the three-year period preceding that day in the United Kingdom and Islands; and (c) his residence in the United Kingdom and Islands has not during any part of that three-year period been wholly or mainly for the purpose of receiving full-time education. Para. 16:As regards migrant workers and members of their families covered by Regulation (EEC) No 1612/68 of the Council of 15 October 1968 on freedom of movement for workers within the Community (OJ, English Special Edition 1968 (II), 475), paragraphs 4 to 6 of Schedule 1 to the Student Support Regulations do not require them to be settled in the United Kingdom and make their eligibility for a student loan subject to the same residence conditions, while considering that they satisfy the condition of ordinary residence in paragraph 8(b) of that schedule from the time when they reside in the European Economic Area. Para. 17: Under the Immigration Act 1971 a person is settled in the United Kingdom if he is ordinarily resident there without being subject to any restriction on the period for which he may remain in the territory. Para.18: However, it is apparent from the case-file that under United Kingdom law a national of another Member State cannot, in his capacity as a student, obtain the status of being settled in the United Kingdom. Para. 19: As regards tuition fees, the Student Support Regulations provide for financial support on the same conditions for nationals of the United Kingdom and those of other Member States.'

11. *Bidar v London Borough of Ealing*. Case C-209/03 (2005) *ECR* I 2119, *supra*, para. 23.

> conditions for granting that assistance would guarantee the existence of a direct link between the recipient of the assistance and the State which finances it.[12]

§4.03 ANALYSIS OF THE JUDGMENT

The CJ held, as regards the first question, namely, whether the matter of assistance to students 'in higher education intended to cover their maintenance costs, in the form of a subsidized loan or a grant, falls outside the scope of the Treaty, in particular the first paragraph of Article 12 EC.' the following: the answer to this question involved the interpretation of Article 12 EC (now Article 18 TFEU) which proscribes discrimination on grounds of nationality 'without prejudice to any special provisions contained therein'. It is submitted that overall, the CJ (ex ECJ) utilized a teleological interpretation of Article 12 EC (now Article 18 TFEU), and notably the words 'any discrimination on grounds of nationality shall be prohibited ... and without prejudice to any special provisions' in order to read down[13] restrictions which exist both in Article 12 EC (now Article 18 TFEU) and in Article 18 EC (now Article 21 TFEU). These restrictions, particularly in Article 18EC (now Article 21 TFEU), concern the words: 'subject to the limitations and conditions laid down in this Treaty and by the measures adopted to give it effect'. Arguably, therefore, the effect of such a reading down of the exceptions is to expand the meaning of the words contained in Article 18EC (Article 21 TFEU). Further, it is clear that the CJ treated the words in Article 12 EC (now Article 18 TFEU) and Article 18 EC (now Article 21 TFEU) as words with ordinary meaning as opposed to words with technical meaning: that is, the CJ (ex ECJ) at no time sought to establish the technical meaning of the words in Article 12 EC (now Article 18 TFEU) and Article 18 EC (Article 21 TFEU) notably, by means of expert evidence introduced either by judicial notice of the wide sort used by Davis,[14] or by means of expert evidence subject to cross-examination led by the parties. In truth, this expansion of the scope of the meaning of the words in Article 12 EC (now Article 18 TFEU) and Article 18 EC (now Article 21 TFEU) cannot be related to or justified by means of any expert opinion or

12. *Ibid.*
13. R Sullivan, *Sullivan and Driedger on the Construction of Statutes*, 4th edn (Vancouver, Butterworths, 2002), *supra*, at 370: 'Reading down is a technique used by courts to give effect to the presumptions of compliance with jurisdictional limits and constitutional norms. In reading down the potential scope of legislation is narrowed to exclude applications that are grammatically possible but would entail invalidity. ... When reading down is used as an interpretive tool, it narrows the scope of legislation without giving the government an opportunity to justify a broader application. For this reason the technique should not be used in interpretation unless the narrow interpretation is appropriate.' By parity of reasoning mutatis mutandis the expansion of the scope of application due to reading down of exceptions and conditions which otherwise would narrow its application, must be 'appropriate' to the domaine of application of a statute particularly when the teleological method of interpretation is used and based exclusively upon the ordinary as opposed to the technical meaning of the words contained notably in the exceptions and conditions. It is clear that the interpretation not only of the ordinary meaning but also the technical meaning will have an effect in addition to the purpose of the statute upon the extent to which its scope may be modified through a wide or narrow interpretation of the wording of the conditions and exceptions.
14. KC Davis, 'Judicial Notice' (1955) *Columbia Law Review* (55) (7) 945, *supra*, passim.

indeed any evidence including very detailed logical or semantic analysis). Therefore, the statutory interpretation constitutes an unjustifiable interpretation in violation of both the principle of rectitude of decision and Article 6 (1) ECHR. Thereby, this interpretation lacks credibility and above all reasonableness such that pursuant to the analysis of Sullivan[15] it can be described, therefore, as absurd. It is submitted that normally, were a technical meaning to have been given to those words, in standard

15. R Sullivan, *Sullivan and Driedger on the Construction of Statutes*, 4th edn (Vancouver, Butterworths, 2002), *supra*, at 235: 'When a court is called on to interpret legislation it is not engaged in an academic exercise. Interpretation involves the application of legislation to facts in a way that affects the well-being of individuals and communities for better or worse. Not surprisingly, the courts are interested in knowing what the consequences will be and judging whether they are acceptable. Consequences judged to be good are presumed to be intended and generally are regarded as part of the legislative purpose. Consequences judged to be contrary to accepted norms of justice and reasonableness are labelled absurd and are presumed to have been unintended. If adopting an interpretation would lead to absurdity the courts may reject that interpretation in favour of a plausible alternative that avoids the absurdity' and at 236 'The modern understanding of the ... presumption against absurdity includes the following propositions: 1) It is presumed that the legislature does not intend it legislation to have absurd consequence. 2) Absurd consequences are not limited to logical contradictions or internal incoherence but include violations of established legal norms such as rule of law; they also include violations of widely accepted standards of justice and reasonableness. 3) Whenever possible an interpretation that leads to absurd consequences is rejected in favour of one that avoids absurdity ...'; and at 249; 'Another important category of absurdity is based on the efficient and orderly administration of justice. He courts have always regarded law enforcement as a matter particularly suited to judicial supervision. In exercising their supervisory role various principles based on the rule of law have been developed to protect individual subjects from arbitrary law enforcement. Apart from this concern for the individual however and potentially opposed to it is a concern for values like efficiency and effectiveness and a desire to promote the smooth operation of law enforcement machinery. Interpretations that interfere with the operation of this machinery or render the enforcement of the law ineffective may be labelled absurd.' Arguably the judgments of the CJ in Sala (*Maria Martina Sala*, case C-85/96 (1998) *ECR* I 2691) and Bidar (*Bidar v London Borough of Ealing.* Case C-209/03 (2005) *ECR* I 2119 *supra*) herein discussed, can be said to be absurd in the wider sense of the concept thereof in so far as the unjustifiably wide interpretation based upon no rational or empirical justification in the body of the judgments interferes in terms of consequences with the 'efficient and orderly' administration of justice notably as regards the following consequences: financing of social and educational services in the context of the members states' responsibilities as opposed to that of the community; an attempt at harmonization which is devoid of any financial analysis following van den Bergh; the unjustified (in the sense of not producing a rational justification' for the reading down of the exemptions provided in the then EC Treaty at that point such that there is a fundamental breach of the rule of law as it pertains to the distribution of powers in the then EC Treaty (now TFEU) and additionally the argument of vires developed by P. Craig: ultimately interference with the efficient administration of justice by completely failing to consider the legal and financial consequences of the application of an excessively widely interpreted concept of equality based upon nationality. And R Sullivan, *Sullivan and Driedger on the Construction of Statutes*, 4th edn (Vancouver: Butterworths, 2002), at 253 'Techniques to Avoid Absurdity: Justifying a restrictive interpretation: absurdity is often relied on to justify giving a restricted application to a provision'. As explained by Gonthier J. in *Ontario v Canadian Pacific* (1995) SCC 1031 at para. 65 'One method of avoiding absurdity is through the strict interpretation of general words ... Where a provision is open to two or more interpretations the absurdity principle may be employed to reject interpretations which lead to negatives consequences as such consequences are presumed not to have been intended.' It is clear that a narrower interpretation of the concept of equality arising in the context of nationalities and as would be provided by an expert opinion would be required to avoid the absurdity of provoking a breach of the rule of law and interference with efficient administration of justice and government.

British English,[16] it would have been narrower than that accorded by the CJ. This is, of course, in contrast to the method of statutory interpretation utilized in the cases which were examined in the judgments of *Sauvé v Canada*,[17] *Re: Polygamy*[18] and *Roper v Simmons*.[19] The CJ in Bidar[20] proceeds on the basis that all of the words contained with Article 12EC (now Article 18 TFEU) and Article 18 EC (now Article 21 TFEU) constitute words the ordinary meaning of which can be ascertained solely by the judges themselves without any assistance from experts either cross-examined or in the form of judicial notice of legislative facts. It is clear that normally, the expert meaning of a term is by necessity narrower in scope than is the ordinary meaning, here the target language being standard British English. The CJ at no time discusses the possibility or the utility of an expert on this matter. In summary, in the view of the judges of the CJ, the words in question apparently contain only ordinary meaning. This decision by the CJ was taken by the judges notwithstanding that the words may well be perceived from their context as possessing not only ordinary meaning but technical meaning: that is, the matter of the source of financing of what might be termed non-host State EU students constitutes an area of what KC Davis[21] referred to as legislative fact which would be subject of expert opinion introduced by judicial notice as used in the Polygamy[22] reference which will be considered later in this section. Accordingly, as regards statutory interpretation, one of the primary questions that must be posed at this precise point is whether or not the method of interpretation of utilized by the CJ is correct: that is, whether the use of the teleological method based exclusively upon the ordinary meaning of the words in contained within Article 12 EC (now Article 18 TFEU) and related to Article 18 EC (now Article 21 TFEU), coupled with Article 3 of Directive 93/96 replaced by Article 24 (2) of Directive 2004/38 provides the most accurate interpretation of the words involved which arguably contain expert meaning in particular as regards the national systems of university financing. As regards the directives 96/93 Article 3 and 2004/38 Article 24 (2) the words are 'any entitlement to the payment of maintenance grants' generally in a free standing sense and in particular in terms of UK (English) legislation. Similarly, as regards Article 18EC (now Article 21 TFEU) and Article 12 EC (now Article 18 TFEU) the operative words which, it is submitted, in the instant case possesses not just an ordinary meaning but a technical meaning, are the following: in the context of entitlement of 'the payment of maintenance grants' they are respectively 'limitations and conditions' and 'special provisions

16. D Crystal, *The Cambridge Encyclopedia of the English Language* (Cambridge, Cambridge University Press, 1995). T McArthur (ed), *The Oxford Companion to the English Language* (Oxford, Oxford University Press, 1992); M McBride, *London's Dialect: An Ancient Form of English Speech* (London, Priory Press, 1910). TW Machan & CT Scott (eds), *English in its Social Contexts* (Oxford, Oxford University Press, 1992); W Mathews, *Cockney Past and Present* (London and Boston: Routledge & Kegan Paul, 1972); J Milroy & L Milroy (eds), *Real English. The Grammar of English Dialects in the British Isles* (London, Longman, 1993).
17. *Sauvé v Canada* (AG) (2002) 3 *SCR* 519, *supra*.
18. *Re: Polygamy* 2011 *BCSC* 1588 Re: S 293 CCC, *supra*.
19. *Roper v Simmons* (2005) 543 *US* 551, *supra*.
20. *Bidar v London Borough of Ealing*, Case C-209/03 (2005) *ECR* I 2119 para. 23, *supra*.
21. KC Davis 'Judicial Notice' (1955) *Columbia Law Review* (7) 945, *supra*.
22. *Re: Polygamy* 2011 *BCSC* 1588 Re: S 293 CCC, *supra*.

contained therein'. As will be noted earlier in both Roper[23] and Re Polygamy[24] expert opinion evidence was introduced into the statutory interpretation of constitutional provisions dealing with, among other things, conditions and restrictions, by means of the wide concept of judicial notice of Davis:[25] that is, the court considered such information to constitute legislative facts of which it could take notice thereby dispensing from the necessity of proof through cross-examination, despite the fact that the meaning is not incontestable. In the Re: Polygamy[26] case at certain points, judicial notice was coupled with the traditional presentation of expert evidence through cross-examination of the expert. In short, the matter of the meaning of the words, that is, whether ordinary or technical, and their proof either through judicial notice involving simply the view of the judge or the introduction of expert evidence and, in some cases, the introduction of experts as witness subject to cross-examination is crucial for the determination of the following issues: first, conformity with the procedural principle of rectitude of decision as developed by Bentham, that is, accurate application of the law to the facts presupposes accurate understanding of the law; and second, whether there has been compliance with Article 6 (1) ECHR in terms of a fair trial and whether the court has carried out a proper evaluation of the facts submitted by the parties such as the UK in Bidar.[27] In the case of Bidar, arguably, the CJ by not using expert information to assist in the determination of the statutory interpretation of the words just considered in the articles of the TFEU (ex EC Treaty) and the EU directives failed to carry out a proper evaluation of the facts submitted by the parties, and notably the United Kingdom as adversary of the applicant Bidar.[28] The essence of the UK defence involved the technical meaning notably of financing of university education in England. Ineluctably, the rules of the CJ which deal with the drafting of the pleadings by the parties in a reference as well as the appointment of an expert, the use of judicial notice by the court in order to simplify the meaning of words in particular technical words, coupled with the utilization of assessors to assist the court in the understanding of expert opinions which bear upon the meaning of technical words will all have an effect upon the CJ's legal compliance Article 6 (1) ECHR, *Kraska v Switzerland*[29] and the principle of the Rule of Law. In so far as a considerable amount of information available and presented notably by the UK was ignored or at least not referred to by the CJ in detail, that is, the CJ did not appoint an expert to examine the claims therein in the context of establishing and applying the technical meaning, notably of the available exceptions pursuant to the requisite articles of the TFEU were not mentioned in the text of its judgment and therefore not utilized by the court concerning the technical aspects of financing the studies of EU students, the following is submitted: namely, that the technical meaning of the words contained notably within therein and in the exceptions to both Article 12 EC (now Article 18 TFEU) and Article 18 (now Article 21 TFEU)was

23. *Roper v Simmons* (2005) 543 *US* 551, *supra*.
24. *Re Polygamy* 2011 *BCSC* 1588 Re: S 293 CCC, *supra*.
25. KC Davis, 'Judicial Notice' (1955) *Columbia Law Review* (55) 7, *supra*, 945 at 978-984.
26. *Re: Polygamy* 2011 *BCSC* 1588 Re: S 293 CCC *ibid*.
27. *Bidar v London Borough of Ealing*. Case C-209/03 (2005) *ECR* I 2119, *supra*, paras 13-19.
28. *Ibid*.
29. *Kraska v Switzerland* (1994) *EHRR* (18) 188, *supra*, at para. 18.

ignored. It is submitted that this method of interpretation violated the rights of the UK as a party to the preliminary reference in so far as it resulted in a breach of Article 6 (1) ECHR, due process, *Kraska v Switzerland*:[30] that is, the duty of a court to examine carefully the legal and evidential merits of the case presented by the parties. For this reason, the scope of the statutory interpretation of propounded by the CJ was much wider than would have been the case if only the technical meaning had been considered.[31] This is in large measure attributable to an inaccurate and incomplete

30. *Kraska v Switzerland* (1994) *EHRR* (18) 188, *ibid.* at para. 18.
31. It is submitted that one of the impediments upon the use of expert evidence results from the jurisprudence of the EU courts themselves, as regards the exclusion of economic considerations in the interpretation of the derogations now incorporated as in *Raymond Kohll v Union des caisses de maladie* Case C-158/96, C-158/96, ECR 1998 I-1931) into secondary legislation such as, Directive 2004/38 ':Limitations on Grounds of Public Policy, Public Security and Public Health, Article 27 General Principles: 1. Subject to the provisions of this Chapter, Member States may restrict the freedom of movement and residence of Union citizens and their family members, irrespective of nationality, on grounds of public policy, public security or public health. These grounds shall not be invoked to serve economic ends.' R Sullivan, *Sullivan and Driedger on the Construction of Statutes*, 4th edn, (Vancouver, Butterworths, 2002), *supra*, at Ch. 9, 235: 'When a court is called on to interpret legislation it is not engaged in an academic exercise. Interpretation involves the application of legislation to fact in a way that affects the well-being of individuals and communities for better or worse. Not surprisingly the courts are interested in knowing what the consequences will be and judging whether they are acceptable. Consequences judged to be good are presumed to be intended and generally are regarded as part of the legislative purpose. Consequences judged to be contrary to accepted norms of justice and reasonableness are labelled absurd and are presumed to have been unintended. If adopting an interpretation would lead to absurdity the courts may reject that interpretation in favour of a plausible alternative that avoids the absurdity.' It is submitted that the refusal to consider the financial aspects of certain exceptions to various rights in the context of statutory interpretation can lead to financial consequences as for example including foreign students whether resident or not within the context of social benefits as was done by the CJ (ex ECJ) in Bidar (*Bidar v London Borough of Ealing.* Case C-209/03 (2005) *ECR* I 2119, *supra*, paras 13-19.) which are financial onerous, disproportionate and therefore unreasonable. Arguably, this is the essence of the criticism by K Hailbronner 'Union Citizenship and Access to Social Benefits' (2005) *CMLRev* (42)1245, *supra*, at 1247; see also, L Clark 'EU Students who attended British universities owe us £ 75m in taxpayer funded loans' www.dailymail.co.uk. It would appear that L Hancher and W Sauter, 'One Step Beyond? From Sodemare to Docmorris: The EU's Freedom of Establishment Case Law Concerning Healthcare' (2010) *CMLRev* (47) 117 at 119 -120 make the same point, namely, the need for rigorous factual analysis, particularly economic analysis in the health as well as other sectors particularly in relation to the application of the principle of proportionality: 'Arguably the goal of realizing an internal market in any particular sector is not just about securing a procedural or good governance approach with a right to reasoned decisions and a right of appeal as has been predominantly the main requirement imposed on national governments in the patient mobility. It is also about ensuring that States apply sound economics to their health care decisions. The application of the free movement rules inevitably occurs as a result of what have been referred to as 'constitutional asymmetries'; and the question arises and the question arises whether a more economics based approach to their application could offer a better way to take this problem. As the stated objective of the free movement rules is the realization of an internal market and if the concept of market access is to be taken seriously it surely follows that there ought to be more economics arguments in the establishment context. This does not necessarily mean that there should be an unquestioned assumption that market access is beneficial as such. Rather it means that where assumptions are make they should be tested on the basis of economic theories which offer useful insights beyond bland declarations in the name of some unspecified or ill-determined public interest objective.' And at p. 144 the two authors observe therein: 'One possible approach could be to expose the economic assumptions underlying the model that is implicit in the public policy justification invoked to

statutory interpretation of Article 12 EC (now Article 18 TFEU) and Article 18 EC (now Article 21 TFEU) and above all the exceptions thereto contained within the EC Treaty (now he TFEU): this, in turn, eventuates in, among other things, an incorrect assessment of what, as noted earlier, Craig[32] refers to as vires and violation of competences established by the aforementioned Treaties. Notwithstanding these observations, it is appropriate to continue the taxonomy of the interpretation of Article 12 EC (now Article 18 TFEU) and Article 18 EC (now Article 21 TFEU) by the CJ. One observes the clear manner in which the CJ embarks upon its teleological interpretation coupled with the reading down of the restrictions contained in the aforementioned

---

date and to identify at a minimum inconsistencies as a counterpoint again the vague claims of the 'unity and balance of the system'. A second approach may be to introduce a more rigorous cost -benefit analysis in the context of the proportionality test: surely if one party provides data to this effect the burden of proof at the other end of the scales will increase too.' At finally at p. 146 Hancher & Sauter (L Hancher & W Sauter, 'One Step Beyond? From Sodemare to Docmorris: The EU's Freedom of Establishment Case Law Concerning Healthcare' (2010) *CMLRev* (47) 117 *ibid.* at 119 -120) focus on an expert economic analysis of the principle of proportionality: 'If this is correct it appears it is in entrants' interest to do so. ... If the proportionality test is refined to embrace a consistency standard underpinned by a more robust economic analysis this could pave the way to substantial improvements in guaranteeing the application of the free movement rules in the health sector. This need not challenge Member States' authority over the standard of heath protection at all. At most it could open up debate on the organization of health care services delivery while potentially improving health outcomes. Finally it might well serve to introduce a more objective approach to defining the public interest and to ensure a more robust examination of the various and often vested interests involved.'

32. P Craig, 'The ECJ an ultra vires Action: A Conceptual Analysis' (2011) *CMLRev* (48) (2) 395: arguably, the concern raised by Craig concerning violations of competences as reflected in vires and ultra vires necessarily in an epistemological requires, as a first step, an accurate statutory interpretation in a semantic sense which in turn requires that the distinction between ordinary and technical meaning be sustained by the use of expert evidence in order to prove such meanings. In this sense, L Hancher & W Sauter 'One Step Beyond: from Sodemare and Docmorris: the EU's Freedom of Establishment Law Concerning Health Care' (2010) *CMLRev* (47) 117, *supra*, at 143 'Arguably the goal of realizing an internal market in any particular sector is not just about securing a procedural or good governance approach with a right to a reasoned decisions and a right of appeal has been predominantly the main requirement imposed on national governments in the patient mobility cases. It is also about ensure that States apply sound economics to their healthcare decisions. The application of the free movement rulers inevitably occurs as a result of what has been referred to as 'constitutional asymmetries' and the question arises whether a more economics-based approach to their application could offer a better way to tackle this problem. As the stated objective of the free movement rules is the realization of an internal market and if the concept of market access is to be taken seriously it sure follows that there ought to be room for more economic arguments in the establishment context. This does not necessarily mean that there should be an unquestioning assumption that market access is beneficial as such. Rather it means that where assumptions are made they should be tested on the basis of economic theories which offer useful insights beyond bland declarations in the name of unspecified or ill-determined public interest objective. 'It is submitted that notably as regards the exceptions to various economic and social rights as well as the application of principle of proportionality, in truth the analysis of Hancher and Sauter basically is a subset the analytic approach of the instant book in that both authors require the use of expert evidence in what is effectively statutory interpretation. R van den Bergh, 'The Subsidiarity Principle in European Community Law' (1994) *Maastricht J Europ Comparative Law* (1) 337 argues that economic analysis which seeks to harmonies or centralize (notably in the hands of the Commission) must be justified by economic analysis. This would surely apply to the courts expansionist interpretation which have the effect of harmonization as in the education and health cases which of course requires the participation of economists.

articles in order to establish that the following: that the financial assistance is part of the rationae materiae of the Treaty through the purpose of the assistance to advancing education for citizens as provided ultimately by Article 18 EC (now Article 21 TFEU); then once that inclusion of the financial assistance within the scope of the Treaty by reason of its purpose to enhance citizenship then such becomes subject to the obligation of equality of access to all citizens to whatever falls within the scope of the Treaty. One of the primary elements of this argument is to be found in the following paragraph of the judgment of Trojani[33] the facts of which are as follows: the claimant, a French national, lived in Belgium at a Salvation Army hostel for which, in return for board and lodging and some pocket money, he did various jobs for about thirty hours a week as part of a personal socio-occupational reintegration programme. He applied for the Belgian minima, a minimum subsistence allowance for persons with inadequate resources, but was refused on the ground that he did not satisfy the conditions of eligibility that he was either of Belgian nationality or a worker in the meaning of Council Regulation (EEC) No 1612/68 on freedom of movement for workers. In proceedings by the claimant, a preliminary ruling was sought on whether he could claim a right of residence as a worker, under Article 39 EC on freedom of movement for workers, or other provisions of Community law. The CJ[34] held as follows:

> Para 43 Second, with regard to such benefits, a citizen of the Union who is not economically active may rely on Article 12 EC where he has been lawfully resident in the host Member State for a certain time or possesses a residence permit.

This paragraph of the judgment, arguably, signifies that as regards non-economically active citizens provided that they have achieved lawful residence for a 'certain time' or possess a 'residence' permit, then 'social assistance benefits' fall within the scope rationae materiae of the Treaty. The CJ developed the concept of a non-economically active citizen who has achieved lawful residence in Baumbast[35] based upon Article 18 EC (now Article 21 TFEU) which was then taken over in Trojani.[36] This concept however, crucially requires the 'reading down' of the conditions specified notably within Article 18 EC (now Article 21 TFEU) by means of the application of certain EU legal principles and, in particular, that of proportionality. Therefore, such a person, following Trojani[37] is able to claim, as a citizen who is lawfully resident, certain

33. *Trojani* Case C-456/02 [2004] *ECR* I-0000, para. 43.
34. L Hancher & W Sauter, 'One Step Beyond? From Sodemare to Docmorris: The EU's Freedom of Establishment Case Law Concerning Healthcare' (2010) *CMLRev* (47) 117 at 119 -120; *Trojani*, Case C-456/02 [2004] *ECR* I-0000, para. 43 *ibid.*
35. Case C-413/99 *Baumbast and R* [2002] *ECR* I-7091 at para. 84: 'As regards, in particular, the right to reside within the territory of the Member States under Article 18(1) EC, that right is conferred directly on every citizen of the Union by a clear and precise provision of the EC Treaty. Purely as a national of a Member State, and consequently a citizen of the Union, Mr Baumbast therefore has the right to rely on Article 18(1) EC.'
36. Trajani C 456/02 [2004] *ECR* I-0000, *supra*, para. 31.
37. Trajani C 456/02 [2004] *ECR* I-0000, *ibid.*, para. 31 'It must be recalled that the right to reside in the territory of the Member States is conferred directly on every citizen of the Union by Article 18(1) EC (see Case C-413/99 *Baumbast and R* [2002] *ECR* I-7091, paragraph 84). Mr Trojani therefore has the right to rely on that provision of the Treaty simply as a citizen of the Union. 32 That right is not unconditional, however. It is conferred subject to the limitations and conditions

laid down by the Treaty and by the measures adopted to give it effect. 33 Among those limitations and conditions, it follows from Article 1 of Directive 90/364 that Member States can require of the nationals of a Member State who wish to enjoy the right to reside within their territory that they themselves and the members of their families be covered by sickness insurance in respect of all risks in the host Member State and have sufficient resources to avoid becoming a burden on the social assistance system of that State during their period of residence. 34 As the Court has previously held, those limitations and conditions must be applied in compliance with the limits imposed by Community law and in accordance with the general principles of that law, in particular the principle of proportionality (*Baumbast and R*, paragraph 91). Para. 35 It follows from the judgment making the reference that a lack of resources was precisely the reason why Mr Trojani sought to receive a benefit such as the minimex. 36 In those circumstances, a citizen of the Union in a situation such as that of the claimant in the main proceedings does not derive from Article 18 EC the right to reside in the territory of a Member State of which he is not a national, for want of sufficient resources within the meaning of Directive 90/364. Contrary to the circumstances of the case of *Baumbast and R* (paragraph 92), there is no indication that, in a situation such as that at issue in the main proceedings, the failure to recognise that right would go beyond what is necessary to achieve the objective pursued by that directive. 37 However, it must be observed that, according to information put before the Court, Mr Trojani is lawfully resident in Belgium, as is attested by the residence permit which has in the meantime been issued to him by the municipal authorities of Brussels. 38 It should be recalled here that it is for the Court to provide the national court with all those elements for the interpretation of Community law which may be of assistance in adjudicating on the case pending before it, whether or not that court has specifically referred to them in its questions (see inter alia, to that effect, Case C-241/89 *SARPP* [1990] *ECR* I-4695, paragraph 8; Case C-315/92 *Verband Sozialer Wettbewerb ('Clinique')* [1994] *ECR* I-317, paragraph 9; and Case C-87/97 *Consorzio per la tutela del formaggio Gorgonzola* [1999] *ECR* I-1301, paragraph 16). Para. 39 In the context of the present case, it should be examined more particularly whether, despite the conclusion in paragraph 36 above, a citizen of the Union in a situation such as that of the claimant in the main proceedings may rely on Article 12 EC, under which, within the scope of application of the Treaty and without prejudice to any special provisions contained therein, all discrimination on grounds of nationality is prohibited. 40 In the present case, it must be stated that, while the Member States may make residence of a citizen of the Union who is not economically active conditional on his having sufficient resources, that does not mean that such a person cannot, during his lawful residence in the host Member State, benefit from the fundamental principle of equal treatment as laid down in Article 12 EC. 41 In that connection three points should be made. 42 First, as the Court has held, a social assistance benefit such as the minimex falls within the scope of the Treaty (see Case C-184/99 *Grzelczyk* [2001] *ECR* I-6193, in particular paragraph 46). 43 Second, with regard to such benefits, a citizen of the Union who is not economically active may rely on Article 12 EC where he has been lawfully resident in the host Member State for a certain time or possesses a residence permit. 44 Third, national legislation such as that at issue in the main proceedings, in so far as it does not grant the social assistance benefit to citizens of the European Union, non-nationals of the Member State, who reside there lawfully even though they satisfy the conditions required of nationals of that Member State, constitutes discrimination on grounds of nationality prohibited by Article 12 EC. 45 It should be added that it remains open to the host Member State to take the view that a national of another Member State who has recourse to social assistance no longer fulfils the conditions of his right of residence. In such a case the host Member State may, within the limits imposed by Community law, take a measure to remove him. However, recourse to the social assistance system by a citizen of the Union may not automatically entail such a measure (see, to that effect, *Grzelczyk*, paragraphs 42 and 43). 46 Consequently, the answer to the second question must be that a citizen of the Union who does not enjoy a right of residence in the host Member State under Articles 39 EC, 43 EC or 49 EC may, simply as a citizen of the Union, enjoy a right of residence there by direct application of Article 18(1) EC. The exercise of that right is subject to the limitations and conditions referred to in that provision, but the competent authorities must ensure that those limitations and conditions are applied in compliance with the general principles of Community law, in particular the principle of proportionality. However, once it is ascertained that a person in a situation such as that of the claimant in the main

benefits for citizens, by reason of the application of the principle of proportionality being used to read down the conditions and limitations provided within Article 18 EC (now Article 21 TFEU). Thus, the Court established that Baumbast[38] was able to directly rely upon his status as a citizen in Article 18 EC (now Article 21 TFEU) such that Article 12 EC (now Article 18 TFEU) then applied to ensure equality of access to all that is contained in terms of benefits within the Treaty.

Of particular interest is the manner in which the 'principle' of proportionality is applied which is used to read down the conditions and limitations in Article 18 EC (now Article 21 TFEU) which therefore widens the scope of the concept of citizenship attributes benefits or rights.

In Trojani,[39] the Court merely observed the following:

> Para 34 As the Court has previously held, those limitations and conditions must be applied in compliance with the limits imposed by Community law and in accordance with the general principles of that law, in particular the principle of proportionality (*Baumbast and R*, paragraph 91).

In Baumbast[40] the Court provides some discussion concerning the actual method of application of the principle of proportionality:

> Para 84 As regards, in particular, the right to reside within the territory of the Member States under Article 18(1) EC, that right is conferred directly on every citizen of the Union by a clear and precise provision of the EC Treaty. Purely as a national of a Member State, and consequently a citizen of the Union, Mr Baumbast therefore has the right to rely on Article 18(1) EC.
> Para85 Admittedly, that right for citizens of the Union to reside within the territory of another Member State is conferred subject to the limitations and conditions laid down by the EC Treaty and by the measures adopted to give it effect.
> Para 86 However, the application of the limitations and conditions acknowledged in Article 18(1) EC in respect of the exercise of that right of residence is subject to judicial review. Consequently, any limitations and conditions imposed on that right do not prevent the provisions of Article 18(1) EC from conferring on individuals rights which are enforceable by them and which the national courts must protect (see, to that effect, Case 41/74 *Van Duyn* [1974] ECR 1337, paragraph 7). I - 7166;
> Para 87 As regards the limitations and conditions resulting from the provisions of secondary legislation, Article 1(1) of Directive 90/364 provides that Member States can require of the nationals of a Member State who wish to enjoy the right to reside within their territory that they themselves and the members of their families be covered by sickness insurance in respect of all risks in the host Member State and have sufficient resources to avoid becoming a burden on the social assistance system of the host Member State during their period of residence.

---

proceedings is in possession of a residence permit, he may rely on Article 12 EC in order to be granted a social assistance benefit such as the minimex.'

38. Case C-413/99 *Baumbast and R* [2002] *ECR* I-7091, *supra*.
39. Case C-456/02 *Trojani* [2004] *ECR* I-0000, *supra*, para. 43.
40. *Baumbast and R*, Case C-413/99 [2002] *ECR* I-7091, *ibid*.

Para 88 As to the application of those conditions for the purposes of the Baumbast case, it is clear from the file that Mr Baumbast pursues an activity as an employed person in non-member countries for German companies and that neither he nor his family has used the social assistance system in the host Member State. In those circumstances, it has not been denied that Mr Baumbast satisfies the condition relating to sufficient resources imposed by Directive 90/364.

Para 89 As to the condition relating to sickness insurance, the file shows that both Mr Baumbast and the members of his family are covered by comprehensive sickness insurance in Germany. The Adjudicator seems to have found that that sickness insurance could not cover emergency treatment given in the United Kingdom. It is for the national tribunal to determine whether that finding is correct in the light of Regulation (EEC) No 1408/71 of the Council of 14 June 1971 on the application of social security schemes to employed persons and their families moving within the Community (OJ, English Special Edition 1971 (II), p. 416). Particular reference should be made to Article 19(1)(a) of that regulation which ensures, at the expense of the competent Member State, the right for an employed or self-employed person residing in the territory of another Member State other than the competent State whose condition requires treatment in the territory of the Member State of residence to receive sickness benefits in kind provided by the institution of the latter State.

Para 90 In any event, the limitations and conditions which are referred to in Article 18 EC and laid down by Directive 90/364 are based on the idea that the exercise of the right of residence of citizens of the Union can be subordinated to the legitimate interests of the Member States. In that regard, according to the fourth recital in the preamble to Directive 90/364 beneficiaries of the right of residence must not become an 'unreasonable' burden on the public finances of the host Member State.

Para 91 However, those limitations and conditions must be applied in compliance with the limits imposed by Community law and in accordance with the general principles of that law, in particular the principle of proportionality. That means that national measures adopted on that subject must be necessary and appropriate to attain the objective pursued (see, to that effect, Joined Cases C-259/91, C-331/91 and C-332/91 *Allué and Others* [1993] ECR I-4309, paragraph 15).

Para 92 In respect of the application of the principle of proportionality to the facts of the Baumbast case, it must be recalled, first, that it has not been denied that Mr Baumbast has sufficient resources within the meaning of Directive 90/364; second, that he worked and therefore lawfully resided in the host Member State for several years, initially as an employed person and subsequently as a self-employed person; third, that during that period his family also resided in the host Member State and remained there even after his activities as an employed and self-employed person in that State came to an end; fourth, that neither Mr Baumbast nor the members of his family have become burdens on the public finances of the host Member State and, fifth, that both Mr Baumbast and his family have comprehensive sickness insurance in another Member State of the Union.

Para 93 Under those circumstances, to refuse to allow Mr Baumbast to exercise the right of residence which is conferred on him by Article 18(1) EC by virtue of the application of the provisions of Directive 90/364 on the ground that his sickness insurance does not cover the emergency treatment given in the host Member State would amount to a disproportionate interference with the exercise of that right.

> Para 94 The answer to the first part of the third question must therefore be that a citizen of the European Union who no longer enjoys a right of residence as a migrant worker in the host Member State can, as a citizen of the Union, enjoy there a right of residence by direct application of Article 18(1) EC. The exercise of that right is subject to the limitations and conditions referred to in that provision, but the competent authorities and, where necessary, the national courts must ensure that those limitations and conditions are applied in compliance with the general principles of Community law and, in particular, the principle of proportionality.

The essence of these aforementioned paragraphs is that according to the CJ, the application of the principle of proportionality the following must be established in para 91:

> That means that national measures adopted on the subject must be necessary and appropriate.

The words 'necessary and appropriate'[41] arguably indicate that expert opinion is required on what are clearly technical issues even basic technical facts such as the following: whether Mr Baumbast who does not have UK coverage for emergency services would be able either individually through his own resources or through his insurance coverage in other countries to cover the eventual likely liability which he could incur for emergency services in the UK; that is, whether or not the policy of Mr Baumbast which covers emergency services in other countries would apply to the UK or if it does, up to what limit, which may be crucial. Similarly, there is no analysis of the matter from a macro-economic point view of what the statistics exist as regards the overall costs to the UK health system, the NHS, for providing coverage in this situation.[42] Accordingly, the application of the principle of proportionality in Baumbast

41. One recalls the observations made by R Sullivan, *Sullivan and Driedger on the Construction of Statutes*, 4th edn (Vancouver, Butterworth, 2002), *supra*, at 110 at as regards general words like 'reasonable' which would include words such as 'necessary and appropriate' in the above ECJ judgment which are general words not suitable for interpretation as ordinary meaning by judges but which can be in some circumstances words with technical meaning referring to legislative standards. As recalled, Sullivan uses a very narrow interpretation of judicial notice which applies only to indisputable facts. Therefore, as regards technical words a judge in the absence of indisputability which would preclude the use of judicial notice would require proof by experts firstly that the word had a technical meaning and secondly what the meaning was. KC Davis 'Judicial Notice' (1955) *Columbia Law Review* (35) (7) 945, *supra*, at 978-984 would permit judicial notice as recalled of disputable legislative facts provided that the defence rights were respected in that contradiction was possible of any finding through judicial notice which affected the rights of the defence.
42. L Hancher & W Sauter 'One Step Beyond? From Sodemare to Docmorris: The EU's Freedom of Establishment Case Law Concerning Healthcare' (2010) *CMLRev* (47) 117, *supra*, at 119-120 make the same point, namely the need for rigorous factual analysis, particularly economic analysis in the health as well as other sectors particularly in relation to the application of the principle of proportionality.

has been carried out in a factual vacuum[43] effectively in violation of ECHR Article 6 (1) as interpreted by *Kraska v Switzerland*.[44] It is submitted that this inadequacy of treatment as regards the facts or more particularly the absence of facts and expert opinion lead to a situation such as that decried, as will be seen in a subsequent chapter herein, by Scalia J. in the judgment of the USSC:[45] it is a judgment which is sustained on nothing more than the opinion of the judges and upon no facts or expert opinion. Further, the net result of this type of reasoning which is devoid of any factual or expert basis is as follows: firstly, to the extent that it is based upon the opinion of the judges themselves, there is legal uncertainty. There is no proof thereof. Moreover, the issue has not been looked at from the economic perspective beyond the immediate case. If it were examined in the context of the macro-economic behaviour involved, the conclusion may well be that such behaviour on a large scale will lead to excessive and therefore unreasonable pressure on the overall national health system. In short, the CJ seeks to apply the principle of proportionality so as to eliminate the application of the conditions provided within Article 18 EC (now Article 21 TFEU) which protect the financial interests of the Member States on the basis of an analysis which is completely deficitory in terms of any expert economic analysis. It is unclear from the judgment in Baumbast what the nature of the submissions which were made by the UK and German governments as well as those made by the Commission were as a matter of law and fact. Accordingly, it is unclear as to whether or to what extent the CJ has through its application of the principle of proportionality to the conditions of Article 18EC (now Article 21 TFEU) which would protect the interests of the Member States financially in notably the instant case has violated Article 6 ECHR: that is by a failure to consider properly the evidence submitted by the parties.[46] Finally, once again following Scalia J. in Simmons[47] which will be considered later in this book, the judgment in Baumbast arguably leads to a teleological interpretation of Article 18 EC (Article 21 TFEU) and Article 12 EC (now Article TFEU 18) the scope of which simply has no factual justification. In short, the absence of all expert opinion as regards the application of the principle of proportionality has led to a situation wherein there is no factual justification for the reading down of the restrictions in particular in Article 18 EC (now Article 21 TFEU). Thus, there is no factual justification for the wide interpretation given not only to the remainder of Article 18 EC (now Article 21 TFEU) but also to the equality provisions of Article 12 EC (now Article 18 TFEU). The terms which possess technical meaning have not been examined from the point of view of what their accurate technical meaning is. Further, the CJ in the context of the interpretation of these

43. See the above mentioned criticism by L Hancher & W Sauter 'One Step Beyond: from Sodemare and Docmorris: the EU's Freedom of Establishment Law Concerning Health Care' (2010) *CMLRev* (47) 117 *ibid.* at 143, as regards the application of the principle of proportionality without proper expert economic opinion and evidence.
44. *Kraska v Switzerland* (1993) 18 *EHRR* at para. 30.
45. *Roper v Simmons* 543 US 551 (2005), *supra*.
46. (1994) *EHRR* (18) 188, *supra*, para. 30.
47. *Roper v Simmons* (2005) 543 *US* 551, *supra*.

technical terms and notably of the exceptions, did not exercise its discretion to appoint an expert to deal with notably the submissions concerning financial and economic aspects involving students. The CJ itself[48] undertook an analysis which ought to have been carried out by an expert, despite the fact that procedurally it has the possibility to appoint experts itself.[49] There was on the facts of the reported case no justification given by CJ for its failure to appoint an expert. In short, the CJ failed to evaluate properly the merits of national defence which required the use of involving experts. Thereby, the CJ breached its duty pursuant to Kraska[50] to evaluate the merits of the case and the submissions of the national intervener, with the requisite due care and attention, that is, properly.

§4.04 EUROPEAN UNION COMPETITION LAW

It is appropriate at this point to consider a different area of EU law which has been the object of concern for many years by various legal scholars such as Prof. V. Korah.[51] The primary concerning as regards EU Competition Law was and remains the absence of cogent economics analysis using expert evidence in both Commission and CJ judgments. The early cases in this field demonstrate arguably, with force the truth of the hypothesis used herein: namely, that the EU courts tend to produce statutory interpretations, notably, of technical words which are more accurate when or if they introduce expert evidence either through the cross-examination of witnesses of by means judicial notice. Indeed, the greater accuracy signifies usually that the scope of the technical word is more narrow than the ordinary word. As regards words with technical meaning Sullivan observes[52] as follows:

> Technical or scientific terms are words or expressions that have no common or popular meaning; their only meaning devices from specialised used by a distinct portion of the community. When technical or scientific terms are used in legislation there is no possibility of confusion; such terms automatically receive their technical or scientific meaning (Note 2 See Perka v R (1984) 2 SCR 232 at 264 per Dickson J 'It is well established that technical and scientific terms which appear in statutes should be given their technical or scientific meaning'.)

The analysis of this particular area of CJ and GC cases, namely, EU Competition Law, will proceed slightly differently than was the case in the previous section: namely, that

48. E Barbier de La Serre & A-L Sibony, 'Expert Evidence before the EC Courts' (2008) *CMLRev* (45) 941, *supra*, and in particular DJ Gerber, 'Courts and Economic Experts in European Merger Law' (2004) *Fordham Corporate Law Institute* (30) 475, *supra*, passim.
49. B Vesterdorf, 'Economics in Court' in M Johansson, N Wahl and U Bernitz (eds) *Liber Amicorum of Sven Norberg* (Brussels, Bruylant, 2006) 511, *supra*, at 527.
50. *Kraska v Switzerland* (1993) EHRR 188, *supra*, para. 30.
51. Prof. V Korah, Barrister, Emeritus Professor of Competition Law, University College London, www.ucl.ac.uk, last used 27.10.2013.
52. R Sullivan, *Sullivan and Drieder on the Construction of Statutes*, 4th edn (Vancouver, Butterworths, 2002) at 40-41.

in addition to analysing certain of the earlier classic or iconic judgments in the field of EU competition law rendered by the CJ and the GC, an additional source of analysis and reflection concerning the use of expert evidence in the application of EU competition law will be considered: namely, some of the writings of Korah. It is felt that such an analysis is of heuristic value in so far as first, the works of Korah are readily available and, second, they extend over the major period of development in terms of the application of EU competition law by the EU courts and the European Commission. More particularly, it is felt that the legal analysis by Korah of CJ and GC judgments carried out over more than forty years can cogently, compendiously, and faithfully be presented in, notably, the context of the procedural analysis attempted herein: that is, an analysis predicated upon expert evidential deficits, in what ineluctably constitutes the statutory interpretation of the Articles 101 and 102 TFEU (ex Articles 85 and 86 EEC). One observes in this regard however, that Korah never specifically focussed her work on statutory interpretation or a particular method thereof. Nor did she endeavour to relate statutory interpretation to considerations arising from General Linguistics as does Sullivan.[53] Nevertheless, it is submitted that it is possible to clearly analyse the work of Korah in the field of EU competition law in a continuous and detailed fashion such that it demonstrates what are effectively major procedural failures on the part of the CJ and the GC: specifically, the non-compliance with the procedural principle of rectitude of decision and Article 6 (1) ECHR leading thereby ineluctably to a breach of the Rule of Law. In short, the failure of the CJ, the GC and above all, the European Commission, to provide sufficient empirical and theoretical foundation to justify to a requisite evidentiary standard, their application of Articles 101 and 102 TFEU (ex Articles 85 and 86 EEC) has led thereby, in many cases, to deleterious practical consequences: the lowering of competitive abilities and structures of business and commercial enterprises within the European Union. This is demonstrated eloquently by among others, a judgment which will be examined herein, My Travel[54] that being said, and as previously noted, the methods of statutory interpretation considered briefly in the preceding chapters as being characteristic of that of the CJ and the GC as regards the TFEU (ex EEC) perhaps remarkably, did not take into consideration any expert opinion. In short, these methods of interpretations even if one used the concept of teleological interpretations were based upon the ordinary meaning of the words in Article 85 (1) and (3) EC (now Article 101 (1) and (2) TFEU) the text of which is as follows but not upon the technical meaning therein which required expert opinion evidence. The relevant words are as follows:

53. *Ibid.*
54. Case T-212/03 *MyTravel Group plc v Commission of the European Communities* (2008) *ECR* II 1967.

> Article 101 TFEU (ex Article 81 TEC ex Art 85 EEC)[55]
> 1. The following shall be prohibited as incompatible with the internal market: all agreements between undertakings, decisions by associations of undertakings and concerted practices which may affect trade between Member States and which have as their object or effect the prevention, restriction or distortion of competition within the internal market, and in particular those which:
> (a) directly or indirectly fix purchase or selling prices or any other trading conditions;
> (b) limit or control production, markets, technical development, or investment;
> (c) share markets or sources of supply;
> (d) apply dissimilar conditions to equivalent transactions with other trading parties, thereby placing them at a competitive disadvantage;
> (e) make the conclusion of contracts subject to acceptance by the other parties of supplementary obligations which, by their nature or according to commercial usage, have no connection with the subject of such contracts.
> 2. Any agreements or decisions prohibited pursuant to this Article shall be automatically void.
> 3. The provisions of paragraph 1 may, however, be declared inapplicable in the case of:
> - any agreement or category of agreements between undertakings,
> - any decision or category of decisions by associations of undertakings,
> - any concerted practice or category of concerted practices, which contributes to improving the production or distribution of goods or to promoting technical or economic progress, while allowing consumers a fair share of the resulting benefit, and which does not:
> (a) impose on the undertakings concerned restrictions which are not indispensable to the attainment of these objectives;
> (b) afford such undertakings the possibility of eliminating competition in respect of a substantial part of the products in question.

In short, it is submitted that historically, as it were, the application of Article 101 TFEU (ex Article 85 EEC) involved certain of the following words being given their ordinary meaning: namely, 'all agreements between undertakings ... which may affect trade between Member States and which have as their object or effect the prevention restriction or distortion of competition'. Significantly, by reason of the fact that the words were considered in terms of their ordinary meaning which would be known to every competent speaker of the English language, the judges of the CJ and the GC would normally not make recourse to experts for the interpretation of the aforementioned Article 101 (1) TEFU (ex Article 85 (1) EEC). Nor, a fortiori, would these judges use of expert evidence to establish the meaning of the terms therein. Sullivan[56] as may

55. Consolidated version of the Treaty on the Functioning of the European Union - PART THREE: UNION POLICIES AND INTERNAL ACTIONS - TITLE VII: COMMON RULES ON COMPETITION, TAXATION APPROXIMATION OF LAWS - Chapter 1: Rules on competition - Section 1: Rules applying to undertakings - Article 101 (ex Article 81 TEC) http://eur-lex.europa.eu/LexUriServ/LexUriServ.do?uri=CELEX:12008E101:EN:HTML last consulted on 25.10.2013.
56. R Sullivan, *Sullivan and Drieder on the Construction of Statutes,* 4th edn (Vancouver, Butterworths, 2002), *supra*, at 20-21.

be recalled from an earlier chapter herein, defines ordinary meaning, in the following manner:

> The expression 'ordinary meaning' is much used in statutory interpretation but not in any consistent way. Sometimes it is identified with dictionary meaning, sometimes with literal meaning and sometimes with the meaning that results after the words to e interpreted are read in total context. Most often however it refers to the reader's first impression meaning the understanding that spontaneously emerges when words are read in their immediate context – the words of Gonthier J. 'the natural meaning which appears when the provision is simply read through (Canadian Pacific Airlines v Canadian Air Line Pilots Assn (1993) 3 SCR 724 at 735). This last sense of 'ordinary meaning' is the one adopted here. ... Courts are entitled to take judicial notice of facts that in their opinion are indisputable. This includes (a) facts that are notorious in the sense that everyone knows and accepts them; they belong to the store of information that ever educated member of the society takes for granted and (b) facts that can be demonstrated to be true b resorting to sources that are easily accessible and whose authority and accuracy are accepted by all. (Note 13 R v Williams (1998) 1 SCR 1128 and 1154). The ordinary meaning of language used in legislation is considered a fact that every competent speaker either knows or knows how to look up. For this reason ordinary meaning is judicially noticed. Under the doctrine of judicial notice[57] it is permissible for judges to declare the ordinary meaning of a work or expression without explaining how they arrived at their conclusion.

Interestingly, Sullivan[58] places some inherent limits upon the use of the ordinary meaning of words:

> Although there are good reasons for courts to prefer the ordinary meaning of a legislative text that meaning is often unhelpful. Even with the benefit of the immediate context words are often ambiguous o uncertain in scope or are otherwise unclear. In such cases the courts have no choice but to look elsewhere for assistance. Ordinary meaning is apt to be unhelpful when the language in which the legislation is drafted is vague, abstract or requires the interpreter to apply a standard rather than a rule. Standards are provisions that set principles or policies to be applied or goals to be sought by the official interpreter of the legislation. Provisions that incorporate normative concepts like 'just' 'reasonable' or appropriate' relative terms like 'under exploitation' or abstract concepts like 'discrimination' 'wrongful' of 'obscene' are all examples of standards. Although it would be possible to look up words like these in a dictionary the result would not be helpful because what is called for is a judgement based on principle or policy rather than an interpretation based on the cared conventions of language.

57. P Roberts & A Zuckerman, *Criminal Evidence*, 2nd edn (Oxford, OUP 2010) presents the narrow interpretation of judicial notice based upon indisputable facts. This is in contrast to the wide view of judicial notice presented by KC Davis, 'Judicial Notice' (1955) *Columbia Law Review* (55) 945, *supra*, which includes both indisputable and disputable facts.
58. R Sullivan, *Sullivan and Driedger on the Construction of Statutes,* 4th edn (Vancouver, Butterworths, 2002) at 36-37.

This is in contrast to the method of interpretation which involves technical words, namely, those which, among other things, contain, as noted by Sullivan, vague or general words which refer to standards. Sullivan[59] observes in this regard:[60]

> In deciding whether to adopt the ordinary or the technical meaning of words courts look to the usual range of factors: the purpose and scheme of the legislation, the consequences of preferring one meaning over another relevant common law principle and so on. .... Whether a term has a technical meaning and what that meaning is are both questions of fact which must be established in a legally acceptable way. When a technical or specialized meaning is not something that everybody knows it cannot be judicially noticed but must be established through evidence, normally expert opinion evidence (see Nova v R (1988) 87 NR 101 (FCA) at 109; Township of Waters(1959) SCR 585 at 587-89; Dentists Supply Co v Deputy MNR (1956) Ex. CR 450, 461-66). Such evidence is required to establish both that

59. R Sullivan, *Sullivan and Driedger on the Construction of Statutes*, 4th edn (Vancouver, Butterworths, 2002), at 41; 'When words are ambiguous in the sense that they could bear either a technical or a non-technical meaning in the context in which they appear the courts presume that the ordinary non-technical meaning was intended' (Noted 4 *R v Mansour* (1979) 2 SCR 916). The presumption in favour of the ordinary non-technical meaning of words is subject to an important qualification. This is explained by Lord Esher in *Unwin v Hanson* (1891) 2 *QB* 115 at 119 'if the Act is directed to dealing with matters affecting everybody generally the words used have the meaning attached to them in the common and ordinary use of language. If the Act is one passed with reference to a particular trade, business or transaction and words are used which everybody conversant with that trade, business or transaction knows and understand to have a particular meaning in it then the words are to be construed as having that particular meaning though it may different from the common or ordinary meaning of the words.' At p. 43, 'Relying on this exception courts have adopted a technical meaning of the words 'sex' in regulations under British Columbia's Horse Racing Act, the words 'opthalmic dispensing' in Ontario's Opthalmic Dispensers Act, the words 'subcutaneous tissues of the human foot in the Ontario Chiropody Act, the word 'earthenware' in a tariff item under the Customs Tariff, the word 'concentrators' in Ontario's Assessment Act, The word 'pipeline' in the Income Tax Regulations and the words 'transmission line' in the Telecommunications Act. ...These varying formulations of the presumption in favour of ordinary non-technical meaning reflect different understanding of the principle underlying the rule. Baron Pollock in the Grenfell case makes audience understanding the key. He assumes that most statutes are addressed to the general public and therefore the common understanding of the words used should prevail. Lord Esher in Unwin v Hanson makes a statue's subject matter the key. ... Even though the Pfizer case is the only recent pronouncement of the Supreme Court of Canada on this issue Pigeon J's approach is generally ignored. This is because it is outdated. Statutes are increasingly written for specialized audiences and deal with highly technical subjects. The following observation by Farber though reflective of an American context is equally applicable in Canada: (Daniel A Farber 'The Inevitability of Practical Reason: Statutes, Formalism and the Rule of Law' (1992) 45 *Van L Rev* 533 at 552-53) [Many] important statutes today are not addressed to the ordinary citizen. They are addressed to more specialized audiences – government agencies, legal specialists particular industries. Less sophisticated individuals often rely on official compliance guides or publications by experts to understand the statute rather than deciphering the statute themselves. The more sophisticated audience approaches the statute with a rich contextual understanding of previous law, the politics of the enactment, the affected activity, the dynamics of implementation in that area. It is artificial to ignore all this in interpretation. Farber's observations suggest that the key consideration in determining whether words should have their ordinary or their technical meaning should be the understanding of the audience at which the legislation is directed. As Lord Diplock said in Black Clawson (1975) *AC* 591 at 638: '... the court must give effect to what the words of the statute would be reasonably understood to mean by those whose conduct it regulates.'
60. R Sullivan, *Sullivan and Drieder on the Construction of Statutes*, 4th edn (Vancouver, Butterworths, 2002), *ibid.*, at 46.

> a term has a technical meaning and the content of that meaning. The expert may introduce specialized dictionaries or encyclopedias, textbooks, publications of regulatory authorities or even legislation to support his or her testimony.[61]

Applying the aforementioned concept of words with an ordinary meaning as opposed to words with a technical meaning, it is useful, at this point, to consider the text of the Sherman Act[62] which is something of an historical precursor of Article 101 TFEU (ex Article 85 (1) EEC), albeit restricted to the US:

> Section 1:
> Every contract, combination in the form of trust or otherwise, or conspiracy, in restraint of trade or commerce among the several States, or with foreign nations, is declared to be illegal.

As regards its application however, one observes that arguably, the expression 'in restraint of trade' is, in reality, treated by the USSC in specific judgments, as a nominal phrase containing words with technical meaning. For this reason, the evidence is admitted as regards the meaning of the phrase 'in restraint of trade' in various circumstances.[63] Thus, in the judgment, Board of Trade of the City of Chicago,[64] Brandeis J. observed:

> No attempt was made by the Government to show that the rule had the purpose or the effect of limiting the amount of gain shipped to Chicago; or of retarding or accelerating shipment; or of raising or depressing prices; or that it resulted in hardship to anyone.[65] Absolutely no evidence had been advanced by the Government to show an adverse effect on market conditions. The Government had rested its case entirety on the mere proposition that a rule or agreement by which men, occupying positions of strength in any branch of trade fixed prices at which they would buy or sell during an important part of the business day is an illegal restraint of trade under the Antitrust Law (*ibid* pa 238). But the legality of an agreement or regulation cannot be determined by so simple a test as whether it restrains competition. Every agreement concerning trade every regulation of trade restrains. To bind to restrain is of their very essence. The true test of the legality is whether the restraint imposed is such as merely regulates and perhaps thereby promotes

---

61. P Craig, 'The ECJ and Ultra Vires Action: A Conceptual Analysis' (2011) *CMLRev* (48) 395 at 437 observes:
> The scope of intra vires action is an endemic problem for any polity that has limited power. The determination of those limits is often contestable more especially in a polity such as the EU where the range of powers accorded to it are broad and certain powers are couched in language that renders it difficult to impose tight constraints on its exercise. The article has contributed to this debate by emphasizing the need for coherence when thinking about the intra or ultra vires nature of EU action. It has also specified criteria through which to test concerns that the EU might be exceeding its ascribed limits and by applying these criteria in specific areas of EU law'. It is submitted that epistemologically, Craig's concepts for an analysis to determine what is intra as opposed to ultra vires clearly require as a first step, accurate statutory interpretation which involves notably the use of expert e evidence to determine in particular the technical meaning of certain words.

62. *The Sherman Antitrust Act* (*Sherman Act*, 2 July 1890, ch. 647, 26 Stat. 209, 15 U.S.C. §§ 1-7).
63. R Joliet, *The Rule of Reason in Antirust Law* (La Haye, Martinu Nijhoff, 1967) Ch. 1.
64. *Board of Trade of the City of Chicago v United States*, 246 US 231, 238 (1918).
65. *Board of Trade of the City of Chicago v United States*, 246 US 231, 238 (1918) *ibid*.

> competition or whether it is such as ma suppress or even destroy competition. To determine that question the Court must ordinarily consider the facts peculiar to the business to which the restraint is applied; its condition before and after the restraint was imposed; the nature of the restraint and its effect actual or probable. The history of the restraint the evil believed to exist the reasons for adopting the particular remedy the purpose and end sought to be attained are all relevant factors. This is not because a good intention will save an otherwise objectionable regulation or the reverse; but because knowledge of intent may help the Court to interpret fact and to predict consequences.

Judge Joliet[66] for his part, observes as follows concerning the aforementioned judgment:

> Obviously the restraint which was upheld by the Court had no significant effect on the market. It was even likely to improve market conditions. Brandeis by analyzing the nature, the scope and the effect of the rule endeavoured to demonstrate this. Stressing the narrow limits of the 'call' rule he listed several reasons why within its narrow limits the rule helped to improve market conditions.

Overall one might say that the net effect of the interpretation of Brandeis J. And the evidence which he used is to narrow the scope of application[67] of the expression 'restraint of trade' by means of the substitution of the technical meaning of that expression for the ordinary meaning thereof. Further, through the use of the empirical data and eventually expert opinion it becomes apparent that the word 'restraint' does not apply to restrictions on intra-brand competition which have the effect of increasing inter-brand competition. Moreover, the term 'restraint of trade' although utilized in legislation is, in reality, destined and intended to be understood by experts: economists and lawyers informed by economists and certain commercially experienced individuals. Such individuals would be the only speakers of the English language capable of understanding without assistance from an external source or a third person, the meaning of 'restraint of trade' in the context of the Sherman Act. Therefore, the semantic change is rather more the substitution of a technical meaning in Economics

66. R Joliet, *The Rule of Reason in Antitrust Law* (La Haye, Martinu Nijhoff, 1967), *supra*, at 36.
67. *Ibid.*, at 23-24: prefers not to view the change of the interpretation of the Sherman Act which led to the development of the rule of reason as being describable as a restriction of the scope of the phrase 'restraint of trade': 'The conflict which led to the Rule of Reason is generally viewed as one between literalists and those who wanted to save the Sherman Act from its vagueness by imparting to it the gloss of history. However this view seems to be oversimplified. Recent students of the Rule of Reason have shown convincingly that the debate was not as to whether the Act should be flexible or rigid but by what criteria its flexibility was controlled'. (Note 1 p. 24 R H Bork 'The Rule of Reason and the Per se Concept: Price Fixing and Market Division', 74 *Yale L J* 775 (1965) and 75 *Yale LJ* 375. With due respect to both Joliet and to Bork, arguably the characterization of the change in the interpretation of the words 'in restraint of trade' depends upon the objective at hand. From the point of view of producing an analysis of statutory interpretation which can in turn be incorporated within a theory of linguistics, clearly a characterization of a restriction of scope based upon the substitution of an expert meaning of 'restraint of trade' for the ordinary meaning is preferable. From the point of view of theories of industrial economics it may be that the description of Bork and the observations of Joliet are preferable.

for the ordinary meaning of restraint of trade thereby resolving what for a linguist[68] would term the ambiguity in the meaning of the phrase 'restraint in trade'. Certainly one of the advantages of envisaging what appears to be a narrowing of the scope of the meaning of 'restraint in trade' by means of the substitution of the technical meaning for the ordinary meaning is as follows: specifically, the need for the use of expert evidence to elucidate the meaning of the term 'restraint of trade' and the specific procedural method for so doing in terms of the Court's rules of procedure. In this regard, Sullivan[69] observes as regards the ineluctable need to utilize expert evidence in order to ensure an accurate interpretation:

> When a court is called on to interpret legislation it is not engaged in an academic exercise. Interpretation includes the application of legislation to facts in a way that affects the well-being of individuals and communities for better or worse. Not surprisingly the courts are interested in knowing what the consequences will be and judging whether they are acceptable. Consequences judged to be good are presumed to be intended and generally are regarded as part of the legislative purpose. Consequences judged to be contrary to accepted norms of justice and reasonableness are labelled absurd and are presumed to have been unintended. If adopting an interpretation would lead to absurdity the courts may reject that interpretation in favour of a plausible alternative that avoids the absurdity. As Mr Justice O'Halloran explained in Waugh v Pedneault. The Legislature cannot be presumed to act unreasonably or unjustly for that would be acting against the public interest. The members of the Legislature are elected by the people to protect the public interest and that means acting fairly and justly in all circumstances. Words used in enactments of the Legislature must be construed upon that premise. That is the real 'intent' of the Legislature. That is why words in an Act of the Legislature are not restricted to what are sometimes called their 'ordinary' or 'literal' meaning but are extended flexibly to include the most reasonable meaning which can be extracted from the purpose and the object of what is sought to be accomplished by the statute.

In truth, this view of Sullivan signifies that in order to achieve a reasonable interpretation consideration of the facts and in certain cases expert opinion is necessary in order to ensure that the application of the law to the facts, the essence of interpretation, produces consequences which are reasonable. This signifies therefore, that a consideration of the facts and eventually expert opinion is necessary in the interpretation of the law in so far as the application of the law involves of necessity an application

68. Linguistics as exemplified in the work of the following scholars: A Martinet, *Eléments de Linguistique Générale*, Paris, Armand Colin 1960; W Croft & D Cruse, *Cognitive Linguistics* (Cambridge, CUP, 2010); R Longacker, *An Introduction to Cognitive Grammar* (Oxford, OUP, 2008); R Brandom, *Articulating Reasons: An Introduction to Inferentialism* (Cambridge Mass,. Harvard University Press (2000); RH Robins, *General Linguistics: An Introductory Survey* (London, Routledge, 1994). N Chomsky, *Aspects of the Theory of Syntax* (Cambridge, Massachusetts, MIT Press, 1965). FJ Newmeyer, *Generative Linguistics: A Historical Perspective* (New York, Routledge, 1996). JR Searle, 'Chomsky's Revolution in Linguistics' (1972), *The New York Review of Books* (18) 12. J Lyons; 'Review of Aspects of the Theory of Syntax by Noam Chomsky' (1966), *The Philosophical Quarterly* 16 (65): 393-395, J Lyons, *Chomsky*, 3rd edn (London, HarperCollins, 1991). J Lyons, *Linguistic Semantics: An Introduction* (Cambridge, CUP, 1995).
69. R Sullivan, *Sullivan and Drieder on the Construction of Statutes*, 4th edn (Vancouver, Butterworths, 2002), *supra*, at 235.

thereof to facts which in certain cases requires consideration of an expert opinion in order to ensure that the consequences are reasonable. In short, in order to ensure that the consequences of an interpretation are reasonable, facts and eventually expert opinion as regards the interpretation of technical words must be considered.

It is now appropriate to consider the evolution of the application of Article 101 (1) TFEU (ex Article 85 (1) EEC) which arguably, has some similarities in content to Section 1 of the Sherman Act but where, semantically and therefore linguistically, the same underlying methods of statutory construction are involved: namely, the substitution of technical words for the initial ordinary meaning in the context of evolving statutory interpretation of Article 101 (1) TFEU (ex Article 85 (1) EEC). This particular instance of the evolution of the statutory interpretation can be profitably utilized as something of a test case for the general hypothesis which underlies the analysis of this book: namely, that overall, the use of the concept of words with technical meaning understood by experts and which can be proved by expert opinion evidence is more likely to produce an interpretation with consequences which are reasonable and objectively acceptable to experts in the particular domain than the following: namely, an interpretation which is predicated effectively upon the ordinary meaning of words where the meaning is not proven by means of expert evidence but rather is based not upon evidence but rather the knowledge possessed by the judges as competent speakers of a particular human language such as English. The legal analysis which best illustrates this process is that of Korah[70] coupled with that Judge Joliet.[71] For reasons

70. V Korah, *An Introductory Guide to EC Competition Law and Practice*, 9th edn (Oxford, Hart, 2007).

71. R Joliet, *The Rules of Reason in Antitrust Law* (La Haye, Martinus Nijhoff, 1967), *supra*, at 189 provides a vivid example of his approach in the following exert; 'So far the mechanical definition of 'restraint of trade' adopted by the EEC Commission has led it to concern itself excessively with exclusive franchise agreements and to neglect horizontal agreements which undoubtedly exist in Europe and can be far more dangerous to the Common Market. This is not only bad law; it is bad policy. At a time when European countries are opening their old boundaries to each other and endeavouring to create larger economic spheres Europe badly needs a vigorous antitrust policy in order to assure European consumers the benefits they expect from a Common Market. ... If the American approach to the concept of restraint of trade i.e. the rule of reason had been adopted the EEC Commission would not have been deluged with thousands of notifications. Most of the registered agreements appear to be simple exclusive franchise agreements and thus must be of no substantial anticompetitive significance. Consequently, they hardly merited so much attention. The time thereby saved would have enabled the Commission to concentrate on horizontal agreements and to counteract more efficiently the more serious conspiracies. My main concern however is not with what is he more liberal rule but with what is the more efficient one. If at the same time it is more liberal let it be so. It is at all events clear that the narrowness of the approach taken by the Commission has not been conducive to efficiency but rather to bureaucratic paralysis. Generally business groups in Europe just as in American complain about the lack of certainty in Antitrust law. At the same time they are included to demand more flexibility. Such demands are irreconcilable. A rule of reason under Article 85(1) would bring about more uncertainty for business men. But some uncertainty appears to be a fair price to pay for an effective antitrust policy. It is inherent in the nature of such policy not to rely on abstract legal criteria but to discriminate between significant and insubstantial restraints of trade'; V Korah in 'EEC Competition Policy-Legal Form or Economic Efficiency' (1986) *Current Legal Problems* (39) 85 at 100 observes in regard to Judge Joliet, 'When he was a university teacher at Liège, Judge Joliet was the first and most cogent advocate of the need for market analysis under Art 85 (1).'

of convenience some of the legal analysis of Korah will be considered in summary form as being representative of the precursors responsible for the evolution of Article EU 101 TFEU (ex Article 85 EEC). The immense work of Korah consisting of many articles, books, years of teaching competition law and professional advising can be considered from many points of view: the economic aspect which is arguably that of a lawyer using the principles of the Chicago School[72] will not be considered here by reason of lack of space. Rather, it is the procedural aspect of the approach to interpreting and applying notably Article 101 TFEU (ex Article 85 EC), specifically, the use of expert evidence albeit of the Chicago School which provides expert opinion as to how Article 85 (1) and (3) are applied. Two observations are to be made at this juncture: first, although the specific economic theory which underpins the legal interpretation of Article 101 TFEU (Article 85 EC) is that of the Chicago School, nevertheless, the procedure utilized is the Rules of Civil Procedure[73] of European Union Courts. In short, it is submitted that Korah's approach although based upon a specific school of economic experts can be utilized by any party by reason of the fact that whatever the type of expert economic opinion, the same rules of civil procedure must be used: namely, those of the Community courts;[74] second, conspicuously the expertise involved is that of an economist or at a minimum, a lawyer, who is extremely familiar with a particular economic theory. Rather, it would appear that in terms of litigation whether before the national courts or the EU Courts procedurally, Korah envisages that the lawyer will work with an economist mirroring in large measure, perhaps, her own earlier professional experiences in the UK. Such collaboration falls naturally, within the ambit of the use of either a party expert notably as provided within the rules of the CJ and the GC; or in the alternate, the use of a court expert, an expert appointed by the court in order to provide an opinion for itself taking into consideration the procedural possibility of an assessor.[75] Indeed, such an expert is appointed by the court in order to assist it in understanding certain of the economic concepts utilized either by the court expert or by the experts of the parties or both. It is submitted that it is specifically the use of the economic expert evidence which is to be utilized by the EU judges, both in contentious and non-contentious litigation involving the application of Articles 101 and 102 TFEU (ex Articles 85 and 86 EEC), which distinguishes Korah's method of interpretation and application of those two articles from that of the Commission and of the EU courts themselves particularly at the early period of the application of the aforementioned articles. It is also submitted that it was the use of the economic expert evidence, in the premises, the Chicago School, which led effectively to considering the component words of Article 101 TFEU (ex Article 85 EEC) in particular, but also Article 102 TFEU (ex Article 86 EEC) as technical words as opposed to words with ordinary. As noted earlier, the introduction of the economic evidence particularly as regards to Article 101

72. RA Posner, 'The Chicago School of Antitrust Analysis' (1979) *University Pennsylvania L Rev* 925; The Law and Economics of Antitrust (U of Chicago Press) GJ Stigler, The Organisation of Industry (Homewood, R D Irwin, 1968);WJ Baumol, J Panzar & RD Willig, *Contestable Markets and the Theory of Industry Structure* (New York, Harcourt Brace Jovanovich, 1982).
73. www.curia.europa.eu, Civil Procedure: CJ and GC: website last used 28 October 2013.
74. *Ibid.*
75. See definition of an assessor in earlier chapters herein.

(1) TFEU (ex Article 85 (1) EEC) led to a reduction of its scope of application. Overall, therefore, the result was that the aforementioned articles of the TFEU (ex EEC) were considered as technical words the meaning of which and the scope of which were directed at a specialist audience composed primarily of experts: economists businessmen and lawyers with a background in economics or assisted by an expert and of course judges assisted by an expert or with training in economics such as Judge Joliet. The advantage of this narrower statutory construction of Article 101 (1) TFEU (ex Article 85 (1) EEC) was substantial: first and most significantly, the use of an economic theory in the form of expert opinion presented to the CJ (ex ECJ) permits the construction of a fully reasoned judgment in conformity with the principles with which the judgments of the EU courts must comply, namely, judgments (particularly of the GC) coupled with reasons which by their existence protect, in the context of litigation, the rights of the defence by providing lucid and clear grounds for appeal in conformity with notably Article 6 (1) ECHR; second, the use of an economic theory to sustain the interpretation of the component words of notably Article 101 (1) TFEU (ex Article 85 (1) EEC) provides at least two new grounds of appeal: on the one hand, that of the accuracy of the application of the economic theory involved, for example, whether or not the market correctly delineated using the criterion of the Chicago School for example, and on the other, what might be termed the accuracy of the theory as a whole, for example the Chicago School, as opposed to the accuracy of an opposing economic theory. Accordingly, the use of the expert evidence serves to protect the rights of the defence much more effectively by providing clear reasons for the statutory interpretation but also specific grounds on various levels as just noted, all thereby enhancing the respect of the rights of the defence. Overall, therefore, it is submitted that statutory interpretation of the aforementioned articles based upon economic expert evidence, when used, can lead to a judgment which is procedurally and in terms of accuracy or rectitude of decision superior to judgments made without the use of economic evidence: this is because the component words of the aforementioned TFEU (ex EEC)articles are considered from the point of view of the ordinary meaning of words where judges do not admit or utilize expert evidence. Therefore, it is now appropriate to consider some of the observations made by Korah in the above context of which the first is the following:

> Both [Articles 85 and 86] are drafted in terms of economic concepts – agreements that restrict competition, dominant position and so on. One might have expected them to be applied only after a careful commercial and economic analysis of the market they affect. Yet many lawyers who appear before both the Community and national courts, the judges and the jurists who become official in the competition department of the Commission tend to find economic analysis difficult although specialist competition lawyers and in-house counsel advising firm on prospective transactions are often better at it and the latter know the markets.[76]

76. V Korah, 'EEC Competition Policy – Legal Form or Economic Efficiency' (1986) *Current Legal Problems* (39) 85 at 92. See also V Korah, *Cases and Materials of EC Competition Law* (London, Hart, 2006); V Korah (ed) *Competition Law of the European Community* (NY, Lexis Publishing, 2001).

> ... To see whether an agreement restricts competition it is not enough to examine its provisions. One needs to know about the market and the commercial reasons for inserting restrictive provisions. .... Neither the Commission nor the Court enquired whether Consten (Consten & Grundig) would have established the market so effectively or at all, without absolute territorial protection from parallel imports no whether UNEF and other imports would have been so successful if it had not. If the answer to both questions was negative then even absolute territorial protection would have been necessary for the development of any competition in France for Grundig products at that time. Indeed it would have helped to integrate the market. The analysis of the Court and the Commission limited to the terms of the transaction and ignoring their effect on the market may have led to the wrong result.[77]

It is clear from these statements that Korah is effectively considering[78] the components of Articles 101 and 102 TFEU (ex Articles 85 and 86 EEC) as technical words which can be only understood by those who have training in economics in that effectively expert opinion evidence in the form of an economic analysis would be presented in litigation or in legal opinions. More specifically, Korah makes a clear distinction between what is in reality, the ordinary meaning of the words which compose Articles 101 and 102 TFEU (ex Articles 85 and 86 EEC) which produces what might be termed their inaccurate application, that is, the 'wrong result' and the contrary: that is, the expert opinion of an economist which, in the particular case at hand, would produce the « correct result ». In order to achieve the latter, according to Korah, 'One needs to know about the market and the commercial reasons for inserting restrictive provisions.' It is also clear that one has access to, henceforth, at least two grounds of appeal so as to protect the rights of the defence: the observation, 'One needs to know about the market and the commercial reasons for inserting restrictive provisions.' effectively implies not only that the knowledge about the market is accurate in the sense that the economic theory has been applied correctly by the expert but in turn, that the economic theory, in the instant case, the Chicago School, can be said to produce appropriate results in relation to other theories. It is these two factors, in particular, which will provide the structure for a seriously reasoned judgment based upon the analysis of the market by means of the application of a particular economic theory.[79] The result is that the

77. V Korah 'EEC Competition Policy – Legal Form or Economic Efficiency' (1986) *Current Legal Problems* (39) *ibid.*, 85 at 93-94.
78. It is clear that Professor Korah did not specifically utilize or analyse the judgments of the then Community Courts (now EU Courts) or the decisions of the European Commission using the terminology which is used in the instant analysis. It is rather that the analysis used here which is based upon a method of statutory interpretation notably that of R Sullivan, *Sullivan and Driedger on the Construction of Statutes*, 4th edn, (Vancouver, Butterworths, 2002), *supra*, appears to describe very effectively and efficiently her analysis as represented by the citations of her work considered herein: in short, the instant work represents an analysis using the method of statutory interpretation of Sullivan of specific citations taken from the published work of Korah.
79. Possible examples of alternate economic theories would be: Austrian School (L von Mises, *Epistemological Problems of Economics*, 3rd edn (translated by G Reisman (L von Mises Institute, Auburn, Alabama, 2003)); Keynsian (JM Keynes, *A Treatise on Money* (Cambridge, CUP, 1979); Post Keynsian (M Kalecki, *Selected Essays on the Dynamics of the Capitalist Economy* (Cambridge, CUP, 1971)); Structuralist Economics (R. Prebish, *The Economics Development of Latin America and its Principal Problems* (New York, United Nations, 1950); Stockholm School

introduction and use of expert economic analysis can lead when used, to the reduction of the scope of application of the aforementioned Article 101 (1) TFEU (ex Article 85 (1) EEC) and in so doing can result in much stronger judgments from the point of view of the rights of the defence by means of the articulation of reasons and conformity with Article 6 (1) ECHR and therefore the Rule of Law and the procedural principal of rectitude of decision espoused by Bentham.[80] As noted earlier, the problem in terms of statutory interpretation notably of the TFEU can be identified as the failure to consider certain of the operative words in Article 101 (1) TFEU (ex Article 85 (1)EEC) as technical words which are to be proved by as matters of fact by evidence and in

(K Wicksell) M Woodford, Interest and Prices: Foundations of Monetary Policy (Princeton, Princeton University Press, 2003)); also Law and Economics: C Veljanovski, *Economic Principles of Law* (Cambridge, CUP, 2007).

80. AAS Zuckerman (ed) *Civil Justice in Crisis: Comparative Perspectives of Civil Procedure* (Oxford, OUP, 1999) at 3-4 'In all systems of procedure doing justice means arriving at decisions which give the parties before the court what is legally due to them. In order to do justice then the court has to determine the true facts and then correctly apply the law to them. In Bentham's terminology, the purpose of procedure is rectitude of decision which requires the correct application of the law to the true facts (Note 1 p. 4 Principle of Judicial Procedure in Collected Works of Jeremy Bentham (ed) Bowring (1938-43) vol. ii; see also W Twining, Theories of Evidence: (Bentham and Wigmore) (1985))'; at p. 5 'Most if not all procedural requirements are concerned to secure rectitude of decision including the requirements of procedural justice. Measures such as the right to be heard or the right to an impartial tribunal are dictated by the desire for rectitude of decision. Of course the appearance of justice is also important but it does not alter the fact that at the foundation of procedures lies the objective of getting at the truth. This objective lies behind e entire procedural organization. Rules such as those dealing with notice of commencement of proceedings with the definition of the issues between the parties with the obtaining of evidence and with the calling of witnesses are all designed to facilitate the correct determination of fact and of law. There is one more observation that needs to be made about rectitude of decision. A partial or prejudiced judge could distort the truth or the application of the law and thus undermine rectitude of decision. But it is not only judges of the law who could distort rectitude of decision: procedures too could do so since as we have seen, procedures are imperfect and liable to some mistakes. Given there is always a risk of error justice demands that this risk should be equally distributed between different litigants. A procedure which imposed a higher risk of error on a certain class of litigants would fail to treat those litigants with equal concern and regard. Being treated as equal is a basic requirement of justice. It is not suggested that plaintiffs and defendants are treated equally vis-à-vis each other. Clearly they are not because one is bound to win whereas the other will lose. The requirement of treating litigants means that none of them is given preferential treatment compared with other. In short it is means that all are equal before the law in the sense that the rules of procedure will not distort the correct application of the law to the true facts in favour of one litigant.' For improvement of the possibilities to ensure the rectitude of decision the Court may uses experts in the procedural sense of assessors who will explain to them the meaning of technical terms used by the experts in their opinion evidence: D Dwyer, 'The Future of Assessors under the CPR' (2006) *CJQ* (25) 219; L Blom-Cooper QC 'Experts and Assessors' (2002) *Civil Justice Quarterly (CJQ)* (22) 341; A Dickey, 'The Province and Function of Assessors in English Courts' (1970) *MLR* (33) 494; SJ Cannon, 'Effective Fact-Finding' (2006) *CJQ* (25) 327; for the dangers of distortion of expert evidence by the experts see: DM Dwyer, 'The Causes and Manifestation of Bias in Civil Expert Evidence' (2006) *CJQ* (25) 425; Sir L Blom-Cooper QC (ed) *Experts in Civil Courts* (Oxford, OUP, 2006); D Dwyer, *Civil Procedure Rules: Ten Years On* (Oxford, OUP, 2009); D Dwyer, 'The Effective Management of Bias in Civil Expert Evidence (2007) *CJQ* (26) 57; on civil procedure: Lord Woolf Access to Justice – Interim Report (1995) Ch. 23; Access to Justice-Final Report Ch. 13; JA Jolowicz, *On Civil Procedure* (Cambridge, CUP, 2005); AAA Zuckerman, *Civil Procedure* (London, Sweet & Maxwell, 2006), *supra*; D Dwyer, *The Judicial Assessment of Expert Evidence* (Cambridge, CUP, 2008).

particular expert evidence. Sullivan[81] observes that the choice of a technical meaning as opposed to an ordinary meaning as well as the method of proof takes place in the following manner:

> In deciding whether to adopt the ordinary or the technical meaning of words court look to the usual range of factors: the purpose and scheme of the legislation, the consequences of preferring one meaning over the other, relevant common law principles and so on.... Whether a technical meaning and what that meaning is are both questions of fact which must be established in a legally acceptable way. When a technical or specialized meaning is not something that everybody knows it cannot be judicial noticed but must be established through evidence normal expert opinion evidence.

As noted earlier, of particular significance however, is the failure to consider technical words such as the « restraint of trade » as technical words which require expert opinion evidence. It is submitted that this failure has two major consequences: first, as regards contentious actions, the object of which is to determine rights, the failure to consider certain words as technical words which require expert evidence arguably sounds as a breach of ECHR Article 6 (1). Fundamentally, the deficit arises because there has been a failure to introduce and to examine expert evidence which is required in order to prove the technical meaning of words in Article 101 (1) TFEU (ex Article 85 (1) EEC): in short, a failure to consider the expert evidence properly which undermines the rights of the defence. Second, this is aggravated by the fact that the rules of procedure of the EU Courts and, notably, that for the appointment of a court expert and for an assessor exist and may be activated as noted previously, by the EU Courts themselves on their own motion. Similarly, there is an absence of active rules of Case Management which are necessary in order to ensure that the necessary facts are pleaded. Essentially, as previously observed, the problem is that the failure to consider certain of the words as technical words which require proof by means of expert evidence is such that the interpretation thereof is incomplete and therefore unfair. In short, an incomplete examination of the meaning of the technical terms has taken place which fundamentally distorts the technical meaning of the word. It is clearly in this procedural sense that Korah is completely accurate in stating that effectively the absence of economic analysis, that is, a deficit of economic expert opinion, renders the examination of the technical meaning of the operative words incomplete if not unreliable:

> Both articles are drafted in terms of economic concepts – agreements that restrict competition, dominant position and so on.... To see whether an agreement restricts competition it is not enough to examine its provisions. One needs to know about the market and the commercial reasons for inserting restrictive provisions.

Arguably, this particular violation is the essence of what Bentham identified as being the fundamental principle of civil procedure: namely rectitude of decision: the correct application of the law to the true facts coupled with compliance with ECHR Article 6

81. R Sullivan, *Sullivan and Dredger on the Construction of Statutes*, 4th edn (Vancouver, Butterworths, 2002), *supra*, at 46.

(1).[82] The interpretation of a technical word as an ordinary word thereby precluding the introduction of economic expert evidence to prove the meaning thereof as opposed to the utilization of the private knowledge used by judges as competent speakers which is appropriate for the meaning of ordinary meaning of words, conspicuously violates two principles: first, that of rectitude of decision and second, the principle of dues process embodied within ECHR Article 6 (1), effectively, the concept of the Rule of Law. Second, there is the fact that the use of procedural principles can assist in determining what constitutes an accurate or a well formed judgment, notably, one with reasons based upon technical words which are interpreted by means of expert evidence. Finally, the evolution which EU competition law has undergone permits a scholar such as Korah[83] to remark several years later:

> My object in this chapter written 45 years after the adoption of the first implementing regulation is to assess some aspects of competition policy and of the institutions that enforce it which I particularly like or dislike. In the past I have complained about the paucity of economic reasoning by the Commission and in this edition I shall discuss some of the steps that Commission and CFI have taken to meet the criticism. I shall express my personal conviction that competition policy and its enforcement have improved dramatically over the last decade and the Commission's initiative to abandon its monopoly over Art 81 (3) has made a vast change largely for the better.

While the current situation may not be perfect with respect to the enforcement of EU Competition law by the EU Courts notably in the context of a litigious context as opposed to the reference procedure nevertheless, it may be that Korah[84] feels that some changes have taken place with respect to the use of expert evidence: namely, the fact that the EU Courts and the Commission are increasingly less reluctant to use expert economic opinion to sustain at least some of their reasoning. Therefore, at least in that respect the enforcement of Articles 101 and 102 TFEU has perhaps improved in the sense of the statutory interpretation of the aforementioned articles becoming, on some occasions at least more accurate by reason of the increasing use of expert opinion evidence both by the Union Courts and of course the Commission. To that limited extent one can state that the application of the application of Articles 101 and 102 TFEU seems, in some cases, to be more accurate and that the Courts in particular have contravened less their duty pursuant to Article 19 TEU 'it [the Court] it shall ensure that in the interpretation and application of the Treaties the law is observed' as well as of course, Article 6 (1) ECHR and the principle of rectitude of decision.

82. AAS Zuckerman (ed), *Civil Justice in Crisis: Comparative Perspectives of Civil Procedure* (Oxford, OUP, 1999) at 3-4.
83. V Korah, *An Introductory Guide to EC Competition Law and Practice*, 9th edn (Oxford, Hart, 2007).
84. One may quaere whether Judge René Joliet who died on 15 July 1995 and who wrote the Forward for the fourth edition of Korah's Introductory Guide to EC Competition Law and Practice in 1990 might well share her comments just cited above in the 9th edition.

Indeed perhaps the substantial heuristic value of the examination of some of the EU Competition judgments most of which involve contentious as opposed to non-contentious proceedings through the preliminary reference procedure, is the magnitude of the violations of that particular duty, namely, Article 6 (1) ECHR, principle of rectitude of decision and Article 19 TEU, in some of the judgments. Arguably, much of the work of Korah can ultimately seen as an attempt to identify, analyse and criticize these early breaches of Article 19 TEU as being derivative of defective methods of statutory interpretation of Articles 101 and 102 TFEU as used by the Union Courts which include, necessarily, their use of their own rules of civil procedure which deal with among other things, expert evidence: that is, TFEU articles whose component words possess technical meaning which require the use of evidence, specifically expert evidence obtainable through the use by the Court where necessary of its own initiative in order to accurately apply the law to the facts following Article 6 (1) ECHR and the allied concept of the Rule of Law and the principle of rectitude of decision. One might add that these major deficiencies in turn have been exacerbated by Court's Rules of Pleading the case notably in regard to the contentious jurisdiction which are deficient in the precision with which they require the drafting of the pleadings.

It is, thus, in this optic that it would be appropriate to consider some of the following examples to illustrate some of both the flaws and the achievements of the CJ and the GC in the enforcement of Articles 101 and 102 TFEU (ex Articles 85 and 86 EEC) over the years as well as some of the criticisms and suggestions made by learned commentators over extended periods. In his extremely helpful presentation of a series of EU Competition judgments, Nazzini[85] provides the following summary of the issues in Consten and Grudig:[86] he commences by referring to Korah's[87] remarks:

> Both Articles 81[88] and 82 and the regulations that implement them as well as the merger regulation must be read in the light of the objectives of the Treaty. Article 2 as amended provides that:

85. R Nazzini, 'Art 81 EC between the Time Present and Time Past: a Normative Critique of 'Restriction of Competition' in EU Law' (2006) *CMLRev* 497.
86. *Etablissements Consten S.a RL and Grundig-Verkaufs GmbH v Commission* (1966) *ECR* 299; it is clear that this judgment involves a direction action in which following P Lasok, *The European Court of Justice: Practice and Procedure*, 2nd edn (London, Butterworths, 1994) there are no specific limitations on evidence.
87. V Korah, *An Introductory Guide to EC Competition Law and Practice*, 9th edn (Oxford, Hart, 2007), *supra*, at p. 8.
88. Flowchart summarizing the procedure under the Council Regulation (EC) No 1/2003, 2

> The Community shall have as its task, by establishing a common market and an economic and monetary union and by implementing the common policies or activities referred to in Articles 3 and 4, to promote throughout the Community a harmonious and balanced development of economic activities, sustainable and non-inflationary growth respecting the environment, a high degree of convergence of economic performance, a high level of employment and of social protection, the raising of the standard of living and quality of life, and economic and social cohesion and solidarity among Member States.

One might think that the Common Market is the mechanism by which the expansion, stability and so forth are to be achieved but market integration has been elevated in competition cases to an aim in itself (note 15 at p. 8, *Consten & Grundig v Commission*, Cases 56.58.64 (1966) ECR 299) and has been pursued in a mechanical way even when this leads to reduced competition and may delay the integration of the market. The ECJ has held more than once that both Articles 81 and 82 should be construed in the light of these provisions even when there is a fairly clear literal interpretation to the contrary.

Article 3 (1) provides:

> For the purposes set out in Article 2, the activities of the Community shall include, as provided in this Treaty and in accordance with the timetable set out therein:
>
> (a) the elimination, as between Member States, of customs duties and quantitative restrictions on the import and export of goods, and of all other measures having equivalent effect; ...
> (g) a system ensuring that competition in the internal market is not distorted;
> .... .

In Continental Can for instance the ECJ interpreted Article 82 not only as a provision under which the conduct of firms already dominant which harmed consumers directly could be regulated but also as one forbidding the weakening of any remaining potential competition by a firm already dominant as this might harm consumers in the longer term.

Nazzini[89] then observes:

> The problem of what constitutes a restriction of competition is of great theoretical and practical significance. From a theoretical point of view, the problem of the definition of 'restriction of competition' under Art 81(1) is closely related to the development of Community law as a whole. This is borne out by the process of internal convergence between the Art 81 (1) jurisprudence and the judicial

---

Article 105 of the TFEU 8
Article 119 of the TFEU 8
Article 346 of the TFEU 9.

89. R Nazzini 'Article 81 EC between Time Present and Time Past: A Normative Critique of 'Restriction of Competition' (2006) *CMLRev* (43) 497, *supra*, at 499.

approach to the analysis of the free movement of goods and the freedom to provide services enshrined in Articles 28[90] and 49[91] EC respectively.

Nazzini[92] interestingly observes the following with regard to the accuracy of the judgment of the Court of Justice in the case of Consten:[93]

> Consten and Grundig has come under severe criticisms for not taking onto account the economics of intra brand restrictions and vertical restraints for relying on abstract and formalistic arguments and for elevating the establishment of the common market from being an instrument to foster competition, economic convergence and efficiency to being an end in itself. (note 41 p 508 V. Korah,[94] *An*

90. CHAPTER 3 of the TFEU PROHIBITION OF QUANTITATIVE RESTRICTIONS BETWEEN MEMBER STATES
Article 34 (ex Article 28 TEC) Quantitative restrictions on imports and all measures having equivalent effect shall be prohibited between Member States.;
91. CHAPTER 3 SERVICES *Article 56* (ex Article 49 TEC) Within the framework of the provisions set out below, restrictions on freedom to provide services within the Union shall be prohibited in respect of nationals of Member States who are established in a Member State other than that of the person for whom the services are intended. The European Parliament and the Council, acting in accordance with the ordinary legislative procedure, may extend the provisions of the Chapter to nationals of a third country who provide services and who are established within the Union.
Article 52 (ex Article 46 TEC) 1. The provisions of this Chapter and measures taken in pursuance thereof shall not prejudice the applicability of provisions laid down by law, regulation or administrative action providing for special treatment for foreign nationals on grounds of public policy, public security or public health.
Art 34 TFEU ex Art 28 is subject to the following derogation:
CHAPTER 3 PROHIBITION OF QUANTITATIVE RESTRICTIONS BETWEEN MEMBER STATES
Article 34 (ex Article 28 TEC) Quantitative restrictions on imports and all measures having equivalent effect shall be prohibited between Member States.
Article 35 (ex Article 29 TEC) Quantitative restrictions on exports, and all measures having equivalent effect, shall be prohibited between Member States.
Article 36 TFEU (ex Article 30 TEC) The provisions of Articles 34 and 35 shall not preclude prohibitions or restrictions on imports, exports or goods in transit justified on grounds of public morality, public policy or public security; the protection of health and life of humans, animals or plants; the protection of national treasures possessing artistic, historic or archaeological value; or the protection of industrial and commercial property. Such prohibitions or restrictions shall not, however, constitute a means of arbitrary discrimination or a disguised restriction on trade between Member States.
92. R Nazzini, 'Article 81 EC between Time Present and Time Past: A Normative Critique of 'Restriction of Competition' (2006) *CMLRev* (43) 497, *supra*, at 508.
93. Cons*ten and Grundig v Commission,* Cases 56 and 58/64 (1966) *ECR* 299.
94. V Korah, 'The Rise and Fall of Provisional Validity – The Need for a Rule of reason in EEC Antitrust' (1981) 3 *NW J Int L and Bus* 320, 354-355: 'The Community Court and Commission have not developed the same theory of per se offences so brilliantly developed in the early cases under the Sherman Act. Naked restraints on pricing market sharing and some kinds of collective boycott ... are likely to be condemned with fairly short reasoning if they are found a capable of restricting trade between Member States but more market analysis is required in the case of ancillary restraints. In Consten and Grundig, the Court seems to have developed a per see rule against absolute territorial protection conferred by export bans, and this has been consistently applied by the Commission despite mounting criticism. For all other restraints, however, the Court seems to be applying a rules of reason requiring an analysis of the actual or intended effects in the light of market conditions. The Commission however habitually analyzes agreements under Article 85 (1) in the formalist way developed by the German case law and condemns any restriction on the conduct of the parties or third parties provided the restriction has or may be expected to have appreciable effects on the market. Only under Art 85 (3) does the

> *Introductory Guide to EC Competition Law and Practice*, 8th edn (2004 Oxford) ... It cannot however be maintained that the Court did not apply Art 81 EC in a way consistent with its economics purpose (Note 42 Oduda 'Interpreting Article 81(1): Demonstrating restrictive effect' 26 EL Rev (2001) 261 a 271-72)

Korah[95] observes in this regard:

> On reading Art 2 of the EEC Treaty one might be forgiven for thinking that the integration of the Common Market is a mechanism for improving efficiency and so achieving an accelerated increase in prosperity stability and so forth. In competition cases however, integration has been elevated by the Commission and the Court to a goal in itself more important that efficiency.

Accordingly it is necessary to consider the relevant section of the judgment in Consten:[96]

> The applicants and the German Government maintain that the Commission has relied on a mistaken interpretation of the concept of an agreement which may

Commission usually try to balance any pro and anti-competitive effects. If national courts adopt the Commission's practice it is feared that many desirable contracts which restrict only competition that could not take without such an agreement or which restrict competition less than they increase it may not be made. The Commission grants few exemptions ... Important agreements are unlikely to be exempted unless certain clauses are altered. These alterations may help one part more than the other and the whole contract may have to be renegotiated after the parties have been implemented it when their relative bargaining power may have been altered as a result of the collaboration. This is a considerable disincentive to notification. There is fear that European firms that may have to compete in world markets may fall behind technologically or have to merge completely so as to reduce the risk of collaboration. Market analyses are difficult especially for lawyers and bureaucrats. But if such analyses are not made agreements that may have overall desirable consequences should not be controlled. This means that national courts will have to be strong in resisting claims that agreements are anti-competitive just because some competitor is harmed.' I Forrester & C Loral, 'The Laicization of Community Law: Self-Help and the Rules of Reason: How Competition Law Is and Could Be Applies' (1984) *CMLRev* (21); R Wish & B Surfing, 'Article 85 and the Rule of Reason' (1987) 7 *YBEL* 12-20, make an interesting attempt at providing what might be justification for specific method for the interpretation of TFEU Art 101 and 102' (ex Articles 81 and 82) because among other things 'We do not consider them to be appropriate forum for deciding upon complex economic issues'. Although intellectually interesting this position notably in the context of Dir 1/2003 does suffer, with due respect to the two scholars involved, from what might be termed an erroneous evaluation of the ability of both the national and the EU courts to evaluate economic evidence. In truth the EU courts as well as certainly the English courts possess the requisite procedural ability to not only introduce expert evidence but also, perhaps more significantly, to evaluate this evidence: that is by means of assessors whose opinions about given to the judges as regards the meaning of expert testimony particularly in economics is communicated to the judges and to but also to the parties in order to conform with the rights of defence provided by the ECHR but also to ensure the duty to provide proper evaluation of the evidence protected by both of those conventions. Whish and Sufrin certainly are right to raise some concern about the effect of the use of economic evidence on the concept of legal certainty, a significant principle in EU law. This principle of legal certainty must, however, be balanced notably with the duty on the part of the courts both Community and national to ensure that the application of the principle of legal certainty is in turn applied taking into consideration ECHR Art 6 (1) due process which requires that all the relevant evidence be carefully examined. See also D Hildebrand, Th*e Role of Economic Analysis in the EC Competition* Rules, 3rd edn (New York, Wolters Kluwer 2009).

95. V Korah 'EEC Competition Policy – Legal Form or Economic Efficiency' (1986)*Current Legal Problems* (39) 85 at 91.
96. *Consten and Grundig v Commission* Cases 56 and 58/64 (1966) *ECR* 299, *supra*, at 341.

> affect trade between Member States and has not shown that such trade would have been greater without the agreement in dispute … .

The concept of an agreement 'which may affect trade between Member States' is intended to define in the law governing cartels, the boundary between the areas respectively covered by Community law and national law. It is only to the extent to which the agreement may affect trade between Member States that the deterioration in competition caused by the agreement falls under the prohibition of Community law contained in Art 85; otherwise it escapes the prohibition.

In this connexion, what is particularly important is whether the agreement is capable of constituting a threat either direct or indirect, actual or potential to freedom of trade between Member States in a manner which might harm the attainment of the objectives of a single market between States. Thus the fact that an agreement encourages an increase even a large one, in the volume of trade between states is not sufficient to exclude the possibility that the agreement may 'affect' such trade in the abovementioned manner. In the present case, the contract between Grundig and Consten on the one hand by preventing undertakings other than Consten from importing Grundig products into France and, on the other hand, by prohibiting Consten from re-exporting those products to other countries of the Common Market indisputably affect trade between Member States. These limitations on the freedom of trade as well as those which might ensure for third parties from the registration in France by Consten of the GINT trade mark which Grundig places on all its products are enough to satisfy the requirement in question.

Consequently the complaints raised in this respect must be dismissed.

One of the primary difficulties with the interpretation of by the CJ of EC Article 85 (1) (now Article 101 TFEU) in Consten is demonstrated by the following sentence in the judgment:

> Thus the fact that an agreement encourages an increase even a large one, in the volume of trade between states is not sufficient to exclude the possibility that the agreement may affect such trade in the above mentioned manner.[97]

This particular sentence, arguably, seeks to preclude the use of a certain type of economics,[98] in the enforcement of Article 85[99] EEC (now Article 101 TFEU): that is, the

---

97. *Consten and Grundig v Commission* Cases 56 and 58/64 (1966) *ECR* 299, *supra*, at 341.
98. V Korah is arguably the major academic exponent of the Chicago School of Economics in the context of EU competition law in the UK. However, in truth, the essence of her position does not consist in the use of a particular school of economics in the practice of competition law and in the judgments and decisions of the CJ and the European Commission but rather the need for use of expert economic evidence in general in enforcement of EU competition law. For Korah this apparently entails, among other things, a thorough analysis of the facts which underlie the use of certain concepts such as market delimitation.
99. 1. The following shall be prohibited as incompatible with the internal market: all agreements between undertakings, decisions by associations of undertakings and concerted practices which may affect trade between Member States and which have as their object or effect the prevention, restriction or distortion of competition within the internal market, and in particular those which:
    (a) directly or indirectly fix purchase or selling prices or any other trading conditions;
    (b) limit or control production, markets, technical development, or investment;
    (c) share markets or sources of supply;

use of restrictions on intra-brand competition which isolate one Member State from another within the European Union in order to stimulate additional extra brand competition and general competition, business and prosperity throughout the Union is precluded because according to the CJ in Consten[100] it 'may affect' trade among the Member States. The CJ observes in this regard:

> In this connexion, what is particularly important is whether the agreement is capable of constituting a threat, either direct or indirect, actual or potential, to attainment of the objectives of a single market between States.[101]

However, the real difficulty, as will be seen shortly, is that the creation of a single market is not one of the objectives which is enumerated in the text of EEC Article 2.[102] This article specifically provides as follows:

> The Community shall have as its task, by establishing a common market and an economic and monetary union and by implementing the common policies or activities referred to in Articles 3 and 4, to promote throughout the Community a harmonious and balanced development of economic activities, sustainable and non-inflationary growth respecting the environment, a high degree of convergence of economic performance, a high level of employment and of social protection, the raising of the standard of living and quality of life, and economic and social cohesion and solidarity among Member States.

It is submitted that the overall problem is as follows: first, the failure of the CJ to utilize expert evidence in the interpretation of ECC Article 85 (1) (now TFEU Article 101 (1) TFEU), and in particular of the verbal phrase 'may affect trade between Member States'; second, this evidentiary and semantic deficit which arguably sounds as a

---

(d) apply dissimilar conditions to equivalent transactions with other trading parties, thereby placing them at a competitive disadvantage;

(e) make the conclusion of contracts subject to acceptance by the other parties of supplementary obligations which, by their nature or according to commercial usage, have no connection with the subject of such contracts.

2. Any agreements or decisions prohibited pursuant to this Article shall be automatically void.
3. The provisions of paragraph 1 may, however, be declared inapplicable in the case of:
   - any agreement or category of agreements between undertakings,
   - any decision or category of decisions by associations of undertakings,
   - any concerted practice or category of concerted practices,

   which contributes to improving the production or distribution of goods or to promoting technical or economic progress, while allowing consumers a fair share of the resulting benefit, and which does not:

   (a) impose on the undertakings concerned restrictions which are not indispensable to the attainment of these objectives;

   (b) afford such undertakings the possibility of eliminating competition in respect of a substantial part of the products in question.

100. *Consten and Grundig v Commission* Cases 56 and 58/64 (1966) *ECR* 299, *supra*, at 341.
101. *Consten and Grundig v Commission* Cases 56 and 58/64 (1966) *ECR* 299, *supra*, at 341 *ibid*.
102. Foreign and Commonwealth Office London, A COMPARATIVE TABLE OF THE CURRENT EC AND EU TREATIES AS AMENDED BY THE TREATY OF LISBON: generally Art 2 and 3 EEC are Art 2 and 3 TFEU: the comparative table must be consulted for the exact equivalences with these two articles. www.official-documents.gov.uk, last consulted on 28.10.2013.

breach of ECHR Article 6 (1) notably in terms of the duty established by *Kraska v Switzerland*[103] to examine properly the submissions of the parties, has led arguably to the unfounded addition of the 'single market' to list of the objectives of EEC Article 85 (now Article 101 TFEU) as set out in EEC Articles 2 and 3.[104] The addition of the 'single market', at least as interpreted by the court, is not based upon any economic expert opinion. In truth, this semantically and grammatically implausible inclusion of single market within the objectives of the EC Article 85 (now Article 101 TFEU) is then used to increase, again without any basis in accurate statutory interpretation based upon the used of expert evidence in the interpretation of technical meaning of words, the scope of the phrase 'may affect trade'. As just noted, the increased scope of that phrase is achieved arguably because the ordinary as opposed to technical meaning of the words has been interpreted. Thus, the prohibition on agreements which are anti-competitive is activated not only when it affects one of the objectives such as economic growth but also if it affects one of the prohibitions on free moment of goods in the context of the single market, even if there is no negative effect on economic growth.[105] This is so because as just observed, the creation of a single market has been transformed into an objective to be achieved under EEC Article 2.[106] In short, the scope of the prohibition in EEC Article 85 (1) (now Article 101 (1) TFEU) is substantially increased particularly by reason of the fact that the 'objectives' have now been increased by the inclusion of the creation of the single market. The demonstration of this unexplained inclusion is to be found in the text of Consten[107] which has been previously noted:

> The Concept of an agreement 'which may affect trade between Member States' is intended to define in the law governing cartels, the boundary between the are respectively covered by Community law and national law. It is only to the extent to which the agreement may affect trade between Member States that the deterioration in competition caused by the agreements falls under the prohibition of Community law contained in Art 85; otherwise it escapes the prohibition.
> In this connexion, what is particularly important is whether the agreement is capable of constituting a threat either direct or indirect, actual or potential to freedom of trade between member States in a manner which might harm the attainment of the objectives of a single market between States. Thus, the fact that an agreement encourages an increase, even a large one in the volume of trade between States is not sufficient to exclude the possibility that the agreement may affect such trade in the above mentioned manner.

It is clear that the CJ does not explain how it is that an interpretation apparently using ordinary meaning of the words contained in EEC Article 85 (1) (now Article 101 (1)

103. *Kraska v Switzerland* (1994) *EHRR* (18) 188, *supra*, para. 30.
104. Foreign and Commonwealth Office London, A COMPARATIVE TABLE OF THE CURRENT EC AND EU TREATIES AS AMENDED BY THE TREATY OF LISBON: generally Art 2 and 3 EEC are Art 2 and 3 TFEU: the comparative table must be consulted for the exact equivalences with these two articles, www.official-documents.gov.uk.
105. *Consten and Grundig v Commission* Cases 56 and 58/64 (1966) *ECR* 299, *supra*, at 341.
106. Foreign and Commonwealth Office London, A COMPARATIVE TABLE OF THE CURRENT EC AND EU TREATIES AS AMENDED BY THE TREATY OF LISBON: generally Art 2 and 3 EEC are Art 2 and 3 TFEU: the comparative table must be consulted for the exact equivalences with these two articles. www.official-documents.gov.uk.
107. *Consten and Grundig v Commission* Cases 56 and 58/64 (1966) *ECR* 299, *supra*, at 341.

TFEU) can justifying including among the objectives provided by EEC Articles 2 and 3[108] that of the creation of a single market, that is, 'the attainment of the objectives of a single market between States'. It is clear that once the creation of a single market which contains its own independent objectives, has been achieved there remains, nevertheless, another step which must be taken: namely, that any effect on the attainment of the objective of the creation of a single market whether positive or negative is prohibited and excluded. Further, it is not apparent on what basis the CJ can justify interpreting 'agreements ... which may affect trade between Member States' in a fashion which is so wide that it includes not only negative effects but positive effects such as the increase of the general prosperity which happens to use barriers to trade which may possibly contravene EC Article 28 (ex EC Articles 28-30 now Articles 34-36 TFEU). This is even more so that such potentially positive restrictions could be justified through a derogation either under public policy or indeed simply benefit from an interpretation of that article which is restrictive in scope as to the word 'all' as in 'all restraints'. The effect of this unjustifiable statutory interpretation and, notably, of the phrase 'which may affect trade between Member States' by the CJ results in the creation of the single market as a political and economic objective where both negative and positive influences may lead, pursuant to EEC Article 85 (2) now (now Article 101 (2) TFEU), to legal and economic consequences: namely the voiding of contracts which may affect the trade in the single market involving Member States. In this regard, one observes the judgment of Consten:

> Thus the fact that an agreement encourages an increase even a large one in the volume of trade between the States is not sufficient to exclude the possibility that the agreement may 'affect' such a trade in the above mentioned manner. In the present case the contract between Grundig and Consten on the one hand by preventing undertakings other than Consten from importing Grundig products into France and on the other hand by prohibiting Consten from re-exporting those products to other countries of the Common Market indisputably affects trade between Member States. These limitations on the freedom of trade as well as those which might ensure for the third parties from the registration in France by Consten of the GINT trade mark which Grundig places on all products are enough to satisfy the requirement in question.

Basically, according to the CJ, the mere fact that a restriction affects trade in what could be a positive (i.e., with an increase in trade) or negative manner (decrease in trade or modification of the market structure) suffices to breach Article 85 (1) (now Article 101 TFEU). It is here that the difficulties arise from the incorrect semantic classification manifests itself: in this regard, it is necessary to consider the actual text in the English translation. Article 85 EEC (now Article 101 TFEU) provides as follows:

> all agreements between undertakings, decisions by associations of undertakings and concerted practices which may affect trade between Member States and which

108. Foreign and Commonwealth Office London, A COMPARATIVE TABLE OF THE CURRENT EC AND EU TREATIES AS AMENDED BY THE TREATY OF LISBON: generally Art 2 and 3 EEC are Art 2 and 3 TFEU: the comparative table must be consulted for the exact equivalences with these two articles, www.official-documents.gov.uk, last consulted on 29.10.2013.

> have as their object or effect the prevention, restriction or distortion of competition within the internal market, and in particular those which ...

It is clear, once again, simply on the ordinary meaning of the words that while there is one category of infraction it has two components: that is, 'agreements .... which may affect trade and have as their object or effect the prevention or ... distortion of competition within the internal market'. The CJ, as noted earlier, transposes this in the following manner:

> In this connection what is particularly important is whether the agreement is capable of constituting a threat either direct or indirect actual or potential to freedom of trade between Member States in a manner which might harm the attainment of the objectives of a single market between States. Thus the fact that an agreement encourages an increase even a large one in the volume of trade between States is not sufficient to exclude the possibility that the agreement may affect such trade in the above mentioned manner.

A major difficulty, here, is that even assuming, which is not the case, that the creation of a common market is an objective of the Treaty, there is no indication as to what its attributes and requirements would be. Most significantly however, is that arguably, the words in Article 85 (1) (now Article 101 TFEU) effectively are directed at a small group of experts, namely, economists, businessmen and anti-trust lawyers. Therefore, they possess a technical and not just an ordinary meaning which in turn will require expert evidence from at a minimum an expert such as an economist in order to be proved. It is submitted that by reason of its failure to consider the technical meaning of Article 85 (1) EC (now Article 101 TFEU) the CJ has created a category of infringing contracts and agreements which is larger than necessary. Accordingly, the then applicable Regulation 17/62,[109] in the context of the above interpretation led to a much larger number of contracts than strictly necessary violating Article 85 (2) (now Article 101 (2) TFEU. Manifestly, by reason of this violation, the contracts became void and therefore, unenforceable. Further, it is necessary to consider what words in particular possess a technical meaning and thereby, would require proof of their meaning by an expert. It is clear that the words such as 'common market' 'distortion' 'may effect' would require at a minimum interpretation by an economist. The CJ proffers no expert evidence to sustain its opinion and ultimately judgment to the effect that barriers in the sense of intra-brand restrictions based upon the boundaries of Member States 'may effect' in a negative manner either the common market or the attainment of the economic objectives provided notably by Articles 2 and 3 EEC.[110] In short, the CJ provides no finding in expert opinion to establish that its manner of interpreting the above terms which form part of Article 85 (1) (now Article 101 (1) TFEU) EEC require of necessity its interpretation which is devoid of any grounding in expert opinion: namely, the

109. Council Regulation No 17 (EEC): First Regulation implementing Articles 85 and 86 of the Treaty [Official Journal No. 013, 21.02.1962].
110. Foreign and Commonwealth Office London, A COMPARATIVE TABLE OF THE CURRENT EC AND EU TREATIES AS AMENDED BY THE TREATY OF LISBON: generally Art 2 and 3 EEC are Art 2 and 3 TFEU: the comparative table must be consulted for the exact equivalences with these two articles. www.official-documents.gov.uk.

expansion of the category of contracts and agreements which may breach Article 85 (2) (now Article 101 (2) TFEU) thereby leading to considerable economic and administrative distress. This is even more so the case that EEC Articles 28 and 30 (now Articles 34-36 TFEU) with which Article 85 (1) (now Article 101 (1) TFEU)may be conveniently construed notably in relation to the restrictions upon the free moment of good within the European Union, clearly do not exclude the possibility either of being interpreted restrictively in the sense of using expert evidence to determine to what categories the prohibitions do and do not apply; and second, the whole regime of prohibitions of restrictions and quantitative restrictions is subject to derogation notably as provided in Article 30 EEC (now Article 36 TFEU) of public policy.[111] In short, the interpretation proposed by the CJ which is not based upon any expertise nor any support of related articles of the Treaty such as Article 30 (now Article 36 TFEU) and can be said to constitute the following problems: namely the failure to use expert evidence in order to

111. See in this regard *Schmidberger* Case 112/00 (2003) *ECR* I 5659 at para. 78 which ultimately permitted the restriction of the TFEU right to move free goods on the basis of violation of Art 10 ECHR: 'First, whilst the free movement of goods constitutes one of the fundamental principles in the scheme of the Treaty, it may, in certain circumstances, be subject to restrictions for the reasons laid down in Article 36 of that Treaty or for overriding requirements relating to the public interest, in accordance with the Court's consistent case-law since the judgment in Case 120/78 *Rewe-Zentral ('Cassis de Dijon')* [1979] *ECR* 649.' Case 112/00 refers to Rewe Case 120/78 at para. 13 'As the Commission rightly observed, the fixing of limits in relation to the alcohol content of beverages may lead to the standardization of products placed on the market and of their designations in the interests of a great transparency of commercial transaction and offers for sale to the public. However this line of argument cannot be taken so far as to regard the mandatory fixing of minimum alcohol contents as being an essential guarantee of the fairness of commercial transactions since it is a simple matter to ensure that suitable information is convened to the purchaser by requiring the display of an indication of origin and of the alcohol content on the packaging of products.' See also the Opinion of AG-Jacobs in Schmidberger Case 112/00 (2003) *ECR* I 5659 at paras 85-118. In the instant case, it is submitted that following the normal practise as regards the application of a derogation to a right guaranteed by the TFEU, as per the right to free movement of goods, the derogation pursuant to public policy would require a restrictive interpretation so as not to undermine the purpose of the right to free moment and the it would be necessary to ensure that the restriction upon the right, in the instant case, an imposition of territorial restrictions which prevented intra-brand competition upon a Member State basis, was both justified and proportional. However, it is here that the derogation in EEC Art 30 as regards public policy would specifically require that its component words be considered as technical words and that therefore, the proof of their meaning would require expert opinion evidence, namely that of an economist. In order to ensure accuracy and conformity of the interpretation of Art 2 and 3 EEC pursuant to its duty to apply the law under Art 19 TFEU, the CJ would in turn be obliged to apply the principles of effectiveness and proportionality with the assistance of expert economist evidence. Schmidberger, *supra*, is notable in that the CJ used ECHR Art 13 right of free assembly which is not an absolute right to restrict the application of the Art 28 EC prohibition of restrictions upon the free moment of good for which there is a derogation under public policy pursuant to Art 30. Accordingly the CJ balanced the interest of the demonstrators to organized a limited blockage of the tunnel to that of the complainants who wished to exercise their right to move goods without restriction but which right can be restricted through statutory derogations such as public policy which must be restrictively interpreted and made subject to the n but which right can be restricted through statutory derogations such as public policy which must be restrictively interpreted and made subject to the application of the principle of proportionality. At no time however, did either the CJ or AG-Jacobs consider the possibility of utilizing the CJ Rule of Procedure Art 45-47 and Art 25 of the Statutes of the Court to appoint a court expert to assist them with the interpretation of the words in the derogation of EC Art 30.

interpret statutes which are composed of words which have technical meaning has led to granting to the words in question an unjustifiably wide scope. This unjustifiably wide scope is of course entirely devoid of any empirical evidence. Moreover, the method of interpretation used by the CJ signally fails by reason of the various errors noted herein. It also does not demonstrate that Article 85 (1) (now Article 101 TFEU) is subject only to one economic interpretation, namely, that developed by the CJ without the presence of experts. Rather, it is clear that the CJ has not yet demonstrated that Article 85 EC (now Article 101 TFEU) cannot be successfully interpreted and applied to various economic theories including that of Chicago economists.[112]

Finally, even if one accepts that the objectives includes the creation of the common market the fundamental flaw arises from the fact that the words have been interpreted in the judgment in their ordinary meaning. There is no demonstration that the creation of the single market notably by means of EEC Articles 28 and 30 (now Articles 34-36 TFEU), and the prohibitions upon barriers to the free movement of good, in terms of economic evidence requires such wide scope. This is a fortiori the case when one considers the derogation provided under EEC Article 30 (now Article 36 TFEU) as regards quantitative restrictions which are possible because their presence may lead to more effective competition and sustained economic grown and thereby enter the parameters of the public policy derogation provided by that article. Finally, one of the essential difficulties which the method of interpretation utilized by the CJ creates is the following: that is, a failure to permit EEC Articles 85 and 86 (now TFEU Articles 101 and 102) to evolve with the passage of time in relation to the changes in certain fields of expertise such as economics which are particularly relevant to the application of these articles.

§4.05 EU MERGER CONTROL AND ACTIONS FOR DAMAGES FOR NON-CONTRACTUAL DAMAGES FOR ERRONEOUS COMMISSION DECISIONS FORBIDDING MERGERS

Merger Control. The last EU competition case, involves an attempt by My Travel Group plc.[113] to recover damages for the losses which it allegedly suffered as a result of the Commission having decided wrongfully to prohibit a proposed merger. This is not a reference pursuant to Article 267 TFEU: rather, it is a direct action for un-liquidated damages founded upon non-contractual liability pursuant to Article 340 TFEU.

In 1999, the European Commission decided that MyTravel Group,[114] previously known as Airtours, could not buy the British tour operator, First Choice, as that would have left three travel companies owning a 79% share of the UK market for package holidays. Three years later, however, the Court of First Instance – now the General

112. The Chicago school of economics is a neoclassical school of economic thought associated with the work of the faculty at the University of Chicago, some of whom have constructed and popularized its principles.
113. Case T-212 /03 *My Travel Group plc v Commission* (2008) *ECR* II-1967.
114. Case T-212/03 *MyTravel Group plc v Commission of the European Communities* (2008) *ECR* II 1967 *ibid.* at paras 74 and 75.

Court – ruled that the Commission had not successfully proved the merger would stifle competition. MyTravel then filed a claim for damages of €644 million, arguing that the Commission's unjustified decision to block the merger had resulted in a loss of profits. A summary of the judgment reads as follows:

> The Court of First Instance (now the GC) held that the possibility cannot be ruled out that manifest and grave defects affecting the Commission's economic analysis which underlies a competition decision may constitute breaches that are sufficiently serious to give rise to the non-contractual liability of the Community. However, the complexity of the situations to be regulated in the control of concentrations, difficulties of application connected with the time constraints imposed on the administration in that regard and the margin of discretion available to the Commission are all factors to be taken into account in assessing whether a sufficiently serious breach exists. In this case, the Court of First Instance (now the GC) found that there was no such breach, with the result that the non-contractual liability of the Community could not be established. The action was therefore dismissed.[115]

One might say therefore, that according to the CFI (now the GC) the errors of assessment of the proposed merger made by the Commission did not constitute a serious breach.[116] In the absence of a serious breach no compensation could be obtained pursuant to Article 340 (2) TFEU which provides for damages resulting from non-contractual liability of Community institutions such as the Commission or the Court.

In truth, the summary discloses, and this will be verified by the wording of the judgment itself, that the CFI (now the GC) did not consider the Commission's breach of the then Community regulation on concentrations to constitute a sufficiently serious breach and this apparently for two reasons: mere errors of assessment and a lack of relevant evidence in the context of an action for annulment cannot constitute a serious breach. Accordingly the CFI (now the GC) evaluated the expert economic analysis made by the Commission of the merger propose by Air Tours (now My Travel[117]). The first question which arises is namely how the CFI (now the GC) carried out this evaluation of the Commission expert analysis of the proposed merger. The second question is the nature and the reason for a lack of evidence. It is submitted that the real difficulty with this judgment is at least at this level, one which deals with the rules of procedure and evidence. It does not concern the substantive scope of Article 340 (2) TFEU.

---

115. ECJ summary of the judgment: European Commission Legal Service: www.ec.europa.eu.
116. *My Travel Group v Commission* Case T 212/035 (2008) *ECR* II 1967 On 29 April 1999, *supra*, para. 1.

    The applicant, the United Kingdom travel company Airtours plc, which has since been renamed MyTravel Group plc, announced its intention to acquire the whole of the issued share capital of First Choice plc, one of its competitors in the United Kingdom, on the stock market. On the same date, the applicant notified the proposed concentration to the Commission with a view to obtaining an approval decision on the basis of Council Regulation (EEC) No 4064/89 of 21 December 1989 on the control of concentrations between undertakings (corrected version OJ 1990 L 257, 13), as amended by Council Regulation (EC) No 1310/97 of 30 June 1997 (OJ 1997 L 180, 1).
117. *My Travel Group v Commission* Case T 212/035 (2008) *ECR* II 1967.

At this point it is necessary to consider two paragraphs of the judgment in My Travel[118] which are the following:

> 2. Findings of the Court
> a) The argument relating to the duty to recognise the limited scope of application of Article 2 of Regulation No 4064/89
> Para 74 The first point to be made is that, in reply to the applicant's argument that the Commission manifestly and gravely disregarded the limits on its discretion by basing its reasoning at least in part on the economic theory known as the theory of unilateral effects as a basis for declaring the Airtours/First Choice concentration incompatible with the common market under Article 2 of Regulation No 4064/89, it must be pointed out – as the Court did in paragraphs 49 to 54 of *Airtours* v *Commission*, cited in paragraph 11 above – that the Commission denies that it adopted a new approach and maintains that it applied the test for collective dominance already used by it in previous cases and approved by the Court of First Instance in Case T-102/96 *Gencor* v *Commission* [1999] ECR II-753.
> Para 75 In the light of that statement by the Commission and in the absence of sufficiently detailed submissions from the applicant as to whether and to what extent that alleged new approach might have had any effect on the Commission's assessment of the Airtours/First Choice concentration on competition, it is unnecessary to adjudicate on the alleged failure to comply with the obligation to recognise the limited scope of application of Article 2 of Regulation No 4064/89.
> b) The arguments relating to the obligation to define the market situation in the absence of the concentration and the obligation to establish the conditions for tacit collusion.

As regards the first aforementioned question the answer appears to be that the CFI (now the GC) decided itself on the basis of its own expertise that the Commission's declaration concerning the type of economic model which it used, contrary to the assertions of the claimant, was true in the sense, presumably, as a matter effectively of economics. This assessment by the CFI (now the GC) of the Commission's argument as to the type of economic model used, which necessarily involved an understanding of economics, contained an additional important element; that is, according to the aforementioned judgment, the claimants had failed to produce sufficiently detailed submissions as to whether and to what extent that alleged new economic mode might have had any effect on the Commission's assessment of the Airtours/ First Choice concentration on competition. There are effectively two essential problems the first of which deals with what appears to be the manner of assessment of the facts put forward by the parties and notably that of the Commission as regards to the type of model used to analyse the submission of the claimants. The affirmation 'in the light of that statement by the Commission "... it is unnecessary to adjudicate on the alleged failure to comply with the obligation to recognise the limited scope of application of Article 2 of Regulation No 4064/89"'[119] would arguably establish various matters concerning the evaluation of evidence. It would appear, that following Gerber,[120] the judges of the CFI

118. *My Travel Group v Commission*, Case T- 212/035 (2008) *ECR* II 1967, *ibid.*
119. *My Travel Group v Commission*, Case T 212/035 (2008) *ECR* II 1967 *ibid.*
120. DJ Gerber, 'Courts as Economic Experts in European Merger Law', in BE Hawk (ed) *Annual Proceedings for the Thirtieth Fordham Corporate Law institute: International Law and Policy* (Huntington NY Juris Publishing, 2004), *supra*, at 47.

(now the GC), themselves, assessed the claim made by the Commission concerning the type of model it used without the use of an expert. The CFI (now GC) of course could have appointed an expert in economics on its own initiative pursuant to notably Article 65 (d)[121] of the Measures of Inquiry of the CFI (now the GC) for two reasons: first, to assist members of the court understand the full nature of the denial by the Commission as regards the use of a specific economic model as well as any and all explanations by the Commission as to the type of economic model it did in fact use; second, to obtain an expert opinion given by an economist concerning, specifically, the type of model which was used by the Commission. The type of economic model used constituted the essence of the claimant's action for breach by the Commission and for the remedy in damages for non-contractual liability sought by the claimant. Accordingly, it is submitted that by failing to appoint an expert to assist with the comprehension[122] and the evaluation of the expert evidence presented by the Commission and by failing to appoint an independent expert to ascertain exactly the type of model which the Commission had used, the CFI (now the GC) conspicuously failed to carry out its duty pursuant to *Kraska v Switzerland*.[123] Thus, by relying upon its own abilities to evaluate the expert evidence, the CFI (now the GC) breached Article 6 (1) ECHR, due process, the principle of rectitude of decision and thereby the concept of the Rule of Law. However, it is necessary to consider the second limb of this particular judgment: namely, the objection by the CFI (now the GC) of an insufficiency of evidence or facts presented in the pleadings by the claimant. This objection is stated as follows:

> Para 75 ... in the absence of sufficiently detailed submissions from the applicant as to whether and to what extent that alleged new approach might have had any effect on the Commission's assessment of the Airtours/First Choice concentration on competition, it is unnecessary to adjudicate on the alleged failure to comply with the obligation to recognise the limited scope of application of Article 2 of Regulation No 4064/89.[124]

---

121. 'RULES OF PROCEDURE OF THE GENERAL COURT Section 2 – Measures of inquiry
Article 65
Without prejudice to Articles 24 and 25 of the Statute, the following measures of inquiry may be adopted:
    (a) the personal appearance of the parties;
    (b) a request for information and production of documents;
    (c) oral testimony;
    (d) the commissioning of an expert's report;
    (e) an inspection of the place or thing in question'. http://curia.europa.eu/jcms/upload/docs/application/pdf/2008-09/txt7_2008-09-25_14-08-6_431.pdf, last consulted on 28.10.2013.
122. To explain as an assessor the meaning of the technical words to the judges. See discussion in a previous chapter herein concerning the definition of the scope and function of an assessor in English law.
123. *Kraska v Switzerland* (1994) *EHRR* 188, *supra*, para. 30.
124. *My Travel Group v Commission*, Case T- 212/035 (2008) *ECR* II 1967, *supra*, at para. 75.

The concerns expressed by Bailey[125] and Dawes and Peci[126] concerning the identification of a clear standard of proof is manifestly intimately related to the nature of the proof which is used: specifically expert evidence and its assessment as expert evidence by judges who either have knowledge of economics or more likely with the assistance of experts and eventually the assistance of expert in the form of assessors whose participation takes place in the context of judicial notice. Conspicuously, the standard of proof cannot be achieved until the evidence tendered is firstly of the most appropriate type: that is, specifically, an expert nature and secondly, the standard will not be attained until the expert evidence is assessed accurate with the use of the parameters of an expert in economics. However, overall, this matter is perhaps clearer in the field of economics as opposed to other social sciences where there exists less mathematical formalization such as in the field of political science and their applications to justifying or resisting laws and government policies as in the case of prisoner rights or the application of the European Convention of Human Rights. As regards the instant case of My Travel,[127] in reality, there exists something of a procedural irony: having failed itself to use its procedural powers to supplement the quantity of expert evidence notably in order to assess the arguments presented by the Commission in its denial of breach the CFI (now the GC), itself, then criticizes the applicant. The criticism is expressed by the CFI (now the GC) of a failure on the part of the applicant to produce information in the form of factual details in his pleading. In reality, the culpability here is that of the CFI (now the GC) which omitted to utilize, seriously, the powers of case management which the Rules of Procedure provide pursuant to Article 64:[128]

---

125. D Bailey, 'Standard of Proof in EC Merger Proceedings: a Common Law Perspective' (2003) *CMLRev* (40) 845.
126. A Dawes & K Peçi, 'Sorry but There's Nothing We Can Do to Help: Schneider II and the Extra Contractual Liability of the European Commission Merger Cases' (2008) *ECLR* 151.
127. *My Travel Group v Commission,* Case T 212/035 (2008) *ECR* II 1967, *supra.*
128. RULES OF PROCEDURE OF THE GENERAL COURT Section 1 – Measures of organisation of procedure

> *Article 64*
> 1 The purpose of measures of organisation of procedure shall be to ensure that cases are prepared for hearing, procedures carried out and disputes resolved under the best possible conditions. They shall be prescribed by the General Court, after hearing the Advocate General.
> 2. Measures of organisation of procedure shall, in particular, have as their purpose:
> (a) to ensure efficient conduct of the written and oral procedure and to facilitate the taking of evidence;
> (b) to determine the points on which the parties must present further argument or which call for measures of inquiry;
> (c) to clarify the forms of order sought by the parties, their pleas in law and arguments and the points at issue between them;
> (d) to facilitate the amicable settlement of proceedings.
> 3. Measures of organisation of procedure may, in particular, consist of:
> (a) putting questions to the parties;
> (b) inviting the parties to make written or oral submissions on certain aspects of the proceedings;
> (c) asking the parties or third parties for information or particulars;
> (d) asking for documents or any papers relating to the case to be produced;
> (e) summoning the parties' agents or the parties in person to meetings.

Art 64 (3). Measures of organisation of procedure may, in particular, consist of:

(a) putting questions to the parties;
(b) inviting the parties to make written or oral submissions on certain aspects of the proceedings;
(c) asking the parties or third parties for information or particulars;
(d) asking for documents or any papers relating to the case to be produced.

There is, in addition, a problem with the uncertainty with the rules of pleading utilized by the CFI (now the GC): specifically an uncertainty as to the amount of detail to be pleaded initially by the litigant. Regretfully, this deficiency at least in the instant case was not rectified by the application of the rules of case management which permit the court to ask for additional detail and particulars of fact in addition to appointing an expert.[129]

It is submitted, therefore, that this deficiency of both expert evidence and detailed pleading produces a resounding breach of the duty by the CFI (now the GC) in My Travel[130] pursuant to Article 6 (1) ECHR under *Kraska v Switzerland*:[131] specifically, a failure on the part of the CFI (now the GC)to properly evaluate the merits of the case as presented by the applicant in light of the rules of procedure which, it, the Court, possesses; and secondly, by reason of the unjustified and unjustifiable[132] omission to use, proportionately, the Rules of Procedure concerning the appointment of experts and case management, the CFI (now the GC) effectively denied the claimant access to the court in violation of Article 6 (1) ECHR.[133] In short, the reason for the failure on the part of the CFI (now the GC) is, arguably, that adumbrated by both Gerber[134] and

---

4. Each party may, at any stage of the procedure, propose the adoption or modification of measures of organisation of procedure. In that case, the other parties shall be heard before those measures are prescribed. Where the procedural circumstances so require, the Registrar shall inform the parties of the measures envisaged by the General Court and shall give them an opportunity to submit comments orally or in writing.
5. If the General Court sitting in plenary session or as the Grand Chamber decides to prescribe measures of organisation of procedure and does not undertake such measures itself, it shall entrust the task of so doing to the Chamber to which the case was originally assigned or to the Judge-Rapporteur.

If a Chamber prescribes measures of organisation of procedure and does not undertake such measures itself, it shall entrust the task to the Judge-Rapporteur. The Advocate General shall take part in measures of organisation of procedure.' http://curia.europa.eu/jcms/upload/docs/application/pdf/2008-09/txt7_2008-09-25_14-08-6_431.pdf, last consulted on 28.10.2013.

129. G Cumming, *Merger Decisions and the Rules of Procedure of the European Community Courts* (Kluwer Law International, The Hague, 2012), *supra*, Chs 2 and 3.
130. *My Travel Group v Commission*, Case T 212/035 (2008) *ECR* II 1967, *supra*.
131. *Kraska v Switzerland* (1993) *EHRR* (18) 188, *supra*.
132. The GC neither explains nor justifies its omission to utilize the rules of procedures which have been cited herein. Further, costs and delay which are indeed involved in the use of expert evidence can nevertheless be controlled in other jurisdictions as evidenced by judgments herein considered, namely, Re: Polygamy 2011 BCSC 1588 Re: S 293 CCC, *supra*; *Sauvé v Canada* (AG) (2002) 3 SCR 519, *supra*; *Roper v Simmons* (2005) 543 US 551, *supra*.
133. *Airey v Ireland* (1979) *EHRR* (2) 305.
134. DJ Gerber, 'Courts as Economic Experts in European Merger Law' in BE Hawk (ed) *Annual Proceedings for the Thirtieth Fordham Corporate Law institute: International Law and Policy* (Huntington NY Juris Publishing, 2004), *supra*, 475; JD Gutierrez, 'Expert Economic Testimony, Economic Evidence and Asymmetry of Information in Antitrust Cases', CEDEX Competition Law and Economics Working Paper No: 07-04, October 2007.

Barbier de La Serre:[135] namely, a feeling by members of the court that they prefer not to make recourse to experts in order to avoid the possibility that the decision making may be effected by the experts and not by the members of the court. This reasoning is untenable given that it is founded upon an inability of the court to properly analyse and understand the expert evidence: that is, the failure to use a court appointed expert in the form of an assessor whose task it is to explain to the judges the technical meaning of the words used by the experts in the case.

§4.06 CONCLUSION

Overall, this section has set forth cases decided primarily by the CJ but also one by the GC involving two areas of EU law: firstly, preliminary references which concerned with citizenship rights notably in the context of students and secondly, non-contractual liability on the part of the Commission concerning errors in the control of mergers. The most notable similarity of all of the cases arises from the fact that neither the CJ nor the GC used expert evidence or indeed availed themselves of the procedural possibility which exists for both courts to appoint of its own motion an expert. The exact reason for the failure of the CJ and the GC to appoint an expert is unclear notwithstanding, that Barbier and Sibony[136] sought to enumerate a series of possible explanations thereon. What is clear however, is that the CJ and the GC failed to use expert evidence and or notably appoint of their own motion an expert to assist them in interpreting the TFEU. Overall, the essential problem was that the statutory interpretation notably, of the technical words contained within the relevant articles of the TFEU and the Merger Control Regulation,[137] did not involve any expert evidence. Nor was any expert evidence utilized by the CJ and the GC by means of the process of judicial notice in the interpretation of the ordinary meaning of words contained within the relevant articles of the TFEU and the Merger Control Regulation.[138] The most significant difficulty encountered through what might be termed the non-evidentially based application of the teleological principle of interpretation which stresses a wide interpretation of the rights and a narrow interpretation of the derogations was of course in the construction of ex Article 85 (1)[139] EEC (now Article 101 TFEU). It is clear that the original interpretation of Article 85 (1) EEC (now Article 101 TFEU) which was interpreted

135. E Barbier de La Serre & A-L Sibony, 'Expert Evidence Before the EC Courts' (2008) *CMLRev* (45) 4, 941, *supra*, at 953, 'The EC courts therefore seem to enjoy a great discretion as to the amount of personal experience or knowledge they can put into their judgements in order to establish the factual background of the case. Judges do use this power and sometimes reach conclusions on the basis of their personal experience even though they concern issues of fact that could warrant additional fact-finding.'
136. E Barbier de La Serre & A-L Sibony, 'Expert Evidence before the EC Courts' (2008) *CMLRev* (45) 941, *supra*, passim.
137. *Council Reg (EC) No 139/2004* of 20.1. 2004 which replaces *Council Reg (EEC) 4064/89* of 21.12.1989.
138. *Council Reg (EC) No 139/2004* of 20.1. 2004 which replaces *Council Reg (EEC) 4064/89* of 21.12.1989.
139. Article 101 TFEU ex Art 81 (1) (ex Article 81 TEC): 1. The following shall be prohibited as incompatible with the internal market: all agreements between undertakings, decisions by associations of undertakings and concerted practices which may affect trade between Member

without reference to expert evidence derived from notably the Chicago School of economic theory included not only agreements between undertakings which were harmful to competition but also agreements (particular intra-brand) competition which overall were beneficial to inter-brand competition. It required the use of the expert opinion in order to restrain the scope of the application of notably the expression 'all agreements' which arguably in the instant context contains a highly technical meaning. The expression 'all agreements' following the expert opinion of the Chicago School would be narrowly construed so as not to prohibit what might be termed 'pro-competitive' agreements as discussed by Korah in detail as previously noted herein.

As the judgments from the USSC,[140] the SCC[141] and the BCSC[142] demonstrate there is no particular reason to restrict the use of expert evidence to the interpretation of Article 101 TFEU and economics. It is submitted that it is both equally possible and desirable to utilize expert evidence in statutory interpretation which involves other aspects of the TFEU such as citizenship and student rights. Similarly, as regards the rights contained within the ECHR which will be considered in the following chapters.

Perhaps the most striking aspect the judgments of the USSC,[143] the SCC[144] and the BCSC[145] is that they all considered expert evidence both by means of judicial notice and sworn expert witnesses in the fields of social and political science unlike the CJ and the GC. Arguably, these judgments of the three aforementioned US and Canadian courts possess a degree of credibility which is very much related to the quality of the expert evidence which was considered by the courts either as submitted by the parties or eventually be the court of its own motion. Regretfully such a measure of credibility based upon expert evidence coupled with detailed logical analysis is absence from the judgments considered herein as rendered by the CJ and the GC.

States and which have as their object or effect the prevention, restriction or distortion of competition within the internal market, and in particular those which:

(a) directly or indirectly fix purchase or selling prices or any other trading conditions;
(b) limit or control production, markets, technical development, or investment;
(c) share markets or sources of supply;
(d) apply dissimilar conditions to equivalent transactions with other trading parties, thereby placing them at a competitive disadvantage;
(e) make the conclusion of contracts subject to acceptance by the other parties of supplementary obligations which, by their nature or according to commercial usage, have no connection with the subject of such contracts.

140. *Roper v Simmons* (2005) 543 *US* 551, *supra.*
141. *Sauvé v Canada* (AG) (2002) 3 *SCR* 519, *supra.*
142. *Re: Polygamy* 2011 *BCSC* 1588 Re: S 293 CCC, *supra.*
143. *Roper v Simmons* (2005) 543 *US* 551, *supra.*
144. *Sauvé v Canada* (AG) (2002) 3 *SCR* 519, *supra.*
145. *Re: Polygamy* 2011 *BCSC* 1588 Re: S 293 CCC, *supra.*

CHAPTER 5

European Court of Human Rights Judgments Hirst (2)* and Scoppola**

§5.01 INTRODUCTION

Having considered the judgments notably of SCC, the USSC and the BCSC, it is now appropriate to now consider two cases of the ECtHR which deal with prisoner rights: the first is Hirst No 2.[1] As noted earlier, by reason of the provisions of Article 6 (2) TFEU[2] the judgments of the ECtHR will exercise a considerable influence in the interpretation of the rights contained with the ECHR as it applies to the CJ and the GC in their application of the TFEU. Essentially, as will be observed from the two judgments, Hirst[3] and Scoppola[4] the procedural problem encountered in the instant judgments of the ECtHR turns on the absence of expert evidence. In this regard, the ECtHR operates in a completely analogous manner to that of the CJ and the GC: namely, a complete failure on the part of the ECtHR to utilize the rules which provide for the use of expert evidence and appoint of an expert evidence in the statutory interpretation of the ECHR. Ironically and unfortunately, the ECtHR contravenes

* *Hirst v UK (No 2)* (2006) 42 *EHRR* 41.

** *Scoppola v Italy (No 3)* (2012) *ECHR* 866.

1. *Hirst v UK (No 2)* (2006) 42 *EHRR* 41 *ibid.*
2. Article 6 TFEU (ex Article 6 TEU) ... 2. The Union shall accede to the European Convention for the Protection of Human Rights and Fundamental Freedoms. Such accession shall not affect the Union's competences as defined in the Treaties. 3. Fundamental rights, as guaranteed by the European Convention for the Protection of Human Rights and Fundamental Freedoms and as they result from the constitutional traditions common to the Member States, shall constitute general principles of the Union's law.
3. *Hirst v UK (No 2)* (2006) 42 *EHRR* 41, *supra.*
4. *Scoppola v Italy (No 3)* (2012) *ECHR* 866.

Article 6 (1) ECHR as interpreted by Kraska[5] through this failure to use expert opinion notably in the domain where political scientists may provide expert opinion as regards its statutory interpretation of the ECHR.

§5.02 JUDGMENT OF HIRST[6]

Mr J. Hirst, a prisoner then serving a sentence for manslaughter, was prevented from voting by section 3 (1) of the Representation of the People Act (1983),[7] which prohibits convicted prisoners from voting during their incarceration in a penal institution. In 2001, Hirst brought a case to the English High Court, but the case was dismissed. He appealed this judgment to the ECtHR[8] where ultimately, the Grand Chamber held on 6 October 2005[9] that the aforementioned section of the Representation of the People Act (1983) violated prisoners' voting rights to which Article 3 of the First Protocol of the ECHR[10] applied.

The ratio of the judgment turns upon the following: having decided that the objective of punishment pursued by the temporary disenfranchisement is valid, the ECtHR holds that effectively, the method of achieving that objective leads to a disproportionate restriction upon the right to vote provided by Article 3 of the First Protocol of the ECHR. This is because S 3 (1) of the Representation of the People Act (1983) provides an automatic disenfranchisement on all convicted prisoners who are incarcerated. The judgment of the ECtHR[11] provides as follows as regards notably the objection of disproportionality of automatic application of the temporary disenfranchisement pursuant to S3 of the Representation of the People Act (1983):

> Proportionality
>
> 76. The Court notes that the Chamber found that the measure lacked proportionality, essentially as it was an automatic blanket ban imposed on all convicted prisoners which was arbitrary in its effects and could no longer be said to serve the aim of punishing the applicant once his tariff (that period representing retribution and deterrence) had expired.

---

5. *Kraska v Switzerland*, Application No. 13942/88, Judgment of 19 April 1993 (1993) *EHRR* (18) 188 at para. 30.
6. *Hirst v UK (No 2)* (2006) 42 *EHRR* 41, *ibid.*
7. Section 3 of the Representation of the People Act 1983 ('the 1983 Act') provides: '(1) A convicted person during the time that he is detained in a penal institution in pursuance of his sentence ... is legally incapable of voting at any parliamentary or local election.' The Convention right allegedly violated provides as follows: Article 3 of protocol No. 1 ECHR'. The High Contracting Parties undertake to hold free elections at reasonable intervals by secret ballot, under conditions which will ensure the free expression of the opinion of the people in the choice of the legislature, www.legislation.gov.uk/1982/, last consulted on 28.10.2013.
8. *Hirst v UK (No 2)* (2006) 42 *EHRR* 41, *supra.*
9. *Hirst v UK (No 2)* (2006) 42 *EHRR* 41, *ibid.*
10. European Convention of Human Rights: Protocols 1. Enforcement of certain Rights and Freedoms not included in Section I of the Convention ... Art 3 The High Contracting Parties undertake to hold free elections at reasonable intervals by secret ballot, under conditions which will ensure the free expression of the opinion of the people in the choice of the legislature. http://www.hri.org/docs/ECHR50.html; site last consulted on 28.10.2013.
11. *Hirst v UK (No 2)* (2006) 42 *EHRR* 41, *supra.*

....

80. It is also evident from the judgment of the Divisional Court that the nature of the restrictions, if any, to be imposed on the right of a convicted prisoner to vote was generally seen as a matter for Parliament and not for the national courts. The court did not, therefore, undertake any assessment of proportionality of the measure itself. It may also be noted that the court found support in the decision of the Federal Court of Appeal in Sauvé (no. 2), which was later overturned by the Canadian Supreme Court.

...

82. Therefore, while the Court reiterates that the margin of appreciation is wide, it is not all-embracing. Further, although the situation was somewhat improved by the 2000 Act which for the first time granted the vote to persons detained on remand, section 3 of the 1983 Act remains a blunt instrument. It strips of their Convention right to vote a significant category of persons and it does so in a way which is indiscriminate. The provision imposes a blanket restriction on all convicted prisoners in prison. It applies automatically to such prisoners, irrespective of the length of their sentence and irrespective of the nature or gravity of their offence and their individual circumstances. Such a general, automatic and indiscriminate restriction on a vitally important Convention right must be seen as falling outside any acceptable margin of appreciation, however wide that margin might be, and as being incompatible with Article 3 of Protocol No. 1.

...

84. In a case such as the present one, where Contracting States have adopted a number of different ways of addressing the question of the right of convicted prisoners to vote, the Court must confine itself to determining whether the restriction affecting all convicted prisoners in custody exceeds any acceptable margin of appreciation, leaving it to the legislature to decide on the choice of means for securing the rights guaranteed by Article 3 of Protocol No. 1 (see, for example, the cases concerning procedures governing the continued detention of life prisoners, where Court case-law and domestic legislation have evolved progressively: Thynne, Wilson and Gunnell v. the United Kingdom, judgment of 25 October 1990, Series A no. 190-A; Singh v. the United Kingdom, judgment of 21 February 1996, Reports 1996-I; and Stafford v. the United Kingdom [GC], no. 46295/99, ECHR 2002-IV).

85. The Court concludes that there has been a violation of Article 3 of Protocol No. 1.

Analysis of the judgment of *Hirst (2) v UK*:[12]

It is submitted that the argument of lack of proportionality is insufficiently analysed and proved: firstly, the objective of increasing the respect for the electoral system and for citizenship through temporary disenfranchisement is not considered in the body of the judgement despite the fact that it has been deemed to be an acceptable objective by the ECtHR.[13] The matter of the imposition of the temporary

12. *Hirst v UK (No 2)* (2006) 42 *EHRR* 41, *ibid.*
13. (a) Legitimate aim: Para. 74. 'The Court points out that Article 3 of Protocol No. 1 does not, like other provisions of the Convention, specify or limit the aims which a restriction must pursue. A wide range of purposes may therefore be compatible with Article 3 (see, for example, Podkolzina, cited above, § 34). The Government have submitted that the measure pursues the

disenfranchisement arguably can constitute, notably as analysed by the minority in Sauvé,[14] a separate civil matter where different considerations from punishment apply: that is, an expression of moral opprobrium on the part of the majority of the electorate. Therefore, in first instance as regards proportionality it would be necessary to prove that the temporary disenfranchisement whether or not the aforementioned civil objective of the expression by the majority of moral reprobation is reasonable or rational which arguably it is, but above all can be sustained as such through the opinion of experts such as political scientists and social psychologists; secondly, the analysis then passes on to ascertain whether the achievement of such an objective can reasonably be attained by utilising the type of sentence imposed: that is, whether or not the automatic temporary disenfranchisement can be appropriately imposed following directly or in tandem with a sentence of incarceration imposed following an individual assessment and consideration of the personal characteristics of the prisoner. As just noted, the disenfranchisement which is related to the electoral process and the upholding of the law can constitute, among other things, a civil expression of societal disapproval for a class of criminals – namely those who are incarcerated. The disenfranchisement which is co-terminus with the length of the incarceration must be viewed in conjunction with the actual sentencing of the prisoner, following Gonthier J and the learned Minority in Sauvé[15] it may be conceived of as an alternative to a longer period of incarceration: that is, as a mollifying factor. In short, the imposition of the temporary disenfranchisement functions in conjunction with a system of sentencing which is individual and takes account of the specific characteristics of the prisoner. It is difficult if not impossible given that no facts concerning the operation of such a system have either been presented or considered by the ECtHR, to assess empirically the effectiveness of such a system in attaining its objective of improving citizenship and protecting the integrity of the electoral system. The essential problem with the argument based upon lack of proportionality utilised by the ECtHR is that no evidence is led to demonstrate that that the use of a legislative approach in the form of a law which automatically disenfranchises prisoners for the period of their incarceration neither achieves the objective and therefore is irrational or if it does, the method constitutes a disproportionate restriction of the right to vote. This absence of any empirical basis for the decision, nevertheless, occurs in a procedural context where the ECtHR itself was able to obtain if necessary on its own initiative facts dealing with this

---

aim of preventing crime by sanctioning the conduct of convicted prisoners and also of enhancing civic responsibility and respect for the rule of law. The Court notes that, at the time of the passage of the latest legislation, the Government stated that the aim of the bar on convicted prisoners was to confer an additional punishment. This was also the position espoused by the Secretary of State in the domestic proceedings brought by the applicant. While the primary emphasis at the domestic level may have been the idea of punishment, it may nevertheless be considered as implied in the references to the forfeiting of rights that the measure is meant to act as an incentive for citizen-like conduct.' Para. 75. 'Although rejecting the notion that imprisonment after conviction involves the forfeiture of rights beyond the right to liberty, and especially the assertion that voting is a privilege not a right (see paragraph 59 above), the Court accepts that section 3 may be regarded as pursuing the aims identified by the Government. It observes that, in its judgment, the Chamber expressed reservations as to the validity of these aims, citing the majority opinion of the Canadian Supreme Court in Sauvé (no. 2) (see paragraphs 44-47 of the Chamber judgment). However, whatever doubt there may be as to the efficacy of achieving these aims through a bar on voting, the Court finds no reason in the circumstances of this application to exclude these aims as untenable or incompatible per se with the right guaranteed under Article 3 of Protocol No. 1.'

14. *Sauvé v Canada (Attorney General)*, [2002] 3 *S.C.R.* 519 *ibid.*
15. *Sauvé v Canada (Attorney General)*, [2002] 3 *S.C.R.* 519 *ibid.*

point through[16] by appointing a court expert pursuant to its own rules of procedure. This situation of paucity of facts has in part arisen because no facts were used to establish the wide inclusive category of the beneficiaries of the voting rights even more so that some logical difficulties appear given that it is recognised that this apparently extremely important right can be restricted in certain circumstances: the right to vote is not an absolute right. Therefore, no pragmatic justification for the wide scope of the interpretation of the class of beneficiaries is given by the ECtHR. This in turn, once again, leads to difficulties in justification given that the category thereof is viewed in terms of the disenfranchisement operating as an additional method of punishment: this is despite the ECtHR having recognised initially, as noted herein, the additional social purpose of what is essentially the collective expression on the part of the electorate of moral opprobrium as regards those who contravene democratically adopted laws. Accordingly, the definition of the scope of the intervention of the ECtHR on the facts is arbitrary in the extreme given that it has not specifically linked the intervention to the control of an unreasonable exercise of power by the UK parliament. In any event, on the few facts available in the judgement, it is difficult to see how the ECtHR could hold that the exercise of the discretion by the UK government to use both the binary system consisting of the punishment of incarceration coupled with an automatic co-terminus application of the moral opprobrium can, together, constitute an unreasonable and, therefore, disproportionate use of legislative discretion: this is even more so that the binary system which consists of the moral opprobrium – temporary automatic disenfranchisement co-terminus with the period of incarceration – serves to attenuate the longevity of the incarceration is coupled with punishment in the form of incarceration which is based upon individual characteristics of the prisoner. In short, the ECtHR has not demonstrated why a system where the temporary disenfranchisement the objective of which is not punishment but rather the expression of societal disapproval of law infringement, requires individual case by case assessment as a method of imposition as opposed to imposition by means of a binary system where the duration of the disenfranchisement is determined automatically by the length of the punishment in the form of the incarceration. Conspicuously, the ECtHR by failing to utilise expert evidence in the form of opinions of political scientists and social psychologists among others, has not appropriately analysed the claim of the UK pursuant to Art 6.1 ECHR that the disenfranchisement serves rather more to enhance civic responsibility and respect for the rule of law which include necessarily the society expression of opprobrium by the electorate: further it serves arguably to reduce or attenuate the actual length of the punishment in the form of incarceration.[17] Given that such objectives are different from those of punishment and deterrence, the element of reasonableness or proportionality as regards their method of implementation will be different from the reasonableness or proportionality of implementing a system where the objective is solely one of punishment not in terms of the legal standard but in terms of the facts which must be considered. In short, the two objectives and their methods of implementation being different the criterion of proportionality must be applied differently. Further, it is clear that had the ECtHR appointed an expert on its own initiative it would have apprehended with more clarity this

16. Rules of Court, 1 July 2013, Registry of the Court Strasbourg: 'Annex Rule A1 – Investigative measures1. The Chamber may, at the request of a party or of its own motion, adopt any investigative measure which it considers capable of clarifying the facts of the case. The Chamber may, *inter alia*, invite the parties to produce documentary evidence and decide to hear as a witness or expert or in any other capacity any person whose evidence or statements seem likely to assist it in carrying out its tasks.' www.echr.coe.int, last consulted on 28.10. 2013.
17. *Sauvé v Canada (Attorney General)*, [2002] 3 *S.C.R.* 519.

> difference between the two objectives in the submissions of the UK government. This is perhaps a defining example of where the ECtHR has breached Art 6.1 ECHR pursuant to Kraska v Switzerland[18] by failing to evaluate accurate by means of using expert evidence the submissions made by the parties, in the instant case, by the UK.

Finally, an alternate manner of analysing the proportionality of the temporary disenfranchisement is to simply argue as did Gonthier J of the learned minority in *Sauvé v Canada*[19] who upheld the finding of the Federal Court of Appeal in Sauvé: namely, that in truth, the temporary disenfranchisement in truth operates when coupled with the individual assessment for punishment in a completely proportionate manner. Gonthier, J observes as follows:

> 171 The approach taken by Linden J.A. for the majority of the Federal Court of Appeal below is sound. He held that the current provision was minimally impairing for a number of reasons: only 'serious offenders', as determined by Parliament, are subject to disenfranchisement; accused persons and those convicted but out on bail are permitted to vote; those out on parole are permitted to vote; and the provision acts proportionately since it is individualized insofar as those with longer sentences will be disenfranchised longer. The provision is reasonably tailored insofar as disenfranchisement reflects the length of the sentence and actual incarceration, which, in turn, reflects the seriousness of the crime perpetrated and the intended progress towards the ultimate goals of rehabilitation and reintegration.[20]

§5.03 ANALYSIS OF SCOPPOLA[21]

Summary:

> Mr. Scoppola was convicted for the murder of his wife and for willfully causing injuries to his son. He was initially sentenced to life imprisonment. Following a finding of violation of arts 6 and 7 of the Convention in Scoppola (no. 2), the penalty was reduced to thirty years. In the Italian criminal law system, the ancillary penalty of the ban from public offices is mandatorily imposed on any person convicted by a final judgment in two hypothesis: for certain defined offences (mainly, against the interests of the administration of the State or of justice), independently of the harshness of the main penalty; and when the

18. *Kraska v Switzerland* (1994) *EHRR* (18) 188, *supra*, para. 30: duty to properly examine the merits of a case. '30. It falls to the Court to decide whether the contested proceedings considered as a whole were fair within the meaning of the Convention. The effect of Article 6 para. 1 (Article 6-1) is, *inter alia*, to place the 'tribunal' under a duty to conduct a proper examination of the submissions, arguments and evidence adduced by the parties, without prejudice to its assessment of whether they are relevant to its decision (see, among other authorities, mutatis mutandis, the Barberà, Messegué and Jabardo v Spain judgment of 6 December 1988, Series A no. 146, 31, para. 68). It has to be determined whether this condition was satisfied in the instant case.'
19. *Sauvé v Canada (Attorney General)*, [2002] 3 *S.C.R.* 519 *ibid.*
20. *Ibid.*, at para. 171.
21. *Scoppola v Italy (No 3)* (2012) ECHR 866.

> offender is sentenced to a term of imprisonment exceeding three years, independently of the nature of the crime committed. The ban may be permanent or temporary depending on cases and entails the loss of the right to vote for the term of its duration. Further, the ban may be terminated if and when the offender is granted rehabilitation. The assessment on the need for application of the ancillary penalty, and of its duration, is entirely made by the legislature, with little room left to judicial assessment. Accordingly, the judicial authorities can have only an indirect influence on the ban: *ex ante* by calibrating the sentence and *ex post* by examining whether the conditions for rehabilitation are met (Art. 179 of the (Italian) Criminal Code).

Therefore, in the applicant's case, there was no question of avoiding disenfranchisement under domestic law. After having exhausted domestic remedies to no avail, he complained before the ECtHR that his right to vote guaranteed under Article 3 of Prot. No. 1 had been violated.

As he had done before domestic courts, before the ECtHR the applicant relied on the Hirst (no. 2)[22] judgment, in which the Grand Chamber of the Court, by a majority vote, found that the automatic disenfranchisement imposed by English law on all convicted offenders in prison, 'irrespective of the length of their sentence and irrespective of the nature or gravity of their offence and their individual circumstances', was a 'general, automatic and indiscriminate restriction' (§ 82) incompatible with Article 3 of Prot. no. 1. On this basis, the ECtHR considering Scoppola's case found that the permanent disenfranchisement imposed by the law on the applicant, in the absence of a judicial assessment of the proportionality of the measure in the specific circumstances of the case, was in breach of Article 3 of Prot. no. 1. When the case was referred to the Grand Chamber, Italy maintained that the measure met the criteria of legality, legitimacy of the aim and proportionality required for implicit limitation to the right to vote to be consistent with Article 3 Prot. no. 1. The ECtHR, after reaffirming the broad margin of appreciation enjoyed by the contracting Parties and the difference in solutions adopted in their domestic legal systems, held as follows: namely, that while proportionality of restrictions on prisoners' voting rights is in principle guaranteed by the intervention of a judge, 'such restrictions will not necessarily be automatic, general and indiscriminate simply because they were not ordered by a judge.' Accordingly to the ECtHR, the principle of proportionality can be respected also when 'the circumstances in which the right to vote is forfeited may be detailed in the law, making its application conditional on such factors as the nature or the gravity of the offence committed' (§ 99). Therefore, according to the ECtHR 'the Contracting States may decide either to leave it to the courts to determine the proportionality of a measure restricting convicted prisoners' voting rights, or to incorporate provisions into their laws defining the circumstances in which such a measure should be applied. In this latter case, it will be for the legislature itself to balance the competing interests in order to avoid any general, automatic and indiscriminate restriction' (§ 102).

22. *Hirst v UK (No 2)* (2006) 42 EHRR 41, *supra.*

The essence of the judgment of Scoppola[23] involves, firstly, the reaffirmation of the judgment Hirst (No 2):[24]

> 96. The Court accordingly reaffirms the principles set out by the Grand Chamber in the Hirst judgment (see paragraphs 85 and 86 above), in particular the fact that when disenfranchisement affects a group of people generally, automatically and indiscriminately, based solely on the fact that they are serving a prison sentence, irrespective of the length of the sentence and irrespective of the nature or gravity of their offence and their individual circumstances, it is not compatible with Article 3 of Protocol No. 1 (*ibid.*, § 82).[25]

Secondly, the finding that the Italian system of disenfranchisement which can be both temporary and permanent is proportionate. The concept of proportionality used by the Court consists in two different periods of disenfranchisement for the Italian system, five years for three to four years of incarceration or permanent disenfranchisement for periods of incarceration in excess of five years which is applied to specific offences. This is as opposed to the English system of one category, namely, incarceration which is co-terminus with the actual period of incarceration imposed by the court as punishment but applies to all offences. The ECtHR observes as follows:

> 105. As to the legal framework, it should be noted that in the Italian system the measure is applied to individuals convicted of a series of specific offences for which express provision is made by law, irrespective of the duration of the sentence imposed (offences against the interests of the State administration, for example – see paragraph 33 above), or to people sentenced to certain terms of imprisonment specified by law. In this latter case, prisoners sentenced by the courts to three years' imprisonment or more forfeit the right to vote temporarily, for five years, while those sentenced to five years or more, or to life imprisonment, permanently forfeit the right to vote (see paragraphs 34 and 36 above).
> 106. In the Court's opinion the legal provisions in Italy defining the circumstances in which individuals may be deprived of the right to vote show the legislature's concern to adjust the application of the measure to the particular circumstances of the case in hand, taking into account such factors as the gravity of the offence committed and the conduct of the offender. It is applied only in connection with certain offences against the State or the judicial system, or with offences which the courts consider to warrant a particularly harsh sentence, regard being had to the criteria listed in Articles 132 and 133 of the Criminal Code (see paragraph 37 above), including the offender's personal situation, and also to the mitigating and aggravating circumstances. The measure is not applied, therefore, to all individuals sentenced to a term of imprisonment but only to those sentenced to a prison term of three years or more. Italian law also adjusts the duration of the measure to the sentence imposed and thus, by the same token, to the gravity of the offence: the disenfranchisement is for five years for sentences of three to five years and permanent for sentences of five years or more.[26]

It is clear that the ECtHR envisages the imposition by the Italian legal system of disenfranchisement as part of a system of punishment as opposed to a separate system,

23. *Scoppola v Italy (No 3)* (2012) *ECHR* 866.
24. *Hirst v UK (No 2) (2006)* 42 *EHRR* 41, *supra*.
25. *Scoppola v Italy (No 3)* (2012) *ECHR* 866 at para. 96.
26. *Ibid.*

the purpose of which is to ensure the integrity of the voting system: this is clear from the expression in the aforementioned paragraph 106:

> It [the disenfranchisement] is applied only in connection with certain offences against the State or the judicial system, or with offences which the courts consider to warrant a particularly harsh sentences regard being had to the criteria listed in Articles 132 and 133 of the Criminal Code including the offender's personal situation and also the mitigating and aggravating circumstances.[27]

The ECtHR does not analyse the proportionality of the English system in the context of it constituting a separate system which operates, namely, a binary system wherein the punishment takes place in the context of individual assessment as regards the specific nature of the sentence and in particular incarceration: the second part of the system, namely, the expression of societal opprobrium is directed to the civil concern and objective of ensuring the integrity of the operation of the electoral system. As noted previously herein, this concern is different from that of punishment. This results, therefore, in the matter of proportionality being calculated differently than is the case with the calculation of the period of incarceration. There is no obvious reason why the same categories as those involved in the calculation of the length of incarceration would or should be involved in the calculation of the societal expression of opprobrium and concern for the effect of the participation of incarcerated criminals in the operation of the electoral system – irrespective of the particular characteristics of the individual convicts. Arguably, as noted in the judgment of Sauvé by Gonthier J.,[28] in the opinion of the learned Minority, the matter of the relationship of incarcerated criminals and the operation of the electoral system is very much determined by the scope of the category of beneficiaries of the right to vote which was not clearly defined either in Hirst (No 2)[29] or in the instant case. Indeed it is submitted that the wider the category of beneficiaries of the right to vote particularly is predicated upon a deficit of reasoning embedded in facts, the more difficult it will be to accept a restriction thereupon in the form of a temporary disenfranchisement operated in a global manner in the context of a binary operating system wherein the actual punishment is calculated as a function of the individual characteristics of the criminal and the circumstances of the case, the 'adjudicative facts' as opposed to the legislative facts. Returning to the judgment the ECtHR in Scoppola[30] proceeds to enumerate the various degrees of categorization in the Italian system:

> 107. In the instant case the applicant was convicted of murder, attempted murder, ill-treatment of his family and unauthorised possession of a firearm (see paragraphs 13 and 14 above). These are serious offences which led the Rome Court of Appeal to impose a life sentence (see paragraph 19 above), which was later reduced to thirty years' imprisonment (see paragraph 32 above).
>
> 108. In the circumstances the Court cannot conclude that the Italian system has the general, automatic and indiscriminate character that led it, in the Hirst (no. 2)

27. *Ibid.*, at para. 106.
28. *Sauvé v Canada (Attorney General)*, [2002] 3 *S.C.R.* 519 *ibid.*, at para. 171.
29. *Hirst v UK (No 2)* (2006) 42 *EHRR* 41, *supra*.
30. *Scoppola v Italy (No 3)* (2012) *ECHR* 866, *supra*, paras 107, 108 and 110.

case, to find a violation of Article 3 of Protocol No. 1. In Italy there is no disenfranchisement in connection with minor offences or those which, although more serious in principle, do not attract sentences of three years' imprisonment or more, regard being had to the circumstances in which they were committed and to the offender's personal situation.

.....

110. Taking the above considerations into account, the Court finds that, in the circumstances of the present case, the restrictions imposed on the applicant's right to vote did not 'thwart the free expression of the people in the choice of the legislature', and maintained 'the integrity and effectiveness of an electoral procedure aimed at identifying the will of the people through universal suffrage' (see Hirst (no. 2) [GC], cited above, § 62). The margin of appreciation afforded to the respondent Government in this sphere has therefore not been overstepped.

Accordingly, in the ECtHR. there has been no violation of Article 3 of Protocol No. 1.

[A] Analysis of Scoppola[31]

The essential difficulty here is being able to distinguish between the operative part of the instant judgment as regards proportionality and the reaffirmation by the ECtHR of its judgment in Hirst (No 2):[32] specifically, there is no clear indication in the judgment as to why the Italian system (as described in the instant judgment) which apparently disenfranchises for two different periods on the basis of the length of the sentence, namely, either for five years or for life can be said to be proportionate in contrast to a system which operates differently. Thus one observes the following:

> the first comment is that according to the judgement, in order to assess the proportionality of the disenfranchisement it is necessary to consider two matters: firstly, the manner of the application of the disenfranchisement and second, the 'the legal framework surrounding it'.

The purpose of course of the disenfranchisement is to 'enhance civil responsibility and the respect for the rule of law and ensure the proper functioning and preservation of the democratic regime'.

In so far as no facts are led it is unclear as to why the Italian system achieves the aforementioned goals either at all or more effectively than the British system and in a proportionate manner given in particular the legal context: the necessity in the Italian legal system for a separate application for reinstatement to the electoral list. It is unclear as to why this procedural addition was not mentioned in relation to the English system wherein the essence of the disenfranchisement is that it can only be temporary. Temporary on the facts means co-terminus with actual period of incarceration. There is no subsistence or remaining period subsequent to liberation. There is no need, procedurally, to embark upon reinstatement which is automatically effected. Accordingly, it would appear that the Italian system potentially, according to the rules as

31. *Ibid.*, passim.
32. *Hirst v UK (No 2)* (2006) 42 EHRR 41, *supra*.

presented in the judgment and as described therein, may permanently disenfranchise in certain cases. The possibility of permanent disenfranchisement is not discussed in the context of the proportional operation of the Italian system. Nor is the extent to which such a system of potential permanent disenfranchisement discussed in terms of effectively attaining the objectives either of enhancing civil responsibility or ensuring the proper functioning and preservation of the democratic regime. This would appear to be a classic instance of where a judgment has been rendered on the basis of an incomplete consideration of the few facts – notably those presented in relation to the UK system of disenfranchisement in Hirst 2[33] and as reaffirmed by the ECtHR; secondly, an incomplete consideration of the operation of the Italian system notably as regards the proportionality and the effectiveness of the permanent disenfranchisement and its ability to achieve the aforementioned objectives. What appears to perhaps represent an attractive form of various categories or period of disenfranchisement has not be examined in terms of its factual ability to effectively achieve the objectives as compare to the British system. Once again, it is clear that the ECtHR could have endeavoured to obtain expert evidence[34] concerning specifically the operation of the permanent disenfranchisement of the Italian system and its control by means of the administrative measure of rehabilitation and insertion on the electoral roll. Both Hirst (2)[35] and Scoppola[36] constitute almost iconic examples of the failure by the ECtHR to carry out its duty to properly assess the facts which may in the circumstances such as in the instant case require experts; further there remains the profound lacuna arising from the omission by the ECtHR to supplement the evidence of the parties involved in order to achieve a better understanding of the original evidence tendered. It is clear that such omission violate Article 6 (1) of the ECHR and notably cases such as *Kraska v Switzerland.*[37] This corresponds to the situation noted earlier in Hirst (No 2)[38] as noted within the analysis thereof.

Finally, one notes the conclusion in following paragraph of the judgment in Scoppola:[39]

> 110. Taking the above considerations into account, the Court finds that, in the circumstances of the present case, the restrictions imposed on the applicant's right to vote did not 'thwart the free expression of the people in the choice of the legislature', and maintained 'the integrity and effectiveness of an electoral procedure aimed at identifying the will of the people through universal suffrage' (see Hirst (no. 2) [GC], cited above, § 62). The margin of appreciation afforded to the respondent Government in this sphere has therefore not been overstepped.

33. *Ibid.*
34. 'Rules of Court, 1 July 2013, Registry of the Court Strasbourg': 'Annex Rule A1 – Investigative measures1. The Chamber may, at the request of a party or of its own motion, adopt any investigative measure which it considers capable of clarifying the facts of the case. The Chamber may, *inter alia*, invite the parties to produce documentary evidence and decide to hear as a witness or expert or in any other capacity any person whose evidence or statements seem likely to assist it in carrying out its tasks', www.echr.coe.int, site last consulted on 29.10.2013.
35. *Hirst v UK (No 2)* (2006) 42 *EHRR* 41, *supra.*
36. *Scoppola v Italy (No 3)* (2012) *ECHR* 866, *supra*, passim.
37. *Kraska v Switzerland* (1994) *EHRR* (18) 188, *supra*, para. 30.
38. *Hirst v UK (No 2)* (2006) 42 *EHRR* 41, *ibid.*
39. *Scoppola v Italy (*No 3) (2012) ECHR 866, *supra.*

It is not clear on what basis the ECtHR uses the verb 'finds' in English[40] in the above quotation. This translation would appear to be rather more equivalent to 'the Court holds' in the sense that the ECtHR has decided exclusively on the basis of its own reasoning – which has not been presented – but certainly not on any facts or expert opinion that the Italian maintained 'the integrity and effectiveness of an electoral procedure aimed at identifying the will of the people through universal suffrage.' It is manifest that the ECtHR contrary to the practise in SCC,[41] the USSC[42] and the BCSC,[43] as witnessed by the judgments considered herein, did not consider any expert evidence despite once again the procedural availability as provided by its rules[44] and the duty upon it pursuant to its own case-law as in *Kraska v Switzerland*[45] to examine the merits of the case properly.

Paragraph 62 of Hirst (2)[46] reads as follows:

> 62. It is, however, for the Court to determine in the last resort whether the requirements of Article 3 of Protocol No. 1 have been complied with; it has to satisfy itself that the conditions do not curtail the rights in question to such an extent as to impair their very essence and deprive them of their effectiveness; that they are imposed in pursuit of a legitimate aim; and that the means employed are not disproportionate (see Mathieu-Mohin and Clerfayt, p. 23, § 52). In particular, any conditions imposed must not thwart the free expression of the people in the choice of the legislature – in other words, they must reflect, or not run counter to, the concern to maintain the integrity and effectiveness of an electoral procedure aimed at identifying the will of the people through universal suffrage. For example, the imposition of a minimum age may be envisaged with a view to ensuring the maturity of those participating in the electoral process or, in some circumstances, eligibility may be geared to criteria, such as residence, to identify those with sufficiently continuous or close links to, or a stake in, the country concerned (see Hilbe v. Liechtenstein (dec.), no. 31981/96, ECHR 1999-VI, and Melnychenko v. Ukraine, no. 17707/02, § 56, ECHR 2004-X). Any departure from the principle of universal suffrage risks undermining the democratic validity of the legislature thus elected and the laws it promulgates. Exclusion of any groups or categories of the general population must accordingly be reconcilable with the underlying purposes

40. *Scoppola v Italy (No 3)* (2012) *ECHR* 866 *ibid*. 'The judgement in French uses the word 'estimer' '110. Au vu de ce qui précède, la Cour estime que, dans les circonstances de l'espèce, les restrictions apportées au droit de vote du requérant se concilient avec le souci de ne pas entraver ' la libre expression du peuple sur le choix du corps législatif 'et de maintenir' l'intégrité et l'effectivité d'une procédure électorale visant à déterminer la volonté du peuple par l'intermédiaire du suffrage universel' (Hirst (no 2) [GC], précité, § 62). La marge d'appréciation reconnue au gouvernement défendeur dans ce domaine n'a donc pas été outrepassée.'
41. *Sauvé v Canada (AG)* (2002) 3 *SCR* 519, *supra*.
42. *Roper v Simmons* (2005) 543 *US* 551.
43. *Re Polygamy* (2011) *BCSC* 1588 Re: S 293 CCC.
44. 'Rules of Court, 1 July 2013, Registry of the Court Strasbourg: Annex to the Rules 1 (concerning investigations) 'Rule A1 – Investigative measures 1. The Chamber may, at the request of a party or of its own motion, adopt any investigative measure which it considers capable of clarifying the facts of the case. The Chamber may, *inter alia*, invite the parties to produce documentary evidence and decide to hear as a witness or expert or in any other capacity any person whose evidence or statements seem likely to assist it in carrying out its tasks.' www.echr.coe.int, site last consulted on 28.10.2013.
45. *Kraska v Switzerland* (1994) *EHRR* (18) 188, *supra*, para. 30.
46. *Hirst v UK (No 2)* (2006) 42 *EHRR* 41, *supra*.

> of Article 3 of Protocol No. 1 (see, mutatis mutandis, Aziz v. Cyprus, no. 69949/01, § 28, ECHR 2004-V).

The essential part of the above cited paragraph for the instant purposes is as follows:

> In particular, any conditions imposed must not thwart the free expression of the people in the choice of the legislature – in other words, they must reflect, or not run counter to, the concern to maintain the integrity and effectiveness of an electoral procedure aimed at identifying the will of the people through universal suffrage. For example, the imposition of a minimum age may be envisaged with a view to ensuring the maturity of those participating in the electoral process or, in some circumstances, eligibility may be geared to criteria, such as residence, to identify those with sufficiently continuous or close links to, or a stake in, the country concerned (see Hilbe v. Liechtenstein (dec.), no. 31981/96, ECHR 1999-VI, and Melnychenko v. Ukraine, no. 17707/02, § 56, ECHR 2004-X).

Regretfully, the ECtHR in Hirst[47] and similarly in Scoppola[48] – albeit to the advantage of the latter – did not embark upon any reasoned analysis of why the operation of the British restriction on voting by incarcerated prisoners demonstrably either in a hypothetic or factual sense either thwarted the integrity and the effectiveness of the British electoral system; or in the case of Scoppola[49] how the Italian system of disenfranchisement achieved on the facts those very objectives. This absence of full reasoning and above the deficiency of facts and particularly expert opinion regretfully substantiates a failure on the part of the court to properly examine the merits of the case of the UK in Hirst (2)[50] and arguably the same in Scoppola[51] although here no loss was suffered by Italy in terms of the cost of endeavouring to comply with such a decision. Arguably, in contrast to the judgments in BCSC[52] and the SCC[53] (and many part of the Majority) the absence of facts in the sense described in both of the aforementioned cases that that following conclusion follows: namely that the European Court of Human Rights conspicuously violated Article 6 (1) as interpreted in *Kraska v Switzerland*[54] given that it did not base its judgment on full reasoning which indicated that it had carefully analysed the facts presented by the UK or the Italian government.

§5.04 CONCLUSION

This brief analysis of the two cases of Hirst[55] and Scoppola[56] arguably demonstrates clearly the failure of the ECtHR to utilize any form of expert evidence as regards interpretation of the ECHR and notably Article 3 which deals with the organization of

47. *Kraska v Switzerland* (1994) *EHRR* (18) 188, *supra*, para. 30.
48. *Scoppola v Italy* (No 3) (2012) *ECHR* 866, *supra*.
49. *Ibid.*
50. *Scoppola v Italy (*No 3) (2012) E*CHR* 866 *ibid.*
51. *Scoppola v Italy (*No 3) (2012) *ECHR* 866 *ibid.*
52. *Polygamy reference: re constitutionality of S 293 of Criminal Code*, 2011 BCSC 1588, *supra*, www.bcla.org.
53. *Sauvé v Canada (Attorney General)*, [2002] 3 *S.C.R.* 519 *ibid.*
54. *Kraska v Switzerland* (1994) 18 *EHRR* 328 para. 33.
55. *Hirst v UK (No 2)* (2006) 42 *EHRR* 41, *supra*.
56. *Scoppola v Italy (No 3)* (2012) *ECHR* 866 *ibid.*

elections and therefore the right to vote. This becomes clear when one compares the judgment of the SCC, Sauvé[57] where although the full deployment and evaluation of evidence took place at the Court of First Instance, the court of final instance also examined the evidence carefully. Perhaps most notably in Sauvé[58] was the reference by Gonthier J. to the specific type of evidence which is required in the stator interpretation of rights such as enfranchisement and prisoners' rights. Although such concepts cannot be established with detailed empirical evidence nevertheless according to the learned Minority – and on this point they was no disagreement with the learned Majority in Sauvé[59] nevertheless, proof thereof is required in the form of logical inferences based upon facts. Regretfully, and taking account of the fact that the rules of procedure of the ECtHR provides as noted above, for the appointment of a court expert on its own motion, that court decided for whatever reasons to avoid endeavouring to consider establishing or relating its reasoning on the basis of expert facts and opinions. Further the logical inference which seeks to establish that the restriction is disproportionate is regretfully insufficiently detailed in the sense of establishing cogently, that is of proving a breach of Article 3 ECHR. By reason of this factual insufficiency which one might term a deficit in expert evidence, the ECtHR has regretfully in both Hirst[60] and Scoppola[61] breached its duty to consider carefully the evidence presented by the parties and also to above all use expert evidence in order to prove the technical meaning of certain words within notably Article 3 ECHR. Once again this deficit of expert evidence occurred despite the availability of the appropriate rules of procedure which are possessed by the ECtHR. Ultimately, this failure upon the part of the ECtHR sounds in a breach of the fundamental procedural principle of rectitude of decisions which requires the correct and accurate application of the law to the true facts. Such inaccurate interpretations of the ECHR attributable to the evidential deficits caused by the reluctance of the ECtHR to use its rules of procedure to obtain expert opinion regretfully operates to exacerbate the type of deficiency in the judgments rendered by the CJ and GC as noted earlier. This in turn aggravates the breach of Article 6 (1) ECHR and of course the principle of rectitude of decision and finally, undermines the Rule of Law.

57. *Sauvé v Canada (Attorney General),* [2002] 3 *S.C.R.* 519 *supra.*
58. *Ibid.*
59. *Ibid.*
60. *Hirst v UK (No 2)* (2006) 42 *EHRR* 41, *supra.*
61. *Scoppola v Italy (No 3)* (2012) *ECHR* 866 *supra.*

Conclusion

This study has concentrated on the failure by the CJ, the ECtHR and marginally, the GC, to use expert evidence for the purpose of statutory construction in certain judgments which were chosen at various chronological periods in the development of EU and ECHR law. The expert opinion evidence if it had been utilized, would have involved, generally, two types of potential areas of expertise: first, the expert evidence drawn from certain social sciences such as political science where the evidence is not precise and is not easily susceptible to formalization and mathematic quantification; the second category of expert evidence consists of more experimental and mathematically quantifiable social sciences such as economics and extends to the physical sciences such as physics. No attempt has been made, in the instant analysis, to observe whether a particular pattern concerning the failure to use expert evidence could be detected other than it would appear that, generally, the absence of expert evidence constitutes the consistent method of the statutory interpretation used by the three courts discussed in the instant analysis. The premise of the instant analysis is, further, that this method of statutory interpretation, that is, one devoid of expert evidence, has a profoundly negative impact upon the factual and legal accuracy of the judgments. Further, one observes ultimately that this factual and jurisprudential deficiency reduces overall the legal and forensic credibility of the judgments rendered by the ECtHR, the CJ and GC. Effectively, the opacity of some of the reasoning therein coupled with vacuity in terms of a lack of grounding in expert evidence diminishes the legal certainty of the judgments as regards application of the TFEU and the ECHR. Certainly, the overall conclusion must be, from the point of view of the parties involved in the cases considered, that that Article 6 (1) and the principles of the Rule of Law and rectitude of decision have been violated. In addition to both of the jurisprudential and epistemological weaknesses of the judgments of the CJ, the GC and the ECtHR, which results from the absence of the use by the three courts of their existing rules of procedures in order to obtain and analyse expert witness a further difficulty arises: as noted in previous chapters of this book, by reason of Article 6 (2) TEU[1] the judgments of the

1. *Treaty on European Union and the Treaty on the Functioning of the European Union* (2010 OJ C831/1 (consolidated version) 6 (2) TEU 'The Union shall accede to the European Convention for

ECtHR will in some manner come to have an effect, perhaps of some type of binding nature, upon the CJ and GC.[2] The exact nature of this relationship is currently being decided. For this reason, it is necessary to consider the judgments of the ECtHR notably in relation to Article 6 (1) ECHR. Suffice to say, however, that in so far as the analysis of the judgments examined herein from the ECtHR disclose exactly the same deficiency of expert evidence as those of the CJ and the GC, this mirror image so to speak can only serve to complicate compliance by both the ECtHR and the EU Courts with notably Article 6 (1) ECHR. More specifically, it has been argued that the aforementioned courts violate a duty which exists upon them pursuant to *Kraska v Switzerland*.[3] Indeed, as noted earlier in this analysis, the nature of this duty is quite straight forward: it establishes that a court, including, necessarily the ECtHR itself, subject to the ECHR is invested so to speak with a duty of care to ensure the proper evaluation of the merits of cases to the adjudication, notably as regards the evidence. As is recalled, Kraska[4] provides as follows:

> Para 30. It falls to the Court to decide whether the contested proceedings considered as a whole were fair within the meaning of the Convention. The effect of Article 6 para. 1 (art. 6-1) is, inter alia, to place the 'tribunal' under a duty to conduct a proper examination of the submissions, arguments and evidence adduced by the parties, without prejudice to its assessment of whether they are relevant to its decision (see, among other authorities, mutatis mutandis, the Barberà, Messegué and Jabardo v. Spain judgment of 6 December 1988, Series A no. 146, p. 31, para. 68). It has to be determined whether this condition was satisfied in the instant case.

The essence of the sentence ' ... under a duty to conduct a proper examination of the submissions, arguments and evidence ...' bearing in mind that 'proceedings [are] considered as a whole' is as, observed earlier, as follows:

> the duty as regards the appointment of experts so as to ensure proper evaluation of the evidence, is as Judge Edward,[5] noted necessarily judicial in nature. Its exercise arises from the function or the operation of the court or tribunal qua court. The duty is not an administrative duty. Its scope arguably, would include in first

the Protection of Human Rights and Fundamental Freedoms. Such accession shall not affect the Union's competences as defined in the Treaties.' One notes also that with the entry into force of the Lisbon Treaty (1 December 2009), *The EU Charter of Fundamental Rights* has become legally binding on the EU's institutions and on Member States when they act in the scope of EU law. It entrenches all the rights found in the European Convention on Human Rights as well as other rights and principles resulting from the common constitutional traditions of the EU Member States, the case law of the European Court of Justice and other international instruments.

2. T Lock, 'EU Accession to the ECHR. Implications for Judicial Review in Srasbourg' (2010) *ELRev* (35) 777.
3. *Kraska v Switzerland* (1994) 18 *EHRR*, *supra*, at para. 30.
4. *Kraska v Switzerland* (1994) 18 *EHRR* 188 *ibid*. at para. 30.
5. Sir David Edward QC, 'Proof, Fact-Finding and the Expert Witness', *Expert Witness Institute* – 29 April 2004 7th Sir Michael Davies Lecture, www.law.du.edu, at 8 'What is the role of the expert in that context? I think the way to put it is this. The expert's report, the expert's investigations, are simply one tool in the judge's armoury of decision-making. They are one way in which a judge may go about deciding on an element in the case that needs to be established one way or another. Ultimately, the procedure, unlike the 'lay' procedure of the common law, is archetypally 'judicial' – the judge decides what are the crucial issues and what is the best way of resolving them.'

> instance, what might be termed a procedural and a substantive duty: namely, the duty on the part of the court to exercise its discretion as regards the operation of the rules of procedures which provide, specifically, for the acquiring and evaluation of expert evidence. Arguably also, the matter of the evaluation of expert evidence comports both a procedural aspect as manifested in the rules concerning the appointment of experts and the introduction of expert evidence as well as a substantive aspect which is in the form of a duty: namely, pursuant to *Kraska v Switzerland*[6] the duty on the part of the court to properly evaluate the merits of the case in terms of the submissions and evidence which arguably is part of the more profound duty, namely, to correctly apply the law to the facts of the case in the context of the standard of proof which is required by the particular legal system. This part of the duty has been described accurately by Bentham[7] as constituting the first objective of civil procedure: specifically, the correct application of the law to the facts subsequent to the correct determination of fact and of law. It is submitted that this procedural principle is reflected in Art 19 TEU[8] which provides for a duty on the part of the court to ensure accurate judgements taking cognisance of both their procedural and substantive aspects as just noted. In addition, however, arguably the aforementioned duty may extend to proper case management.[9] Moreover, the procedural rules of both the CJ GC and the ECtHR provide for the introduction of expert evidence by the court, if necessary of their own motion therefore in addition to the evidence which may be presented the parties.

With respect to the two aforementioned EU courts, Judge Versterdorf[10] observed as follows:

> The Rules of Procedure of the CFI contain adequate tools for the production of sufficient economic evidence before the courts. The review and use of this evidence can be improved through two ways: better presentation of such evidence by the parties and more specialisation of the judiciary so that it is more capable of understanding and using this evidence.

This study has dealt exclusively with expert evidence in the context of a procedural deficit. However, the rules of case management contained within the rules of civil procedure involve the evaluation of the case in terms of its submissions, arguments and evidence in terms not only of production of both expert and non-expert evidence but

6. *Kraska v Switzerland* (1994) 18 *EHRR* 188 *ibid.* at para. 30.
7. A Zuckerman, 'Justice in Crisis: Comparative Dimensions of Civil Procedure' in A Zuckerman, S Chiarloni & P Gotwald (eds), *Civil Justice in Crisis: Comparative Perspectives of Civil Procedure* (New York, OUP, 1999), 4. 'In Bentham's terminology, the purpose of procedure is rectitude of decisions which requires the correct application of the law to the true facts ... Most if not all procedural requirements are concerned to secure rectitude of decisions including the requirements of procedural justice. Measures such as the right to be heard or the right to an impartial tribunal are dictated by the desire for rectitude of decision. Of course, the appearance of justice is also important but it does not alter the fact that at the foundation of procedure lies the objective of getting at the truth. This objective lies behind the entire procedural organization.'
8. Article 19 TEU It is based in Luxembourg. Art. 19 TEU provides that the role of the European Court of Justice (ECJ) is '(...) to ensure that in the interpretation and application of the Treaties the law is observed.
9. G Cumming, *Merger Decisions and the Rules of Procedure of the European Community* Courts (Wolters Kluwer, Alphen an den Rijn, 2012) Ch. 3 131-179.
10. B Versterdorf 'Economics in Court', in M Johansson, N Wahl & U Bernitz (eds) *Liber Amicorum in Honour of Sven Norberg* (Brussels, Bruylant, 2006) 511 at 527.

also the rules of pleading notably factually based pleading. Cumming[11] argues that the rules of case management which exist in both the CJ and the GC have been used insufficiently by those courts and that this insufficient use arguably violates Article 6 (1) ECHR: specifically, the duty of the court to properly examine in a procedural and substantive sense the arguments, submissions and the parties. Accordingly, with this broader interpretation of the duty pursuant to Article 6 (1) ECHR which would include case management, any defects therein would necessarily aggravate the violations of the duty through a deficiency of expert evidence. For heuristic reasons of clarity, there has been no specific attempt to link, in the instant work, the breaches of the duty pursuant to Kraska[12] provoked by deficient use of expert evidence with factual deficiencies which arise from defective case management. It is felt that for the purposes of this study at least initially, it is appropriate to consider the two types of deficits, namely, that of expert evidence and that of case management – fact management – separately.

In themselves, the violations of the ECHR which have been identified in the judgments cited herein by the CJ, the GC and ECtHR are profoundly perturbing. However, the gravity thereof is arguably augmented or at least rendered more patent by the brief comparisons which have been undertaken herein with judgments respectively of the USSC, *Roper v Simmons*,[13] the SCC, *Sauvé v Canada*[14] and the BCSC, Re Polygamy.[15] These three courts are national courts. Perhaps for this reason as well as the specific history of each of the courts, a very substantial use is made of the rules of procedure in order to produce statutory interpretation which is based upon expert evidence. The utilization of the Brandeis Brief as well as Judicial Notice involving the use of an expert as the reliable source of information for the judge is very well established. Both of these approaches seek to deal with one of the procedural problems involved in using expert evidence, which is costs and time.[16] By reason of the introduction of expert evidence through these two methods in particular in addition of course to the conventional cross-examination of expert witnesses, the criticisms of the learned minorities in both Roper[17] and Sauvé[18] could be focused upon something patent and clear: the standard of proof or more particularly the insufficiency of the expert evidence as decried by the learned minority in both judgments. This is in contrast to the judgments examined herein rendered by the CJ, the GC and the ECtHR. It is submitted that the aforementioned judgments in the sense of applying visibly the

11. G Cumming, *Merger Decisions and the Rules of Procedure of the European Community Courts* (Wolters Kluwer, Alphen an den Rijn, 2012) *ibid.*, passim.
12. *Kraska v Switzerland* (1994) 18 *EHRR* 188, *supra*, at para. 30.
13. *Roper v Simmons* (2005) 543 *US* 551, *supra*.
14. *Sauvé v Canada* (AG) (2002) 3 *SCR* 519, *supra*.
15. *Re Polygamy* 2011 *BCSC* 1588 Re: S 293 CCC, *supra*.
16. A Zuckerman, 'Justice in Crisis: Comparative Dimensions of Civil Procedure', in A Zuckerman, S Chiarloni & P Gotwald (eds) *Civil Justice in Crisis: Comparative Perspectives of Civil Procedure* (New York, OUP, 1999), *supra*, 6, 'There are further dimensions of justice which while having no direct bearing on rectitude of decision have a powerful influence on both the justice of the system and the individual outcomes. These are time and costs.'
17. *Roper v Simmons* (2005) 543 *US* 551, *supra*.
18. *Sauvé v Canada* (AG) (2002) 3 SCR 519, *supra*.

law to facts which have been examined carefully with the addition of expert opinion accords an element of judicial security which lack in the judgments of both the CJ, GC and ECtHR. Specifically, the manner in which the law has been interpreted and applied to the facts becomes apparent and accordingly, the application thereof is rendered more predictable notably as regards possible changes where expert evidence is used by reason of the fact that the latter is necessarily cited within the judgments. Further, by relating closely the statutory interpretation to the expert evidence, arguably the US and Canadian courts in the judgments considered herein, have succeeded in attaining a degree of credibility which is absent as regards the judgments considered herein of the ECtHR and the CJ and GC. Once again, the opinions of the Minority as noted both in Roper,[19] Sauvé[20] and Re: Polygamy[21] can be clearly analysed from the point of view of the actual expert evidence used and its evaluation by the courts involved. Regretfully, this is not the case, however, with the judgments examined herein which were rendered by the ECtHR or the GC and the CJ. Perhaps the combination of Hirst (2)[22] and Scoppola[23] demonstrates most easily this point as regards the finding by the ECtHR that the temporary disenfranchisement practised by the UK as regards incarcerated prisoners constitutes a disproportionate restriction of the right to vote as guaranteed by the ECHR.[24] It is clear that if the temporary disenfranchisement were linked to a concept of the freedom to vote which is less inclusive than that proposed but without explanation, by the ECtHR and coupled with a wide concept of societal disapproval of criminals which is associated to an individualized imposition of a criminal punishment then the UK method of temporary disenfranchisement could be declared, to consist in the following: namely, a binary system composed of general societal reprobation on the one hand, and on the other hand, coupled with an individualized punishment and incarceration. The actual length of the societal reprobation is automatically coterminous with the individualized period of incarceration but in itself, significantly, it does not constitute an actual part of the individualized punishment in the form of incarceration. Conspicuously, the proportionality of the concept of a uniform societal disapprobation depends for its legitimacy in part, on the category of beneficiaries of the right to vote being narrow and, therefore, not necessarily including prisoners; or as a group of beneficiaries of the right coupled with a wide exception which recognizes such societal disapprobation of criminals as being both acceptable inherently and one which for its effectiveness requires automatic application. This is even more so that its use may serve to reduce the actual length of the incarceration at least per Gonthier J.[25] Following the reasoning of the latter learned judge in Sauvé, it is clear that the position of the UK

19. *Roper v Simmons* (2005) 543 US 551, *supra.*
20. *Sauvé v Canada* (AG) (2002) 3 SCR 519, *supra.*
21. *Re: Polygamy* 2011 BCSC 1588 Re: S 293 CCC, *supra.*
22. *Hirst v UK (No 2)* (2005), *ECHR* 681, *supra.*
23. *Scoppola v Italy (No 3)* (2012) *ECHR* 868, *supra.*
24. Council of Europe, The European Convention on Human Rights, ROME 4 November 1950 and its Five Protocols Article 3 'The High Contracting Parties undertake to hold free elections at reasonable intervals by secret ballot, under conditions which will ensure the free expression of the opinion of the people in the choice of the legislature', www.hri.org, this site was last used on 28 October 2013.
25. *Sauvé v Canada (AG)* (2002) 3 *SCR* 519, *supra.*

ultimately is rational in the sense of being not only coherent but also one which is demonstrably relatable to a political theory of the operation of parliament and societal duties. This position can be perceived as proportionate in the context of the operation of the binary system of an individualised punishment coupled with automatic societal moral disapproval, which, by contrast to the penal incarceration, is entirely civil in nature, and manifested in the temporary disenfranchisement calculated in relation to the actual duration of the incarceration as opposed to the overall sentence. At a minimum one concludes, following Gonthier J., that in truth, given the nature of actual evidence which could have been but was not introduced one has competing theories involving social and political ideas, namely, that of the UK Government and that of the ECtHR. Regretfully, the conclusion must be that in Scoppola[26] and Hirst (2)[27] the ECtHR tacitly refused to admit that the political theory animating the UK legislation was rational and that, ultimately, the impugned legislation pursued an acceptable objective in a proportionate manner: that is, that the UK legislation was ultimately predicated upon either a restricted category of beneficiaries of electoral rights which does not include prisoners can be legitimate ipso fact or a wide category of beneficiaries of the right to vote which includes incarcerated prisoners but which may be varied in order to achieve, in a proportionate manner, certain objectives. Analysed in this manner, the temporary disenfranchisement provided by the UK legislation at bar, as just noted, expresses collective societal moral disapproval of criminals participating in the democratic process which they have contravened through their penalized acts. This societal expression of moral disapproval requires for its effective operation, uniform as opposed to individual application of the actual criminal punishment: this is because as a civil expression of societal indignation it is directed at the incarceration and the duration thereof which reflect the gravity of the crimes and therefore of the violations against the democratic order. The actual period of incarceration is by contrast manifestly imposed on an individual basis proportionate to the crime committed and in consonance with the individual characteristics of the prisoner. The disenfranchisement also does not form part of the punishment, the incarceration, in that is serves, once again, to express the indignation of society for certain types of criminal behaviour, *ipso facto*, which have been sanctioned by any period of incarceration irrespective of the personality type involved. Overall, this temporary expression of society disapprobation although pursuing a civil objective of the expression of moral and political indignation is nevertheless coupled with an individualised criminal system of punishment which for its effectiveness, requires individualised treatment of each prisoner. Conspicuously, the two aforementioned judgments of Hirst (2)[28] and Scoppola[29] of the ECtHR cannot admit the legitimacy and proportionality of the concept of a societal expression of disapproval of prisoners participating in the democratic process which their convictions have arguably undermined, and which for its effectiveness requires automatic implementation. It is submitted that this is so because, once again, the original concept

26. *Scoppola v Italy (No 3)* (2012) *ECHR* 866, *supra.*
27. *Hirst v UK (No 2)* (2006) 42 *EHRR* 41, *supra.*
28. *Hirst v UK (No 2)* (2005) *EHRR* 681, *supra.*
29. *Scoppola v Italy (No 3)* (2012) EHRR 868, *supra.*

of the beneficiaries of the electoral right utilized by the ECtHR was extremely wide and this, it is submitted, arises by reason of the absence of any apparent use of expert evidence couple with clear logical argumentation. Specifically, contrary to, in particular, the minority in *Sauvé v Canada*[30] led by Gonthier J, the majority in the ECtHR does not articulate the particular theory or theories or collection of ideas disparate or organized which may be used to prove in the context of the social science its reasoning in the judgment. In truth, the political concept underlying the position of the UK as observed, was not properly examined in detail by the ECtHR: that is, either in the sense of either detailed and prolonged logical or factual refutation. Therefore, it is submitted that Article 6 (1) ECHR as interpreted by the ECtHR itself in *Kraska v Switzerland*[31] is contravened by the ECtHR by its judgments in Hirst (2)[32] and its reaffirmation in Scoppola.[33] Once again, in contrast to the judgments in *Sauvé v Canada,*[34] *Roper v Simmons*[35] and *Re Polygamy,*[36] it is impossible to discern the exact reason that particular political concepts of the UK Government at bar in Hirst (2)[37] violate the ECHR or what it should do to avoid contravention in the future.

It is also necessary to consider the analysis herein in relation to the original principles which, in part, animated this study, namely those of Rasmussen.[38] In one sense, the conclusion of this study is of perhaps more restricted than that proposed by Rasmussen who wrote:

> What I undertook to demonstrate was that the Court of Justice's lawmaking activities defiant of much European tradition in that respect were regularly preceded by deep involvements in making choices between competing public policies for which the available sources of law did not offer the Court judicially applicable guidelines. In the absence thereof, the Court turned to essentially political guidelines contained in the Preamble of the Rome Treaty. I think that it is a tenable conclusion of my study that the Court actually transgressed the borderline to the Community's judicial function.

The reason that the conclusions of this analysis are more restricted than those of Rasmussen is that it seeks to identify how, from a procedural point of view, at least in some instances and at some periods, not only the CJ but also ECtHR apply the linguistic process of statutory interpretation particular as regards the use of expert evidence: that is, the failure on the part of both courts to use expert evidence in order that carry out statutory interpretation which involves not only technical words contained within the TFEU and the ECHR but also words with ordinary meaning. The latter involves as regards the use by the judge of the process of Judicial Notice where proof may be directly obviated provided that the signification of the word or words can be said to be

30. *Sauvé v Canada (AG)* (2002) 3 *SCR* 519, *supra.*
31. *Kraska v Switzerland* (1994) 18 *EHRR* 188, *supra,* at para. 30.
32. *Hirst v UK (No 2)* (2005) *EHRR* 681, *supra.*
33. *Scoppola v Italy (No 3)* (2012) *EHRR* 868, *supra.*
34. *Sauvé v Canada (AG)* (2002) 3 *SCR* 519, *supra.*
35. Roper *v Simmons* (2005) 543 *US* 551.
36. Re Polygamy 2011 BCSC 1588 Re: S 293 CCC.
37. *Hirst v UK (No 2)* (2005) *EHRR* 681, *supra.*
38. H Rasmussen, *On Law and Policy in the European Court of Justice: A Comparative Study in Judicial Policymaking* (Dordrecht Maritnus Kijhoff 1986), *supra,* 508.

indisputable either directly or indirectly in the sense of readily ascertainable from an indisputable source such as an expert. The overall result, arguably, of the failure to use expert evidence from the point of view of statutory interpretation would appear to be that the scope of the application of words with a technical meaning contained in the TFEU and the ECHR, particularly as regards 'rights', may well be wider than would be the case were empirical studies or indeed, a detailed semantic[39] and logical[40] analysis of the meaning were carried out. This is particularly so in the field of the social sciences where cogent and probative factual demonstration is more difficult to establish as noted by Gonthier J. on behalf of the minority in the judgment of *Sauvé v Canada*.[41] In so far as the judges do not use such sources of indisputable and objective authenticity particularly in the form of experts, the result is that the statutory interpretation given is semantically defective: that is, ordinary meaning as opposed to technical meaning is used by the judges. Accordingly, it may well be that the deficiency of expert evidence of the CJ, GC and the ECtHR, as compared to the methods of interpretation utilized by the Canadian and US Supreme Courts and as exemplified in the three cases analysed, can very easily provide the mechanism for the implementation of specific political series of values for the following reason: there is no grounding in detailed factual analysis particularly in the sense of expert evidence or thorough logical analysis. It is

39. Semantics which can best be comprehended systematically in the context of research in General Linguistics: J Nerbonne, *Handbook of Contemporary Semantic Theory* (Blackwell, Camb MA, 1996); HR Nielsen, *Semantic with Applications: A Formal Introduction* (Wiley and Sons, Chichester,1995); K Kearns, *Semantics* (Palgrave, London, 2000); A Cruse, *Meaning and Language: An Introduction to Semantics and Pragmatics*, Oxford Textbooks in Linguistics, Oxford, 2004).
40. Logical in the sense of application to hypothetical situations: P Kitcher & WC Salmon, *Scientific Explanation* (1989 University of Wisconsin Press). Further, jurisprudentially, it is submitted that the position expressed by Gonthier J effectively, in terms of evidence admits, as such, logical determinations which include what might be termed deontological ethics evidenced by authors such as E Kant (TL Beauchamp, *Philosophical Ethics: An Introduction to Moral Philosophy*, 2nd edn (New York, McGraw Hill, 1991))and J Rawls, *A Theory of Justice* (Camb Mass, Harvard, 1971): that is where, in contrast to utilitarian arguments based upon effects measured and analysed in facts various ways, arguments based upon deontological ethics are not measureable in an empirical manner unlike with utilitarian arguments but they do, for accurate use, require application by means of logic to facts. Regretfully, the scope of the category of beneficiaries of rights utilized but not defined by the ECtHR notably in *Hirst v UK (No 2)* (2005) *ECHR* 681, *supra*, appears to be related to a utilitarian origin as opposed to the concept of the UK which is, it is submitted, more derivable from the deontological ethics; that is, where in the instant case of temporary prison disenfranchisement, the category of beneficiaries is subject to moral restraints the effectiveness of which are not necessarily measureable in an utilitarian sense. However such moral restraints can be logically related to the category of beneficiaries and can be related to facts in a given situation which do not lead to contradictions with the moral principles. The implicit use by the ECtHR of an utilitarian concept of prisoner rights which gave a very wide scope to the category of beneficiaries and arguably by definition excludes a narrower scope based upon moral restraints the effects of which are not immediately verifiable under the utilitarian model. Once again this is a classic instance of two competing theories which are logically tenable but where neither can effectively be used to eliminate each other and in so far as the context is one of government policy, the rational policy of the government is to be preferred on what might be termed a restrictive concept of effectively judicial review by an extra national tribunal, the ECtHR.
41. *Sauvé v Canada (AG)* (2002) 3 *SCR* 519, *supra*.

in this sense that the analysis of Rasmussen[42] is interpreted in this instant work. In short, if such political values are used either personally or collectively, subliminally or overtly by the judges in their judgments, then in terms of statutory interpretation such is rendered possible or at least, facilitated, by the omission on the part of the court to use expressly expert evidence. As a matter of procedure this is perspicuous from a consultation of the judgments herein considered. In the case of the CJ, GC and the ECtHR, as noted in earlier chapters of this analysis, the three courts possess the procedural ability to appoint experts notably on their own initiative court: that is, firstly, to provide a supplement of information which may be required in order to comprehend the case as presented by the parties notably in the context of a reference; and secondly, the rules of procedure permit the courts in both cases to appoint an expert proprio motu who will be able to explain where necessary the technical terms used by any expert led in particular by the parties. As observed earlier, in the English system of procedure[43] such an expert is termed an assessor[44] and is utilized in large measure in the context of judicial notice. However the rules of the English CPR 35.15[45]

42. H Rasmussen, *On Law and Policy in the European Court of Justice: A Comparative Study in Judicial Policymaking* (Dordrecht Maritnus Kijhoff 1986), *supra*, 508.
43. Civil Procedure Rules, www.justice.gov.uk, last consulted 20 October 2013.
44. Etymologically assessor signifies a person who is authorized to sit with others in order to assist directly in the taking of decisions. In practice the role of the assessor may vary widely. Indeed for some such as Viscount Simon L.C. an assessor may intervene exclusively on matters which require an explanation of the meaning of technical terms. Moreover, an assessor being unsworn, may not give evidence. Others such as Viscount Dunedin in *Richardson v Redpath Brown & Co Ltd* (1944) *AC* 67 at 70 believe that an assessor may provide a source of facts beyond simply the meaning of words.
45. Assessors CPR 35.15 (1) This rule applies where the court appoints one or more persons under section 70 of the Senior Courts Act 1981[1] or section 63 of the County Courts Act 1984 as an assessor. (2) An assessor will assist the court in dealing with a matter in which the assessor has skill and experience. (3) An assessor will take such part in the proceedings as the court may direct and in particular the court may direct an assessor to – (a) prepare a report for the court on any matter at issue in the proceedings; and (b) attend the whole or any part of the trial to advise the court on any such matter. (4) If an assessor prepares a report for the court before the trial has begun – (a) the court will send a copy to each of the parties; and (b) the parties may use it at trial. (5) The remuneration to be paid to an assessor is to be determined by the court and will form part of the costs of the proceedings. (6) The court may order any party to deposit in the court office a specified sum in respect of an assessor's fees and, where it does so, the assessor will not be asked to act until the sum has been deposited. (7) Paragraphs (5) and (6) do not apply where the remuneration of the assessor is to be paid out of money provided by Parliament: Practice Directions: Assessors 10.1 An assessor may be appointed to assist the court under rule 35.15. Not less than twenty-one days before making any such appointment, the court will notify each party in writing of the name of the proposed assessor, of the matter in respect of which the assistance of the assessor will be sought and of the qualifications of the assessor to give that assistance. 10.2 Where any person has been proposed for appointment as an assessor, any party may object to that person either personally or in respect of that person's qualification. 10.3 Any such objection must be made in writing and filed with the court within 7 days of receipt of the notification referred to in paragraph 10.1 and will be taken into account by the court in deciding whether or not to make the appointment. 10.4 Copies of any report prepared by the assessor will be sent to each of the parties but the assessor will not give oral evidence or be open to cross-examination or questioning.

www.justice.gov.uk/courts/procedure-rules/civil/rules. This site was last used on 28 October 2013.

may require modification[46] in order to permit cross-examination of the expert in the contexts identified by Davis[47] in legislative facts. The appointment of an expert as noted by Edward[48] is quintessentially judicial in nature and is necessarily subject to certain legal restraints such as the application of Article 6 (1) ECHR as regards due process equally in the ECtHR, the CJ and the GC. It was argued in the course of the instant analysis that this article applies so as to impose upon these courts, pursuant to *Kraska v Switzerland*,[49] a duty to properly evaluate the merits of a case. Therefore, depending upon the facts of the case and the statute involved, the duty pursuant to Article 6 (1) ECHR will be such that it will require the courts in certain circumstances to utilize expert evidence. The cases examined involving the CJ, the GC and the ECtHR sounded, it was argued, in a breach of ECHR Article 6 (1) by reason of the failure to utilize expert evidence notably in the construction of words with technical meaning or even in some cases, with ordinary meaning through judicial notice involving an expert. The third consequence of statutory interpretations which are effectively inaccurate because they are devoid of any serious factual justification is of course, as noted vigorously by Scalia, J.,[50] a democratic deficit. The court exceeds effectively the boundaries of its jurisdiction.[51] Its inaccurate and factually devoid statutory interpretation in the form of a judgment replaces a law or policy which has been adopted by a democratically elected body. In the case of Sauvé[52] in the case Gonthier J. the matter

46. Sir Louis Blom-Cooper 'Experts and Assessors: past Present and Future' (2002) *CJQ* 341 at 347; 'The assessor system being advice by an expert not under oath given to the court on matters not disclosable for cross examination by either party would be regarded today as being incompatible under S 3(1) of the Human Rights Act 1988 as a violation of Art 6 (1) ECHR' and A Zuckerman *Civil Procedure*, 2nd edn (London, Thomson, 2006), *supra*, at 743 ... The court will define the role of the assessor and may direct the assessor to prepare a report for the court on a particular matter... The assessor advises the court on the issues and may well have considerable influence on the outcome. The parties must therefore have an adequate opportunity to respond to the assessors advice in much the same way as they must have an opportunity to challenge expert evidence. Compliance with Art 6 (1) ECHR requires that the court should first seek counsel's reactions to the questions that it proposes to put to the assessors and disclose the assessor's reactions to the questions it proposes to put to the assessors and disclose the assessor's answers in order that any appropriate submission could be made as to whether the judge should accept the advice. Fairness requires Burnton J explained, that assessors who advised a tribunal on issues of fact should do so openly in the presence of the parties and before the tribunal made its decision. Assessors should be normally asked to give their advice after the conclusion of the evidence and before submissions. It is clearly undesirable for assessors to express an opinion on a matter that is beyond their remit.' Finally, D Dwyer 'The Future of Assessors under the CPR' (2006) CJA (25) 219 observes that 'it is settled law that an assessor acting in a normal civil capacity or under a particularly statutory form of proceedings is not an evidentiary source and almost certainly constitutes part of the tribunal as a scientific adviser under S 70(3) Supreme Court Act (1981) and CPR 35.15'.
47. KC Davis 'Judicial Notice' (1955) *Columbia Law Review* (55) 7, *supra*, 945 at 978-984.
48. Sir David Edward QC, 'Proof, Fact-Finding and the Expert Witness', Expert Witness Institute – 29 April 2004, 7th Sir Michael Davies Lecture. www.law.du.edu, at 8 *supra*.
49. *Kraska v Switzerland* (1994) 18 *EHRR* 188 *ibid.*, at para. 30.
50. *Roper v Simmons* (2005) 543 *US* 551, *supra*.
51. See also P Craig 'The ECJ and Ultra Vires Action: A Conceptual Analysis' (2011) *CMLRev* (48) 395 at 436-473, *supra*. T Horsley, Reflections on the Role of the Court of Justice as the 'Motor' of European integration: Legal Limits to Judicial Law Making' (2013) *CMLRev* (50) (4), *supra*, 931.
52. *Sauvé v Canada* (AG) (2002) 3 *SCR* 519, *supra*.

becomes one of an attempt to impose one view containing certain values where in reality the situation gives rise to various competing systems of values: a plurality of rational views where ultimately procedurally the view of the legislature is to be preferred provided that it is rational even if its content is contestable. Clearly the *Re: Polygamy*,[53] *Sauvé v Canada*[54] and the *Roper v Simmons*[55] judgment considered briefly herein demonstrate firstly, that it is possible for courts to utilize expert evidence even in cases which involve concepts of a political nature such as freedom to vote where evidence may not be that of an empirical nature; secondly, even where such courts do utilize evidence of a broad kind ranging from empirically precise to detail rational political arguments, difficulties may arise. However, the difficulties are immediately evident. They are identifiable and almost quantifiable. They are problems of insufficiency of evidence preventing the achievement of the requisite standard of proof. Such a problem is something which can be remedied on a long-term basis. It is much more difficult to identify the problems which ultimately concern the same subject of insufficiency of evidence where no expert evidence has been led at all as was the case in the judgments of the CJ, GC and the ECtHR examined herein. It is submitted, moreover, that such an evidential deficiency fundamentally undermines the credibility of the judgment in terms of the value thereof for third parties in addition to contravening Article 6 (1) ECHR.

Ultimately the conclusion is that the appropriate rules of procedure exist in both of the CG, the GC and the ECtHR such that the courts are able to deal not only with expert evidence led by the parties but above all, through their own motion. It is clear that the deficit of expert evidence can be very easily rectified by the decision on the part of the judges to exercise their discretion so as to use the rules of procedure to appoint court experts to assist them when dealing with in particular the interpretation of technical meaning of words but also the ordinary meaning of words through judicial notice involving experts as an indisputable source of accuracy and expertise. Above all, it is the use of the overall system of Case Management which facilitates the enforcement of the courts' duty pursuant to Kraska[56] to ensure pursuant to Article 6 (1). ECHR that they examine properly the merits of the case. It was noted in this regard that the English CPR Article 1.4 (1)[57] provides for a duty for case management which is active in the sense of 'actively managing cases'.[58] Arguably however, some caution must be used particularly bearing in mind the American and Canadian cases considered herein concerning any recommendation for wholesale adoption of a procedural mechanism such as case management for the following reasons: there will not be an attempt to utilize comparative law, notably, the existence of procedural dispositions in the English

53. *Re Polygamy* 2011 *BCSC* 1588 Re: S 293 CCC, *supra*.
54. *Sauvé v Canada* (AG) (2002) 3 *SCR* 519, *supra*.
55. *Roper v Simmons* (2005) 543 *US* 551, *supra*.
56. *Kraska V Switzerland* (1993) 18 *EHRR* 188 para. 30.
57. CPR 1.4 '(1) The court must further the overriding objective by actively managing cases. (2) Active case management includes – ... (b) identifying the issues at an early stage; (c) deciding promptly which issues need full investigation and trial and accordingly disposing summarily of the others; . ...' www.justice.gov.uk/courts/procedure-rules/civil/rules.
58. CPR 1.4(1) 'The court must further the overriding objective by actively managing cases'. www.justice.gov.uk/courts/procedure-rules/civil/rules.

CPR which provide for a duty for case and fact management on the part of the court which is active. Rather the position of Zuckerman[59] will be adopted. Specifically, it is appropriate to consider each legal system as an individual entity which has its own specific features and characteristics. While it is possible to utilize what might be termed general or universal categories of analysis such as the rectitude of decision, costs and time, in truth each legal system has its own method of deal with each of therewith: specially, each legal system does appear to have specific considerations as regarding the achievement of rectitude of decision as well as dealing with the effluxion of time as well as the costs of litigation. As such, it is necessary to take account of the entirety of the operation of each system before seeking to introduce modifications particularly if they emanate from other legal systems. Zuckerman[60] observes in this regard:

> 10-11 It will have become clear that measuring the success of procedures in doing justice calls for a complex judgment. It is not enough to ask whether the system produces correct judgments. We have also to ask how timely judgments are because a judgment given too late may amount to denial of justice even though it involves the correct application of the law to the true facts. Cost too is relevant to the assessment of procedural systems. The resources available to the system will influence its global level of rectitude of decision. Cost will affect access to justice and lastly high litigation costs may enable rich litigants to acquire a procedural advantage against their opponents. Each of these aspects is clearly relevant to the assessment of any system of civil justice. Each procedural system discussed in this volume has devised methods for attempting to achieve justice in all its dimensions though none of them is fully realizable. There is no perfect rectitude of decision, justice cannot be dispenses instant without some delay and justice cannot be absolutely free of costs constraints. It follows that when we come to look at the different systems we should not merely compare how particular aspects of procedure are treated by different systems. .... A comparison of systems calls therefore for a holistic approach: that is for an assessment as a whole. Each individual system needs to be judged by reference to the three dimension justice criteria that have been outlined [rectitude of decision, time, costs]. However we have to be clear about the limitations of such a comparative approach. A three dimension investigation may reveal the strengths and weaknesses of individual systems but it will not necessarily tell us which system is better. Just because a procedure gives greater weight to rectitude of decision that it is better that a differing system which sacrifices rectitude for the sake of delivering quicker and more timely judgments. As we have seen the mere fact that discovery is a good method of obtaining the truth is not a conclusive argument for importing discovery into a system that prefers to keep down costs. Each system of procedure has its own preferences which it comes to making choices between the different dimensions of justice. It does not follow however that a comparison of systems is useless. By looking at other systems we can evaluate different ways of resolving conflicts between competing demands of justice.

59. AA Zuckerman, S Chiarloni & P Gottwald (eds) *Civil Justice in Crisis: Comparative Perspectives of Civil Procedure* (Oxford, OUP, 1999), *supra*, 4-5.
60. *Ibid.*, passim.

Zuckerman[61] further observes as regards the principle of rectitude of decision which appears in all legal systems:

> In all systems of procedure doing justice means arriving at decisions which give the parties before the court what is legally due to them. In order to do justice, then the court has to determine the true facts and then correctly apply the law to them. In Bentham's terminology, the purpose of procedure is rectitude of decisions which requires the correct application of the law to the true facts. While rectitude of decision or truth is the aim of civil procedure it is acknowledged that our procedures are not perfect. They are always limitations to the ability of procedure to achieve rectitude of decision. A system of procedure can strive to determine what happened in the past and to apply the law precisely but it cannot guarantee that errors will never occur. It is the mark of legal procedures that while the criterion of justice is external to the procedure the procedure itself cannot always achieve a perfect correspondence between individual decisions and this criterion. Accordingly, a procedure may be just even if individual decisions arrived at by this procedure are sometimes erroneous. We cannot expect perfect justice but we can and should expect a just procedure. That question therefore arises: what is just procedure? Since rectitude of decisions is as we have seen, the most basis requirement a system of procedure must take sufficient steps to arrive at decisions which are correct in law and fact. A procedure in which the courts do not even try to at the truth is manifestly an unjust procedure because it fails in its main task of giving whose who seek the court's help what is due to them by right. We can therefore take it for granted that all procedures seek to achieve rectitude. Yet not all procedures are necessarily just. To be just we have to be satisfied that the system of procedure produces results which are broadly correct. Most if not all procedural requirements are concerned to secure rectitude of decision including the requirements of procedural justice. Measures such as the right to be heard or the right to an impartial tribunal are dictated by the desire for rectitude of decision. Of course the appearance of justice is also important but it does not alter the fact that at the foundation of procedure lies the objective of getting at the truth. This objective lies behind the entire procedural organization. Rules such as those dealing with notice of commencement of proceedings with the definition of the issues between the parties, with the objecting of evidence and with the calling of witnesses are all designed to facilitate the correct determination of fact and of law.

Zuckerman particularly notes in the above quotation the following:

> Since rectitude of decisions is as we have seen, the most basis requirement a system of procedure must take sufficient steps to arrive at decisions which are correct in law and fact. A procedure in which the courts do not even try to at the truth is manifestly an unjust procedure because it fails in its main task of giving whose who seek the court's help what is due to them by right.

The essential difficulty is that the judges of the CJ, GC and the ECtHR arguably do not try to achieve rectitude of decision as regards the use of expert evidence. This is despite the recognition noted earlier by Judge B Vesterdorf[62] that the rules of procedure

61. AA Zuckerman, S Chiarloni & P Gottwald (eds) *Civil Justice in Crisis: Comparative Perspectives of Civil Procedure* (Oxford, OUP, 1999), *supra* at 1-2.
62. B Vesterdorf 'Economics in Court' in M Johansson N Wahl and U Bernitz (eds) *Liber Amicorum in Honour of Sven Norberg* (Brussels, Bruylant 2006) 511, *supra*, at 527.

certainly of the CJ, GC and implicitly the ECtHR contain sufficient procedural disposition such that economic evidence may be presented to the courts. What is required is better presentation therefore by the parties and more specialization of the judiciary so that the judges may understand the expert evidence. Thus, by reason of the fact that the aforementioned courts apparently do not even try to ensure rectitude of decision in respect of expert evidence one can only conclude that the courts themselves are violating not only Article 6 ECHR but the fundamental procedural principle of rectitude of decision. The evidential deficit arguably does not arise from the rules of the procedure utilized by the GC, the CJ and the ECtHR but rather as noted by Judge Versterdorf: that is, the judges and the parties. The rules of procedure in themselves, it is submitted, could be applied if the parties but above all the judges were so minded. Indeed, as noted earlier the resolution of this problem of evidentiary deficit particularly of expert evidence although identifiable as a breach of a fundamental procedural principle is probably not solvable most effectively by means of the straight forward introduction of a rule involving for example 'active case' law such as exists in English procedure. Not only are legal systems most appropriately analysed as separate, independent and coherently complete in truth, change through the introduction of rules introduced from other legal systems may not be successful. In short, as Kahn Freund[63] argues, it is necessary to consider the whole context in which a legal disposition exists before it may be modified by external borrowings, that is not only the purely legal but the historical, the societal and above all the political. It is the latter factors in particular which may affect profoundly the success of the introduction of a legal disposition from one legal system to another. In regard to the rules of civil procedure Kahn Freund notes that they may be among the most difficult to change for the following reason:

> All rules which organise constitutional legislative administrative or judicial institutions and procedures are designed to allocate power rule making decision making above all policy making power. These are the rules which are the closest to the 'organic' end of our continuum they are the ones most resistant to transplantation. Nothing shows it more clearly than the futile attempts to export British parliamentary institutions into countries which do not share the very peculiar features of history of social structure and of political consensus characteristics of this country. .... All I have wanted to suggest is that its use requires a knowledge not only of the foreign law but also of its social and above all its political context.[64]

This hesitation on the part of Kahn-Freund to make recourse to what might be termed legal harmonization based upon comparative law based upon the inherent legal peculiarities of each legal system as entirely legitimate individualised responses to

63. O Kahn Freund, 'Uses and Misuses of Comparative Law' (1974) *MLR* (37)1 at 27.
64. *Ibid.*, at 17 and at 27. See also P Legrand, 'The Same and Different', in P Legrand & R Munday (eds). *Comparative Legal Studies: Traditions and Transitions* (Cambridge, CUP, 2003). D Nelken (ed), *Comparing Legal Cultures* (Aldershot, Dartmouth, 1997). PG Monateri (ed), *Methods of Comparative Law* (Cheltenham, Edward Elgar, 2012). B Markesinis. *Comparative Law in the Courtroom and Classroom* (Oxford, Hart, 2003). W Menski, *Comparative Law in a Global Context*, 2nd edn (Cambridge, CUP, 2006). E Örücü & D Nelken, *Comparative Law: A Handbook* (Oxford, Hart, 2007). B Markesinis & J Fedtke, *Engaging with Foreign Law* (Oxford, Hart, 2009).

particular characteristics of the specific legal, political and economical characteristics in which he operates finds confirmation in the work of Van den Bergh:[65]

> Market integration is not synonymous with the highest possible degree of uniformity? Divergent legal rules are better able to satisfy heterogeneous preference of a large population and may thus contribute to increased welfare in the European internal market. The lawyers' blind concern for legal certainty diverts their attention away from the important benefits of competition between legislators. Such competition may initiate more efficient rules. The costs of decentralised law making may be lower than those of enacting rules at the central level whilst the latter rules bring fewer economic benefits ... When preferences are heterogeneous Member State laws may be able to satisfy more references than European law: that is in the absence of overriding motives for harmonisation and unification diversity in rules should thus be preserved.

That being said, certainly the rules of the GC[66] in particular do provide for case management although they are not articulated as specifically being 'active' as is the

65. R van den Bergh, 'Subsidiarity as an Economic Demarcation Principle and the Emergence of European Private Law' (1998) *MJL* 129, *supra*, at 130.
66. 'Chapter 3 MEASURES OF ORGANISATION OF PROCEDURE AND MEASURES OF INQUIRY Section 1 – Measures of organisation of procedure

> *Article 64*
> 1. The purpose of measures of organisation of procedure shall be to ensure that cases are prepared for hearing, procedures carried out and disputes resolved under the best possible conditions. They shall be prescribed by the General Court, after hearing the Advocate General.
> 2. Measures of organisation of procedure shall, in particular, have as their purpose:
> (a) to ensure efficient conduct of the written and oral procedure and to facilitate the taking of evidence;
> (b) to determine the points on which the parties must present further argument or which call for measures of inquiry;
> (c) to clarify the forms of order sought by the parties, their pleas in law and arguments and the points at issue between them;
> (d) to facilitate the amicable settlement of proceedings.
> 3. Measures of organisation of procedure may, in particular, consist of:
> (a) putting questions to the parties;
> (b) inviting the parties to make written or oral submissions on certain aspects of the proceedings;
> (c) asking the parties or third parties for information or particulars;
> (d) asking for documents or any papers relating to the case to be produced;
> (e) summoning the parties' agents or the parties in person to meetings.
> 4. Each party may, at any stage of the procedure, propose the adoption or modification of measures of organisation of procedure. In that case, the other parties shall be heard before those measures are prescribed.
> Where the procedural circumstances so require, the Registrar shall inform the parties of the measures envisaged by the General Court and shall give them an opportunity to submit comments orally or in writing.
> 5. If the General Court sitting in plenary session or as the Grand Chamber decides to prescribe measures of organisation of procedure and does not undertake such measures itself, it shall entrust the task of so doing to the Chamber to which the case was originally assigned or to the Judge-Rapporteur.

If a Chamber prescribes measures of organisation of procedure and does not undertake such measures itself, it shall entrust the task to the Judge-Rapporteur. The Advocate

case with the English CPR. Arguably, and although this study is limited to the deficiency of expert evidence in statutory interpretation, the rules of the CJ[67] do also provide for a form for case management also although once again there is no specific mention of 'active' management as in the English CPR. Nor is any specific exclusion of case management to be found in those of the ECtHR. It could be said that the rules which provide for investigative measures in that court constitute a form of case management in embryonic form.[68] It is clear that active case management could be

---

General shall take part in measures of organisation of procedure. http://curia.europa.eu/jcms/upload/docs/application/pdf/2008-09/txt7_2008-09-25_14-08-6_431.pdf, last consulted on 28.10.2013.

67. 'MEASURES OF ORGANISATION OF PROCEDURE AND MEASURES OF INQUIRY Section 1. Measures of organisation of procedure

> *Article 61*
> Measures of organisation prescribed by the Court
> 1. In addition to the measures which may be prescribed in accordance with Article 24 of the Statute, the Court may invite the parties or the interested persons referred to in Article 23 of the Statute to answer certain questions in writing, within the time-limit laid down by the Court, or at the hearing. The written replies shall be communicated to the other parties or the interested persons referred to in Article 23 of the Statute.
> 2. Where a hearing is organised, the Court shall, in so far as possible, invite the participants in that hearing to concentrate in their oral pleadings on one or more specified issues.
> *Article 62*
> Measures of organisation prescribed by the Judge- Rapporteur or the Advocate General
> 1. The Judge-Rapporteur or the Advocate General may request the parties or the interested persons referred to in Article 23 of the Statute to submit within a specified time- limit all such information relating to the facts, and all such documents or other particulars, as they may consider relevant. The replies and documents provided shall be communicated to the other parties or the interested persons referred to in Article 23 of the Statute.
> 2. The Judge-Rapporteur or the Advocate General may also send to the parties or the interested persons referred to in Article 23 of the Statute questions to be answered at the hearing.'

68. 'Annex to the Rules 1 (concerning investigations)

> Rule A1 – Investigative measures
> 1. The Chamber may, at the request of a party or of its own motion, adopt any investigative measure which it considers capable of clarifying the facts of the case. The Chamber may, *inter alia*, invite the parties to produce documentary evidence and decide to hear as a witness or expert or in any other capacity any person whose evidence or statements seem likely to assist it in carrying out its tasks.
> 2. The Chamber may also ask any person or institution of its choice to express an opinion or make a written report on any matter considered by it to be relevant to the case.
> 3. After a case has been declared admissible or, exceptionally, before the decision on admissibility, the Chamber may appoint one or more of its members or of the other judges of the Court, as its delegate or delegates, to conduct an inquiry, carry out an onsite investigation or take evidence in some other manner. The Chamber may also appoint any person or institution of its choice to assist the delegation in such manner as it sees fit.
> 4. The provisions of this Chapter concerning investigative measures by a delegation shall apply, *mutatis mutandis*, to any such proceedings conducted by the Chamber itself.
> 5. Proceedings forming part of any investigation by a Chamber or its delegation shall be held in camera, save in so far as the President of the Chamber or the head of the delegation decides otherwise.
> 6. The President of the Chamber may, as he or she considers appropriate, invite, or grant leave to, any third party to participate in an investigative measure. The President shall

effected by the GC, the CJ and the ECtHR which would assist enormously in the eventual use of the rules of procedure of that court as regards the appointment of experts notably on its own motion. Indeed, even without the use of comparative law and taking into consideration the views of Kahn Freud[69] as regards the difficulty of immediately adapting rules of procedure developed for one court in that of another, the fact that case management is specifically provided for in the rules of the GC, is also clearly present in those of the CJ and is similarly, discernible in those of the ECtHR is profoundly useful for achieving compliance with ECHR Article 6 (1) and the procedural principle of Bentham, rectitude of decision. Arguably the rules indicate that case management is indeed possible not only in the GC but in the CJ with its inquisitorial system as well as arguably in the ECtHR as well.

In conclusion, following Judge Vesterdorf,[70] hopefully, the analysis herein presented will contribute to convincing the learned judges of the aforementioned courts as well as legal counsel to use expert evidence more frequently in order to strengthen the quality of their judgments in order to ensure compliance with ECHR Article 6 (1), the principle of rectitude of decision and above all, the notion of the Rule of Law discussed earlier herein.

lay down the conditions of any such participation and may limit that participation if those conditions are not complied with.' http://curia.europa.eu/jcms/upload/docs/application/pdf/2008-09/txt7_2008-09-25_14-08-6_431.pdf, last consulted on 28.10.2013.

69. O Kahn Freund, 'Uses and Misuses of Comparative Law' (1974) *MLR* (37) 1, *supra*, at 17 and at 27.
70. B Vesterdorf, 'Economics in Court' in M Johansson N Wahl & U Bernitz (eds) *Liber Amicorum in Honour of Sven Norberg* (Brussels, Bruylant 2006) 511, *supra*, at 527.

Bibliography

Alston, P., M. Bustelo & J. Henan. *The EU and Human Rights*. Oxford: Oxford University Press, 1999.

Akmajian, A., et al. *Linguistics: An Introduction to Language and Communication*. Cambridge MA: MIT Press, 2010.

Andreangeli, A. *EU Competition Enforcement and Human Rights*. Cheltenham: Edward Elgard, 2008.

Andrews, N. *English Civil Procedure: Fundamentals of the New Civil Justice System*. Oxford: Oxford University Press, 1999.

Arnull, A. *The European Union and Its Court of Justice*. Oxford: Oxford University Press, 1999.

Barnard, C. *The Substantive Law of the EU: The Four Freedoms*. 3rd edn. Oxford: Oxford University Press, 2010.

Bates, E. *The Evolution of the European Convention of Human Rights: From Its Inception to the Creation of a Permanent Court of Human Rights*. Oxford: Oxford University Press, 2010.

Bell, J. & G. Engle (eds). *Cross on Statutory Interpretation*. 3rd edn. London: Butterworths, 1995.

Bennion, F. *Bennion on Statutory Interpretation*. 5th edn. London: Lexis Nexis, 2008.

Blom-Cooper Sir L. (ed). *Experts in Civil Courts*. Oxford: Oxford University Press, 2006.

Brennan, L. & W. Blair (eds). *Bullen & Leake & Jacob's Precedents of Pleadings*. 15th edn. London: Sweet & Maxwell, 2004.

Brüggemeier, G., A. Colombi Ciacchi & G. Comandé. *Fundamental Rights and Private Law in the European Union*. Vols 1 and 2. Cambridge: Cambridge University Press, 2010.

Chalmers, D. et al. *European Union Law*. Cambridge: Cambridge University Press, 2006.

Chalmers, D. *European Union Law: Cases and Materi*als. Cambridge: Cambridge University Press, 2010.

Chase, O., et al. *Civil Procedure in Comparative Context*. New York: Thomson West, 2007.

Chomsky, N. *On Language*. New York: The New Press, 1998.

Clayton, R. QC & H. Tomlinson QC. *The Law of Human Rights*. Vols 1 & 2. Oxford: Oxford University Press, 2009.

Craig, P. *EU Administrative Law*. 2nd edn. Oxford: Oxford University Press, 2012.

Craig, P. *EU Administrative Law*. Collected Court of the Academy of European Law. Col XVI/I. Oxford: Oxford University Press, 2006.

Cumming, G. *Merger Decisions and the Rules of Procedure of the European Community Courts*. Alphen aan den Rijn: Kluwer Law Books, 2012.

Cumming, G. & M. Freudenthal. *Civil Procedure in EU Competition Cases before the English and Dutch Courts*. The Hague: Kluwer Law International, 2010.

Dembour, M.-G. *Who Believes in Human Rights and Reflections on the European Convention*. Cambridge: Cambridge University Press, 2006.

Dougan, M. *National Remedies before the Court of Justice, Issues of Harmonisation and Differentiation*. Oxford: Hart, 2004.

Douglas-Scott, S. *Constitutional Law of the European Union*. London: Longman, 2002.

Dworkin, R. *Justice in Robes*. London: Belknap Press, 2006.

Dworkin, R. *Taking Rights Seriously*. London: Duckworth, 1977.

Edmond, G. (ed). *Expertise in Regulation and Law*. Burlington: Ashgate, 2004.

Freeman, M.D. *Lloyd's Introduction to Jurisprudence*. London: Sweet & Maxwell, 2008.

Guinchard, S., F. Ferrand & C. Chanais. *Procédure Civile : Droit Interne et Droit Communautaire*. 29th edn. Paris: Dalloz, 2008.

Hart, H.L. *The Concept of Law*. Oxford: Clarendon Press, 1961.

Hartley, T.C. *The Foundations of European Union Law*. Oxford: Oxford University Press, 2010.

Hodgkinson, T. & M. James. *Expert Evidence: Law and Practise*. 2nd edn. London: Sweet & Maxwell, 2010.

Horspool, M. & M. Humphreys. *European Union Law*. Oxford: Oxford University Press, 2010.

House of Lords European Union Committee, 14th Report, *The Workload of the Court of Justice of the European Union*. www.publications.parliament.uk.

Isac, D. & C. Reiss. *Language: An Introduction to Linguistics as Cognitive Science*. 2nd edn. Oxford: Oxford University Press, 2013.

Jackson, L.J. (ed). *White Book Service*. London: Sweet & Maxwell, 2013.

Jans, J., R. de Lange & S. Prechal. *Europeanisation of Public Law*. Amsterdam: Europa Publishing, 2007.

Joliet, R. *The Rule of Reason in Anti-Trust Law: American, German and Common Market Laws in Comparative Perspective*. Liège, Faculté de Droit de l'Université de Liège, 1967.

Jolowicz, A. *On Civil Procedure*. Cambridge: Cambridge University Press, 2000.

Jones, O. *Bennion on Statutory Interpretation – Supplement*. 5th edn. London: Lexis Nexis, 2010.

Keane, A. T*he Modern Law of Evidence*. Oxford: Oxford University Press, 2012.

Korah, V. *An Introductory Guide to EC Competition Law and Practice*. Oxford: Hart, 2007.

Korah, V. *Intellectual Property Rights and EC Competition Rules*. Oxford: Hart, 2006.

Lasok, P. *The European Court of Justice: Practice and Procedure*. 2nd edn. London: Butterworths, 1994.

Lasok, P., T. Millett & A. Howard. *Judicial Control in the EU: Procedures and Principles*. Richmond: Richmond Law and Tax, 2004.

Layton, A. QC & H. Mercer (eds). *European Civil Practice*. Vols 1 & 2. London: Sweet & Maxwell - Thomson, 2004.

Legrand, P. & R. Munday (eds). *Comparative Legal Studies: Traditions and Transitions*. Cambridge: Cambridge University Press, 2003.

Lenaerts, K., et al. (eds). *European Union Law*. London: Sweet & Maxwell, 2011.

Lester of Herne Hill QC, Lord, Lord Pannick QC & J. Herberg. *Human Rights Law and Practice*. 3rd edn. London: Lexis Nexis, 2009.

Lianos, L. *La Transformation du Droit de la Concurrence par le Recourse à L'Analyse Economique*. Brussels: Bruylant, 2007.

Malek, H.M. (ed). *Phipson on Evidence*. 17th edn. London: Sweet & Maxwell, 2010.

Markesinis, B. *Comparative Law in the Courtroom and Classroom*. Oxford: Hart, 2003.

Markesinis, B. & J. Fedtke. *Engaging with Foreign Law*. Oxford: Hart, 2009.

Menski, W. *Comparative Law in a Global Context*. 2nd edn. Cambridge: Cambridge University Press, 2006.

Monateri, P.G. (ed). *Methods of Comparative Law*. Cheltenham: Edward Elgar, 2012.

Monti, G. *EC Competition Law*. Cambridge: Cambridge University Press, 2007.

Morgan, B. & K. Yeung. *Introduction to Law and Regulation*. Cambridge: Cambridge University Press, 2006.

Mulcahy, L.-A. (ed). *Human Rights and Civil Practice*. London: Sweet & Maxwell, 2001.

Murray, P. & R. Stürner. *German Civil Justice*. Durham: Carolina Academic Press, 2004.

Nazzini, R. *Concurrent Proceedings in Competition Law, Procedure, Evidence and Remedies*. Oxford: Oxford University Press, 2004.

Nelken, D. (ed). *Comparing Legal Cultures*. Aldershot: Dartmouth, 1997.

Örücü, E. & D. Nelken. *Comparative Law: A Handbook*. Oxford: Hart, 2007.

Plender, R. (ed). *European Courts Practice and Precedents*. London: Sweet & Maxwell, 1997.

Rand Corporation, Institute for Civil Justice. *Just, Speedy and Inexpensive: An Evaluation of Judicial Case Management under the Civil Justice Reform Act (1996)*. www.Rand.org/pubs/monograph_report/MR800.

Rawls, J. *A Theory of Justice*. Oxford: Clarendon Press, 1972.

Robins, R.H. *An Introduction to Linguistics*. 4th edn. London: Longman, 2001.

Roberts, P. & M. Redmayne (eds). *Innovations in Evidence and Proof: Integrating Theory: Research and Teaching*. Oxford: Hart, 2007.

Rose, V. & D. Bailey (eds). *Bellamy and Child: European Union Law of Competition*. Oxford: Oxford University Press, 2013.

Sales, B. & D. Shuman. *Experts in Court: Reconciling Law, Science and Professional Knowledge*. New York: American Psychological Association, 2005.

Scalia, A. *A Matter of Interpretation: Federal Courts and the Law*. Princeton: Princeton University Press, 1997.

Sime, S. *A Practical Approach to Civil Procedure*. Oxford: Oxford University Press, 2002.

Simon, D. *Le système juridique communautaire*. 3rd edn. Paris: Presses Universitaires de France, 2001.

Simpson, A.W.B. *Human Rights and the End of Empire: Britain and the Genesis of the European Convention*. Oxford: Oxford University Press, 2001.

Sullivan, R. *Statutory interpretation*. 2nd edn. Toronto: Irwin Inc., 2007.

Sullivan, R. *Sullivan and Driedger on the Construction of Statutes*. 4th edn. Vancouver: Butterworths, 2002.

Tapper, C. *Cross & Tapper on Evidence*. 12th edn. London: Butterworths, 2010.

Trocker, N. & V. Varano (eds). *The Reforms of Civil Procedure in Comparative Perspective*. Torino: Giappichelli, 2005.

Van Hoecke, M. (ed). *Epistemology and Methodology of Comparative Law*. Oxford: Hart, 2004.

Wägenbaur, B. *Court of Justice of the European Union: Commentary on Statute and Rules of Procedure*. Nomos: CH Beck, Hart, 2013.

Ward, A. *Judicial Review and the Rights of Private Parties in EC Law*. 2nd edn. Oxford: Oxford University Press, 2007.

Weiss, F. (ed). *Improving WTO Dispute Settlement Procedures*. London: Cameron May, 2000.

Zuckerman, A. & P. Roberts. *Criminal Evidence*. Oxford: Oxford University Press, 2010.

Zuckerman, A.A.S. *Zuckerman on Civil Procedure: Principles of Practice*. London: Sweet & Maxwell, 2006.

Zuckerman, A.A.S. (ed). *Civil Justice in Crisis*. Oxford: Oxford University Press, 1999.

Zweigert, K. & H. Kötz. *An Introduction to Comparative Law*. 3rd edn. New York: Oxford University Press, 1998.

Index

EUROPEAN MONOGRAPH SERIES

1. Lammy Betten (ed.), *The Future of European Social Policy,* 1991 (ISBN 90-654-4585-4).
2. Annemarie Loman, Kamiel Mortelmans, Harry H.G. Post & Stewart Watson, *Culture and Common Law: Before and After Maastricht,* 1992 (ISBN 90-654-4638-9).
3. John A.E. Vervaele, *Fraud against the Community: The Need for European Fraud Legislation,* 1994 (ISBN 90-654-4634-6).
4. Philip Raworth, *The Legislative Process in the European Community,* 1993 (ISBN 90-654-4690-7).
5. Jules Stuyck, *Financial and Monetary Integration in the European Economic Community,* 1993 (ISBN 90-654-4718-0).
6. Jules Stuyck & A.J. Vossestein (eds), *State Entrepreneurship, National Monopolies and European Community Law,* 1993 (ISBN 90-654-4773-3).
7. Jules Stuyck & A. Looijestijn-Clearie (eds), *The European Economic Area EC-EFTA,* 1994 (ISBN 90-654-4815-2).
8. Rosita B. Bouterse, *Competition and Integration: What Goals Count?,* 1995 (ISBN 90-654-4816-0).
9. René Barents, *The Agricultural Law of the EC: An Inquiry into the Administrative Law,* 1994 (ISBN 90-654-4867-5).
10. Nicholas Emiliou, *Principles of Proportionality in European Law: A Comparative Study,* 1996 (ISBN 90-411-0866-1).
11. Eivind Smith, *National Parliaments as Cornerstones of European Integration,* 1996 (ISBN 90-411-0898-X).
12. Jan H. Jans, *European Environmental Law,* 1996 (ISBN 90-411-0877-7).
13. Síofra O'Leary, *The Evolving Concept of Community Citizenship: From the Free Movement of Persons to Union Citizenship,* 1997 (ISBN 90-411-0878-5).
14. Laurence W. Gormley (ed.), *Current and Future Perspectives on EC Competition Law,* 1983 (ISBN 90-411-0691-X).
15. Simone White, *Protection of the Financial Interests of the European Communities: The Fight against Fraud and Corruption,* 1998 (ISBN 90-411-9647-1).
16. Morten P. Broberg, *Broberg on the European Commission's Jurisdiction to Scrutinise Mergers,* 4th Edition, 2013 (ISBN 978-90-411-3339-7).
17. Doris Hildebrand, *The Role of Economic Analysis in the EC Competition Rules: The European School,* 2nd Edition, 2002 (ISBN 90-411-1706-7).
18. Christof R.A. Swaak, *European Community Law and the Automobile Industry,* 1999 (ISBN 90-411-1140-9).

19. Dorthe Dahlgaard Dingel, *Public Procurement: A Harmonization of the National Judicial Review of the Application of European Community Law,* 1999 (ISBN 90-411-1161-1).
20. John A.E. Vervaele (ed.), *Compliance and Enforcement of European Community Law,* 1999 (ISBN 90-411-1151-4).
21. Martin Trybus, *European Defence Procurement Law: International and National Procurement Systems as Models for a Liberalized Defence Procurement Market in Europe,* 1999 (ISBN 90-411-1167-0).
22. Helen Staples, *The Legal Status of Third Country Nationals Resident in the European Union,* 1999 (ISBN 90-411-1277-4).
23. Damien Geradin (ed.), *The Liberalization of State Monopolies in the European Union and Beyond,* 1999 (ISBN 90-411-1264-2).
24. Katja Heede, *European Ombudsman: Redress and Control at Union Level,* 2000 (ISBN 90-411-1413-0).
25. Ulf Bernitz & Joakim Nergelius (eds), *General Principles of European Community Law,* 2000 (ISBN 90-411-1402-5).
26. Michaela Drahos, *Convergence of Competition Laws and Policies in the European Community,* 2002 (ISBN 90-411-1562-5).
27. Damien Geradin (ed.), *The Liberalization of Electricity and Natural Gas in the European Union,* 2001 (ISBN 90-411-1560-9).
28. Gisella Gori, *Towards an EU Right to Education,* 2001 (ISBN 90-411-1670-2).
29. Brendan P.G. Smith, *Constitution Building in the European Union,* 2001 (ISBN 90-411-1695-8).
30. Friedl Weiss & Frank Wooldridge, *Free Movement of Persons within the European Community,* 2nd Edition, 2007 (ISBN 978-90-411-2545-3).
31. Ingrid Boccardi, *Europe and Refugees: Towards an EU Asylum Policy,* 2002 (ISBN 90-411-1709-1).
32. John A.E. Vervaele & André Klip (eds), *European Cooperation Between Tax, Customs and Judicial Authorities,* 2001 (ISBN 90-411-1747-4).
33. Wouter P.J. Wils, *The Optimal Enforcement of EC Antitrust Law: Essays in Law and Economics,* 2002 (ISBN 90-411-1757-1).
34. Damien Geradin (ed.), *The Liberalization of Postal Services in the European Union,* 2002 (ISBN 90-411-1780-6).
35. Nick Bernard, *Multilevel Governance in the European Union,* 2002 (ISBN 90-411-1812-8).
36. Jill Wakefield, *Judicial Protection through the Use of Article 288(2) EC,* 2002 (ISBN 90-411-1823-3).
37. Sebastiaan Princen, *EU Regulation and Transatlantic Trade,* 2002 (ISBN 90-411-1871-3).

38. Amaryllis Verhoeven, *The European Union in Search of a Democratic and Constitutional Theory,* 2002 (ISBN 90-411-1872-1).
39. Paul L.C. Torremans, *Cross Border Insolvencies in EU, English and Belgian Law,* 2002 (ISBN 90-411-1888-8).
40. Malcolm Anderson & Joanna Apap (eds), *Police and Justice Cooperation and the New European Borders,* 2002 (ISBN 90-411-1893-4).
41. Christin M. Forstinger, *Takeover Law in EU and USA: A Comparative Analysis,* 2002 (ISBN 90-411-1919-1).
42. Antonio Bavasso, *Communications in EU Antitrust Law: Market Power and Public Interest,* 2003 (ISBN 90-411-1974-4).
43. Fiona G. Wishlade, *Regional State Aid and Competition Policy in the European Union,* 2003 (ISBN 90-411-1975-2).
44. Gareth Davies, *Nationality Discrimination in the European Internal Market,* 2003 (ISBN 90-411-1998-1).
45. René Barents, *The Autonomy of Community Law,* 2003 (ISBN 90-411-2251-6).
46. Gerhard Dannecker & Oswald Jansen (eds), *Competition Law Sanctioning in the European Union,* 2004 (ISBN 90-411-2100-5).
47. Nauta Dutilh (ed.), *Dealing with Dominance: The Experience of National Competition Authorities,* 2004 (ISBN 90-411-2211-7).
48. Stefaan van den Bogaert, *Practical Regulation of the Mobility of Sportsmen in the EU Post Bosman,* 2005 (ISBN 90-411-2327-X).
49. Katalin Judit Cseres, *Competition Law and Consumer Protection,* 2005 (ISBN 90-411-2380-6).
50. Philipp Kiiver, *The National Parliaments in the European Union: A Critical View on EU Constitution Building,* 2006 (ISBN 978-90-411-2452-4).
51. Alexander Turk, *The Concept of Legislation in European Community Law,* 2006 (ISBN 978-90-411-2472-2).
52. Dimitrios Sinaniotis, *The Interim Protection of Individuals before the European and National Courts,* 2006 (ISBN 978-90-411-2498-2).
53. M. Holoubek & D. Damjanovic, M. Traimer (eds), *Regulating Content: The European Regulatory Framework for the Media and Related Creative Sectors,* 2006 (ISBN 978-90-411-2597-2).
54. Anneli Albi & Jacques Ziller (eds), *The European Constitution and National Constitutions: Ratification and Beyond,* 2006 (ISBN 978-90-411-2524-8).
55. Gustavo E. Luengo, *Regulation of Subsidies and State Aids in WTO and EC Law: Conflicts in International Trade Law,* 2007 (ISBN 978-90-411-2547-7).
56. Eniko Horvath, *Mandating Identity: Citizenship, Kinship Laws and Plural Nationality in the European Union,* 2007 (ISBN 978-90-411-2662-7).

57. Rass Holdgaard, *External Relations Law of the European Community: Legal Reasoning and Legal Discourses,* 2007 (ISBN 978-90-411-2604-7).
58. Jill Wakefield, *The Right to Good Administration,* 2007 (ISBN 978-90-411-2697-9).
59. Dimitry Kochenov, *EU Enlargement and the Failure of Conditionality: Pre- accession Conditionality in the Fields of Democracy and the Rule of Law,* 2008 (ISBN 978-90-411-2696-2).
60. Despina Mavromati, *The Law of Payment Services in the EU: The EC Directive on Payment Services in the Internal Market,* 2008 (ISBN 978-90-411-2700-6).
61. Anne Meuwese, *Impact Assessment in EU Lawmaking,* 2008 (ISBN 978-90-411-2720-4).
62. Ulf Bernitz, Joakim Nergelius & Cecilia Cardner (eds), *General Principles of EC Law in a Process of Development,* 2008 (ISBN 978-90-411-2705-1).
63. Johan van de Gronden (ed.), *The EU and WTO Law on Services: Limits to the Realisation of General Interest Policies within the Services Markets?,* 2008 (ISBN 978-90-411-2809-6).
64. Alina Tryfonidou, *Reverse Discrimination in EC Law,* 2009 (ISBN 978-90-411-2751-8).
65. Mikael Berglund, *Cross-Border Enforcement of Claims in the EU: History Present Time and Future,* 2009 (ISBN 978-90-411-2861-4).
66. Theodore Konstadinides, *Division of Powers in European Union Law: The Delimitation of Internal Competence between the EU and the Member States,* 2009 (ISBN 978-90-411-2615-3).
67. Mattias Derlén, *Multilingual Interpretation of European Union Law,* 2009 (ISBN 978-90-411-2853-9).
68. René Barents, *Directory of EU Case Law on the Preliminary Ruling Procedure,* 2009 (ISBN 978-90-411-3150-8).
69. Yan Luo, *Anti-dumping in the WTO, the EU and China: The Rise of Legalization in the Trade Regime and its Consequences,* 2010 (ISBN 978-90-411-3207-9).
70. Patrick Birkinshaw & Mike Varney (eds), *The European Union Legal Order after Lisbon,* 2010 (ISBN 978-90-411-3152-2).
71. Thomas Gr. Papadopoulos, *EU Law and Harmonization of Takeovers in the Internal Market,* 2010 (978-90-411-3340-3).
72. Bas van Bockel, *The* Ne Bis In Idem *Principle in EU Law,* 2010 (978-90-411-3156-0).
73. Veljko Milutinović, *The 'Right to Damages' under EU Competition Law: From* Courage v. Crehan *to the White Paper and Beyond,* 2010 (978-90-411-3235-2).

74. Amandine Garde, *EU Law and Obesity Prevention*, 2010 (978-90-411-2706-8).
75. Leonard Besselink, Frans Pennings & Sacha Prechal (eds), *The Eclipse of the Legality Principle in the European Union*, 2011 (978-90-411-3262-8).
76. Sacha Garben, *EU Higher Education Law: The Bologna Process and Harmonization by Stealth*, 2011 (978-90-411-3365-6).
77. Dimitry Kochenov (ed.), *EU Law of the Overseas: Outermost Regions, Associated Overseas Countries and Territories, Territories Sui Generis*, 2011 (978-90-411-3445-5).
78. Pablo Ibáñez Colomo, *European Communications Law and Technological Convergence: Deregulation, Re-regulation and Regulatory Convergence in Television and Telecommunications*, 2012 (978-90-411-3829-3).
79. Elise Muir, *EU Regulation of Access to Labour Markets: A Case Study of EU Constraints on Member State Competences*, 2012 (978-90-411-3823-1).
80. Tim Corthaut, *EU Ordre Public*, 2012 (978-90-411-3232-1).
81. Oana Ştefan, *Soft Law in Court: Competition Law, State Aid and the Court of Justice of the European Union*, 2013 (978-90-411-3997-9).
82. Francesco Rossi dal Pozzo, *Citizenship Rights and Freedom of Movement in the European Union*, 2013 (978-90-411-4660-1).
83. Jens Hartig Danielsen, *EU Agricultural Law*, 2013 (978-90-411-3280-2).
84. Ulf Bernitz, Xavier Groussot & Felix Schulyok (eds), *General Principles of EU Law and European Private Law*, 2013 (978-90-411-4683-0).
85. Michelle Everson, Cosimo Monda & Ellen Vos (eds), *European Agencies in between Institutions and Member States*, 2014 (978-90-411-2843-0).
86. Stefan Leible & Matthias Lehmann (eds), *European Contract Law and German Law*, 2014 (978-90-411-2588-0).
87. Piero Leanza & Ondrej Pridal, *The Right to a Fair Trial: Article 6 of the European Convention on Human Rights*, 2014 (978-90-411-4855-1).
88. Patrick J. Birkinshaw, *European Public Law: The Achievement and the Challenge*, 2014 (978-90-411-4744-8).
89. George Cumming, *Expert Evidence Deficiencies in the Judgments of the Courts of the European Union and the European Court of Human Rights*, 2014 (978-90-411-4123-1).

www.ingramcontent.com/pod-product-compliance
Lightning Source LLC
Chambersburg PA
CBHW071242230926
51849CB00001B/200
9789041141231